KU-431-137

NAM — For HIV information

This directory is one of five that makes up the NAM Manual. The Manual helps professionals in HIV sectors around the world with their work by providing the latest information on treatment and care, prevention, the social impact of the epidemic, and comprehensive listings of organisations in the UK, Europe and the world.

The Manual is dedicated to the memory of Martin Fright, Mike Rhodes, Simon Mansfield and Barry Jackson as a tribute to their inspirational contributions to NAM's development and to the broader community response to AIDS.

NAM was founded by Peter Scott in 1987. He was working at the heart of the community affected by HIV - at the London Lesbian and Gay Switchboard. At that time it was important to produce a clear, plain language resource in the face of extensive misinformation about HIV and AIDS, much of it confused and homophobic.

The Manual soon became the UK's primary source of high quality information on all aspects of the epidemic. As its users have grown and diversified within the UK and abroad, so it has been constantly revised, rewritten and adapted to take account of new needs.

NAM now also publishes a wide range of printed, audio and electronic materials for all communities of people with HIV and publishes on the internet at www.aidsmap.com. The work is rooted in the experiences of those most affected by the epidemic.

NAM believes information enables people to take control of their lives and healthcare, develop better dialogues with their healthcare staff and so live longer, healthier lives.

" The harsh mathematics of this epidemic proves that prevention is essential to expanding treatment. Treatment without prevention is simply unsustainable. **"**

Bill Gates
16th International AIDS Conference, Toronto, 2006

Over the past ten years, much of the focus in the UK and beyond has been on HIV treatment: how to take it, what to take, how to get it and how to increase access to it.

Yet, as Bill Gates points out, while strategies to increase access to treatment are beginning to prove successful, improved strategies to prevent HIV infection are urgently needed.

At the most basic level, a wider understanding of the evidence for the effectiveness of some HIV prevention is needed.

Calls for evidence-based HIV prevention have been growing in recent years. This volume summarises key evidence on HIV prevention in an up-to-date in and accessible way, without an ideological or moral bias, but informed by the need to respect human rights, and with a dedication to identifying what works – and what doesn't.

Preventing HIV also looks at technologies and innovations still being investigated, such as circumcision, microbicides and pre-exposure prophylaxis. It's essential that everyone involved in HIV prevention has some understanding of these potential interventions, which could have a significant impact on the way that individuals choose to avoid HIV infection and think about the risk of infection over the next few years.

This volume covers prevention of sexual transmission of HIV. Prevention of mother to child HIV transmission is covered in the *HIV & AIDS Treatments Directory*, and prevention of HIV transmission through injecting drug use is covered in the *HIV & AIDS Reference Manual*.

Keith Alcorn

Senior Editor, NAM

Table of Contents

Introduction

Why prevention still matters 2
Examples of success 5
Why does prevention fail? 5
References 7

A is for abstinence

Abstinence in people with HIV 9
Does abstinence work to reduce HIV transmission? . . .10
Abstinence in Africa 11
References 13

B is for being faithful and behaviour change

Behaviour change in people with HIV 20
References 21

C is for condoms

Condom usage rates 24
Condom controversies 29
Safer sex 30
Condom do's and don'ts 31
Types of condoms 32
Lubricants 34
Female condoms 35
References 38

D is for disclosure, serosorting and negotiated safety

The internet as disclosure venue 41
Does serosorting work? 42
Viral load and negotiated safety 43
HIV-negative serosorting? 44
Talk, Test, Test, Trust 44
Disclosure:
an HIV-positive-controlled safer sex strategy? 45
References 46

E is for emergent prevention technologies

The need for better protection 48
No magic bullet 49
Conclusion 51
References 51

The role of HIV testing in HIV prevention

Making HIV testing routine .54
   1. Make HIV testing a routine part of medical care .54
   2. Use new models for diagnosing HIV
   infection outside of traditional medical settings 54
   3. Prevent new infections by working with people
   diagnosed with HIV and their partners 54
   4. Continue to decrease perinatal HIV transmission. 55
   Reservations 55
   Should we test everyone for HIV? 55
   The position in the UK 57
Home testing 58
   The home tests available in the USA 58
   Rapid self-testing 59
References 60

C is also for Circumcision

References 62

Using antiretrovirals for HIV prevention

Post-exposure prophylaxis 64
   The cost-effectiveness of PEP 67
   Putting PEP into practice 67
   Ethical and practical issues 68
   How soon should PEP be used? 68
   UK guidelines - the draft 69
   Campaigns and controversy 69
   The BASHH Guidelines .70
   International guidelines 72
   References 72

Pre-exposure prophylaxis: the challenge

The need for PrEP 76
'Doing a T' - underground PrEP 76
The evidence so far 77
The Seattle consultation 79
Access 80
Conclusion 80
References 80

Microbicides

An introduction to microbicides 81
Do we already have a microbicide? 83
Lesson one : lemon juice as a microbicide 83
Lesson two: nonoxynol-9 84
Current microbicide efficacy trials 85
Microbicides in development .86

How will microbicides be delivered? 89

Rectal microbicides 90

Challenges to microbicide development 92

Who will control microbicides? 95

The search for an HIV vaccine

What an HIV vaccine would have to do 98

Humoral immunity 99

Cellular immunity 99

Mucosal immunity 100

Broadly neutralising antibodies 100

Vaccines against viral proteins 101

The hurdles to climb 101

Types of HIV vaccines 101

Vaccines - a summary of the issues 103

Mobilising support worldwide 105

Ethical issues in trial design .107

Trials that 'fail' 109

Ethical implications for people with HIV 110

Ethical implications for HIV-negative people 110

Securing global access 110

An evolving programme 111

Conclusions 111

References 112

HIV prevention: which methods work?

How do we know HIV prevention efforts have worked?114

What works? Two meta-reviews 114

The theory and philosophy of HIV prevention 118

Differing philosophies of HIV prevention 122

The limitations of the evidence-based approach 125

Measuring effectiveness 127

Can randomised, controlled trials be used in HIV
prevention research? 130

What is known about the effectiveness of interventions?130

Research on the effectiveness of interventions for specific
communities 131

What is known about the effectiveness of specific
approaches 131

Mass media campaigns 131

Small media 132

Counselling and HIV antibody testing 132

Peer education 133

Workshops 133

Outreach work 133

Group cognitive/skills interventions 134

Individual cognitive interventions 135

Community mobilisation 135

Social marketing 136

Internet interventions 137

What interventions can be recommended? 138

Needs assessment and evaluation: further reading . . .139

Positive prevention 139

Introduction

The first thing that needs to be stated in any publication on HIV prevention is that it works.

HIV has become a pandemic because it has a lethal combination of properties:

- transmission via that most taboo, intractable and instinctive of human activities, sex;

- and a long asymptomatic incubation period during which people are healthy, sexually active - and infectious.

Changing sexual behaviour involves revolutionising cultural attitudes, confronting taboos, reaching out to the most marginalised and despised populations and including them in dialogue, and helping people make rational decisions about their health at the very moments when they are least rational.

HIV prevention can include a myriad of activities, but falls into five broad classes:

- **Biomedical** approaches include HIV treatment, because antiretrovirals reduce people's infectiousness (a study in San Francisco (Porco) calculated that the average viral load, and therefore infectiousness, of gay men in the city had been cut by two-thirds since highly active antiretroviral therapy became available). Post-exposure prophylaxis - taking HIV drugs immediately after a risky exposure to prevent HIV - is another intervention. Needle exchange is another, as is circumcision. Barrier methods like condoms are biomedical, though programmes to ensure their use are not, and the

same will apply to developing prevention technologies such as microbicides.

- **Individual** approaches include one-to-one counselling (including voluntary counselling and testing), cognitive behavioural therapy, face-to-face detached or outreach work, telephone helplines and certain internet interventions.

- **Group** approaches are those delivered to small groups of individuals, often from the same peer group, and are usually facilitated in some way. They include school sex education and small-group work that usually includes both information and risk reduction skills training.

- **Community** interventions are delivered to the whole population or (more frequently) a target audience; the difference from the previous interventions being that individuals do not need to seek out the programme. They include media stories and small-media resources (eg leaflets and posters), condom distribution schemes, the empowerment and development of communities (including communities of people with HIV), and some internet interventions like chat rooms.

- **Sociopolitical** interventions include legal change such as the decriminalisation of homosexuality or intravenous drug use; legal sanctions such as the criminalisation of transmission; and policy interventions which may permit other types of prevention work, such as allowing needle exchange.

It is tempting to conclude at times that only biomedical interventions such as treatment and vaccines can ever have an effect on HIV. But, to give just one example, a meta-review of prevention interventions for gay men in the USA (Johnson 2002) found that the overall effect of group- and community-level behavioural interventions targeted at gay men was a reduction of 26% in unprotected sex acts.

The largest meta-review of HIV interventions ever conducted (Albarracin 2005) only measured condom use but found that 'active' interventions (getting people to practice skills) increased condom use by 38% relative to baseline and passive ones (where people just watched or listened to training) by 16%. Because baseline condom use was 32.3% this means that there was only an absolute increase of 7.8% in people who 'always' used condom and of 17% in ones who stated using them 'sometimes'. (For other meta-analyses of the effectiveness of prevention programmes, see **HIV prevention - what methods work?**)

This may not sound like a great reduction. But no public health intervention is ever 100% successful. In addition public health measures may take decades to have an effect. For instance, in the USA, the proportion of driving deaths caused by drunk drivers declined from 57% in 1982 to 45% in 1992. This 10% reduction was considered a major victory for public awareness campaigning and legal changes.

One paper (Stryker, 1995) put it this way: "Given experience in other health behaviour change endeavours, no interventions are likely to reduce the incidence of HIV infection to zero; indeed, insisting on too high a standard for HIV risk-reduction programmes may actually undermine their effectiveness."

However small, correctly timed reductions in HIV incidence may make a great deal of difference. To take an example: the first generation of topical microbicides is unlikely to prevent more than 50 to 60% of HIV infections when used. But, according to the Global Campaign for Microbicides, (2005) "Researchers have developed a mathematical model that shows that if even a small proportion of women in lower income countries used a 60% efficacious microbicide in half the sexual encounters where condoms were not used, 2.5 million HIV infections could be averted over 3 years."

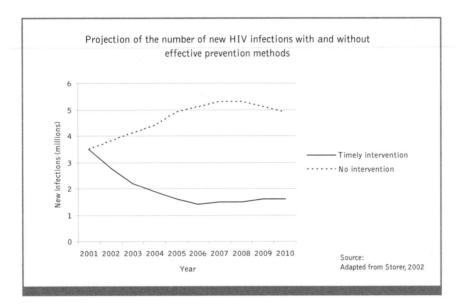

Projection of the number of new HIV infections with and without effective prevention methods

Source: Adapted from Storer, 2002

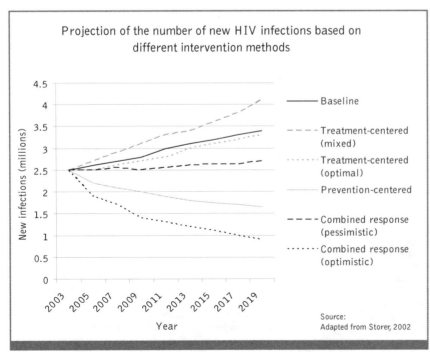

Projection of the number of new HIV infections based on different intervention methods

Source: Adapted from Storer, 2002

Why prevention still matters

Prevention without treatment

A 2002 paper (Stover 2002) modelled mathematically what would happen to the global epidemic if a package of twelve prevention initiatives was adopted by each of 126 low- and middle-income countries. For the package and the assumptions built into it about effectiveness (which have been culled from different controlled trials of the interventions), see table *Success of interventions by method* on page 3.

Stover and colleagues did a systematic review of published work on the prevention of HIV/AIDS and other sexually transmitted infections (STIs) in the developing world, using a total of 86 studies to ascertain the effectiveness of interventions in reducing HIV transmission both through sex and needle-sharing. The effect for each activity was a pooled estimate of the results of these studies. They separately modelled the effect on 51 high-prevalence countries (comprising 92% of the HIV-positive population) and pooled the effect on the other 75 by grouping them into countries with common features to their epidemic, using twelve categories of likely response according to their current prevalence levels, whether HIV prevalence was increasing slowly or rapidly, and the predominant mode of transmission.

Stover calculated that the proportion of expected infections

Success of interventions by method

Intervention	Condom Use (reduction in non-use)			Treatment for sexually transmitted disease (reduction in non-treatment)			Number of sexual partners (reduction in number of partners)			Age at first sexual intercourse (increase in age at first sexual intercourse)			Unsafe drug injections (increase in safe use of clean needles)		
	High Risk	Medium Risk	Low Risk	High Risk	Medium Risk	Low Risk	High Risk	Medium Risk	Low Risk	High Risk	Medium Risk	Low Risk	Low Risk	Medium Risk	Low Risk
Mass media campaigns		17%	17%												
Voluntary counselling and testing programmes for HIV/AIDS	50%	34%	16%												
Peer counselling - CSW	39%	42%					3%								
School-based programmes		34%						33%		0.30					
Programmes for out-of-school youths															
Workplace programmes	39%	34%	19%					23%							
Condom social marketing	21%	11%	5%								0.12				
Public sector condom distribution	57%	10%	5%	11%			35%								
Harm reduction programmes								33%					60%*		
Peer outreach to homosexual men	33%						-17%								
Treatment for sexually transmitted disease	54%	14%		47%		22%	50%								
PMTCT	50%	34%	16%												

* We assumed a 60% decrease in the average number of partners with whom needles are shared and a 60% increase in the fraction of shared needles that are cleaned.

CSW=commercial sex worker; PMTCT=prevention of mother-to-child transmission of HIV-1.

Source: Adapted from Storer, 2002

averted would range from a low of 40% in countries with stable or declining prevalence, such as Senegal and Thailand, to a high of 70% in countries with rapidly growing epidemics, such as Cameroon and China.

This would cost an estimated $4.8 billion out of the $9.2 billion that UNAIDS calculated would be needed at the time to reduce HIV prevalence by 25% by the year 2005 (as pledged in the UNGASS Declaration of Commitment on HIV/AIDS in 2001), or about $1000 per infection averted. However it would cost $27 billion to sustain the programme to 2010 - halted prevention would result in a resurgent epidemic. Stover illustrated the results in a very simple graph thus:

Prevention with treatment

Stover's paper was written just before the Barcelona World AIDS Conference and before treatment programmes started providing relatively widespread access to antiretrovirals in the developing world. It is an illustration of how prevention could affect incidence in a 'pure' epidemic where the infections that are *not* averted lead inevitably to AIDS.

As we have found in the developed world, the provision of treatment has had a paradoxical effect on HIV incidence - one explored three years later in a more sophisticated analysis.

In a paper in 2005 Joshua Salomon of the Harvard Center for Population and Development Studies demonstrated that effective HIV prevention programmes are essential for controlling the epidemic in the era of treatment. Using mathematical modelling, he found that, at least in situations of generalised epidemics as in Africa, relying on the scale-up of

antiretroviral treatment alone would most likely not only result in increased HIV prevalence but in increased deaths due to AIDS, despite the effectiveness of antiretrovirals.

Salomon (see below) used an epidemiologic model of HIV and AIDS to investigate a range of possible positive and negative health outcomes under alternative scenarios that reflected varying implementation of prevention and treatment (see diagrams).

The potential impacts of prevention efforts at a given coverage level were based on Stover's comprehensive package of twelve interventions, although Stover and colleagues also included interventions such as harm reduction for injecting drug users and peer outreach for men who have sex with men, which Salomon did not include in his model for Africa.

In the two scenarios representing treatment-centred strategies, with different assumptions about the impact of treatment on transmissibility and behaviour, the change in the total number of new infections expected by the year 2020 ranged from a 10% increase to a 6% reduction from the baseline level expected at 2020.

But because the absolute number of new HIV infections in Africa under a 'business as usual' scenario of no increased treatment provision are expected to rise from 2.6 million in 2005 to 3.8 million by 2020, in both treatment-based scenarios there would be a net increase in the number of people living with HIV. Indeed annual incidence in Africa would increase to 4.3 million by 2020 if current rates of treatment roll-out were unaccompanied by effective prevention strategies.

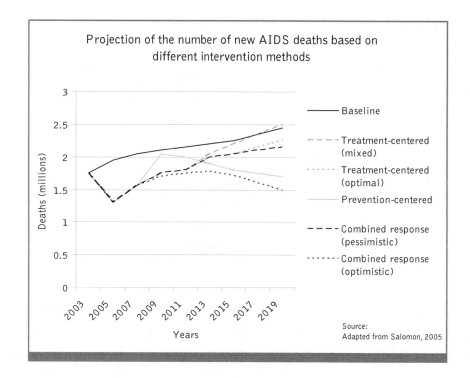

Projection of the number of new AIDS deaths based on different intervention methods

Y-axis: Deaths (millions) — 0, 0.5, 1, 1.5, 2, 2.5, 3
X-axis: Years — 2003, 2005, 2007, 2009, 2011, 2013, 2015, 2017, 2019

Legend:
— Baseline
– – – Treatment-centered (mixed)
· · · · Treatment-centered (optimal)
——— Prevention-centered
— — — Combined response (pessimistic)
· · · · · · Combined response (optimistic)

Source:
Adapted from Salomon, 2005

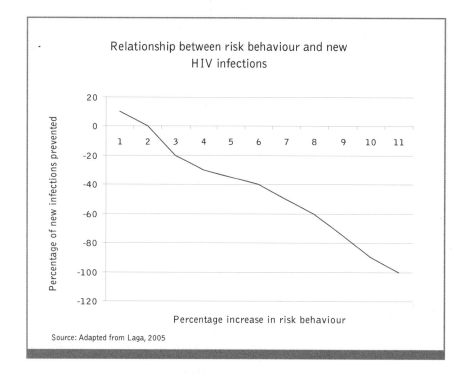

Relationship between risk behaviour and new HIV infections

Y-axis: Percentage of new infections prevented — 20, 0, -20, -40, -60, -80, -100, -120
X-axis: Percentage increase in risk behaviour — 1, 2, 3, 4, 5, 6, 7, 8, 9, 10, 11

Source: Adapted from Laga, 2005

Salomon then looked at the potential synergy between treatment and prevention. If they were to enhance each other in a combined response, the expected benefits would be a 55% reduction in annual incidence (a total of 29 million averted infections) and a 27% reduction in mortality (ten million lives saved) by 2020.

However, if treatment scale-up led to prevention efforts being less effective (because of behaviour change or greater infectivity), the benefits of a combined response would be considerably smaller - a 17% reduction in incidence (nine million averted infections) and a 16% reduction in AIDS deaths (six million lives saved).

What assumptions did Salomon build into his model? The number of people being treated in 2020 ranged from 9.2 million in a treatment-only scenario, to 4.2 million if treatment and prevention worked synergistically together to reduce new infections.

It's worth noting that the 'pessimistic' assumption for the effectiveness of prevention campaigns assumed a 25% effectiveness - pretty close to the figure found in the Johnson study above. This included assumptions such as the reduced fear of death leading to a 10% reduction in condom use - a pretty conservative estimate given reductions seen among groups such as gay men in the west.

Nonetheless, Salomon's model indicates that, in a generalised epidemic at least, only if prevention accompanies treatment can there be control of HIV.

Why is this, given that some studies (Porco) have found that, on a population level, antiretroviral treatment, by reducing viral loads, has reduced the average infectiousness of the HIV-positive individual by as much as two-thirds?

Similarly, the annual number of AIDS deaths relative to the expected 2020 baseline under a treatment-only strategy would decline by 9% to 13% (meaning a net increase of 450,000 to 1.15 million AIDS deaths) but would actually increase if not-very-pessimistic assumptions are made about decreased condom use and the increased longevity of people with HIV resulting in more transmissions.

In contrast, a prevention-only strategy, based on Stover's recommendations, with no increased rollout of antiretrovirals at all, provided greater reductions in incidence (36%) than using treatment. It also provided mortality reductions similar to those of the treatment-centred scenarios by 2020, but more modest mortality benefits over the immediate next five to ten years.

This is because it takes only a small increase in sexual risk behaviour to abrogate the effect of antiretrovirals. In a paper presented at the 2005 International AIDS Society conference that quoted Salomon, Marie Laga of the Antwerp Institute for Tropical Diseases showed that anything more than a 5% increase in risk behaviour would cancel out the life-saving effects of antiretrovirals (see *Relationship between risk behaviour and new HIV infections*).

This is because HIV transmission is not a simple, linear phenomenon. A disproportionate number (though exactly what proportion is disputed) of new infections occur due to transmission by people who are recently infected themselves and therefore have a high viral load and are ignorant of their infection.

There is also a non-linear relationship between the number of *concurrent* sex partners people have within a population and the frequency of HIV transmission. In a situation where people are serially monogamous - the predominant pattern among heterosexuals in the west - new HIV transmissions can only happen when one relationship stops and another starts. But in cultures where concurrent relationships are more common - as in some African and other non-western cultures, within the gay community, and among certain other groups such as sex workers and some young people - one person who is infected can quickly become the 'index case' for a cluster of infections.

Nicole Crepaz, in a 2004 meta-review of 21 studies, found that when individuals started taking antiretroviral therapy, there was no significant change in their sexual risk behaviour. However this does not include how the behaviour of people remaining off treatment in the same population may change when antiretroviral use becomes common in others, let alone how undiagnosed people may change their behaviour when AIDS is no longer seen as an inevitable death sentence.

In response to Salomon's paper, Stover wrote another (Stover 2006) in which he factored in an optimistic scenario of 80% global coverage of antiretroviral treatment by 2010.

His new estimate of the cost of his comprehensive prevention package was nearly five times greater than his previous one, reflecting new understandings about the complexities of sustaining prevention efforts. It would, he estimated, cost $122 billion to sustain comprehensive prevention from 2005 to 2010, or $3923 per infection averted.

However he estimated that the HIV treatment that would be necessary (as 80% coverage) for infections that would occur if the prevention package was *not* put in place would cost $4,707 per lifetime, leading to a net saving of $784 per infection averted or $24.38 billion in total.

The comprehensive prevention package could also prevent 30 million people becoming infected with HIV.

To summarise these modelling studies:

- We stand a chance of reversing the course of the HIV epidemic only if comprehensive prevention packages are combined with treatment access.

- Though costly, comprehensive worldwide prevention programmes could still be cost-effective.

Examples of success

The 26% reduction typical of prevention interventions found by Johnson is of course an average. Although it included many interventions that did *not* work, the history of the epidemic shows that specific interventions targeted accurately and at the right time can work much more dramatically.

To cite three of the most widely-quoted examples:

- In **Uganda**, a countrywide programme of AIDS awareness-raising initiated by the Ugandan president in 1986 led to demonstrable reductions in risky behaviour and at least contributed to a two- to four-fold reduction in HIV prevalence. Similar, more recent reductions have been seen in other African countries such as Kenya and Zimbabwe (see **The Epidemiology of HIV**)

- In **Thailand**, a single-minded campaign to institute 100% condom use in commercial sex establishments brought down the HIV incidence in young men from 2.5% in 1991 to 0.5% in 1993

- The **UK** has its own major triumph. In 1986 HIV prevalence among injecting drug users in Edinburgh was approaching 50%. Reversing a police policy of confiscating needles and instituting needle exchange forced annual HIV incidence among UK drug users down to two per cent. Just seven per cent of Britons with HIV have caught it from needle-sharing, as opposed to 28% in the USA and 80% in Russia.

Why does prevention fail?

Given, then that (for instance) a combination of reduction programmes and HAART should have reduced HIV incidence in gay men in the developed world, why, in many cases, has it not - to the extent that many commentators talk of the 'failure' of HIV prevention?

Although it is important that a country's HIV prevention 'package' includes as wide a variety of interventions as possible (because what is appropriate to a heterosexual virgin teenager is not appropriate to a gay male sex worker), it's also important to be aware that HIV interventions are not necessarily synergistic, (reinforce each others' effects). On the contrary, they may be antagonistic.

To take some examples:

- The advent of HAART has reduced fear of death among the community at large and gay men in particular, and has also increased the population of healthy, sexually active people with HIV. Between them, these contribute to cancelling out the net drop in infectiousness in the community, as shown above.

- Opponents of condom distribution programmes say that providing condoms only encourages sexual activity.

- Doctors fear that providing post-exposure prophylaxis will lead to greater risks being taken.

- Some studies of peer-led and facilitated group interventions have found that their effectiveness is compromised by the 'shame factor' - participants being reluctant to discuss times when they have deviated from the group norm of sexual behaviour.

In addition, the target audience dictates the message, and HIV prevention interventions devised for gay men in the pre-treatment era are no longer appropriate for a large proportion of the world's vulnerable population.

It is interesting to speculate how HIV prevention would have developed in the world's richer countries if the group most affected from the start had been young heterosexual women, as in Africa and other parts of the developing world, instead of gay men.

- Would an HIV prevention strategy based on an essentially male-controlled device - the condom - have been the primary focus of prevention?

- Would strategies encouraging sexual abstinence or monogamy have been more prominent?

- Would the invoking of criminal sanctions against infection have happened earlier?

- And would a general presumption of 'shared responsibility' in sexual relationships and negotiation have been tempered much earlier by questions of power and inequalities of gender, age and income?

Because of the complex synergies and antagonisms possible between interventions, in the last decade HIV prevention, at least in the UK and the developed world, has been utterly transformed from what was essentially the social marketing of a simple message - 'Choose Safer Sex' - into a complex, contradictory and extremely politicised set of dialogues featuring heated debates between proponents of:

- abstinence versus comprehensive sex education

- the promotion of condoms versus the promotion of monogamy

- harm reduction versus risk elimination

- 'normalising' disclosure and HIV testing versus confidentiality and patient rights

- and whether HIV-negative or HIV-positive people are the best targets for - and the best originators of - prevention messages.

As well as becoming more complex, as an endeavour HIV prevention has also come to be seen by many as less effective.

HIV infection continues to climb in much of the developing world, and certain experts continue to forecast that countries like India and Russia are at the 'tipping point' for the development of generalised epidemics. Although prevalence has fallen in some African countries, there are fears that the cost of providing global access to antiretrovirals may impact adversely on community prevention initiatives - and there are equal fears that an American-led emphasis on abstinence as the mainstay of prevention rather than a balanced programme will lead to a resurgence of HIV. According to UNAIDS by July 2005 only one in five people needing HIV prevention had access to prevention programmes and only one in ten people had been tested for HIV.

These fears are best exemplified by the 2002 paper (Marseille, 2002) in *The Lancet* by Elliot Marseille and colleagues, who argued that HIV prevention is 28 times more cost-effective than providing treatment in the developing world, and that "funding HAART at the expense of prevention means greater loss of life."

Although Marseille's views were criticised as placing a false opposition between prevention and treatment, concerns continue to be expressed that over-emphasising treatment at the expense of prevention is not cost-effective.

As recently as July 2005, in an opinion column in *Forbes Magazine*, economist Emily Oster said that the cost of global access to antiretroviral drugs in the developing world was $365 per life-year saved. In comparison, she said, a blanket programme of STI treatment would cost $3.65 per life-year saved and a national HIV education programme would cost $16.

There is also concern that treatment without proper education will lead to increased transmission of drug-resistant HIV in the developing world, with a resultant rapid loss of sustainability of cheap antiretroviral regimens.

However these arguments ignore the fact that providing antiretroviral drugs provides hope, which is in turn a major generator of positive prevention behaviours such as increased testing, increased disclosure of HIV status, reduction of stigma, and an examination of community sexual norms. In one district in Uganda, for instance, the arrival of antiretrovirals in the area led to a 23-fold increase in the number of people coming forward for testing, and some studies (eg Holtgrave and Anderson) have shown that, when diagnosed, people with HIV reduce the amount of unsafe sexual encounters they have by at least 50%.

In the developed world, HIV prevention work faces an uphill battle both against the loss of funding due to the cost of HAART and changes in behaviour leading to a greatly increased incidence of sexually transmitted diseases and, in some cases, HIV, especially among gay men, .

The USA has started to see an increasing degree of inequality when it comes to HIV vulnerability between ethnic minority - particularly African-American people - and the white majority. A recent survey of gay men (Centers for Disease Control, 24 June 2005), for instance, found that HIV prevalence among

Afro-American men who have sex with men was more than twice what it was in whites; among Afro-Americans in general it is four times that of the general population: and four out of five women diagnosed with HIV (Centers for Disease Control, 16 June 2005) is black or Hispanic.

There has been a loss of certainty about how to do effective HIV prevention work with poor black women and also with men who, while having sex with men, may not identify as gay. With gay men in general there have been concerns that two decades of prevention success could be wiped away by recreational drug use.

Gay prevention campaigners are concerned that the global emphasis on HIV is obscuring the fact that men who have sex with men are still the most vulnerable population for infection in most developed countries. For instance, 80% of the people who acquired their HIV in the UK last year were gay men. Sexually active gay men, who form no more than one in 40 of the UK population, are at least 200 times more likely to catch HIV in the UK than heterosexuals (Health Protection Agency, 2005).

While European countries have not seen the same development of HIV health inequality as the USA, increasing HIV prevalence among immigrant populations, who may have limited access to HIV treatment and to prevention messages, has led to fears of a 'second generation' epidemic among minorities, though there are only very early signs so far that this is materialising.

This widely-held feeling that HIV prevention has lost its way and that we no longer live in a simple 'safer sex' world has led to an increased focus on the development and testing of new prevention technologies such as pre-exposure prophylaxis and microbicides.

The changes in HIV prevention work have been predicated upon two huge historical changes.

The 'feminisation' of AIDS. This has transformed HIV educators' views of the position of the HIV-negative partner in sex. Almost all countries have seen increased numbers of women diagnosed with HIV, to the extent of women now forming the majority of people affected in sub-Saharan Africa. The fact that for many of these women - a lot of whom are wives - it is quite simply culturally and personally impossible to negotiate condom use with male partners has led on the one hand to the drive to develop microbicides and other female-controlled technologies, and on the other for proponents of abstinence and monogamy to say that these are the only strategies that protect vulnerable women against male sexual dominance.

Post-HAART optimism. Although studies (Stolte 2004; Huebner 2004) have produced contradictory results as to whether 'treatment optimism' is responsible for the observed decreased condom use and increased levels of STIs, especially among gay men, it makes intuitive sense that when the extreme threat of a universally fatal disease that has killed lovers and friends is lifted, some people in vulnerable communities who might previously have maintained safer sex become prepared to take risks. The increased numbers and improved state of health of HIV-positive people has also meant that more continue to be sexually active, and for longer. This has led to a new and anxious concentration on people with HIV as sexual beings and vectors of disease.

In this chapter, we will therefore look at HIV prevention as a much broader set of techniques and messages than just 'choose safer sex'. To bring some order to a complex field we will use the template of the African 'A-B-C' prevention model, with a couple of additions, without implying that this is an endorsement of it as *the* HIV prevention approach.

A is for Abstinence looks at whether there is evidence that programmes which encourage sexual abstinence or delay sexual debut in young people help to reduce HIV infection.

B is for Being faithful and Behaviour change looks at the degree to which HIV prevention projects have changed sexual behaviour in general, especially in adults.

C is for Condoms and other barrier methods looks at the evidence for the effectiveness of male and female condoms in preventing HIV and other STIs and will review recent evidence on the effectiveness of programmes to encourage condom use.

D is for disclosure, negotiated safety and serosorting looks at measures people with and without HIV take to reduce risk as an alternative to, or in addition to, using condoms

E is for Emergent technologies reviews available and potential new prevention technologies.

References

Albarracin D et al. *A test of major assumptions about behaviour change: a comprehensive look at the effects of passive and active HIV-prevention interventions since the beginning of the epidemic.* Psychological Bulletin 131(6): 856-897, 2005.

Centers for Disease Control. *A Glance at the HIV/AIDS Epidemic. Centers for Disease Control.* See http://www.cdc.gov/hiv/dhap.htm. 16 June 2005.

Centers for Disease Control. *HIV Prevalence, Unrecognized Infection, and HIV Testing Among Men Who Have Sex with Men --- Five U.S. Cities, June 2004--April 2005.* CDC Mortality and Morbidity Weekly Report. See http://www.cdc.gov/mmwr/preview/mmwrhtml/mm5424a2.htm.%2024%20June%202 005.

Crepaz N et al. *Highly active antiretroviral therapy and sexual risk behavior: A meta-analytic review* .JAMA292: 224-236, 2004.

Elford, J et al. *Peer education has no significant impact on HIV risk behaviours among gay men in London.* AIDS 15(4): 535-538, 2001.

Global Campaign for Microbicides Factsheet: *Frequently asked questions about microbicides.* See http://www.global-campaign.org/clientfiles/FS2-FAQs-May05.pdf. Revised May 2005.

Health Protection Agency Quarterly HIV/AIDS Surveillance tables. See http://www.hpa.org.uk/infections/topics_az/hiv_and_sti/hiv/epidemiology/files/quarterly. pdf.%20June%202005.

Holtgrave DR, Anderson T. *Utilizing HIV transmission rates to assist in prioritizing HIV prevention services.* Int J STD AIDS 15(12): 789-792, 2004.

Huebner D et al. *A longitudinal study of the association between treatment optimism and sexual risk-behaviour in young adult men who have sex with men.* Fifteenth International AIDS Conference, Bangkok, abstract D11585, 2004.

Johnson W et al. *HIV prevention research for men who have sex with men: a systematic review and meta-analysis.* JAIDS 30 (suppl. 1), S118-129, 2002.

Laga M. *Synergy between prevention and care in Africa.* Third International AIDS Conference on HIV Pathogenesis and Treatment, Rio de Janeiro, abstract MoFo0104, 2005.

Marseille E, Hofmann PB, Kahn JG. *HIV prevention before HAART in sub-Saharan Africa.* Lancet 359: 9320, 1851-1856. 2002.

Porco TC et al. *Decline in HIV infectivity following the introduction of highly active antiretroviral therapy.* AIDS 18(1): 81-88. 2004.

Salomon JA et al. *Integrating HIV prevention and treatment: from slogans to impact.* PLos Medicine, 2(1): 50-56, 2005.

Stolte I et al. *Homosexual men change to risky sex when perceiving less threat of HIV/AIDS since availability of highly active antiretroviral therapy - a longitudinal study.* AIDS 18: 303-309, 2004.

Stover J et al (2002). *Can we reverse the HIV/AIDS pandemic with an expanded response?* Lancet 360: 73-77, 2002.

Stover J et al (2006). *The global impact of scaling up HIV/AIDS prevention programmes in low- and middle-income countries.* Science 311: 1474-1476, 2006.

Stryker J et al. *Prevention of HIV infection. Looking back, looking ahead.* JAMA 273(14), 1995.

A is for abstinence

Delaying a young person's sexual debut, or at least the age at which they start having full intercourse, could be a very effective HIV prevention measure in certain populations.

In the developing world young women are much more vulnerable to HIV than young men. In southern Africa, for instance, HIV prevalence among young women aged 15 to 24 is three times higher than among young men, and among under-20s up to ten times higher (UNAIDS 2004.). This is attributed partly to culture - with a pattern of older men seeking out younger women for sex - but also partly to nature; the immature genital tract of young women is more susceptible to HIV and other sexually transmitted infections (STIs).

One population among whom delayed debut of intercourse would serve to reduce HIV infections is young gay men.

In the 2002 Gay Men's Sex Survey *Out and About* (Hickson 2003), the authors comment on the finding that the median sexual debut age of young gay men is 16 and the age of first anal intercourse is 17:

"The median age of first heterosexual sex among the male population in the UK is 14 years and median age of first vaginal intercourse is 18. This suggests that gay men have to wait longer before starting to experience sex with men than their heterosexual counterparts do with women, but proceed to intercourse quicker. This is congruent with gay men having been denied opportunities to 'date' or 'court' while a teenager and being left to enter the adult world of sexuality with little practice, support or guidance."

Unfortunately, lesbians and gay men are largely excluded from abstinence education programmes - explicitly so in the case of 'abstinence only until marriage'.

Abstinence in people with HIV

Another population that in some cases appears to be practising abstinence as an HIV prevention method is HIV-positive people. One US survey (Weinhardt 2004), for instance, found that 18.5% of gay men and 26% of heterosexual men and women had not had sex in the three months prior to the survey. Although much of this lack of a sex life will be due to illness, stigma or fear of rejection, some individuals with HIV have taken a willed choice to remain sexually abstinent in order not to pass on their HIV. This appears to be particularly the case with women. The Padare Project (Chinouya 2003), for instance, a survey of HIV-positive Africans living in London, found that while only 10% of men had not had sex in the previous four weeks, among women the proportion rose to one-third.

Even some positive gay youth appear to be trying abstinence, in the absence of any encouragement to do so. A survey of HIV-positive gay men aged 15-24 in Los Angeles (Lightfoot 2005) found that 12% of this group had had no sex with anyone in the three months preceding the study.

Another survey in 2006 looked at the sex lives of people with HIV from the US HIV Cost and Services Utilization Study (HCSUS).

Of the 1,339 HCSUS respondents whose data were analysed, 415 participants reported being sexually inactive in the previous six months. Of those, 201 were deliberately abstinent. More women (18%) and heterosexual men (18%) were deliberately abstinent than gay/bisexual men (11%).

The investigators found that the likelihood of deliberate abstinence was higher among women and heterosexual men, older participants, and those with a stronger sense of responsibility. It was lower among those with a primary relationship partner/spouse, those on antiretroviral therapy, subjects with CD4 counts of 50 or higher, and drinkers.

The researchers found that higher perceived responsibility for limiting disease transmission and non-drinking status were related to deliberate abstinence only among gay men. Worse health was associated with deliberate abstinence only among heterosexual men.

Does abstinence work to reduce HIV transmission?

Does encouraging abstinence work? And does it lead to lower HIV incidence? The data are contradictory, and clouded by differing interpretations of the data.

One study (Bessinger 2003) found that the proportion of urban young women aged 15-19 in Uganda who said they had 'never had sex' increased from 44 to 60% between 1990 and 2000, with an even sharper increase in young men from 33 to 66%. The same study found similar declines in Zambia but not in Zimbabwe or among young women in Cameroon and Kenya.

However another study (Wawer 2005) from the rural province of Rakai, Uganda found that abstinence rates in teenagers had *declined* from 60 to 50% in women and 32 to 28% in men between 1990 and 2002. The same study found that a decline in HIV prevalence from 17.6 to 11.4% during the same period was largely due to more people dying of AIDS than becoming infected with HIV. Rakai has a mature epidemic, being the first district of Uganda from which AIDS was reported, in 1982.

In the USA the Clinton administration was the first to set aside $50 million a year specifically for abstinence education, though the Christian Education Centre had first mooted abstinence education as a way of reducing HIV and STIs in 1987 and programmes such as True Love Waits had been running since 1992.

By 2005 under George W Bush this funding had risen to $167m, with an 18.5% increase promised for 2006 and $204 million for 2007, and with no comparative funding set aside directly for comprehensive, non-abstinence-based sex education in schools.

Conservative think-tank the Heritage Foundation (Pardue 2004) said this was still only one-twelfth of the money spent on all condom provision and comprehensive sex education, and that a large proportion of the federal money was in fact being spent by 'abstinence plus' programmes which taught abstinence as the preferred option in a comprehensive sex education package.

In June 2006, however, more than 200 organisations, representing all 50 states and the District of Columbia, launched a nationwide *No More Money* campaign in an effort to stop federal funding for abstinence-only-until-marriage programs. The campaign was co-ordinated by the Sexuality Information and Education Council of the U.S. (SIECUS). Its vice-president, for public policy, William Smith, said: "Now that it is clear that there is no sound research supporting these programs, no support in the public health community, and no support by the American people, we are asking Congress to stop funding these harmful programs." (see http://www.nomoremoney.org/).

Whether abstinence programmes have made any difference is up for interpretation. One undisputed fact is that the teenage pregnancy rate - seen as an indicator of STI rates - declined in the USA during the 1990s from 117 per 1,000 in 1990 to 84

per 1,000 in 1999, and is now lower than the overall UK rate though it is still five times the rate in the Netherlands.

The national rate declined by 27% (Haddock, 2005) - but in California, which is the sole state to have refused federal funds for abstinence-only education, it fell by 40%, and the national rate has not declined further since 2000.

There is no definitive answer as to whether abstinence-only programmes will impact on HIV incidence in American youth.

Evidence against the effectiveness of abstinence programmes

The most rigorous published review to date (Kirby 2001) of 28 sex education programs in the United States and Canada aimed at reducing teen pregnancy and STIs, including HIV, found that none of the three abstinence-only programs that met inclusion criteria for review demonstrated evidence of efficacy for delaying sexual debut. Furthermore, these three programs did not reduce the frequency of sex or the number of partners among those students who had ever had sex.

However, this same review found that nine abstinence-*plus* programmes (meaning abstinence education as part of comprehensive sex education) showed efficacy in delaying sexual debut, as well as reducing the frequency of intercourse and increasing condom use once sex began.

The largest study so far undertaken specifically of abstinence-only programmes (Bearman 2005) also suggests that while they may significantly delay the age of sexual debut, the long-term effect on sexual health is neutral.

The study interviewed 20,000 teenagers aged 12-18 in 1995, and again in 1997 and 2002. At this point 11,550 of them also provided a urine sample so researchers could find any evidence of STI infections.

One in five teenagers said they had taken a virginity pledge. Despite this, 61% of 'consistent' pledgers had had sex before marriage or before the final 2002 interviews.

The study did find that youth who took abstinence pledges started having sexual intercourse on average 18 months to two years later than youth who did not - though without a proper longitudinal study with baseline attitudes measured, it's impossible to say whether they would have been the kind of young people who would have delayed sex anyway.

The study authors commented: "Pledgers have fewer partners than nonpledgers. Whereas the typical nonpledger male has had 2.4 partners, male pledgers have 1.5 partners on average (p < .0009). The same pattern holds for females as well, 2.7 for nonpledgers and 1.9 for pledgers (p <.0009).

"Nor are pledgers exposed to STI risk for as long as nonpledgers. The average number of years of sexual activity, or time of exposure, is shorter for pledgers than for others. Consistent pledgers were sexually active for an average of 4.2 years, compared with nonpledgers with 5.9 years (p < .0009). Thus, with respect to both the number of partners and cumulative exposure, pledgers are at lower risk to acquisition of an STI than nonpledgers."

However the same study found that 'pledgers' were one-third less likely to use contraception (barrier or otherwise) when they did have sex than 'non-pledgers'. It found that pledgers were slightly but significantly less likely to use a condom at first sex (55% versus 60% condom use, p= <.018). And teenagers' STI rates once they married were the same regardless of whether they had had premarital sex.

It also found that there was evidence that teenagers who took abstinence pledges were "technically" avoiding loss of virginity by having more oral and anal sex. Just two per cent of non-pledgers reported having no vaginal sex but having oral sex: in pledgers the proportion was 13%.

More worryingly, although the absolute figures were small, more pledgers had anal sex as an alternative to vaginal sex too: 1.2% of pledgers and 0.7% of non-pledgers.

Another survey, (Goodson 2004) of five abstinence-only programmes from 59 schools in Texas, which interviewed 726 students aged 11 to 17, found that abstinence-only education apparently made no difference to the proportion of teenagers who were sexually active. It found that 23% of year nine (14 year-old) girls and boys were sexually active before attending an abstinence programme. Afterwards, 28% of girls were sexually active, and when boys were asked a year later at age 15, a total of 39% were active. Other programmes have reported even more substantial increases in sexual activity after programmes, indicating that they have made little or even a negative difference to the natural tendency of more teenagers to start having sex as they get older.

Evidence for the effectiveness of abstinence programmes

The supporters of abstinence programmes, however, including the Heritage Foundation (Rector 2002), pointed to studies which found that at least ten programmes had produced success, by some measures, though in some cases this was more to do with changing teenagers' attitudes towards abstinence than their actual behaviour. It did find, among other things, a steeper decrease in the teenage pregnancy rate in Monroe County, New York, where an abstinence-only programme called 'Not Me, Not Now' had been operating, compared with surrounding non-abstinence-only counties. It found that a programme in Little Rock, Arkansas "reduced the sexual activity rate of girls from 10.2 to 5.9% and of boys from 22.8 to 15.8%." And it found that 14 year-old boys who had not attended a programme in Georgia were three times as likely to have begun having sex by the end of eighth grade as boys who had attended it.

A study by Dr Robert Lerner published in *Adolescent and Family Health* evaluated the effectiveness of the Best Friends abstinence education programme. It found that students in it were significantly less likely than their peers to engage in high-risk behaviours.

The Best Friends program began in 1987 and currently operates in more than 100 schools across the United States. Its curriculum consists of a character-building programme for girls in the fifth or sixth grade, including at least 110 hours of instruction, mentoring, and group activities throughout the year. Discussion topics include friendship, love and dating, self-respect, decision-making, alcohol abuse, drug abuse, physical fitness and nutrition, and AIDS/STIs. The predominant theme of the curriculum is encouragement to abstain from high-risk behavior, including sexual activities. A companion programme for boys, Best Men, began in 2000.

Specifically, girls who participated the Best Friends program had:

- A 52% reduction in the likelihood that they would smoke
- A 90% reduction in the likelihood that they would use drugs
- A 60% reduction in the likelihood that they would drink alcohol
- An 80% reduction in the likelihood that they would have sex

The study compared several years of data on girls from Washington, D.C., who participated in the Best Friends programme with data on Washington, D.C., girls of the same age from the Centers for Disease Control's (CDC) Youth Risk Behavior Survey (YRBS).

Using multiple logistic regressions, which controlled for grade, age, race, and survey year, the study found a significant decrease in the incidence of high-risk behaviours among Best Friends girls as compared to YRBS girls.

Abstinence supporters said that two other studies (Mohn; Santelli) supported the contention that abstinence was largely responsible for the decline in teenage pregnancy rates.

Mohn found that increased abstinence among 15 to 19 year-old teens accounted for at least two-thirds (67%) of the drop in teen pregnancy rates. Increased abstinence also accounted for more than half (51%) of the decline in teen birth rates.

Santelli found that 53% of the decline in teen pregnancy rates from 1991 to 2001 could be attributed to decreased sexual experience among teens aged 15 to 17, while only 47% of the decline was attributed to increased use of contraception among teens.

Same data, differing interpretations

However Santelli also found that when teenagers had sex, condom use increased during this period from 40% to 51%, that teenagers who used no method of protection fell from 17% to 13% and that ones who tried to use withdrawal (without a condom) as their method declined from 20% to 13%. So these findings back the promotion of condom use as well as abstinence.

However although abstinence programmes may reduce rates of sexual activity, opponents of them say that many do so by spreading disempowering and negative messages about sex and condoms.

The Heritage Foundation document quoted above (Rector, 2002) documents significantly higher rates of depression and suicide in teenagers who have sex versus teenagers who don't, while failing to establish the direction of causation: does sex make teenagers depressed, or do depressed teenagers turn to sex for comfort or due to a history of sexual abuse?

And the fact that condoms prevent 85% of HIV infections if used consistently, and 30% of herpes infections (because herpes can be transmitted through touch) is used as evidence that condoms are not a 'safe' protection method against HIV and that they 'never or rarely' prevent herpes. This led to pressure on the US Centers for Disease Control and Prevention (the CDC) to take down temporarily from its website information on the effectiveness of condoms, and was the spur to various legislative changes, such as the State of Louisiana withdrawing all state-financed condom distribution in 2004.

Clearly, abstinence or at least delayed sexual debut could prevent a lot of HIV and STI infections in younger people if it was 'used properly' as a strategy, but equally clearly the evidence we have so far points to it being used more inconsistently than condoms.

Mindful of public controversy about the amount of money spent on abstinence-only programmes, the US government is currently conducting a large survey of their effectiveness.

Abstinence in Africa

Meanwhile in Africa, the lobbying group Human Rights Watch (Human Rights Watch 2005) criticised an apparent policy shift towards abstinence-only programmes, saying that the Ugandan Government had removed critical HIV information from primary school curricula, including information about condoms, safer sex and the risks of HIV in marriage. Uganda's Minister of State for Primary Health Care was quoted as saying: "As a ministry, we have realised that abstinence and being faithful to one's partner are the only sure ways to curb AIDS. From next year, the ministry is going to be less involved in condom importation but more involved in awareness campaigns; abstinence and behaviour change."

Uganda's first lady, Janet Museveni, leads an abstinence programme called the National Youth Forum, describing her approach as "a blend of African and Christian values." However a spokesman for her husband, President Yoweri Museveni, said the government was merely being consistent in advocating for its multi-pronged 'ABC' strategy against AIDS: "Those who are sexually active should be faithful to their partners, others who are single should abstain until marriage, and those who cannot abstain should use condoms."

There has certainly been an increase in the age of sexual debut in Uganda - see chart below - and this may have contributed to reports of declining HIV incidence (see 'Being faithful' below). But the sharpest decline happened in the mid-90s, long before abstinence-only as an approach had been adopted in this country, but around the time the HIV epidemic was maturing and large numbers of family members were dying. The fear of death may be a greater incentive to abstinence than exhortations to stay 'pure'.

HIV activist and prevention advocates in Uganda expressed concern that the new emphasis on abstinence-only programmes and restrictions in condom supply were reversing two decades of successful HIV prevention work, after a survey found that HIV prevalence was starting to increase again, according the *The Lancet* (Wakabi). The national serostatus survey for 2004/05 showed that average national prevalence was 6.4%, slightly up from 6.2% just over a year previously. Infection was shifting from the youth to adults aged between 30 and 40 years. Prevalence rates have traditionally been higher among younger people, so the new trend has baffled health workers. There are at least 1.4 million Ugandans living with HIV.

Two incidents had led to condoms being de-emphasised as the main weapon in the fight against HIV/AIDS. The first was Janet Museveni's campaign.

Secondly, a recall of some brands of condoms in 2004/05 due to concerns about their quality led to a national shortage.

A 2005 study by researchers at the local Makerere University and the AIDS Information Centre showed that when condoms were used by most Ugandans aged 19-25, they were primarily considered contraceptive tools rather than protection against infections.

These findings have added weight to calls from local and international health groups for President Museveni and his government to commit to promoting the ABC strategy properly, rather than trying to downplay the utility of condoms in HIV prevention.

The US Leadership against HIV/AIDS, Tuberculosis, and Malaria Act of 2003 which set up the President's Emergency Plan for AIDS Relief (PEPFAR) recommended that 20% of funds designated to fulfilling the law be designated to prevention. Of that 20%, the law mandated that 33% should be dedicated to abstinence-until-marriage programmes.

In April 2006, the United States Government Accountability Office (GAO) released a report reviewing how the Office of the U.S. Global AIDS Coordinator (OGAC) administers funds for HIV prevention through PEPFAR. The GAO report found that 10 of the 15 PEPFAR focus countries had requested exemptions from fulfilling the abstinence 'earmark' between September 2005 and January 2006, citing the following challenges:

- reduced spending for Preventing Mother-to-Child Transmission (PMTCT):

- limited funding to deliver appropriate prevention messaging to high-risk groups:

- lack of responsiveness to cultural and social norms:

- cuts in medical and blood safety activities:

- and elimination of care programmes.

The report found that OGAC was over-interpreting the abstinence-until-marriage earmark by applying it to all prevention funding although, by law, it only applies to funds appropriated to the Global HIV/AIDS Initiative account, which amounted to an additional $33 million in fiscal year 2006.

It found that the lack of clarity from OGAC on how to implement Abstinence, Be Faithful, Use Condoms (ABC) programmes had caused major confusion and challenges for US government staff and partners implementing programmes in PEPFAR countries.

A lack of clarity about what is permitted in regard to "C" (condom activities) had created a culture of fear amongst PEPFAR implementing partners who are concerned about "crossing the line between providing information about condoms and promoting or marketing condoms." One PEPFAR partner NGO said that "although the organisation views condom demonstrations as appropriate in some settings it believes that condom demonstrations, even to adults, are prohibited under PEPFAR."

Seventeen of the 20 PEPFAR country teams interviewed reported that the earmark "presents challenges to their ability to respond to local epidemiology and cultural and social norms."

Despite the fact that OGAC's guidance on ABC programs requires the programs be integrated, "about half of the 15 focus country teams reported that meeting the abstinence-until-marriage earmark undermines their ability to integrate ABC programs as required." Country teams went even further to say that segregating AB from other prevention funding compromises prevention programmes for at-risk groups that need comprehensive messages.

In June 2006 the *Protection Against Transmission of HIV for Women and Youth Act of 2006*

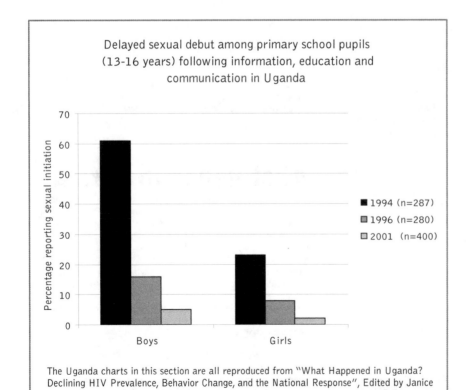

Delayed sexual debut among primary school pupils (13-16 years) following information, education and communication in Uganda

Percentage reporting sexual initiation

- ■ 1994 (n=287)
- ■ 1996 (n=280)
- □ 2001 (n=400)

The Uganda charts in this section are all reproduced from "What Happened in Uganda? Declining HIV Prevalence, Behavior Change, and the National Response", Edited by Janice Hogle, USAID, 2002.

(http://www.advocatesforyouth.org/pathway_hr5674.pdf)(PATH WAY) (http://www.advocatesforyouth.org/pathway_hr5674.pdf), a bill that would remove the abstinence-only-until-marriage funding earmark from PEPFAR, was sponsored by Republican and Democrat members of the House of Representatives. It required "the President and the Office of the Global AIDS Coordinator to establish a comprehensive and integrated HIV prevention strategy to address the vulnerabilities of women and girls in countries for which the United States provides assistance to combat HIV/AIDS, and for other purposes."

References

Bearman, P and Brückner, H. *After the promise: the STD consequences of adolescent virginity pledges.* Journal of Adolescent Health, 36(4): 271-278, 2005.

Bessinger Ret al. *Sexual behavior, HIV, and fertility trends. A comparative analysis of six countries. Phase I of the ABC study.* Washington, DC: U.S. Agency for International Development, Measure Evaluation, 2003.

Bogart LM et al. *Patterns and correlates of deliberate abstinence among men and women with HIV/AIDS.* AM J Publ Health 96(6): 1078-1984, 2006.

Chinouya, M. & Davidson, O. *The Padare Project: assessing health-related knowledge, attitudes and behaviours of HIV-positive Africans accessing services in north central London.* African HIV Policy Network, February 2003.

Government Accountability Office. *Spending requirement presents challenges for allocating prevention funding under the president's emergency plan for AIDS relief. GAO report, April 2006. Can be downloaded from:* http://democrats.reform.house.gov/Documents/20060404121414-18003.pdf

Goodson P et al. *Abstinence education evaluation phase 5: technical report.* Department of health and kinesiology, Texas A&M University, College Station, Texas, 170-172, 2004.

Haddock, Vicki. *Key to Sex Education: discipline or knowledge - advocating abstinence and safe sex may both cut pregnancies.* San Francisco Chronicle, May 22 2005.

Hickson F et al. *Out and About:, Findings from the United Kingdom Gay Men's Sex Survey 2002.* Sigma Research, 2003.

Hogle J. *What happened in Uganda? Declining HIV prevalence, behavior change, and the national response,* USAID, 2002.

Human Rights Watch. *The less they know, the better: Abstinence-only HIV/AIDS programs in Uganda.* Human Rights Watch. See http://hrw.org/reports/2005/uganda0305/index.htm.%20March%202005.

Kirby D. *Emerging Answers:: research findings on programs to reduce teen pregnancy.* Washington D.C.: The National Campaign to Prevent Teen Pregnancy, 2001.

Lerner P. *Can abstinence work? An analysis of the best friends program.* Adolescent and Family Health, 3(4): 185-192, 2004.

Mohn J et al. *An analysis of the causes of the decline in mon-marital birth and pregnancy rates for teens from 1991 to 1995.* Adolescent and Family Health, 3(1): 39-47, 2003.

Pardue Melissa G. et al. *Government spends $12 on safe sex and contraceptives for every $1 spent on abstinence.* Heritage Foundation backgrounder #718. See http://www.heritage.org/Research/Family/bg1718.cfm. 2004.

Rector Robert E. *The effectiveness of abstinence education programs in reducing sexual activity among youth.* Heritage Foundation backgrounder #1533. See http://www.heritage.org/Research/Family/BG1533.cfm.%202002.

Santelli JS et al. *Can changes in sexual behaviors among high school students explain the decline in teen pregnancy rates in the 1990s?* Journal of Adolescent Health, 35(2): 80-90, 2004.

UNAIDS. *AIDS Epidemic Update.* See http://www.unaids.org/html/pub/gcwa/jc986-epiextract_en_pdf.pdf. , December 2004.

Wakabi W. *Condoms still contentious in Uganda's struggle over AIDS.* The Lancet 367(9520): 1387-1388, 2006.

Wawer MJ et al. *Declines in HIV Prevalence in Uganda: Not as Simple as ABC.* Twelveth Conference on Retroviruses and Opportunistic Infections, Boston, 2005, abstract LB27, 2005.

Weinhardt L et al. HIV *Transmission risk behavior among men and women living with HIV in 4 cities in the United States.* JAIDS 36(5): 1057-1066, 2004.

B is for being faithful and behaviour change

B, which stands in the original 'ABC' model for 'Be faithful', but also involves partner reduction as well as strict monogamy, has been called "The neglected middle child of 'ABC'"(Shelton 2004). It is difficult to gather evidence on whether HIV prevention programmes have influenced target populations in the direction of monogamy and reduction of the number of sexual partners, and there has been remarkably little research into, or co-ordinated campaigns promoting, partner reduction as an end in itself.

This is to be regretted, because the rate of spread of HIV in a population is more sensitively dependent on the rate of partner change, whether relationships are concurrent and consecutive, and whether partners are drawn from the local village or the global community, than on any other variable. The spread of HIV is crucially dependent on the establishment of sexual 'networks': remove a few links from those networks and the chain of infection can no longer be maintained. One paper (Garnett 1998) put it this way:

"Heterogeneity in sexual behaviour is vital to generate a high sexual activity 'core group' within which HIV spreads rapidly. How far out of this core group the virus will spread depends on the patterns of mixing within populations."

Another important aspect of reducing the rate of partner change is that it reduces the number of times people are likely to come across partners in early HIV infection. One paper (Pilche, 2004) calculated that, because people in acute HIV infection have much higher viral loads, up to a quarter of all HIV infections are spread by people within two months of themselves being infected,

and the proportion could be even higher if concurrent STIs are taken into consideration.

One problem with research into monogamy and reduction in the number of sexual partners is that it takes two people to be monogamous. An example of the traps the faithful partner of an unfaithful one can fall into is illustrated by an April 2005 study (Thorburn, 2005) which found that among Afro-American heterosexual men and women, lower levels of condom use and contraception were found among people who agreed with the statement 'known partners are safe partners' than among ones who agreed that '*trusted* partners are safe partners'.

In the developed world, far from the number of partners being reduced amongst the general population, the trend in the 1990s was the opposite way. For instance, in the UK, comparing the 1990 and 2000 National Surveys of Sexual Attitudes and Lifestyles (NATSAL), the average number of lifetime sexual partners increased from 8.6 to 12.7 in men and from 3.7 to 6.5 in women, with a particularly sharp increase in the proportion of women reporting more than five lifetime partners, and an equally sharp decrease in the number reporting that they had only had one (see the chart on the next page).

In the developed world, several factors work against reductions in the number of partners and an increase in 'faithfulness'. An increasing sexualisation of 'pop culture' has gone hand in hand with increasing opportunities to access non-marital sex, via channels like the internet. Increasing numbers of people saying that they had had same-sex partnerships (both men and women) attest to this too.

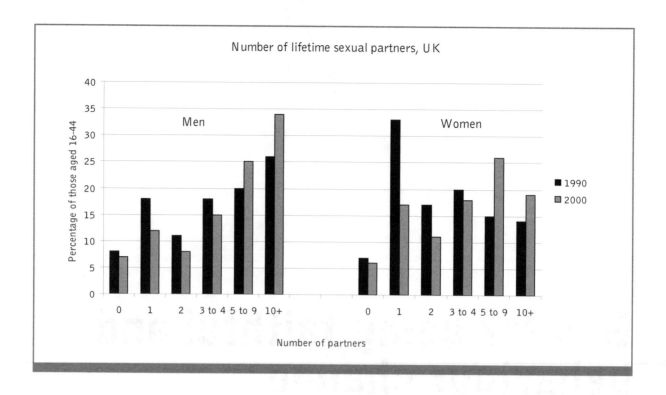

Number of lifetime sexual partners, UK

The early 1990s may also have been an exceptional period with historically low points of sexual risk behaviour - as the data on sexually transmitted infections suggest - in that they coincided with the peak of public concerns about what was then an untreatable AIDS epidemic.

However it is probably true to say that monogamy or partner reduction, in itself (as opposed to abstinence until marriage and an assumption that marriage subsequently implies monogamy) has not been a target of HIV prevention campaigns in the developed world.

One of the few places where a reduction in the number of partners can be teased out as a contributor to lower HIV incidence and prevalence is, once again, in Uganda. That HIV prevalence has fallen no one disputes (except in the war-torn north of the country). But the evidence as to the contribution of partner reduction and increased monogamy to the decline in the figures is still indirect.

According to the USAID report cited in the previous section: "In the mid 1990s, two large randomised trials at Rakai and Masaka in Uganda attempted to look at the impact of STI treatment on reducing HIV prevalence. Although both interventions reduced the rates of some STIs, there was no significant reduction in HIV incidence.

"According to an expert panel at the 2002 World AIDS Conference in Barcelona, the main reason for the lack of effect on HIV from STI treatment was the large decrease in risky sex/multiple partner trends that had occurred in Uganda by the time the STI trials began. Most HIV transmission therefore now occurs within monogamous regular partnerships, where one partner has undiagnosed HIV, but where bacterial STIs tend to be rare."

Certainly a considerable reduction in the amount of 'casual sex' among the population had occurred by 1995, with 50-70% declines in the number of people reporting it (see *Percentage of people reporting casual sex in the past twelve months, Uganda* to the loft) and Uganda was the only country in the area to report such declines around that time.

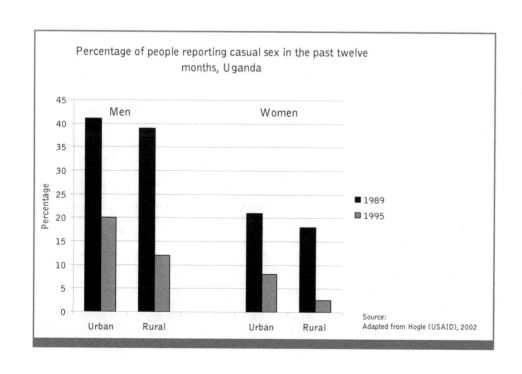

Percentage of people reporting casual sex in the past twelve months, Uganda

Source:
Adapted from Hogle (USAID), 2002

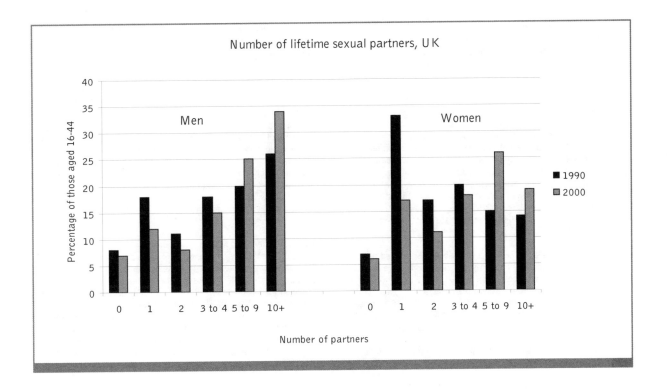

Number of lifetime sexual partners, UK

This decline appears to be evidence that it was not merely the ending of war and the restoring of civil order on Museveni's accession in 1986, which would involve men returning from the army and militias to their families, which created this change in behaviour patterns.

According to Stoneburner and colleagues (2000), "Ugandans are relatively more likely to receive AIDS information through friendship and other personal networks than through mass media or other sources, and are significantly more likely to know of a friend or relative with AIDS. Social communication elements, as suggested by these kinds of indicators, may be necessary to bridge the motivational gap between AIDS prevention activities and behavior change sufficient to affect HIV incidence."

In other words, Stoneburner is arguing that the social diffusion model (see *HIV Prevention: Which Methods Work?*) in which there is (a) a wide personal acquaintance with HIV/AIDS in the population and (b) the encouragement and willingness to speak about it and pass knowledge on in informal social networks is the method that has worked to influence behaviour change, almost uniquely so far for an African country, in Uganda. The first is the inevitable consequence of a developing untreated epidemic: the second, however, can be influenced by political leadership and widespread awareness-raising work. Such work was, supporters say, initiated by Museveni when he started his AIDS awareness campaign in 1986, which included his famous 'Zero Grazing' policy, which urged monogamy on all Ugandans.

However there is recent evidence that this shift in behaviour in Uganda may have essentially happened in the decade from 1985 to 1995, but that in the last ten years a more 'westernised' pattern of behaviour involving the resurgence of extra-marital sex, but an increased use of condoms, has become more common.

In the Wawer study cited above (Wawer, 2005), which looked at behaviour change in the Rakai district from 1993 to 2004, the main driver of reduced HIV prevalence was found to be attrition of the HIV-positive population due to AIDS deaths, with a smaller contribution from increased condom use. During the study period, HIV prevalence had decreased from 17.5 to 11%, but the annual incidence of HIV had *not* declined, and may have even slightly increased, from 1.3 to 1.7% a year.

During the decade the age of sexual debut got younger again; 50% of 19 year-old men had had sex in 2004 compared with

40% in 1994. The proportion of men reporting two or more sexual partners had gone up from 20 to 27%, and among who tested HIV-positive in the study from 40 to 68%. However condom use had doubled during the same time, from 19 to 38%, a high figure for Africa.

Is there evidence of partner reduction in other countries? In Zambia, there was a dramatic fall in HIV prevalence in young pregnant women (15-19) between 1993 and 1998, where the proportion living with the virus halved, from 28.4% to 14.8%. A study (Fylkesnes, 2001)found "a dominant declining trend in HIV prevalence that corresponds to declines in incidence since the early 1990s attributable to behavioural changes," which predominantly means a decline in casual sex.

More recently steep, and apparently real, declines in HIV prevalence have been observed in Zimbabwe - in contrast to neighbouring Botswana, where prevalence remains high.

The study (Gregson) that found the declines pointed to the multifactorial nature of the apparent reasons for the decline:

"We report a decline in HIV prevalence in eastern Zimbabwe between 1998 and 2003 associated with sexual behavior change in four distinct socioeconomic strata. HIV prevalence fell most steeply at young ages - by 23 and 49%, respectively, among men aged 17 to 29 years and women aged 15 to 24 years - and in more educated groups. Sexually experienced men and women reported reductions in casual sex of 49 and 22%, respectively, whereas recent cohorts reported delayed sexual debut. Selective AIDS-induced mortality contributed to the decline in HIV prevalence."

At the 2006 PEPFAR Implementers' Meeting in Durban, Dr Owen Murungi from Zimbabwe's Ministry of Health and Child Welfare teased out some of the reasons for the decline (Gregson and Murungi).

The research is also available in a UNAIDS report published in November 2005 (UNAIDS 2005).

According to Dr Murungi, after the dramatic decline in HIV prevalence during 2004 was registered in Zimbabwe, nearly everyone was shocked. "The big question to all of us was, is this real? What's happened?" he said. A review was therefore conducted to determine whether other available data corroborated the finding, and whether the cause for the decline was due to high mortality rates or an actual decrease in incidence. Then, if there was a decline in incidence, could it be explained by natural dynamics of the epidemic or by behaviour changes?

The Ministry pulled together data from 30 different sources, all of which seemed to agree that the fall in HIV prevalence was real. According to antenatal clinic (ANC) data, in the year 2000, the HIV prevalence in Zimbabwe was 32.1% and in the following two years it hovered around 30%. No data were available for 2003 but in 2004 the HIV prevalence had fallen to 23.8% and the test for the trend was statistically significant (p<0.001). This trend was corroborated by data from the ZVITAMBO study, which included pregnant and post-natal women from Harare followed over several years. In this study population the HIV prevalence actually peaked around 1996 (at over 36%) and had been falling ever since (to somewhere around 21% in the middle of 2004).

A study from Manicaland in eastern Zimbabwe also looked at men between the ages of 17 and 44 years old, where there was also a decrease in prevalence, from 19.5% to 18.2% (p=0.01), with declines in all age groups except men over 35. Very few of the younger men were infected, but in the years 1998-2000 close to 50% of the men between the ages of 30-34 were HIV-infected, falling to around 40% in the next survey.

The data that Dr Murungi presented painted a complex picture for the decline in prevalence.

A very large part of the reduction in HIV prevalence was actually due to the very high mortality rate for people with HIV in the country. In Manicaland, the death rates in men peaked in the year 2000 at around 31-32 deaths per 1000 person years falling to around 26 deaths per 1000 person years in 2002/3. In women, rural death rates peaked in 2001, at just below 25 deaths per 1000 person years, falling to around 23 deaths per 1000 person years, although in both cases the confidence intervals overlap.

However, by itself, the mortality rate could not effect a reduction in prevalence unless there had also been a reduction in incidence of HIV infection. At some point in the last few years, people with HIV must have begun dying at a higher rate than new people were becoming infected.

Over the years, a number of studies have looked at HIV incidence in Zimbabwe. In the first one, Mbizvo et al., in 1993, the incidence was around 5% in antenatal women. Around the year 2000, the ZVITAMBO study observed an incidence that was around 3.6%. Among men, a survey in male factory workers, that the Zimbabwe AIDS prevention survey (ZAPS) conducted in 1994, found the incidence to be about 3.5%. Seven years later (2001), a similar survey in male factory workers reported an incidence of less than 2%.

So the cross-study data do suggest a falling incidence - at least between 1993/4 and 2001. If the current incidence is roughly around 2%, at the current mortality rate, the prevalence would decrease substantially each year.

Reductions in HIV incidence could be the result of natural dynamics of the HIV epidemic. Over time, any epidemic is somewhat self limiting. Mortality plays more than one part in this, because it doesn't only decrease prevalence directly, it can decrease incidence as well, by decreasing the pool of infectious individuals who can spread the infection.

But it can be due to behaviour change too. Dr Murungi said that colleagues at Imperial College in London had run simulations suggesting that other factors besides natural dynamics were needed to explain the changes in incidence observed in Zimbabwe.

Over the last few years, there does appear to have been a clear and substantial fall in the percentage of young men who reported having had sex during the last twelve months with non-regular partners. In the Manicaland study, statistically significant changes in reported sexual behaviour were observed for both

males and females in 1) the age of sexual debut, 2) new partners in the last year/month and 3) the number of current partners.

The UNAIDS report did not find statistically significant evidence of increase in the age of sexual debut. But it found substantial evidence of partner reduction, especially in men under 30, where the proportion of men saying they had had 'non-regular' sexual partners in the previous twelve months declined from 58% in 1999 to 21% in 2003. Among women of the same age the trend was less significant but the proportion reporting non-regular partners declined from 17% to 8% in the same period. Since men are much more likely to have casual and commercial sex anyway, a decline in the number of partners men have is likely to have a larger effect on HIV incidence than a decline in the number women have, as we are usually starting from a much higher baseline.

However differences between the indicators of "faithfulness" used in the different surveys meant that it was not possible to find a single indicator for which data were available over a wide range of time points. The table below show the estimates that could be obtained for having one or more non-regular partners in the past twelve months. The data suggest a reduction in non-regular partnerships in the past twelve months occurred between 1999 and 2003, particularly amongst men. However, some caution is warranted since the indicator had to be calculated by combining responses to a number of different questions in 2003 whereas it was asked directly in 1999 and 2001 (see table below):

Proportions of respondents aged 15-29 years at interview reporting a non-regular sexual partner in past twelve months

	Men	Women
DHS data, 1999	≈ 58%	≈ 17%
PSI data, 2001	≈ 33%	≈ 18%
PSI data, 2003	≈ 21%	≈ 8%

Reported condom use with non-regular partners had also increased in the last five years. Dr Murungi noted that there has also been a steady increase in the number of condoms in circulation, particularly socially marketed condoms (rather than public sector condoms).

A chart similar to the one above, detailing increases in condom use in Zimbabwe, is in **C is for condoms.**

What sort of prevention messages were being spread in Zimbabwe in the late-1990s and early 2000s - and who was doing it? It's interesting to compare and contrast what has happened in Zimbabwe with what is going on in Botswana, where despite massive efforts and funding spent on ABC-based prevention messages, the HIV prevalence in Botswana remains extremely high (38.5%).

Again the effects of such a high mortality rate in Zimbabwe need to be considered. History has shown that observing large numbers of people sick and dying of HIV can be a powerful motivator for changing behaviour. There could also be a host of other negative "enabling" factors that played a part in the reported behaviour change. Since the year 2000, Zimbabwe's economy has ground to a halt; the country suffered from floods, followed by severe drought and endemic food insecurity. As a result of Zimbabwe's economic contraction, many of the old hotspots for HIV trans-mission - near the factories and mines, at truck stops along the highway - could be dwindling or people no longer have a reason or the means to go there. Many of those with the means to get out and look for work have poured into neighbouring countries, including Botswana, and South Africa. Hundreds of thousands of adults in their prime working years (who may represent a substantial proportion of the sexually active and possibly HIV-infected population) have simply left the country. And yet, so far, no one has addressed what impact emigration might have had on Zimbabwe's HIV prevalence and incidence - and what might happen should they all return home for treatment (see below) which is increasingly available.

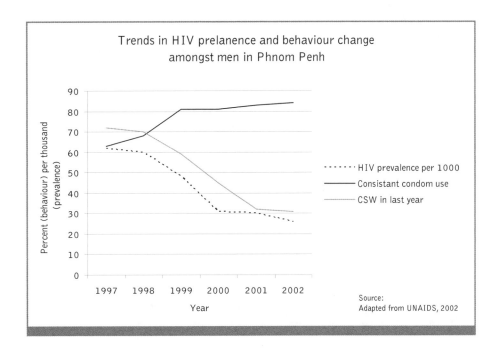

Dr Murungi stressed that Zimbabwe still has a long way to go "We acknowledge the fact that the prevalence rates are still very high in Zimbabwe. We still have a lot to do. 20% is still very, very high."

In Ethiopia (Mekonnen, 2003), a country with a more recent HIV crisis, the proportion of men who reported casual sex at two centres fell in just two years (1997 to 1999) from 17.5 to 3.5%, and the proportion reporting visiting sex workers from 11.2 to just 0.75%.

In Cambodia (UNAIDS, 2002), HIV prevalence halved between 1997 and 2002, as did the proportion of men who reported visiting a sex worker over the year, while condom use, already high, increased less dramatically (see above).

There is one paradox that one needs to be aware of in encouraging monogamous behaviour. In certain HIV-prevalence situations it can make no difference to HIV incidence at all. For instance, in Zimbabwe and South Africa steep declines in the incidence of bacterial STIs like syphilis and gonorrhoea have not been accompanied by declines in HIV. This fact was noticed by an unorthodox researcher, David Gisselquist, who used it as evidence for his theory that the majority of HIV in Africa is being spread by unsterilised medical needles (Gisselquist, 2003).

But the real reason is probably to do with the fact that in these countries prevalence is so high that transmission within marriage or a monogamous relationship is now just as likely as it is during a casual encounter. A monogamous marriage only reduces HIV

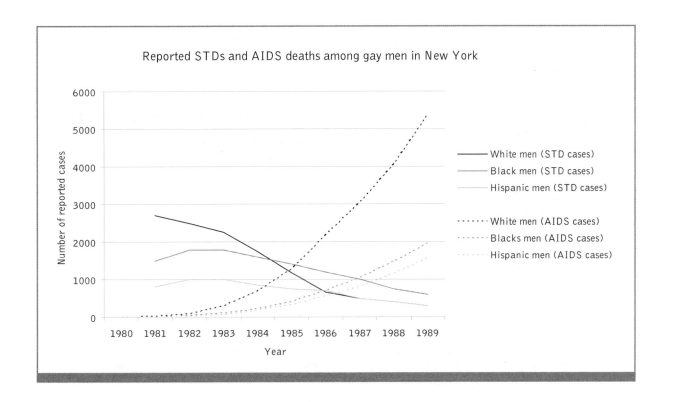

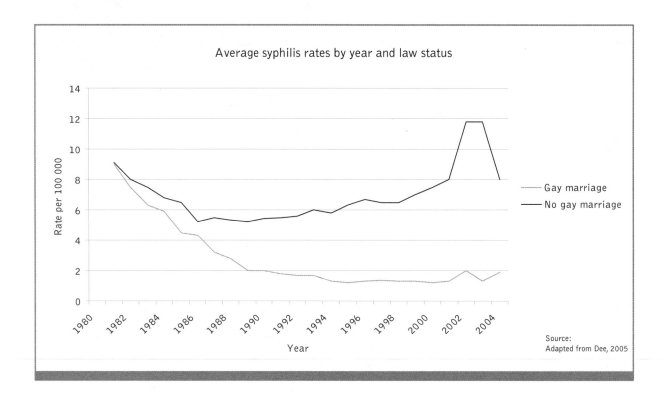

Average syphilis rates by year and law status

Source:
Adapted from Dee, 2005

transmission risk if both partners going into it have the same HIV status, and in countries where HIV testing is the exception rather than the rule, encouraging monogamy may in certain circumstances have the effect of spreading HIV from a core group of sexually active men and their female partners into the female population at large.

What about vulnerable populations in the developed world? There is evidence from the early days of the epidemic(Low-Beer, 2003) that gay men rapidly adjusted their sexual behaviour as soon as the first reports of AIDS appeared. Rates of sexually transmitted diseases and HIV incidence started falling almost immediately, particularly among the more socially cohesive white gay community, though we do not know what proportion of these declines were due to condom adoption, having fewer partners, or abstinence from sex.

The authors of the paper from which the chart on the previous page comes from comment that "these responses preceded and exceeded HIV prevention." However another way of looking at it, using a broader definition of prevention, is that they *were* the first examples of community-led HIV prevention. A chain of 'grapevine knowledge' spread by word of mouth through a closely-knit community is exactly the kind of response to AIDS President Museveni was trying to set up in Uganda.

In the post-HAART era, is a similar behaviour change in gay men possible? There is one intriguing piece of evidence that it might be. US researcher Thomas Dee (2005) used a mathematical model to relate changes in the rates of syphilis, gonorrhoea, TB and malaria in European countries to whether a country had legalised gay marriage or civil partnership.

Dee found a 24% reduction in syphilis incidence and a non-significant reduction in gonorrhoea compared with countries with no gay marriage legislation, and found that the reduction in syphilis started at the same time the marriage legislation was introduced. The rates of the non-sexually transmitted diseases did not change at the same time: neither did HIV diagnoses, but being a non-acute condition, these are subject to a 'time lag'.

This is obviously a highly indirect piece of evidence and cannot say directly whether gay marriage leads to fewer extra-marital partners. It also compares gay marriage with STI rates in the

entire population, though in the case of syphilis, it was gay men during this era who were most affected. However Dee's analysis is conservative: he eliminated from his analysis every other possible variable such as improvements in other health and economic indicators which might also cause falls in STIs, and the difference in syphilis rates on the raw data alone is striking: the 'gay marriage' countries seem so far largely to have avoided the large increases in syphilis seen in countries like the UK. (see above)

If it really is true that, as Dee says "gay marriage will encourage [gay men] to form emotional and legal commitments.that will promote sexual fidelity and possibly reduce STI prevalence," then it again demonstrates that the activities which most successfully reduce HIV incidence and/or risk behaviour may be very far from ones that look like most people's idea of HIV prevention.

Behaviour change in people with HIV

In a country like Zimbabwe, where despite an increase in HIV testing, only a minority of people as yet know their HIV status, it is not possible to relate knowledge of status to behaviour change.

However in the developed world several surveys point to the fact that people with HIV, once diagnosed, substantially reduce their sexual risk behaviour. In the USA the CDC has estimated that people with HIV reduce the number of HIV transmission risk incidents they take part in by 57% after diagnosis (Marks).

In Marks's 2006 study in *AIDS* (Marks) it was estimated that even if HIV-positive people did not reduce their average number of partners post-diagnosis, factors such as reduction in viral load due to HAART would reduce the proportion of HIV spread by people knowing their status such that only 46% of HIV transmissions would be spread by the 75% of people in the USA aware they had HIV, compared with 54% by the 25% of people unaware of their status. This means that a person with HIV who is unaware of their status would be over 3.5 times more likely to transmit HIV than a person aware of it.

However if HIV-positive people also reduced their number of partners generally, then this effect would be accentuated. For instance, if people with HIV reduced the number of HIV-negative partners they had unprotected sex with by 33% relative to the unaware group (or, to put it another way, if the unaware people had 50% more at-risk partners), then the 75% of people aware they had HIV would only be responsible for 37% of infections and the 25% unaware for 63% of them. This means that a person unaware of their status would be more than five times more likely to transmit HIV than a person aware of it.

A 33% reduction in partners was pretty much exactly what was observed in one study of how gay men's sexual behaviour changed after diagnosis (Gorbach).

Gorbach interviewed 113 HIV-positive gay men a month after diagnosis and then again three months afterwards. She found during that period that the average number of partners in the three months prior to interview had declined from 7.9 to 5.2 - a 34% decline.

This was not generalised over the whole group, however. Nearly half (47%) of the men interviewed reported a decrease in the number of partners they had, a third reported an increase. However there was also a very significant shift among those who had unprotected sex to doing it with partners they knew had HIV - see **Disclosure, serosorting and negotiated safety** for details.

References

Dee, Thomas. *Forsaking all others? The effects of "gay marriage" on risky sex.* National Bureau of Economic Research working paper no. 11327. See http://www.nber.org/papers/w11327. 2005.

Fylkesnes K et al. *Declining HIV prevalence and risk behaviours in Zambia: evidence from surveillance and population-based surveys.* AIDS 15(7): 907-916, 2001.

Garnett GP. *The basic reproduction rate of infection and the course of HIV epidemics.* AIDS Patient Care STDs 12: 435-449, 1998.

Gisselquist D et al. *Let it be sexual: how health care transmission of AIDS in Africa was ignored.* Int J STD AIDS 14(3): 148-161, 2003.

Gorbach PM. *Transmission behaviors of recently HIV-infected men who have sex with men.* JAIDS 42(1): 80-85, 2006.

Gregson S et al. *HIV decline associated with behavior change in Eastern Zimbabwe.* Science 311(5761): 664-666, 2006.

Gregson S and Murungi O. *HIV decline accelerated by reductions in unprotected casual sex in Zimbabwe? Evidence from a comprehensive epidemiological review.* The 2006 HIV/AIDS Implementers' Meeting of the President's Emergency Plan for AIDS Relief, Durban, South Africa, abstract 29, 2006.

House of Commons Select Committee on Health third report, 2002-3 session. See www.publications.parliament.uk/pa/cm200203/cmselect/cmhealth/69/6902.htm for details.

Low-Beer D, Stoneburner R. *Behaviour and communication change in reducing HIV: is Uganda unique?* African Journal of AIDS Research 2(1): 9-21, 2003.

Marks G et al. *Estimating sexual transmission of HIV from persons aware and unaware that they are infected with the virus in the USA.* AIDS 20(10): 1447-1450, 2006.

Mekonnen Y et al. *Evidence of changes in sexual behaviours among male factory workers in Ethiopia.* AIDS 17(2): 223-231, 2003.

Pilcher CD et al. *Brief but efficient: acute HIV infection and the sexual transmission of HIV.* J Infect Dis. 189(10): 1785-1792, 2004.

Shelton James D et al. *Partner reduction is crucial for balanced "ABC" approach to HIV prevention.* British Medical Journal 328: 891-893, 2004.

Stoneburner R et al. *Enhancing HIV prevention in Africa: Investigating the role of social cohesion on knowledge diffusion and behavior change in Uganda.* Paper presented at Thirteenth International AIDS Conference, Durban, 2000, (no abstract cited).

Thorburn S et al. *HIV prevention heuristics and condom use among African-Americans at risk for HIV.* AIDS Care 17(3): 335-344, 2005.

UNAIDS 2002. *Report on the global HIV/AIDS epidemic 2002.* Geneva: WHO, 2002.

UNAIDS 2005. *Evidence for HIV decline in Zimbabwe: a comprehensive review of the epidemiological data.* ISBN 92 9 173461 6. Can be downloaded from http://data.unaids.org/publications/irc-pub06/zimbabwe_epi_report_nov05_en.pdf

Wawer MJ et al. *Declines in HIV prevalence in Uganda: not as simple as ABC.* Twelveth Conference on Retroviruses and Opportunistic Infections, Boston, abstract LB27, 2005.

C is for condoms

Efficacy and effectiveness

The crucial question to ask about condoms is not whether they work, but whether they get used.

This distinction is the difference between efficacy - whether an intervention works in ideal circumstances - and effectiveness - whether it reduces disease incidence.

Firstly, however, questions of efficacy have to be addressed, as in recent years condoms' ability to stop HIV has been brought into question by people opposed to their use on religious or moral grounds.

In one of the most highly-publicised statements (Bradshaw, 2003), in October 2003, the President of the Vatican's Pontifical Council for the Family, Cardinal Alfonso Lopez Trujillo, said: "The AIDS virus is roughly 450 times smaller than the spermatozoon. The spermatozoon can easily pass through the 'net' that is formed by the condom.

"These margins of uncertainty...should represent an obligation on the part of the health ministries and all these campaigns to act in the same way as they do with regard to cigarettes, which they state to be a danger."

These statements are quite simply untrue. When condoms are used consistently, their efficacy in preventing HIV and bacterial sexually transmitted infections (STIs) is in the order of 85 to 90%

The most rigorous review (Weller, 2002) of the evidence looked at 16 cross-sectional and twelve longitudinal studies and contrasted the HIV incidence rates between couples who said they 'always' used condoms and ones who said they 'never' did.

The more rigorous longitudinal studies followed condom users for an average of two years among serodiscordant couples and registered seroconversions among the negative partner. They were all among heterosexual couples (three of them people whose main HIV acquisition factor had been intravenous drug use).

The cross-sectional studies assessed HIV status among a high-risk group, and then asked them about their previous condom usage. Four of the cross-sectional studies were among heterosexuals, three of whom were also intravenous drug users. The other nine studies were of gay men. The cross-sectional studies will obviously tend to yield lower apparent efficacy rates, as HIV-positive people who report 'always' using condoms will tend to misreport or misremember their behaviour.

This yields the following efficacy rates for condoms, when the seroconversion rate among 'always used' is calculated as a proportion of the 'never used' rate:

- Gay men, retrospective: 63.6%

- Female to male, retrospective: 36%

- Female to male, longitudinal: 80.5%

- Male to female, longitudinal: 92.8%

- Hetero, direction not stated, longitudinal: 90.8%

This allowed the researchers to calculate a true **efficacy** rate from the longitudinal studies of **86.6%,** on the assumption that the 'always' users did use condoms consistently and correctly, and any seroconversions were due to the inevitable accidents such as slippage and splitting.

The **effectiveness** rate in gay men - that is, the degree to which condom use at the time of the surveys was reducing HIV incidence - can also be approximated. It can be seen that the seroconversion rate between 'sometimes' and 'never' users is very similar. If we assume that the 'always' condom users were gay men who *tried* always to use condoms, and the 'sometimes' gay men were so inconsistent as to make little difference to their HIV seroconversion risk, then this yields an **effectiveness** rate - among the gay community at the time of the surveys, namely from 1986 to 1992 - of around **60%.**

That is, at this early point in the history of the epidemic, condom use as a strategy might have been stopping a maximum of six out of ten potential infections. This is a maximum, because some of those infections might have been stopped by men who use condoms also using other strategies like cutting down on the number of partners, having less anal sex, and so on.

Another study (Winer 2006) has found that condoms offer significant protection against a much more contagious virus than HIV, namely the genital wart- and cervical/anal cancer-causing human papilloma virus (HPV). This is a significant finding because it is a refutation of claims by anti-condom, pro-abstinence campaigners in the USA that condoms did not protect against this kind of infection, and previous studies had appeared to back up this claim (Winer 2003, Ho).

Winer and colleagues found that consistent use of male condoms effectively reduced the risk of male-to-female genital human papilloma virus (HPV) transmission. In contrast to the earlier studies, this was a longitudinal study designed specifically to look at the temporal relationship between condom use and HPV infection.

The authors followed a cohort of female undergraduates ranging in age from 18-22 years, who had either never had vaginal intercourse prior to enrolment or who had just started on their first (heterosexual) relationship.

A total of 126 incident HPV infections were identified in 40 of the 82 women eligible for analysis. The incidence of genital HPV when condoms were used 100% of the time was 37.8 per 100 patient-years, compared with 89.3 per 100 patient-years at risk when condoms were used less than 5% of the time.

Condom usage rates

The degree to which people have taken up the use of condoms during the HIV epidemic varies hugely according to a whole number of different factors. These include the following:

- The degree to which people know that an activity carries an HIV transmission risk

- Whether they think their partner is likely to have HIV

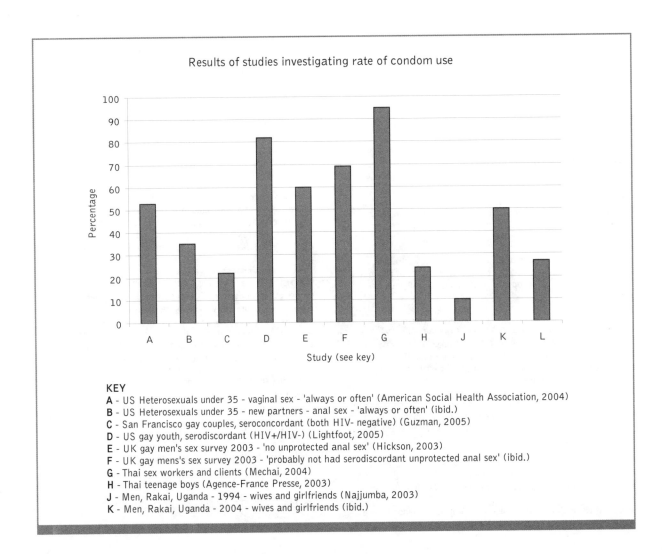

Results of studies investigating rate of condom use

KEY
A - US Heterosexuals under 35 - vaginal sex - 'always or often' (American Social Health Association, 2004)
B - US Heterosexuals under 35 - new partners - anal sex - 'always or often' (ibid.)
C - San Francisco gay couples, seroconcordant (both HIV- negative) (Guzman, 2005)
D - US gay youth, serodiscordant (HIV+/HIV-) (Lightfoot, 2005)
E - UK gay men's sex survey 2003 - 'no unprotected anal sex' (Hickson, 2003)
F - UK gay mens's sex survey 2003 - 'probably not had serodiscordant unprotected anal sex' (ibid.)
G - Thai sex workers and clients (Mechai, 2004)
H - Thai teenage boys (Agence-France Presse, 2003)
J - Men, Rakai, Uganda - 1994 - wives and girlfriends (Najjumba, 2003)
K - Men, Rakai, Uganda - 2004 - wives and girlfriends (ibid.)

- Whether they are having casual or commercial sex or are in a steady relationship

- Whether they are HIV-positive themselves

- Whether risky sex is linked to using alcohol or drugs, which impair people's ability to make healthy decisions

- Whether their behaviour is influenced by chronic mental health problems such as depression, low self-esteem or learned behaviour due to sexual abuse

- Whether they are in a position to insist on the use of condoms

The main factors that influence condom use (other than drugs and mental health) can be illustrated by taking, more or less at random, a selection of condom usage figures from different population groups and exploring the differences between them (see chart opposite)

A risk has to be seen as a risk

The first two columns (A and B) relate to a 2004 telephone survey of heterosexuals under 35 conducted by the US Association for Social Health.

It found that 47% of respondents 'sometimes or never' used condoms for vaginal sex. It also found that of the approximately seven per cent of heterosexuals that said they had anal sex, an even higher proportion did not use condoms - some 65%.

This provides an interesting insight into the under-researched world of heterosexual anal sex and condom use. Firstly, the figure for vaginal sex is quite close to the figures for UK gay men when it comes to consistent condom use for sexual intercourse. Secondly, it shows that a minority sexual behaviour which is in fact a higher HIV transmission risk can result in lower condom usage if HIV prevention messages do not acknowledge that risk. A similar survey from South Africa also found that among the majority of heterosexuals who had anal sex, condom use was lower.

Thirdly, it also sheds light on to how cautious one needs to be in interpreting condom usage results. The only other survey ever done among US adults in the general population (Erickson 1995) found similar rates for anal intercourse but found that among those who had anal sex, only 40% did not use condoms.

Condom use is usually lower in long-term relationships

The next two columns (C and D) contrast condom use between two different populations of gay men. The first were HIV-negative men in long-term relationships living in San Francisco. Among them condom use was the exception not the rule, with only just over one in five couples always using them. Fifty per cent of couples 'allowed' sex outside the relationship, and the main purpose of the study was to see how couples negotiated rules around the safety of 'extra-marital' sex and to what degree these rules were observed or broken.

In contrast, the second group of gay men - in column D - were gay youth (aged 15-25) living with HIV recruited in four US cities, who in the main did not have steady partners. The high condom use figure (82%) was in fact even higher when it came to sex that carried a risk of HIV transmission: with partners whose HIV status was negative or unknown, condom use was 93%.

Unprotected sex is not necessarily unsafe sex

The next two columns (E and F) come from the same data set, the UK Gay Men's Sex Survey of 2003. They represent (E) the proportion of gay and bisexual men who said they had not had unprotected anal intercourse with anyone over the last year (60.2%) and (F) the proportion who said they had 'probably or

definitely' not had unprotected sex with someone of a different HIV status (69.3%).

The nine per cent difference between these two figures represents people who were pretty sure they were having unprotected sex with people whose HIV status was the same as theirs, and were therefore not at risk of being infected or infecting someone with HIV (though they were at risk of other STIs). It might be asked how these men knew their partners' HIV status and whether many in that nine per cent were people making wrong assumptions about their partners' HIV status.

But this nine per cent also excludes the 24% or respondents who were less certain about whether they'd had unprotected sex with a person of differing HIV status. Only 10.3% of the men in the survey were fairly sure that had had serodiscordant unprotected sex, and thus represent the highest population at highest risk of HIV acquisition or transmission.

In recent years the emphasis on condom use has tended to change from a blanket insistence on 100% condom use to a much more nuanced recognition that decisions as to whether or not to use condoms are often arrived at through a complex series of assumptions, calculations and conversations between people. This is discussed in the next section on disclosure, serosorting and negotiated safety.

However this is not an uncontroversial shift in emphasis. In the same way as opponents of condom distribution say that providing condoms only encourages more sex, some prevention experts worry that supporting harm-reduction strategies such as trying to only have sex with people of the same HIV status ('serosorting') spreads confusing messages and encourages people to rationalise about having unsafe sex. More on this below.

Risk populations change - prevention targets must, too

The next two columns (G and H) contrast condom use in Thai men visiting sex workers, which was as near to 100% as any use of condoms is likely to get, and the proportion of teenage boys in one province who used condoms during sex with girlfriends.

As cited already, the "100% condom campaign" in 1990-92 in Thailand is often seen as one of the most successful HIV prevention programmes of all time. It slashed HIV incidence among young men from 2.5% a year to 0.5%, reduced prevalence among army recruits from 10% to 2.5%, and it is estimated that HIV prevalence in Thailand today is still - a decade after the campaign ended - 50% lower than it would have been if it had not happened.

Its success was partly due to good timing and an accurate perception that a widespread culture of commercial sex was responsible for the rapid growth of HIV at the time. It was also partly due to it being an easily enforceable target. The campaign put pressure on brothel owners to enforce 100% condom use in their establishments and ensured that ones not conforming to this rule were closed by the police.

Since then, however, the continued impact of tourism and the global media, and the growing affluence of Thailand, has led to a change in sexual behaviour. A pattern whereby men would marry young but also have extramarital commercial sex has given way to a more 'westernised' pattern of teenagers having pre-marital sexual relationships. The report that only 25% of Thai teenagers were using condoms led to a campaign to have condom machines placed in colleges and a counter-campaign resisting this - with both demands coming from students themselves. As sexual and drug-using cultures change, HIV prevention has to fight the same battle many times again on behalf of new populations.

Men can change...

That populations can adapt their safer-sex behaviour to continue to protect themselves when their habits change is evidenced by the Wawer study quoted above (Wawer, 2005). In her study of adults in Rakai, Uganda Wawer found that although HIV prevalence had declined by 75% between 1993 and 2004, HIV incidence had not, and was running at a steady annual seroconversion rate of 1.5% or so. The decline in the number of people living with HIV in the area was almost entirely due to the thinning of the population by AIDS.

She found evidence that people were actually having more extramarital sex and having it younger in 2004 than in 1993, and that the behavioural changes of the early 1990s were being reversed. For instance, the proportion of 15 to 19 year-olds who were sexually active had gone up from 40 to 50%, and the number of adult men reporting two or more partners a year had increased from 20 to 27%.

What was keeping the incidence rate steady in the face of this 'liberalising' of sexual behaviour was an increased level of condom use. Condom use among men in general with casual partners had increased from 10% in 1993 to 50% in 2004 - a figure described by Wawer as 'incredibly high by African standards' (see columns J and K above).

This figure of 50% was skewed by a 95% rate of condom use in the few per cent of men who admitted having commercial sex. But even in male teenagers, who by and large did not use sex workers, it had gone up from 19 to 38%.

Other recent surveys have reported figures of about 50% of men in South Africa (Peltzer, 2000) and Uganda (Najjumba, 2003) saying they had 'ever' used condoms, with considerably higher usage in sex that was perceived to be risky.
Increased condom use is also apparently partly responsible for what appears to be a genuine, and marked, decrease in HIV prevalence in Zimbabwe in the last five years (UNAIDS 2005). A full investigation of the many possible factors behind the fall in Zimbabwean HIV prevalence is under B is for Being Faithful.

One of the factors, however, appeared to be increased condom use within casual sex. In 1999, men's condom use with non-regular partners was already high at about 75%, but by 2004 this had increased to 85%. Among women there was a much bigger rise: from around 50% in 1999 to at least 75% in 2004. Given that this is casual and non-regular relationships we are talking about, this may (hopefully) reflect an increasing ability of women to ask, or men to permit, the use of condoms within commercial and transactional sexual situations.

...but women can't always make them

The final column (K) represents the figure from the same Ugandan survey by Najjumba which reported 50% condom use among men. Surveys consistently show women reporting lower condom use than men. In this survey 51% of men and 36% of women who perceived themselves to be 'at high risk' or HIV said they had ever used a condom in sex. In those who saw themselves as low risk the figures were 36 and 11% respectively.

Are men lying about how often they use condoms? Or women forgetting about them? The answer is that men are using condoms in high-risk sexual situations such as with sex workers and casual sex with men or women, but not using them with wives and regular partners. Since women in general have fewer partners than men, the average woman is less likely to encounter a man who wants to use a condom during sex.

Rates of condom use among married couples in Africa vary from around 16% for regular or occasional use in one study from KwaZulu Natal (Maharaj, 2005) to the Wawer study above, in which women reported using condoms 28% of the time with casual partners but only one per cent of the time with their husbands.

Similar results have been reported from other parts of the world. In a pioneering study of sexual risk among men who have sex with men in Andhra Pradesh, India, (Dandona, 2005) 42% of the MSM were married, half had had sex with a woman as well

as a man in the last three months, but only 16% had used a condom in sex with a woman.

However even in India there is evidence that increased condom use in crucial populations may be having a positive impact on HIV transmission. A survey of four high-prevalence Indian states (Kumar) examined HIV prevalence among 294,000 women aged 15 to 34 attending antenatal clinics in four states in southern India and 14 states in the north, as well as prevalence among 59,000 men aged 15 to 34 attending clinics for sexually transmitted infections in the same regions.

The researchers found that among women ages 15 to 24 attending prenatal clinics in the southern states of Tamil Nadu, Andhra Pradesh, Maharashtra and Karnataka, HIV prevalence decreased from 1.7% in 2001 to 1.1% in 2004, a relative decline of 35%. Among men aged 20 to 29 attending STI clinics, the researchers recorded a 36% relative decline in HIV prevalence over the same time period.

The study found no significant decrease in HIV prevalence among women ages 25 to 34 or among men and women in the northern states, where the epidemic is driven by injection drug use. The researchers said the study's findings might signify a decrease in the number of new infections acquired through heterosexual contact in India, and they credited the decline among young people to an increase in condom use among commercial sex workers and their clients in the southern part of the country.

The researchers comment:

> What could account for the reduction of HIV-1 prevalence in the South? Mathematical models of sex-work-based networks find that the prevalence is very sensitive to increases in abstinence from sex work or in condom use with sex work. Use of condoms between married couples is probably not relevant to the reductions seen in the south; it is well below 3% in the south and has changed little from 1992 to 1999. HIV-1 trends in young men attending STI clinics provide an imperfect snapshot of high-risk men, including those who have recently visited sex workers.
> The fall in the south could be explained by increased condom use or increased abstinence, and is probably not due to STI antibiotic treatment, since reductions also occurred in men with ulcerative, and presumably viral, STIs.

> In 2004, about 70-80% of female sex workers in Maharashtra and Tamil Nadu reported condom use with their last client, with lower percentages for all recent partners, and lower percentages still with regular non-paying partners. Data for male abstinence from sex workers are not well reported: indirect evidence from surveys of female sex workers in Tamil Nadu in 1996-2004 has shown increases in condom use, but no change in the number of clients per day (see AIDS Prevention and Control Project).

Why don't men use condoms, and why don't women make them?

Although this question is framed in a heterosexist way, the same question can just as well apply to gay men too, although there is more of a (possibly incorrect) assumption that in gay male relationships sexual roles are more fluid and the power to enforce condom use is more equally shared between the two partners.

However we find that in gay men the same pattern applies as among heterosexuals: men in steady relationships, whether of the same HIV status or not, are far less likely to use condoms. This gives us a clue as to the primary psychological driver behind unsafe sex and the decision to use, or not to use, condoms.

Take two examples. A study from the Netherlands (Davidovich, 2000) found that 55% of gay men had unprotected sex with their regular partner but only 20% had it with casual partners.

A London study (Elford, 2001) a year later stratified the same results by HIV status of participants. It found that in

HIV-negative men 28.5% had unprotected sex within relationships but only five per cent with casual partners. HIV-positive men, by contrast, were just as likely to have unprotected sex with regular and casual partners (22.2 vs. 20.6%). The researchers argued that HIV-negative men cannot be sure of the HIV status of partners without mutual testing HIV-positive men, on the other hand, can find out their partners' HIV status by the simple act of mutual disclosure. However it was not ascertained whether disclosure was what was driving up higher rates of casual unprotected sex in positive men.

We will look at evidence like this in the next section to understand how gay men are using disclosure to minimise HIV transmission risk. For the time being we are looking at the psychology of what condoms symbolise and why they tend not to get used in primary relationships.

An interesting insight into this was provided by a study from New York (Simoni, 2000) which examined whether HIV-positive women had safer sex and if so, whether they did so more often in primary relationships. The authors hypothesised that women would be more likely to maintain condom use in steady relationships in order to protect partners.

They found the opposite to be the case. Forty-six per cent of women maintained condom use in all sex (in this study oral sex without a condom was counted as 'unprotected'). But of the remainder, 61% had had at least one episode of unprotected sex in the past 90 days with a steady partner compared with 16% who had done it with a casual partner. Women in steady relationships were three times more likely to have unprotected sex with a steady than with a casual partner.

Was this because steady partners were more likely to be known to be HIV-positive themselves? No, because unprotected sex was just as common with HIV-negative male partners as HIV-positive ones.

On further investigation, condom use had a bipolar distribution. Condom use was significantly higher in women who had casual partners - but also within the most committed relationships, when these were defined by length (over one year), by being within a legalized marriage, or by partners living together. Condom use was a lot lower with primary partners who were new or who did not live with the women.

The researchers theorised: "Women in our study who were married and in the longest, most supportive relationships may have possessed the power to broach or insist upon consistent condom use."

Conversely, they add: "Perhaps in [more recently established] steady partnerships, condom use implies, not primarily protection, but mistrust, suspicion, lack of emotional and physical intimacy, or denial of potential motherhood."

Ugandan President Yoweri Museveni used almost the same words when he address the Bangkok World AIDS Conference in 2004: "The best way to fight AIDS is with relationships based on love and trust, instead of institutionalised mistrust, which is what the condom is all about."

Museveni's words were attacked at the time by activists such as fellow-speaker Mabel van Oranje of the Open Society Foundation, who commented that his opinion "seems slightly drawn by ideology rather than an assessment of needs on the ground."

But he may have been saying something more perceptive about human psychology and the reason why condoms can only ever form part, rather than the whole, of HIV prevention.

A more recent study among gay men in the UK provides similar insights. The INSIGHT study (Elam) is the name of the study conducted by the UK's Health Protection Agency (HPA), which aims to tease out differences in the behaviour and motivations of gay men who catch HIV and ones who stay negative.

The HPA's Dr Gillian Elam took a group of 75 gay men who had tested positive within two years of a previous negative test and compared them with 159 men whose most recent test was negative, again within two years of their previous negative one.

Unsurprisingly, she found that the HIV-positive ones had taken more sexual risks.

Eight out of ten of the positive men had had unprotected sex as the passive partner since their last test, and seven out of ten as the active partner: just under half of the HIV-negative men had done the same.

But it was the interviews Elam did with a subset of men about their reasons for having unsafe sex that were really revealing. They showed that gay men have a multiplicity of reasons for taking sexual risks, so that no one prevention strategy will fit all.

Elam divided gay men into various groups:

- Men who had caught HIV within a steady partnership, of whom:

  - Some caught HIV through being mistaken about their partner's or each other's serostatus

  - Some caught HIV through being in a serodiscordant relationship and taking a positive decision to risk unsafe sex

  - Some caught HIV when one partner seroconverted during the relationship and the couple was faced with the decision of whether to start using condoms

- Men who had caught HIV in casual sexual situation, of whom:

  - Some took a positive decision to have and even seek out unprotected sex

  - Some ended up having unprotected sex even though they had tried not to and it was contrary to their health beliefs

First there were men who'd caught HIV while in a steady relationship. A common theme was that condoms were seen as a barrier to intimacy, love and trust. Men made comments such as: "We've got this thing in the way", "It makes it feel like a process", "It takes away a lot of the emotion".

There were steady partners who thought each other was negative. Here the risk was where men thought their partner was monogamous and he wasn't, or where they decided to drop condoms too soon in a relationship to really establish trust. A common theme was that people didn't think they or their partner was the 'type' to get HIV. One said: "It shouldn't have really been me...my friends have lots of sexual partners and take drugs ... I'm the most reserved out of the people I know."

There were couples where one knew he was positive from the start, and the negative partner decided to risk unsafe sex. Here having unprotected sex was a conscious trade-off between the risk of HIV and the need for intimacy. People also rationalised that repeated negative test results meant they were 'immune'.

Then there were couples where one partner seroconverted during the relationship. One common finding here was that the other partner suddenly felt 'distant' from them. One said: "There was no 'fuck me without a condom, I want to be positive sort of thing'. It is the intimacy ... We had that intimacy and then it was just suddenly taken away."

Then there were people who caught HIV through casual sex. Elam divided these into men who had intentionally not used condoms and ones where they felt they should have done, but had allowed unprotected sex to happen without one in the heat of the moment.

Intentional non-users were seeking positive things through not using condoms: they saw it as a signal of love and trust, at least potentially. Elam commented that the need for 'love and trust' and for 'submission, sleaze and adventures' often went together.

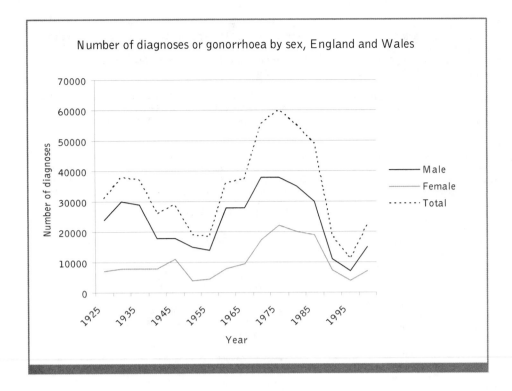

Number of diagnoses or gonorrhoea by sex, England and Wales

not in the sense of condoms splitting, but in giving up their normal safer-sex behaviour in the heat of the moment. Some talked about wanting to please a particularly attractive or confident partner. This was the group who were most likely to talk about depression, drink and drugs as being factors in HIV infection. One said: "Depression really influenced my sexual behaviour. You go out, you want to be abused, almost... you might as well let anybody do what they want to do to you."

Elam said there were themes common to all. Many men talked of condoms reducing intimacy, about not

One said: "There's sort of hope for something," meaning that having 'bareback' sex was a sort of signal that he was emotionally available. Men rationalised their way into unsafe sex. Younger men told themselves that if a partner was well-groomed and 'fit', he would not have HIV. Older men told themselves that HIV would not have such a negative impact because HIV would have no worse an impact than other facets of ageing.

Then there were the 'accidental' non-condom-users. There were men who normally tried to use condoms but who had accidents,

being the 'sort' who caught HIV, and about negative test results giving a sense of false security. Many 'tops' thought they were at no risk, not lower risk. Above all was the sense that giving people more information about HIV risk was not the answer: Elam's interviewees had high levels of knowledge about HIV transmission.

If there was a common theme, it was that catching HIV often involves a conscious decision to trade safety for the possibility of love, approval and fun.

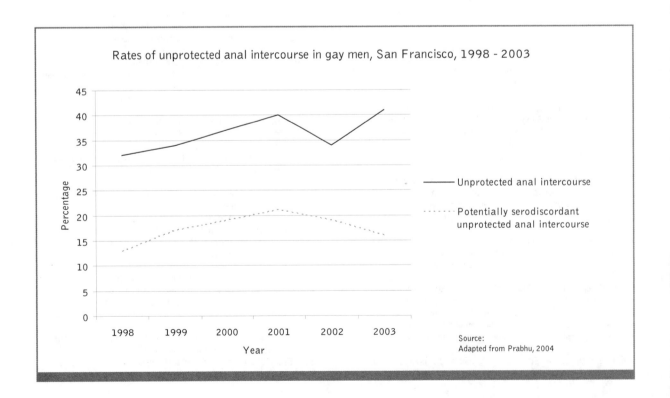

Source:
Adapted from Prabhu, 2004

Has condom use declined in the developed world?

The decade in which AIDS was both widespread and untreatable in the developed world - roughly 1985 to 1995 - marked a historic low point in diagnoses of sexually transmitted diseases in countries like the USA and UK. See above, for instance, for gonorrhoea diagnoses, which peaked briefly after World War Two and then for a prolonged period from 1970-85 (see graph on page 28).

HIV incidence has also increased among risk groups. For instance, according to UNAIDS (UNAIDS, 2001), HIV incidence (new diagnoses) in gay men increased from 0.6% a year in the late 1990s in Vancouver to 3.7% a year in 2000; from 1.16% in 1996 in Madrid to 2.16% in 2000; and from 1.1% in 1997 in San Francisco to 1.7% in 2000. Increases were also reported in London

But was this due to decreased condom use? Among the UK population in general, the 1990 and 2000 National Surveys of Sexual Attitudes and Lifestyles (NATSAL) (Johnson, 2001) found that consistent condom use among the sexually active population as a whole increased from 17 to 24% during the 1990s, even as the rate of STIs also increased.

NATSAL found that the effect of increased condom use had been more than cancelled out by other demographic changes - to which the increased condom use was probably consequent.

- The mean number of lifetime partners had increased from 8.6 to 12.7 in men and from 3.7 to 6.5 in women

- Concurrent relationships - which are an extremely important factor in the spread of STIs, and which are cited as an important contributing factor to the HIV rate in Africa - increased from 12 to 14% in men and from 5 to 8% in women

- Age at first sex declined from 21 in women and 17 in men in the 1990 survey to 16 for both sexes for teenagers included in the 2000 survey.

- The proportion of British men who had a male partner increased from 3.6 to 5.4 %.

This is a reminder that many other risk factors, some of them modifiable and others hardly so, or which it would be difficult to change, produce changes in the rates of STIs.

But condom use in gay men certainly declined during the late 1990s, with the rates of unprotected sex increasing almost as soon as combination therapy became available in 1996 (in the USA) and in 1997 (in Britain). A survey in San Francisco (Centers for Disease Control, 1999), for instance, found that the proportion of gay men who sometimes did without condoms when having anal sex increased from 30.4% in 1994 to 39.2% in 1997.

These figures were almost exactly mirrored, with a year's time lag, by the figures in the annual UK Gay Men's Sex Surveys (Gay Men's Sex Surveys, 1999-2003) and their predecessors. From about 33% of gay men who had unprotected anal sex in the early 1990s, this increased from 1997 onwards and reached a peak of 45% in 2000.

Since then, however, there is some evidence that the amount of unprotected sex among gay men has reached a plateau, at least in the relatively unmarginalised gay populations of US urban centres. A more recent survey from San Francisco (Prabhu, 2004) found some evidence of a levelling-off of unprotected sex after 2001. More importantly, the amount of unprotected sex which was or could potentially be between partners of different HIV status (serodiscordant) showed a more distinct decline since that date (see graph on page 28).

An annual survey of gay men using London gyms (Elford, 2005a) found that the percentage of gay men reporting 'high-risk behaviour' with a casual partner increased from 6.7 to

15.2% between 1998 and 2001 but remained stable after that, with the figure for 2004 being 14.7%.

The evidence from the large annual UK Gay Men's Sex Survey is harder to interpret as questions are not always asked in standardised ways. But this appears to indicate a continued increase in unprotected sex between gay men in general, rather than a levelling off, from 33% in 1993 to 54.4% in 2003. UAI in itself does not imply HIV transmission, but there is also incomplete evidence that rates of potentially and definitely serodiscordant sex are increasing.

However an unpublished study by Jonathan Elford (Elford, 2005b) suggests that rates of serodiscordant sex between gay men in London are levelling off, and may be falling in HIV-positive men - see the next section for details.

One consistent finding from all these surveys has been that HIV-positive men have a great deal more unprotected sex than HIV-negative men. Data from the 2004 San Francisco Department of Public Health HIV Epidemiology Annual Report (2004) show that the increase in unprotected anal intercourse among gay men since 1998 is entirely among HIV-positive men.

We will revisit the subject of exactly why HIV-positive gay men have more unprotected sex, who they are having it with, and what the implications are for HIV, in the next section.

Condom controversies

Condoms as a method both of contraception and of reducing the transmission of HIV have always been controversial. Opponents of condoms, when not simply against their use for religious reasons, consistently suggest (either explicitly or implicitly) that the free or subsidised provision of condoms will simply encourage people, particularly young people, to have sex and take sexual risks they might not otherwise have done.

As we saw above under *A is for abstinence*, the opponents and proponents of comprehensive sex education and condom promotion often use the same data to reach different conclusions about the relative contribution of their favoured prevention method on HIV and STI incidence. In fact all types of behaviour change are more likely to work together to reduce HIV incidence and should ideally be promoted together in a comprehensive package, rather than narrowly focusing on one. See, in particular, Santelli 2004, where the contribution of sexual abstinence to lower teenage pregnancy rates in the USA was calculated to be slightly higher than increased condom use (a finding seized on by pro-abstinence campaigners), but where increased condom use among teenagers who did have sex was also a significant factor.

We will not spend a great deal of time on the arguments for and against condoms here, many of which are conducted from positions informed by ideology rather than evidence. What opponents of condom use have lacked, however, is a 'smoking gun' study that shows that in some circumstances condom provision can increase rather than decrease HIV risk.

Such a study may have been provided by a team from Makerere University in Uganda (see Kajubi).

It found that providing young men with condoms and lessons on how to use them certainly increased condom use, when compared with a control group of men who just had a general talk on HIV and AIDS. However, it also found that the young men had a greater number of sexual partners and more unprotected sex than the control group.

The researchers took 378 young men aged 18-30 from two urban communities near Kampala and split them randomly into two groups. One group attended a three-hour workshop teaching them about how condoms stopped HIV and STIs, how to put on a condom, strategies for negotiating condom use with partners and talking about barriers to having safer sex. They were then given vouchers to redeem for free condoms provided by young people in their local community

The control group was just given a general lecture on the HIV situation in Uganda and given the free vouchers but no condom tuition.

The men taught how to use condoms certainly used more - 110 per man in the six-month period after the study compared with 13 per man in the control group.

However the public health benefit of this was potentially offset by the fact that they had an increased number of partners, whereas the control group reduced their partners.

Men taught condom use increased their average number of partners from 2.13 to 2.44 in the six months whereas the control group decreased their number of partners from 2.20 to 2.03. This was highly statistically significant.

The control group ended up having fewer regular and casual partners; the condom group reduced their number of casual partners slightly but had considerably more regular partners.

This would not matter if condom use was consistent; but while the amount of unprotected sex the control group had was reduced with both regular and casual partners, the condom group only reduced unprotected sex with all partners slightly and actually slightly increased the amount of unprotected sex they had with casual partners.

After adjusting for the fact that men in the condom group were on the whole somewhat older and more likely to be married, the researchers calculated that providing the men with condom lessons actually led to them having 48% more unprotected sex relative to the ones without lessons.

The study had many limitations. It was small and the two groups compared were not identical. And of course it does not show that providing condoms makes you have unsafe sex. But it may demonstrate that condom provision in the absence of other measures encouraging behaviour change are an incomplete answer are an incomplete answer to HIV transmission, at least in the African situation.

The researchers commented: "Prevention interventions in generalised HIV epidemics need to promote all aspects of sexual risk reduction to slow HIV transmission."

Meanwhile, however, despite all the above reservations and complexities of behaviour, it is important to remember that condoms remain the most effective and most widely used HIV prevention method by sexually active people, and that in high-risk populations where condoms are widely available, half of all acts of sexual intercourse take place with a condom.

It's also important to know, as we said above, that that properly-implemented HIV prevention programmes have been shown to consistently increase condom use. For more on this see HIV prevention: which methods work?

This leads us to the best way to use them.

Safer sex

Condoms and lubricants

Using condoms

There are many other kinds of sexual activities which you can enjoy other than penetration, but if like many people you want to keep on having penetrative sex, either anally or vaginally, then learning to use condoms properly, and using them consistently, is the major step in adopting safer sex.

Reliability of condoms

Condoms are not totally safe sex. Remember that according to the statistics quite above, they stop 85 to 90% of STIs (with the exception of contagious viruses like herpes and HPV which can be spread via the fingers). Experience with birth control shows that over a period of a year about six per cent of women who use condoms as their sole form of contraception will get pregnant. Although this is not all down to condom failure - a proportion of the pregnancies are no doubt due to failure to use condoms every time - this is still quite a high failure rate. Moreover, it is important to bear in mind that whilst condoms are required to provide protection during one week of each month in order to prevent pregnancy (the week during which a woman is ovulating), a condom must provide protection on each and every occasion of sexual intercourse if it is to be a reliable form of protection against HIV infection and other STIs.

However, the main reason that condoms fail is because they are used incorrectly - they are torn during opening, oil-based lubricants are used, or they are put on incorrectly, for example.

In general, condoms provide an effective barrier against HIV and other STIs, and given that so many people practice penetrative sex as part of their sex lives, it is important that they are used properly. They are still the most effective barrier to HIV transmission during sexual intercourse.

In this section, we outline how to use condoms and lubricants most effectively, which cuts down on the already small risk of something going wrong.

Condom reluctance

Condoms can be uncomfortable, they can reduce the sensation during sex, and can often interrupt your fun when you have to find a condom, open the packet, find the lubricant and put it on. Nobody is saying that condoms are perfect, or that sex will be just as good if you use them. But, frankly, they are the best thing we have now to cut down on HIV transmission during sex.

A lot of blame has been placed on men's reluctance to use condoms. This ignores the fact that many women also prefer condomless sex, and, as indicated by the Simoni study above (Simoni, 2000), there may be deep psychological reasons to do with the demonstration of trust and closeness why both sexes may find them difficult to use consistently.

It also does not explain the deeper reasons for specifically male reluctance. One clue was given by a recent study of 78 HIV-positive gay men(Cove, 2004) in London. It found that while 38% of the men reported some degree of erectile dysfunction. But this went up to 51% in the context of trying to use condoms - in other worlds, more than half of the men experienced difficulty in getting or sustaining an erection when trying to put a condom on. Furthermore 90% of the 37 men whose erectile dysfunction was associated with condom use reported inconsistent condom use during insertive sex, compared with 28% of those who did not report condom-related erectile dysfunction.

If other groups of men have anything in common with gay men, we may be underestimating performance anxiety and the terror of impotence (often disguised with bravado) as a driver of men's reluctance to use condoms.

Strategies for women whose partners will not use condoms

Women cannot control condom use. Women who perceive themselves at special risk of acquiring HIV should consider the following strategies:

- Ask their partner to wear a condom and use water-based lubricant which does not contain nonoxynol-9

- Use a female condom (vaginal pouch) and lubricant. Although women may insert the female condom, this is not like a female-controlled prevention technology (such as the diaphragm). It is not discreet - your partner will always know you are using it - and it's possible to insert the penis between the wall of the vagina and the female condom, in which case it will offer no protection

■ The effectiveness of the female condom with regard to preventing HIV infection has not been established

■ Withdrawal: the European Study Group on Heterosexual Transmission of HIV(De Vincenzi, 1994) reported in 1994 that HIV-positive men who always withdrew before ejaculating had not infected their partners, even after 18 months. This suggests that if loss of sensation is the problem, intercourse without condoms may not present a significant risk unless ejaculation takes place, and may in some cases be an agreeable solution for both partners. However, Australian AIDS organisations have mounted specific campaigns to warn gay men against this strategy, after research suggested that a significant proportion of (an admittedly small number) of new infections were occurring among men who were using this technique instead of condoms.

Using condoms properly

Although everyone is happy to talk about condoms, very few people can tell you how to use them properly. The best demonstration of condom use that most people get is seeing a rubber placed hurriedly onto a banana. That kind of prudishness is no help to anyone, and can lead to people taking needless risks when they use condoms.

Using a condom properly is easy, once you have learnt how. And one of the best ways you can improve your safer sex life is to spend a little time getting it right. Although condoms will not let HIV pass through them under laboratory conditions, they can break, leak, or (and this is the most common reason for failure) *slip off* during sex, and if they do, they offer much less, or no, protection.

Golden rules of condom use

Later in this section we give a full explanation of how to get used to, and use, condoms, as well as explaining why they can break, what brands to choose and what lubricants to buy. But if you want a quick, easy shorthand to condom use, try to remember the Golden Rules we've listed below. Remember, condoms are not difficult to use, but do take a bit of practice to learn.

■ Practise and be prepared.

■ Choose a condom which carries the British Kitemark.

■ Use the right kind of lubricant (water-based) and not the wrong kind of lubricant (oil-based).

■ Always expel any air by holding the teat between thumb and forefinger.

■ Apply lubricant over the outside of the whole condom, re-apply if necessary.

■ Look after the condom - do not leave unused condoms in direct sunlight, be careful of tearing, using old condoms, leaving space or air in the condom, or not using enough lubrication.

■ Unroll the condom all the way to the base of the penis after it is hard and before starting sex.

■ When pulling out, hold the condom tight to the base of the penis, to prevent leakage.

■ Never re-use a condom. Once it is used, throw it away and put on a new one if you start again.

Condom do's and don'ts

Step-by-step guide to using a condom

Open the packet carefully to avoid damaging the condom (jewellery, long fingernails or careless teeth could tear it). The condom comes out rolled up forming a ring which will fit over the penis

■ Put the condom on after the penis is hard and before any kind of penetration begins

■ Check the condom is the right way up; you can test with a finger that it rolls out and down

■ Keep the penis completely free of grease and lubricant for best 'holding power'

■ Squeeze the closed end between the thumb and forefinger to expel the air. Air bubbles can make condoms break

■ Hold the condom over the tip of the penis and with the other hand carefully unroll it down to the base. It may help to stretch the condom width-ways in order to ease it down the penis and to ensure that it remains in place once penetration begins. But be careful not to pierce the condom with your fingernails when doing this

■ If you have a foreskin pull it back before covering the head of the penis with the condom. Don't try to cover the testicles with a condom

■ Smooth the condom to eliminate any air bubbles

■ Some men withdraw to check the condom, occasionally. If you need more lubrication (and you should use plenty), use more water-based lubricant

■ **Never use two condoms at once**. This more is likely to lead to breakage because of rubber rubbing against rubber

■ If you lose your erection the condom may slip. *This is the biggest single cause of condom failure.* Fingers held round the base of the condom will help it stay put

■ If the condom does break or slip off withdraw as soon as you find out! Obviously you will need to use a new one if this happens

■ A condom is more likely to break if sex lasts a long time, (longer than 45 minutes). Consider changing the condom during a long sex session

■ After coming (ejaculation) withdraw the penis before it becomes soft (otherwise semen could leak out of the condom). To prevent the condom slipping off your penis at this stage, hold it firmly round the base as you withdraw

■ Throw used condoms away. Dispose of them thoughtfully, e.g. wrapped up in tissue paper and then thrown in the rubbish. They shouldn't be flushed down the loo, since this may cause blockages in sewage disposal, according to water companies

■ Never use a condom more than once

■ Never use the same condom on two people in succession.

Practise and be prepared

Practise putting a condom on when you are masturbating on your own. Making it part of masturbation will help you to get used to the feel and look of a condom, and can be a turn-on in itself. You can take your time, following instructions step-by-step, so that you know exactly what you are doing. That way, when it comes to using condoms during penetration, you will know what to do.

You can also practise putting a condom on your partner, on a banana or on a dildo. Some people like to put condoms onto their partner's penis during sex, and this is a way of getting used to it. But never use a condom that you have practised with by inflating or stretching. Use a new one instead.

You never know when you will strike lucky. Carry some around with you all the time. Remember that this is not 'loose' but responsible behaviour. And leave condoms around your flat - in the bedroom, the bathroom, in fact wherever you have sex at home. They will also advertise the fact that you expect to use condoms when you have sex.

Types of condoms

Which condom is safest?

Unfortunately we cannot give an easy answer to this question. There is no national watchdog agency overseeing the safety of all condoms sold in the UK. There is no independent comparative sampling and testing of condoms as actually sold in packets. And it is not illegal to market condoms which don't measure up to the British Standard BS EN600, which lays down requirements for good quality condoms.

Which condom should I choose?

The best advice is to choose a condom which carries the Kitemark. The Kitemark indicates that the condom brand is recognised under the British Standards Institution's (BSI) scheme. The BSI is responsible for drawing up the British Standard (known as BS4074:2002) and its testing division polices the scheme. A manufacturer who wants their brand to carry the Kitemark has to agree that BSI inspectors may regularly test samples of the brand and ensure that those samples will pass the tests laid down in the British Standard.

It's not compulsory for condoms to comply with the British Standard. What's more, any condom manufacturer can claim that his product conforms to the British Standard, but not sign up to the Kitemark scheme to have the claim checked by the BSI. Even if this claim appears to be backed up by a set of laboratory test results, the testing may not have been independent and may reflect only a one-off testing of a sample of condoms from one given batch at one given moment, rather than regular checking of multiple batches over time. So consumers can only be confident that a brand does meet the British Standard on an ongoing basis if it does carry the Kitemark.

During the 1990s, standards organisations throughout Europe have been working together to agree a pan-European condom standard. This was finally approved in early 1996, and European Union member states are obliged to replace their existing national standards with the new European one (known as EN600:1996).

AIDS organisations usually recommend consumers to stick to Kitemarked brands, but this can cause confusion when they also endorse certain brands such as HT Special that don't have a Kitemark. That's because Kitemarking is a British scheme, and condoms that are not formally marketed by their manufacturer in the UK are unlikely to be submitted for Kitemarking regardless of their quality.

Standard thickness condoms

The only difference between condoms listed in this section and the thicker condoms listed below is the thickness of the rubber. On average the condoms listed below are 30% thinner than the thickest brands such as HT Special and Durex Ultra Strong, and around 25% thinner than the other brands listed above.

Male condoms

DUREX

Gossamer
Hypoallergenic, non-spermicidal, regular-sized condom

Close fit
Narrower condoms designed for a closer fit for those who have problems with regular- sized condoms. Non-spermicidal.

Comfort Fit
Extra-long and wide, non-spermicidal

CONDOMI

Nature
Lubricated with silicon-based lube, regular-sized

Ultra THIN
Ultra thin, non-spermicidal, regular-sized condom

XXL
Longer and wider than the average condom, lubricated with a silicone-based lubricant.

CONFIDENT

Classic
Non-spermicidal, slightly longer condom

Feelings
Non-spermicidal, slightly longer, ribbed and textured.

MATES

Crystal
Dermatologically tested, thinner, with a straight profile, and non-spermicidal lube. Mates Crystal condoms have undergone a unique treatment to reduce the risk of an allergic latex reaction and are thinner.

Conform
Non-spermicidal, one of the narrowest brands on the market.

Large
Flared shape at the closed end of the condom, to provide comfort for those who find condoms too tight. Non-spermicidal lube

Pleasure
An oversize tip on a uniquely shaped condom. Non-spermicidal lube

BOOTS

Ultra safe
Non-spermicidal lube, slightly thicker for extra reassurance.

Multi-ribbed
Textured to enhance stimulation for ultimate intensity, non-spermicidal lube with reservoir.

RFSU

Okeido
Longer, wider and slightly fuller than our other condoms. Non-spermicidal

Profile
Non-spermicidal, regular-sized

TROJAN

Ultra Pleasure
Extra thin, non-spermicidal, wider than average from top to bottom

EX S

Natural
Non-spermicidal, regular-sized

SAFEX

Natural
Non-spermicidal, regular-sized

Sensitive
Fine sheath for increased sensitivity, non-spermicidal

NOT RECOMMENDED (lubricated with nonoxynol-9)

Condomi Supersafe
Trojan Supra
Safex Natural Spermicidal
Mates Ultra Safe
Mates Ribbed

The thickest condoms

Since the introduction of the harmonised European standard, condoms that claim to be extra strong have had to pass more a more stringent tensile breaking force test than those that do not make such a claim. There is no difference between the air-burst test requirements for standard versus strong condoms.

In early 1996 Rubberstuffers commissioned the British Standards Institution's laboratories to test condoms that claimed to be extra strong to the new standard. Over 200 condoms from each brand were subjected to tests for holes by filling with water, stretched until broken and inflated until they burst. In late 1996 the Consumers Association published in *Health Which?* the results of tests on a range of condom brands including some (but not all) of the brands tested by Rubberstuffers. Both sets of tests reached the same conclusions. There was little difference in strength between any of the following brands:

EXTRA STRONG CONDOMS:

CONDOMI
- **Strong**
  Non-spermicidal lube, recommended for gay men

DUREX
- **Ultra strong**
  For maximum security. Lubricated with non-spermicidal lubricant. Made from natural rubber latex.
- **Avanti**
  Non-allergenic, non-spermicidal polyurethane condom, which is much thinner than the latex condom

EX S
- **Boys Own**
  Independently tested and approved for gay men's use. Silicone lubricated and manufactured to EN 600 and certified to the ec directive mark, non-spermicidal
- **Ultra Strong**
  non-spermicidal

Another brand marketed to gay men in the UK is SAFEGUARD FORTE. In both sets of tests, these condoms just failed to meet the tensile breaking force requirements for condoms that claim to be extra strong, as defined in the British Standard. Safex Supplies claim that they have since improved their manufacturing processes, but there have not yet been any independent tests to verify this claim.

Notwithstanding their name, the Dutch GAY SAFE condoms performed poorly in both Rubberstuffers' and the Consumers Association's tests, and cannot be considered an extra-strong brand.

Both these brands were also thinner than the others, reinforcing the impression that the thicker condoms are generally the stronger.

Which strength condoms for anal sex?

It is one of the scandals of this epidemic that only in recent years have any of the condoms available in the UK been marketed for anything other than vaginal use. For example, only *Boys Own* and *Safeguard Forte* condoms are currently promoted by their manufacturers towards the gay community.

Naturally, they are regularly used in very large numbers for anal sex as well as for vaginal sex. But because there are no standards for anal sex condoms, nor any guidelines on how to use them for this purpose, those using `vaginal' condoms for anal sex may not be using the best brands, or using them in the safest way.

It may be that in the same way the female condom will also serve as an anal condom, though the same issues that apply to women using female condom also apply to gay men being penetrated with one. See the section on female condoms for further detail.

At the thirteenth International AIDS Conference in Durban, a team of researchers from London's City University (Golombok 2001, Harding, 2000) presented data from a study of 283 gay male couples who had been randomised to use either standard or thicker condoms for anal sex and additional water-based lubricant. Each couple were provided with nine condoms and completed a questionnaire after each sexual act.

The researchers found that condoms broke for the same reasons as previously identified in studies among heterosexual couples; unrolling the condom before fitting it to the penis, longer duration of intercourse (longer than 45 minutes), and absence of additional lubricant. Use of additional inappropriate, (oil-based lubricant or saliva) was also associated with condom breakage. Penis length was also associated with condom breakage, yet girth was not.

The study found **no significant differences** between the two types of condoms with respect to breakage or slippage. Condoms were more likely to slip if lubricant was placed on the penis under the condom. A low incidence of clinical breakage was reported for both condom types during appropriate use.

In order to use standard condoms most effectively, the researchers recommended that gay men be reminded of the following:

- unroll the condom *after* fitting it to the penis

- use additional lubricant

- apply the lubricant to the *outside* of the condom only

- apply the lubricant in and around the anus.

The findings of this study call into question the long-standing UK recommendation that gay men should use extra-strong or thicker condoms wherever possible. The researchers have proposed that gay men should be advised to use Kitemarked condoms, and note that inexperience in the use of condoms and use of inappropriate lubricants were far more important factors in explaining condom failure.

In North America and Australia (yet not in Europe) HIV prevention messages have always offered the alternative of standard condoms for anal sex. This trial has seemingly offered the first piece of evidence to confirm this approach to HIV health promotion.

The authors concluded that the data concerning the predictors of failure should be used in health promotion "to reduce the incidence of condom failure among gay men".

For the past 15 years one of the cornerstones of gay men's HIV prevention in the UK has been the recommendation to use extra-strong condoms for anal sex.

However, this view is not universally shared. Around the world, the UK is almost unique in recommending extra-strong condoms to gay men, with HIV prevention agencies in both the USA and Australia happy to say that it's okay for gay men to use standard strength condoms for anal sex. Only Germany and the Netherlands share the UK's insistence on extra-strong condoms.

Based on this research GMFA designed and launched a mass media campaign which says that standard strength condoms are just as reliable for anal sex as extra-strength ones.

Not everybody involved in UK HIV prevention agreed, most notably and vocally, the then Team Leader of Camden and Islington's HIV and Sexual Health Promotion Service, who now run Freedoms. This meant that gay men in the UK were being offered conflicting advice on condoms by two equally well respected HIV prevention agencies. A debate organised in 2002 between the two sides failed to reach a resolution.

The advice now (2005) offered by Camden and Islington and Freedoms is still that they recommend extra-strong condoms for anal sex, and extra-strong condoms are described as 'gay condoms' on their shop site. But David Smith the current team leader says: "We're cautious about changing that advice. Nut the important thing is to have people using condoms correctly, not failing to use them because they can't find an extra strong one or don't like them."

WARNING: SPERMICIDES

A spermicide is a chemical substance which is designed as a form of birth control by inactivating sperm to prevent conception. Some are also effective against HIV in some circumstances (see *Uncertainty about spermicidal lubricants* below). Spermicides may be introduced in lubricant on condoms, lubricating gels, pessaries etc.

The most frequently used spermicide is nonoxynol-9. **CONDOMS THAT CONTAIN NONOXYNOL-9 ARE NO LONGER RECOMMENDED FOR ANAL SEX OR FOR WOMEN THAT HAVE A LOT OF VAGINAL SEX, LIKE SEX WORKERS.**

Several scientific trials have now shown that that nonoxynol-9 may actually facilitate HIV transmission rather than provide added protection. The clinching trial was the COL-1492 trial nonoxynol-9 as a candidate microbicide in West Africa in 2002. This showed that using N-9, which kills HIV in the test tube, in fact doubled the rate of HIV transmission in frequent users because it damaged the mucous membrane lining the vagina (and has an even worse effect on anal and rectal membranes).

There is now a consensus among organisations concerned with sexual and reproductive health that nonoxynol-9 has no role in preventing HIV and other sexually transmitted infections, and its use should be discouraged by anyone perceived to be at risk. At the same time, there continues to be a role for spermicides containing N-9, as readily-available but moderately effective non-hormonal contraceptives, for women and couples who are at very low risk of HIV or other STIs.

It is particularly important that products containing N-9 should not be used for anal sex.

There has been resistance from condom manufacturers to calls to remove 'spermicidal lubrication' with N-9 from their products, as they perceive that it 'meets a demand' for 'extra safety' from some users. Expert opinion is that the low dose of N-9 in that lubricant does not add to their contraceptive value and might even distract women from the need for emergency back-up contraception if condoms fail. Durex have now removed sprmicidal lubrication from all their condoms, but some *Mates* brands still contain it - see list above.

The dose of N-9 in spermicidally lubricated condoms might still cause problems if such condoms are used for anal sex. Since many heterosexual couples practise anal sex on occasion, it seems unreasonable to expect them to decide in advance, when buying condoms, on what sort of sex they are going to have.

There is an even greater risk for gay men, since in many settings they are more likely to be exposed to HIV, yet there is evidence that gay men continue to use N-9 products despite publicity that these are dangerous.

A survey of gay men in San Francisco was carried out in 2001, a year after the publication of data showing that nonoxynol-9 increased the risk of HIV transmission. This found 349 men out of 573 had heard of nonoxynol-9. Among these, 55% had used products containing it in the previous year, for anal sex. In fact, it had been used in a median of 50% of acts of anal sex in the past twelve months. 23% had used it without a condom in the belief that it reduced their risk of HIV infection. On being informed that N-9 exposure caused disruption of the rectal mucosa, the great majority said they would be less likely to use it.

Brands to use if you are allergic to rubber
The vast majority of condoms are made of latex. If you are allergic to latex:

- Try Durex Allergy: it contains less of what makes you allergic to rubber condoms

- Try Femidoms which are made of plastic rather than latex

- Try polyurethane condoms if they are available.

There is no evidence that lambskin condoms prevent the transmission of HIV.

Teatless condoms
Some condoms are manufactured without a teat at the end. In the past the teat has always been considered necessary to contain semen and prevent the condom from bursting under the force of ejaculation. However, there is no conclusive evidence that teatless

condoms are more prone to bursting, and research in Holland during the development of a stronger condom suitable for anal sex showed that a teatless condom was more acceptable to gay men (it looked less artificial) and performed just as well in strength trials.

Larger and snugger fitting condoms
Men who have experienced difficulty in using condoms quite often complain that condoms split because they are not large enough, or that they slip off because they do not fit snugly enough. There are quite considerable variations in penis size amongst men in the UK which are related to some extent to ethnicity. It was recently estimated that a third of penises in the UK exceed the size designated as 'average' in the UK condom standard. A London GUM clinic recently investigated this variation and found that black men experienced the problem of condoms splitting more frequently, whilst Asian men were more likely to report problems with condoms slipping off.

This list above notes differences between the length and width of the standard strength condoms tested by the Consumers Association.

If you cannot afford condoms
Free supplies are often available from:

- NHS Family Planning Clinics
- Brook Advisory Centres
- Needle exchanges and drugs agencies
- Some GUM clinics
- Some local HIV/AIDS services and self help groups
- And increasingly from some GPs
- Gay pubs and clubs in London participating in the health-authority funded free condom scheme Freedoms.

All these sources should also be able to supply you with free water-based lubricant.

Lubricants

Why use plenty of water-based lubricant?
Condoms are vital to safer sex. They act as a barrier to body fluids, and help to protect us from HIV. But often people use condoms 'dry', that is without any lubricant on them, and this can create problems. The condom is more likely to slip, or tear, because of increased friction.

Anal sex without lubricant can not only be hugely painful, it also greatly increases the risk of tears and cuts to the lining of the rectum as well as the risk of breakage of the condom.

During vaginal intercourse, a woman produces natural lubricating fluids, but these may not be enough for safer condom use. The amount of fluid a woman produces changes throughout the menstrual cycle, and is influenced by several factors. It is quite natural for women to need additional lubrication for comfort as well as for safer sex.

The most important thing to remember is: - don't use oil-based lubricants with condoms: they weaken condoms drastically and dangerously within minutes! Often an oil-covered condom will split whilst you are having sex, so that you never realise it is burst or torn until after the event. If you are desperate to have sex, and only have oil-based lubricant to hand, then still don't use it. Spit is preferable.

On the other hand it is important to ensure that you are not having 'dry sex'. The increased friction from this puts extra strain on the condom. Adequate lubrication can sometimes be ensured in vaginalintercourse by means of plenty of `foreplay' but this is not always effective. Spit or water are not very good lubricants.

The wrong lubricants: oil-based
Anything made of rubber, from tyres to condoms, begins to rot and split when it comes into contact with anything oil-based. For many years, people have used oil-based `lubricants' that are found in any home as an aid to penetration.

But if you want to practice safer sex, or help to avoid pregnancy, by using condoms, then you should switch to using water-based lubricants. Examples of the wrong lubricants are:

- Oil
- Baby oil
- Corn oil
- Butter
- Margarine
- Crisco and other `vegetable fats'
- Vaseline
- Petroleum jelly
- Hand cream and body lotion.

It is important not to rely upon whether the lubricant will wash off your hands or not. There are certain lubricants that are oil-based which will wash off, giving the false impression that they are water-based.

Many ointments, creams, gels, vaginal pessaries or suppositories come in an oil-based medium as well. Your doctor will be able to tell you which prescribed treatments are oil-based. A leaflet detailing which ones are oil-based is also produced by Durex.

If you want to keep having sex, but have to use oil-based products, then you may want to consider using a Femidom instead of condoms (see *female condoms and spermicides* below).

The right lubricants: water-based
- Liquid Silk
  Doesn't contain glycerine, available in sachets/pump

- Eros
  Silicone-based, oil-free formulation - safe for use with all condoms

- ID Millennium
  Silicone-based

- ID Pleasure
  Silicone-based, contains amino acid Arginine

- ID Glide
  Water-based

- Wet Stuff
  Water-based lubricant, available in bottle/tube/pump/sachets

- Oncore
  Homeopathic, water-based gel, available in tube/pump

- Boots Lubricating   Jelly
  Water-based

- K-Y Jelly
  Water-based

- K-Y Liquid
  Water-based, ideal for use with condoms

You can buy water-based lubricants, such as KY, Wet Stuff, Comfort, Probe, Astroglide or 121 at many chemists.

The new **silicone-based** lubricants such as *Millennium ID* and *Eros* are more expensive than water-based ones. But they are also condom-friendly, do not feel sticky or dry out so fast, and are economical (a little goes a long way).

There are also lubricants, such as Boots's own brand which explain that they are water-based on the packaging. Some people like different lubes because they stay wet for longer, and you might want to experiment.

Replens
A recently-launched product on the market, *Replens* is a `super lubricant', designed to help post-menopausal women who find that their vaginal juices are too limited to help with sex or who are generally dry and need lubrication. *Replens* lasts for a long time, and although based on palm oil, it does not affect rubber. Tests by Durex on *Replens* with condoms registered no damage.

Don't use nonoxynol-9 coated condoms

In September 2002 the Global Campaign for Microbicides launched a public `Call to discontinue nonoxynol-9 for rectal use'. This is based on concerns, set out by the US Centers for Disease Control and Prevention and the World Health Organization (WHO), that this widely-used spermicide causes damage to the lining of the rectum when used for anal sex, significantly increasing the risk of HIV and other STI transmission.

The call has been backed by leading scientists in the field and by many HIV, AIDS, gay and women's organisations including all of the main microbicide advocacy groups, the American Foundation for AIDS Research (amFAR), the Family Planning Association (UK), International HIV/AIDS Alliance, International AIDS Vaccine Initiative, National AIDS Trust, Terrence Higgins Trust, and the US Gay and Lesbian Medical Association.

The call demands that manufacturers discontinue the sale of condoms and sexual lubricants containing nonoxynol-9, while continuing to supply over-the-counter spermicides containing nonoxynol-9 in forms designed for vaginal use. The argument is that a public education campaign, to persuade individual consumers to check the labels and avoid products containing nonoxynol-9, would not be as effective in bringing about change as a simple change to the products.

While gay men may generally be at the highest risk of HIV transmission through anal sex, there are many heterosexual couples who sometimes have anal sex and therefore many women who are also potentially at risk.

Female condoms
The most effective method to prevent HIV acquisition and transmission, the condom, is worn by men. Many women do not have relationships of equality with the men they have sex with, and they can experience difficulties `persuading' men to use condoms. This can be particularly difficult in situations where HIV is not the priority concern (for example, when the woman experiences violence). However, it is also problematic for women in more equal relationships, since many men find condoms unpleasant, and as women are more vulnerable to HIV than men from vaginal intercourse, they may not afford the same priority to condom use.

The female condom is the first product which has been developed to offer women more control over HIV prevention methods. However, it is not a method entirely within women's control. Although, in general, the woman inserts the device, it requires compliance and consent from the man for it to be used. It is extremely visible - many would say unattractive - as it extends beyond the labia. It is possible for the man to avoid it and penetrate between the female condom and the vaginal wall, and it is unlikely that the woman would be aware if he was doing this.

Since there are no methods entirely within women's control, and as the vulnerability to HIV from vaginal sex increases for women, the need for new prevention methods is urgent. Microbicides (previously known as virucides) have been spoken about for several years, and are now receiving a fair degree of attention from some policy makers (such as WHO) and sectors of the research community. Currently no proven safe and effective microbicides are available, but research is underway. Microbicides are also beneficial because they offer the potential to protect against sexually transmitted infections, which are a significant contributor to death, illness and infertility around the world.

For more information on the development of microbicides see *Microbicides* in *Emergent prevention technologies*.

Trials in the United States and Britain show a pregnancy failure rate of 2.4% when the female condom is used properly, and 12.2% when not used properly and consistently (source: Chartex). That compares to a 2% pregnancy failure rate for properly used `kitemark' condoms, rising to up to 15% for improperly used condoms (source: Durex).

Advantages

Since it does not fit the penis snugly like a male condom, several men report that it is more pleasurable because it is not constricting. The female condom can be inserted before sexual activity begins and so it may be less of an interference than the male condom. Because it is made of polyurethane, the female condom can be used with oil-based or water-based lubricants.

It has been suggested that some women (for example, sex workers) would find the female condoms an easier way of practising safer sex, by keeping it in for a period of time. However, women who have tried this report that it can be uncomfortable, and it is also important to check the female condom at regular intervals for tears in the plastic. Using a female condom on a number of occasions may present few problems with a single sexual partner, but it is clearly different if used for multiple partners (e.g. for a sex worker). There would be risks to multiple partners who came into contact with infected semen in the female condom deposited by previous men.

The manufacturers also warn against taking out the female condom, washing it and then re-inserting it, since this doesn't guarantee hygiene, and the product would need re-lubricating. They advise using a new female condom on each occasion. There are plans to develop the product so that it can be used on several occasions, like the diaphragm.

The female condom is expensive, although it is increasingly available for free from outlets, such as health clinics, which also provide free male condoms. You may need to ask for the female condom if you don't see it on disply at some clinics, since they may prefer to give out male condoms, which are cheaper.

There are some reported problems with using the female condom. Some women report losing the inner ring inside their vagina whilst others fear that, because the female condom is seamed, it may be more liable to tearing. Some cases of tearing have been noted.

Trials not sponsored by the company have tended to show a lower rate of acceptability. The female condom is very visible, and many women find it unattractive (and comic) because the appliance hangs down beyond the labia. Some women experience irritation to the vulval area because of the outer ring, which fits over the labia to hold the device in place.

The sound of trapped air in the female condom has irritated some users. Other activities, in particular oral sex, are not feasible with it in place. Some men have found the inner ring uncomfortable as they thrust into it - this problem can be solved by either removing the inner ring, or inserting the female condom on the penis (rather than the woman inserting it like a diaphragm).

Use of the female condom in the developing world

Studies conducted in Africa, Asia, Latin America, Europe and North America have found good initial acceptability of the device. A recent review by the World Health Organization of 41 acceptability studies indicated that the degree of acceptance varies widely, from 41 to 95% of study participants. Research indicates that counselling helps overcome women's initial difficulties in using the device, that directing promotion campaigns to men and providing women with negotiation skills are important to overcome men's resistance to use, and that over time, use tends to become concentrated among a subset of women or couples with high motivation to use it.

Among the many acceptability studies, recent UNAIDS-supported research in Costa Rica, Indonesia, Mexico and Senegal found that women who introduced the female condom into a relationship reported it allowed them to communicate more successfully about safer sex. In a study involving 377 women in the Dominican Republic, Mexico and United States, about four of every five women liked the device and said they would recommend it to others.

In Zambia and Zimbabwe, mass marketing campaigns and some educational support have made the female condom available in urban areas. A year after the Zimbabwe campaign began, a survey of more than 1,600 people at retail outlets concluded that single women and men with partners outside of marriage seemed to benefit most from the female condom introduction. After six months in the Zambia campaign, a random sample of 1,570 persons at 52 retail outlets found that those who had already discussed the female condom with a partner were more likely to use it in the future.

Nine hundred women were provided with both male and female condoms at STI clinics in the US. After six months, 8% had used only the female condom. Another 73% had used both the male and female condom. About a third of those used ten or more female condoms. The researchers concluded that women at risk of STIs find the female condom acceptable, with many using either the male or female condom consistently over time.

Two studies among women at high risk of HIV infection indicated successful sustained use. A study in Zambia found that the devices were used in one quarter of coital acts at three, six and twelve months. In a study among sex workers in Thailand, some 250 women offered both male and female condoms used female condoms in 12% of all sexual acts, a level that continued for the entire six-month study period.

Instructions for use

1   Find a comfortable position, for example, lying down, sitting with your knees apart, or standing with one foot up on a chair

2   Open the female condom packet by tearing down from the notch, and remove the product. You will see that the female condom is pre-lubricated. Make sure that the flexible inner ring is at the closed end of the female condom

3   Squeeze the lower half of the inner ring between your thumb, index and middle fingers. This should give you a confident grip and narrows the inner ring to ease insertion

4   With the other hand, spread the labia (folds of skin around your vaginal opening). Insert the squeezed ring of the female condom into the vagina, and push inside as far as you can

5   Then put your finger inside the female condom until you can feel the bottom of the inner ring. Push the ring up into the vagina

6   You can tell if it is in place when the inner ring is up past the pubic bone. You can feel your pubic bone by curving your finger (towards the front) when it is a couple of inches inside your vagina

7   The outer ring and a small part of the female condom will stay outside your vagina. This is quite normal so don't worry

8   Another method is to use the female condom as a penile (male) condom. It may be best to leave the inner ring at the

far end of the Female condom, as this will hold it around the cervix. Since the ring helps to guide the device when it is inserted first into the vagina, and it can cause discomfort, another option is to remove the inner ring. This method could also be used for anal sex

9   Add extra lubricant during sex if one of you needs it. If the outer ring is being drawn into the vagina, or if the penis starts to enter between the vagina and the female condom, then stop. The man should withdraw and add extra lube to the inside of the female condom

10 Removing the female condom: because the female condom lines the inside of the vagina the man doesn't have to withdraw immediately after coming. You can remove the sheath when it suits you, making sure that no semen is spilt. Twist the outer ring to keep the semen inside, then pull gently. Throw away the used female condom. Do not throw it down the toilet as it may cause a blockage.

It is also possible to use the female condom like a baggy penile condom (see below). Although it would make sense for this method to be as safe as the one described, trials have not been conducted to assess the efficacy of using it in this way.

Female condoms for anal sex

Like condoms, it appears that, although not designed for the purpose, female condoms do work as an effective barrier during anal sex. A study in the United States of 14 male couples using the equivalent of the female condoms found that, although no leaks or tears were found in any of the sheaths used, all of the men found design and usage difficulties, 'which were primarily due to lack of experience and knowledge' of the product.

Provisional guidelines for anal sex with female condoms

1   The easiest way to use the female condom for anal sex is to wear it like a 'male' (penile) condom. Put lubricant in the female condom and then place it over the penis (or a dildo). Use plenty of lubricant on the outside of the female condom or around your partner's anus before penetration.

2   Alternatively, you could try to insert the female condom in the rectum first, as for vaginal penetration. Use plenty of lubricant around the anus, and loosen it with a finger in readiness for the female condom. Make sure your fingernails are cut short.

3   After removing the female condom from its wrapper, hold the inner ring between your thumb, index and forefinger, and squeeze it so that it forms an oval. Don't remove the inner ring, as this will lead the female condom to become tangled, and could lead to breakage.

4   Push the female condom up into your rectum as far as you can, using the inner ring as a guide, whilst spreading your anus with your other hand. You may find this easier if you raise one leg onto the side of the bath, or a stool.

5   Then put your index finger inside the female condom, until you feel the bottom of the inner ring. Push up as far as you can, but do not insert the outer ring.

6   You will find that the outer ring, and perhaps a small part of the female condom, are on the outside of your anus. That's meant to happen, and should stop the female condom from slipping inside.

7   Use more lubricant inside the female condom, to keep it moist, and add it whenever you need it during sex.

8   Check every now and again during sex that the outer ring of the female condom hasn't slipped inside your anus, or that his penis hasn't slipped between the female condom

and your anus. If it has, stop, remove the female condom, and use a new one before starting again.

9   Don't re-use the female condom. Some gay men are reported to have used a female condom as a semi-permanent barrier to HIV, having sex with multiple partners. The female condom is designed for vaginal sex and for single use. If you use it more than once for anal sex, we don't know the strains that it could put on the sides of the sheath, which might easily tear. And if you get a lot of semen in the female condom, we don't know how effective it is in holding it in, or whether any seepage into your rectum could take place. It is likely that intercourse in somebody else's cum would also be dangerous for your partners

10 Removing the female condom. Because the female condom lines the inside of the rectum, your partner doesn't have to withdraw immediately after coming. You can remove the sheath when it suits you, making sure that no semen is spilt. Twist the outer ring to keep the semen inside, then pull gently. Throw away the used female condom.

Gay men's use of female condoms

Female condoms were the first product developed to offer women more control over HIV prevention methods. The *Reality* condom was approved in the USA in 1992 for vaginal contraceptive use. Latex male condoms have been associated with usage problems including, breakage, slippage, latex allergies and lack of control by receptive partners. Although female condoms are essentially not designed for the purpose, some gay men have used them and it seems they do provide an effective barrier during anal sex.

A 1999 study (Renzi, 2001) among gay men in San Francisco gave *Reality* condoms to 100 men attending an STI clinic. Eighty-six men said they would use the *Reality* condom again and 54 said they preferred it to penile condoms. Acceptability was greatest among HIV-positive men and men in serodiscordant relationships or non-monogamous ones. Problems cited included difficulty inserting (33%), irritation (17%), bunching up (12%), unpleasant texture (10%), and noise (9%). Breakage was reported three times in 334 episodes of use.

Research published in the March 2003 edition of the journal *AIDS* has assessed the safety and acceptability of a brand of female condom called *Reality* for anal sex among gay men. The study enrolled 56 monogamous seroconcordant gay male couples who had not used condoms in the past three months were randomised to use latex male condoms or the *Reality* female condom for anal sex. On study entry the men were given ten *Reality* or lubricated male condoms to use with lubricant during the following six weeks. In the second six weeks the couples crossed over and began using the other condom type.

The *Reality* condom has two polyurethane rings and a thin, loose-fitting polyurethane sheath which in laboratory studies has been shown to be impermeable to viruses and less likely to rupture than latex condoms. Since it is made of polyurethane it can be used with both water-based and other kinds of lubricant. In this study couples were advised to remove the inner ring to reduce potential rectal trauma and bleeding.

Receptive partners were more likely to report pain or discomfort with the *Reality* rather than the male condom. Both partners were significantly more likely to report *Reality* condom slippage during use or withdrawal. Rates of condom breakage were similar for Reality and male condoms.

After using both sets of condoms , both active and passive partners were significantly less likely to be willing to use *Reality* condoms in the future with partners of unknown HIV status than they were to be willing to use male latex condoms; (21% of receptive and 26% of insertive partners would be willing to use *Reality* condoms, compared to 61% of both receptive and insertive partners who were willing to use latex condoms. The main reason reported by those who would be willing to use the

Reality condom with future partners of unknown HIV status were that the *Reality* condom was more comfortable, easier to use, and perceived to be stronger and safer.

The researchers suggested that gay men who are considering using the *Reality* condom might require training relating to slippage and methods for avoiding semen spillage that might expose the anal mucosa. They added "further work is warranted on design modifications, safety and acceptability of the *Reality* condom in HIV-negative gay men".

References

Agence-France Presse. THAI TEENAGERS SHUNNING CONDOMS, HEALTH MINISTRY WARNS. 16 November 2003.

AIDS Prevention and Control Project. Voluntary health services: executive summary of BSS report wave IX report. Tamil Nadu. India, 2005.

American Social Health Association Press Release: SURVEY SUGGESTS LACK OF AWARENESS HEIGHTENS RISK FOR SEXUALLY TRANSMITTED DISEASES. See http://www.planetout.com/health/hiv/?sernum=2778. 6 April 2004.

Bradshaw S. Vatican: condoms don't stop Aids, *The Guardian, 9 October 2003.* See http://www.guardian.co.uk/aids/story/0,7369,1059068,00.html

Centers for Disease Control and Prevention, Communicable Disease Weekly 148(03): 45-48, 1999.

Cove J, Petrak J. *Factors associated with sexual problems in HIV-positive gay men.* Int J STD AIDS. 15(11): 732-736, 2004.

Dandona L. *Sex behaviour of men who have sex with men and risk of HIV in Andhra Pradesh, India.* AIDS. 19(6): 611-619, 2005.

Davidovich U et al. *Assessing sexual risk behaviour of young gay men in primary relationships: the incorporation of negotiated safety and negotiated safety compliance.* AIDS 14(6): 701-706, 2000.

De Vincenzi I. *A Longitudinal Study of Human Immunodeficiency virus Transmission by Heterosexual Partners.* NEJM 331(6): 341-346, 1994.

Elam G et al. *Intentional and unintentional UAI among gay men who HIV test in the UK: qualitative results from an investigation into risk factors for seroconversion among gay men who HIV test (INSIGHT).* HIV Med 7 (supplement 1), abstract O27, 2006.

Elford J et al. *HIV positive and negative homosexual men have adopted different strategies for reducing the risk of HIV transmission.* Sexually Transmitted Infections 77: 224-225, 2001.

Elford J. *High risk sexual behaviour among London gay men: no longer increasing?* Eleventh Annual BHIVA Conference, Dublin, abstract O14, 2005a.

Elford J et al. *High-risk sexual behaviour among London gay men: no longer increasing.* AIDS, 2005 (in press). 2005b.

Erickson P. *Prevalence of anal sex among heterosexuals in California and its relationship to other AIDS risk behaviours.* AIDS Education & Prevention 7(6): 477-493, 1995

Gay Men's Sex Surveys 1999-2003: See http://www.sigmaresearch.org/

Golombok S et al. *An evaluation of a thicker versus a standard condom with gay men.* AIDS 2001, 15: 245-250, 2001.

Guzman, R et al. *Negotiated safety relationships and sexual behaviour among a diverse sample of HIV-negative men who have sex with men.* JAIDS 38(1): 82-86, 2005.

Harding, R et al. *A clinical trial of a thicker versus a standard condom for gay men.* Thirteenth International AIDS Conference, abstract WePpC1395, Durban, 9-14 July 2000.

Hickson F et al. *Out and About: Findings form the UK Gay Men's Sex Survey 2002.* Sigma Research, 2003.

Ho GY et al. *Natural history of cervicovaginal papillomavirus infection in young women.* N Engl J Med 338(7): 423-428, 1998.

Johnson AM et al. *Sexual behaviour in Britain: partnerships, practices, and HIV risk behaviours.* Lancet 358(9296):1835-1842, 2001.

Kajubi P et al. *Increasing condom use without reducing HIV risk: results of a controlled community trial in Uganda.* JAIDS 40(1): 77-82, 2005.

Kumar R, et al. *Trends in HIV-1 in young adults in south India from 2000 to 2004: a prevalence study.* Lancet367: 1164-1172, 2006.

Lightfoot M et al. *The influence of partner type and risk status on the sexual behaviourr of young men who have sex with me living with HIV/AIDS.* JAIDS38(1), 61-68, 2005.

Maharaj P and Cleland J. *Risk preception and condom use among married or cohabiting couples in KwaZulu-Natal, South Africa.* International Family Planning Perspectives 31(1), 2005.

Najjumba M. *Risk perception and condom use in Uganda.* African Population Studies 18(1), 2003.

Peltzer K. *Factors affecting condom use among senior secondary school pupils in South Africa.* Cent Afr J Med. 46(11): 302-308, 2000.

Mechai Viravaidya. *Personal communication with author,* 2004.

Prabhu R. et al. *The bisexual bridge revisited: sexual risk behavior among men who have sex with men and women, San Francisco, 1998-2003.* AIDS 18(11), 1604-1606, 2004.

Renzi, C. et al. *Safety and acceptability of the Reality* [TM] *condom for anal sex among men who have sex with men.* AIDS17(5) 28: 727-731, 2003.

San Francisco Department of Public Health - HIV Epidemiology Annual Report 2004 - see http://www.dph.sf.ca.us/Reports/HlthAssess.htm.%202004.

Santelli JS et al. *Can changes in sexual behaviors among high school students explain the decline in teen pregnancy rates in the 1990s?* Journal of Adolescent Health, 35(2): 80-90, 2004.

Simoni J M et al. *Safer sex among HIV+ women: The role of relationships.* Sex Roles 42: 691-708, 2000.

Weller S, Davis K. *Condom Effectiveness in Reducing Heterosexual Transmission.* The Cohrane Database of Systematic Reviews, issue 1, 2002.

UNAIDS: AIDS Epidemic Update, December 2001.

UNAIDS 2005. *Evidence for HIV decline in Zimbabwe: a comprehensive review of the epidemiological data.* ISBN 92 9 173461 6. Can be downloaded from http://data.unaids.org/publications/irc-pub06/zimbabwe_epi_report_nov05_en.pdf

Winer RL et al. *Genital human papillomavirus infection: incidence and risk factors in a cohort of female university students.* Am J Epidemiol 157(3): 218-226, 2003.

Winer RL et al. *Condom use and the risk of genital human papillomavirus infection in young women.* N Engl J Med354(25): 2645-2654, 2006.

D is for disclosure, serosorting and negotiated safety

Compare the two charts from the San Francisco Department of Public health's 2004 HIV Epidemiology Report(2004):

The first shows that unprotected anal sex (any episode over the previous six months) was practised by about a third of HIV-negative men consistently from 1998 to 2004, with very little change. In contrast the proportion of HIV-positive men having unprotected sex went up during the same period from 38 to 52%.

The second chart, however, shows that these high and (in positive men) increasing levels of unprotected sex did not translate into increasing levels of unsafe sex. The amount of *potentially serodiscordant* sex - the true measure of the degree of HIV risk

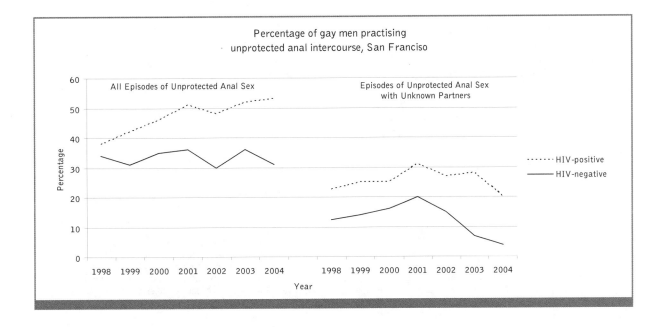

Percentage of gay men practising
unprotected anal intercourse, San Franciso

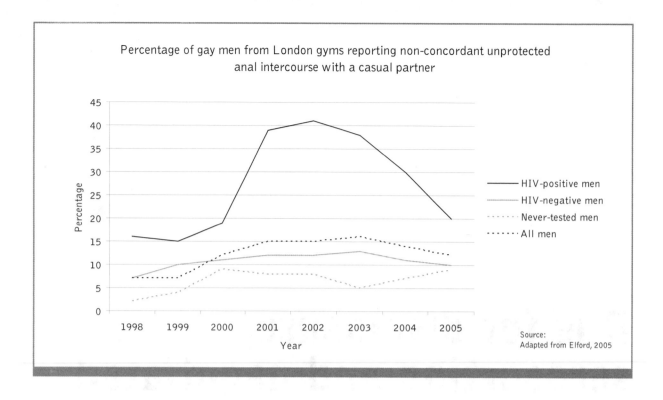

Percentage of gay men from London gyms reporting non-concordant unprotected anal intercourse with a casual partner

- HIV-positive men
- HIV-negative men
- Never-tested men
- All men

Source:
Adapted from Elford, 2005

among a community - has declined from a peak in 2001 among both positive and negative men.

Similarly, in the UK, a decline in serodiscordant unprotected sex may be starting to happen too, and amongst gay men. And among positive men the decline appears to be more dramatic. The annual survey of gay men using London gyms (Elford 2005b) between January and March each year, in which so far more than 5,000 gay men have participated, found last year that the amount of serodiscordant unprotected sex increased between 1998 and 2002, but has remained stable since then or slightly declined among HIV-negative men, and has declined significantly (p=<0.05) in HIV-positive men, from a peak of 41% in 2002 to 20% in 2005. (see chart above)

How can gay men be having *more* unprotected sex while at the same time having *less* sex of the kind that could spread HIV?

Clearly, by increasing the proportion of unprotected sex they have with men with the same HIV status.

The phenomenon by which HIV comes to be brought under better control by people seeking out sex partners with their own HIV status has become called **Serosorting,** and is usually applied specifically to situations where unprotected sex is being sought.

Serosorting may be one reason why an increase in STIs in gay men, especially syphilis, has not led to a concomitant increase in HIV infections. This has shaken an assumption previously used by many HIV epidemiologists - that increases in STI rates can be used as surrogate markers or predictors of increases in HIV. This has been found not to be the case. In the US huge increases in syphilis in gay men have not coincided with equally big increases in HIV. (Conversely, in certain African countries like Zimbabwe, STI rates have gone down while HIV incidence has not, because more HIV infections are now occurring within marriages and fewer within casual encounters)(Gisselquist 2003).

This was first noticed in 2003 when two US cities, Seattle and San Francisco, noticed that HIV incidence among gay men attending for HIV tests was starting to decline even though syphilis rates had increased 25-fold (Buchacz, 2004). At the time this was partly put down to a lot of syphilis being spread via oral

sex, and particularly among gay men, as they were unaware of this transmission route. However only 25% of syphilis, it was thought, was being spread orally. Syphilis is also more contagious than HIV so can spread more rapidly through a connected network of sexual partners.

But Dr Jeffrey Klausner, San Francisco Health Department's Director of STI Prevention, commented at the Eleventh Retrovirus Conference where these findings were presented that there was a lot of evidence that much of the lack of a rise in HIV was due to serosorting.

This phenomenon - of concentrating the unprotected sex you have with people of the same HIV status - was previously thought to be rare.

Serosorting is one example of 'negotiated safety'. In the previous edition of the *AIDS Reference Manual* it was thought, as an HIV prevention strategy, to be quite uncommon, particularly in the UK. It quoted findings from Edinburgh and Glasgow that negotiated safety in the light of full knowledge about HIV status was still rare. Research conducted in 1996 showed that only 16% of men questioned were having unprotected anal sex in a relationship were doing so in the light of knowledge about both partner's HIV status, compared with 60% of men in Australia.

However serosorting may be an important way by which HIV-positive men attempt to reduce the risk of their passing on HIV to others. In one US study (Lightfoot, 2005) of young US gay men (most of them black or Latino) aged 15-24, about 34% of youth with multiple partners and 28% with one primary partner had unprotected anal intercourse.

However they were overwhelmingly more likely to have unprotected sex with other partners *perceived* to be HIV-positive than with partners whose HIV status was negative or unknown.

In some cases the perception was probably accurate. The estimated number of instances of unprotected sex was 32 times greater among youth in a committed relationship if their regular partner was thought to be positive than if he was thought to be negative but at high risk of having other STIs (eg in an open relationship), and 18 times more if he was thought unlikely to have STIs (eg if thought monogamous). In at least some of these cases, the HIV status of the partners must have been known, rather than just a perception.

However, it is the word 'perceived' that has made HIV prevention workers very wary of encouraging serosorting as an HIV prevention technique. Attempting to guess a partner's HIV status, many studies have shown, is doomed to failure, especially as many so-called 'negotiations' do not take place with words. In a backroom or anonymous sex situation, people's HIV status is deduced by their actions. The lack of insistence on a condom is assumed by a positive man to be a sign that the other is positive ("He must be positive or he wouldn't let me do that"). A negative man makes the opposite assumption ("If he was positive he would protect me and use a condom").

The 2002 UK Gay Men's Sex Survey *Out and About* makes the false assumptions of gay men about other's status very clear - and underlines the disincentive many HIV-positive men have to disclose.

A summary of the survey's findings on **Aidsmap** says:

"Of the participants whose most recent HIV test was negative, two-thirds (65.3%) said they would expect an HIV-positive man to disclose his status before having sex. Even more men who had never tested for HIV had the same expectation (77%). In contrast only just over a third of HIV-positive men expected that a partner would disclose their HIV status.

44% of HIV-negative or untested men said they would not want to have sex with the man who'd just disclosed his HIV status to them - and this rose to 56% of men who had never had an HIV test.

Report authors Sigma Research comment: "Expectations that men with HIV will tell a prospective sexual partner their HIV status are still widespread. Over a third of men not tested [HIV] positive both expected a positive partner to disclose their status prior to sex and would not want to have sex with them if they did.

"In this climate, it is difficult to see what incentive men with HIV have for disclosing their status."

In addition, significant numbers of gay men do not know their HIV status. In the year 2000 Gay Men's Sex Survey (*Time for More*), 44% of respondents had never tested for HIV, but of those only 1.3% thought they were 'probably or definitely positive'.

Even if a lot of the others are correct that they are negative, this is still only an eighth of the 10.9% prevalence reported from another survey of gay men in UK cities (Dodds, 2004). Of the HIV-positive men in this survey, who were tested anonymously with an oral saliva test, a third (32.5%) were unaware of their infection and over one in five (21.2%) said their last HIV test was negative.

In these circumstances, how can making safer-sex decisions on the basis of a partner's HIV status possibly be a way of not being infected or infecting someone? The idea that serosorting or making other safer-sex decisions on the basis of a partner's HIV status can possibly contribute to HIV prevention is a challenge to orthodox HIV prevention approaches, and makes many people deeply uneasy:

- As above, people may be making decisions on the basis of assumptions or inaccurate information

- It relies on disclosure - something still practised by a minority of gay men with HIV. In one unpublished survey by Gay Men Fighting AIDS, only 20% of respondents said they always disclosed their HIV status (positive or negative) to partners, forty per cent said they sometimes did, and forty per cent said they never did.

- It is seen as diluting the 'use a condom' message and providing ways for men to rationalise unsafe behaviour

- 'Serosorting' men can do things that at first look like ways of wilfully increasing their HIV risk rather than reducing it. For instance, gay men who advertise for 'bareback' sex may seem

to be nothing other than irresponsible. If however 'bareback' is a code for 'HIV-positive', or if bareback discussions lead to disclosure of HIV status, the net result may be a paradoxical isolation of HIV within a specific group.

- Even if this is the case, HIV-positive men having unprotected sex together are still vulnerable to other STIs and possibly (especially during the first three years of infection) to infection with a second strain of HIV ('superinfection').

- All 'negotiated safety' unprotected sex strategies between men of differing HIV status are likely to involve a considerably greater risk or HIV infection than protected sex does.

However there is indirect evidence that a lot of HIV-positive men, in particular *are* at least attempting to restrict their unprotected sex to other HIV-positive men. The debate around this kind of 'negotiated safety' centres on this dilemma:

- Should prevention messages concentrate on the fact that these practices still involve considerable HIV risk, and should therefore be discouraged?

- Or, since the gay men (and heterosexuals, though negotiated safety among heterosexuals is less well studied) who use these strategies to minimise HIV risk are unlikely to be persuaded back to consistent condom use, should prevention messages encourage behaviours that enable them to happen, such as disclosure of HIV status?

In one analysis of the ongoing survey of gay men attending London gyms (Elford, 2001), the authors detected two very different strategies being adopted by HIV-positive and negative gay men to avoid infection.

In HIV-negative men what the authors call "concordant UAI" and we call serosorting was mainly restricted to main partners. Over one in four (28.6%) practised it with their primary partner and only five per cent with casual partners.

In HIV-positive men concordant UAI was equally practised with main partners (22.2%) and with casual partners (20.6%).

These unprotected sexual encounters were those restricted to ones where men were fairly sure their partner was of the same HIV status. If all men had an equal tendency to be uncertain or to be making decisions on the basis of assumption, the authors argue, one would expect the lower proportion of unprotected encounters with *casual* partners to apply to both HIV-negative and positive men. The significantly greater difference can only be explained, at least in part, by the fact that it is possible for HIV-positive men to disclose their status with certainty:

"Seroconcordance among negative men can only be established with confidence if both men test for HIV together. For this reason it is difficult for HIV-negative men to establish concordance with a casual partner.

"On the other hand, HIV-positive men can establish concordance, be it with a casual or regular partner, simply by mutual disclosure. This requires no confirmatory test."

They add a caution: "Although seroconcordant UAI among positive men carries no risk of HIV transmission to an uninfected person, it raises the possibility of reinfection and drug resistance for the men themselves."

But is this disclosure actually taking place?

The internet as disclosure venue

Concern has been expressed in recent years that the huge increase in sexual encounters being arranged on the internet may be facilitating an upsurge in unprotected sex. This concern has been fuelled by the rise in the number of explicit 'barebacking' sites.

In a more recent study by the same group of researchers (Bolding, 2005), four groups of gay men (internet chatroom users, London gym users, HIV-positive men attending clinics, and HIV-negative men attending for an HIV test) were asked about their patterns of unprotected sex and internet use.

HIV-positive men in the clinic and gym samples who used the internet to look for sex were significantly more likely to report unprotected anal sex with men of the same HIV status than other men (p < 0.05).

The investigators also established that in both the clinic and gym samples, HIV-positive and HIV-negative men who used the internet to find sex were more likely to report non-concordant unprotected anal sex with a casual partner than other men (p < 0.05).

So far, this looks as if the internet is facilitating increased levels of unsafe sex.

But the investigators found that internet users were also more likely to have *concordant* unprotected sex, i.e. to 'serosort'.

In all samples, HIV-positive men who looked for sex through the internet were significantly more (p <0 .05) likely to report concordant unprotected anal sex with a partner they met online rather than offline. For example, 10% of the clinic sample reported concordant unprotected unprotected anal sex with a man they met online, and only four per cent said they had had concordant unprotected sex with a man met offline.

What's more, the investigators found that amongst the HIV-positive clinic sample, men said that they were more likely to disclose their HIV status to men met online (24%) than men met offline (14%, p < 0.001).

They also found that the apparent causal link between internet use and *serodiscordant* unprotected sex was an artefact. When asked directly about *how they met* partners they subsequently had unprotected sex with, there was no evidence that gay men, whether HIV-positive, negative or untested, were more likely to meet partners for discordant unprotected anal sex online rather than offline.

For example, among HIV-negative men in the internet sample, 10% reported non-concordant unprotected anal sex with men met online only, 11% with men met offline only, and six per cent with men met on- and offline. "In fact," note the investigators, "for HIV-negative men in the clinic and gym samples, the reverse pattern was seen; they were more likely to report non-concordant unprotected anal sex with a casual partner met offline."

In other words internet meets were more likely to result in unprotected sex which was concordant: serodiscordant unprotected sex was at least as likely to occur during casual encounters.

"What is new about this study is that we can establish whether the excess risk of HIV and sexually transmitted infections seen among gay men who looked for sex through the internet actually occurred with the men they met online", write the investigators.

"In our study, HIV-positive men who looked for sex through the internet were more likely to meet other HIV-positive men with whom they had (concordant) unprotected anal intercourse online rather than offline ", note the investigators. They add "Men who looked for sex through the internet were no more likely to meet their non-concordant unprotected anal intercourse partners online than offline. This was seen for HIV-positive, HIV-negative and never-tested men alike."

The investigators suggest that the internet may provide a safe space for HIV-positive men to disclose their health status, 'thus facilitating "filtering" or "serosorting' of sexual partners'.

This is not the only study that suggests the internet is being used by HIV-positive men as a safe place in which to disclose and negotiate the level of sexual safety they want.

A study presented at the 2005 Retrovirus Conference(Chiasson, 2005) of users of 14 US-based gay websites found that 28.5% of men had unprotected sex during their last encounter.

However twice as many instances of unprotected sex happened after casual offline encounters that after internet meets.

And online meets, however, were more likely to involve discussion of HIV status. More than half of the men who had met online had discussed their HIV status before sex as opposed to a third of partners who met offline.

The authors comment: "The large number of men online and the diversity of their risk and ways of meeting partners show that the Internet provides a unique opportunity for far-reaching behavioural interventions."

Does serosorting work?

No rigorous longitudinal study has yet been done to find out if HIV-positive serosorters transmit HIV less often, and given that research on serosorting has mainly been carried out on gay men who may have multiple casual partners, this may be difficult to establish. However there is epidemiological evidence that serosorting has *some* impact on HIV incidence - or, at least, has done so in San Francisco (Russell).

This impact, however, is relatively slight and may be cancelled out by other demographic or behavioural changes.

In March 2006, San Francisco Department of Public Health epidemiologist Dr Willi McFarland concluded that estimates of ongoing HIV incidence among gay men in the city should be reduced by a 'disappointing' 10% per year.

This was disappointing because 2005 results from HIV clinics (see Centers for Disease control) had suggested that HIV incidence in among gay men in the city had declined from 2.2% a year - an estimate unchanged since 2000 - to 1.2% in 2004, a difference attributed to the increased practice of serosorting.

"It hasn't changed that much," McFarland told the *San Francisco Chronicle*, "but the fact is, we've reversed a trend. There is some evidence that our efforts at prevention are working."

In fact, the new estimates did conclude that the actual infection rate among gay men in San Francisco had declined substantially, by about 20% since 2001. However it also found that this decrease has been offset by a 25% increase in the city's gay male population during those five years.

Hopes were raised in June 2005 that the city's rate of new infections might be lowered as much as 40% after the Centers for Disease Control study came out. However, after months of analysing fresh data from a dozen programs that track the epidemic in the city, McFarland opted for a more conservative revision.

Since 2001, the city's official estimate has been that each year 1,084 residents become infected with HIV, the virus that causes AIDS. The new estimate is 976 - 87% of them gay men.

McFarland stressed that the science of making these estimates is far less precise than the un-rounded numbers might suggest. Into the mix of data used to make these estimates are new HIV cases reported from public clinics, scattered reports from private doctors and centres that provide anonymous tests, and findings that track trends in sexual behavior that may affect future infection rates.

McFarland said the most surprising finding in his analysis was the increase in the population of gay men in San Francisco. Because there are no census data based on sexual orientation, it has always been difficult to come up with a number. Based on nine surveys, the health department estimates that the number of gay men living in San Francisco is 58,000, a 25% increase from 47,000 in 2001.

It is easier to make an estimate of the degree to which 'serosorting' - most of which might more properly be called negotiated safety - works in HIV-negative people, as one can ask HIV seroconverters about whether they had attempted to restrict their sexual risk behaviour to other HIV-negative people.

At a study presented at CROI, Matthew Golden of the University of Washington, Seattle Center for AIDS and Sexually Transmitted Diseases came up with a figure: he estimated that serosorting among HIV-negative gay men was reducing the number of infections that might otherwise have occurred by about 40%.

Golden looked at what he called "the practice of preferentially choosing sex partners, or deciding not to use condoms with selected partners, based on their disclosed, concordant HIV status."

Data from Golden's clinic found that HIV-positive patients were particularly likely to serosort. Forty and 49% of his HIV-positive patients, respectively, had unprotected receptive and insertive sex with HIV-positive partners but only 3% and 6%, respectively, with HIV-negative partners.

In his HIV-negative patients 31% and 37%, respectively, had unprotected receptive and insertive sex with HIV-negative partners, and 19% and 15% respectively had unprotected receptive and insertive sex with HIV-positive partners - less, though still a surprisingly high figure.

"Where the whole system breaks down," however, Golden commented, "is where the other partner is of unknown status." Here partners were almost equally likely to have unprotected insertive sex regardless of their own status or if the partner's was unknown. In the case of receptive sex, there was some evidence that positive gay men were attempting to adopt 'strategic positioning'. HIV-positive men were somewhat more likely (31% vs 24%) to have unprotected receptive rather than insertive sex with partners of unknown status; conversely HIV-negative men were somewhat less likely (16% vs 22%. Golden did not say whether any of these differences reached statistical significance.

Golden then investigated whether serosorting was actually reducing the number of serodiscordant partners that gay men had, regardless of condom use. The answer was yes. In a population like Seattle where 15% of gay men have HIV (not dissimilar to London), if gay men chose partners completely at random, and if they all had close to the mean number of partners rather than a few having many and many having a few, you would expect 54% of gay men to have at least one serodiscordant relationship per year (with the figure obviously lower for people with few partners and higher for those with many).

In fact about 35% of gay men had had at least one serodiscordant partner, so serosorting appeared to be reducing the number of serodiscordant relationships by about 40%, though Golden also suggested some of this was due to the fact that gay men tend to have sex with men fairly near their own age, and that because young men are less likely to have HIV than older men, some of this concordance was purely due to age similarity. Golden also found that 13-18% of gay men were 'exclusive serosorters', i.e. only had unprotected sex with seroconcordant partners.

Is serosorting actually protective? When it comes to HIV-negative men, Golden found that the rate of new HIV diagnosis among patients who had unprotected sex but tried only to do it with same-status partners (2.6%) was intermediate between men who had unprotected sex regardless (4.1%) and men who attempted always to use condoms (1.5%).

Adjusting for the number of partners, whereas condom use was 76% effective in preventing new HIV infections, serosorting was about 40% effective.

As a 'control', Golden also looked at the rate of STIs and in this case, as you would expect, there was no difference in the STI rates between serosorters and non-serosorters.

Viral load and negotiated safety

HIV status is not the only thing that can be disclosed by men attempting to minimise their HIV risk. Several recent studies have found that gay men are questioning each other about their HIV viral load in order to try and establish if they are infectious. "Are you undetectable?" is becoming as common a chatroom question as "are you poz?"

In a study from San Francisco (Goldhammer, 2005) 78% of 507 gay men questioned were familiar with the term 'viral load' and one third (111 of the total sample) had discussed viral load with a partner of a different HIV status during the previous year in order to make decisions about which sexual practices to engage in.

Of those who had discussed viral load, more than half estimated that they used viral load disclosure to guide sexual decision-making in at least 70% of their sexual encounters.

In another study from Sydney (Van de Ven, 2005) researchers asked 119 men who were in an HIV-serodiscordant regular relationship about whether they used viral load as a basis for their decisions on condom use. Twice as many (39.4%) reported unprotected anal intercourse when the partner's HIV last viral load test was undetectable as when it was detectable (20.8%).

HIV-negative couples and negotiated safety

Another major way in which HIV testing is already affecting sexual behaviour has been described as 'negotiated safety' by Australian researchers. (This has also been called 'serosorting' or 'HIV-negative serosorting').

'Negotiated safety' refers to an agreement between partners about sexual practices which takes into account the HIV antibody status of both partners. Australian and British researchers observed that gay men who had taken the HIV test were having unprotected sex, and doing so with other men who also knew their antibody status. These men had worked out agreements about sexual activity outside the relationship that were designed to minimise the risk of infection within the relationship if it was not sexually exclusive.

These strategies were a consequence of the availability of HIV antibody testing from 1985 onward, but they were not promoted by HIV prevention campaigns. Indeed, most HIV prevention campaigns around the world have consistently promoted the message "Positive or negative, it's all the same" as a means of encouraging solidarity between infected and uninfected men.

Nevertheless, despite such messages, a significant minority of gay men adopted 'negotiated safety strategies' because they were preferable to the continued use of condoms.

Since such strategies were first identified many people have argued that it is unreasonable to assume that long-term condom use is sustainable for the majority of gay men (Odets; King). A proportion of gay men will still continue to have unprotected sex, and the job of HIV prevention ought to be to facilitate the safe practice of unprotected sex, they argue.

This has been a difficult notion to accept in some quarters, for it appears to undermine the continued promotion of condom use. Yet research suggests that in practice gay men in particular are already using information about their HIV status to guide sexual practice, and that many gay men are much more careful about condom use with casual partners than they are with primary partners (Coxon). In his review of the SIGMA cohort data, Tony Coxon identified a number of worrying trends that are particularly important to consider in relation to debates about 'negotiated safety':

- Those who engage most frequently in unprotected sex generally restrict their unprotected sexual activity to one partner who has the same HIV status

- But, nearly 50% of all men interviewed invert any notion of 'negotiated safety' by having unprotected sex with casual partners and regular partners, or else using condoms with their regular partner whilst having unprotected sex with one-off casual partners

- Those not tested tend to have the highest-risk sex, primarily with those known to be negative.

However, Coxon also observes:

- The non-use of condoms is often as much a matter of waiting for the partner to object as it is a pre-negotiated condition (i.e. it happens by default)

- "paradoxically the group which overwhelmingly exhibits close conformity to the ideal of choice, responsibility and negotiation...are those already diagnosed HIV- positive."

These findings present a number of significant problems. They suggest that much unprotected sex is unnegotiated (verbally, at least), and whilst it may not lead to HIV infection with any greater frequency than unprotected sex with regular partners, it will present significant problems to anyone trying to develop 'negotiated safety' approaches to HIV prevention.

For example, negotiated approaches rely on trust. One of the major criticisms of this approach is the degree to which it relies upon the honesty and trust of both partners. Given the degree to which personal relationships are bedeviled by problems of honesty and trust, it is a little difficult to imagine such agreements working well for some people.

Many partnerships have agreements about no sex outside the relationship, but these agreements are broken frequently. Sometimes the other partner will find out, but often they will not, because the partner who has been 'playing away' is scared of the consequences for the relationship. If any agreement about unprotected sex outside the relationship is tied up with an agreement about no other sexual activity outside the relationship, this may reduce the incentive for honesty if a lapse in the agreement does occur.

When does negotiated safety work?

Australian researchers recently looked at whether making explicit agreements about unprotected sex had any effect on the likelihood that men would have unprotected sex outside their primary relationship. They looked at 165 men in seroconcordant HIV-negative relationships. 61% had engaged in unprotected anal intercourse at some point. The researchers found that amongst this group the following factors were associated with a lower likelihood of having unprotected sex with casual partners and with a primary partner (Kippax).

- Having an agreement about unprotected sex outside the relationship

- Agreement included no anal sex with casual partners.

Men who found condom use unacceptable were more likely to have unprotected anal sex with their casual partners. No other demographic or behavioural factors were found to be significant.

HIV-negative serosorting?

There is also some evidence from Australia that HIV-negative men may be beginning to find it possible to engage in what one might call 'true serosorting' rather than negotiated safety. That is, increasingly disclosing and attempting to establish their partner's status in casual as opposed to committed unprotected sex situations.

Limin Mao and colleagues from Sydney looked at the serosorting behaviour of gay men known to be HIV-negative between 2002 and 2005. Although these men were not explicitly asked if they had "serosorted," this behaviour was inferred from information they provided about unprotected sex with casual partners.

The 302 men enrolled in the study were asked to provide details of the total number of casual partners they had unprotected anal sex with in the previous six months, and to provide information on their partner's HIV infection status.

Although there was an overall decrease in the amount of unprotected anal sex with casual partners in the six months before the study interview, the investigators noted that when they looked at the results according to the HIV status of casual partners, the mean number of HIV-negative casual partners who individuals had sex with actually increased (p < 0.001). The proportion of casual unprotected anal sex partners reported to be HIV-negative increased from 6% in 2002 to 25% in 2005.

The proportion of casual unprotected sex partners whose status was unknown also reduced, from 85% to 60%: butthe investigators emphasised that this still meant that the majority of casual unprotected sex among HIV-negative men was occurring with partners of unknown status.

"Serosortin especially is used as a deliberate strategy to replace consistent condom use with casual partners, is highly problematic", write the investigators. They note that even if both partners are indeed HIV-negative there is still the risk of other sexually transmitted infections.

Talk, Test, Test, Trust

Australian approaches to negotiated safety have used the slogan 'Talk, Test, Test, Trust' to highlight the issues involved in making such a commitment. This approach is useful because it highlights the issue of trust, and makes it a talking point amongst the target audience. It implies that an agreement about unprotected sex is a serious matter.

The Australian approach has also used advertising about the testing procedure to follow if you want to come to an agreement about unprotected sex. This advertising emphasises that negotiated safety is a complex process, and shouldn't depend on assumptions about HIV status or short-cuts to abandoning condom use.

Several other factors are likely to distort the strategy of negotiated safety:

- Ability to negotiate and assert: some individuals may find it less easy to assert their doubts about the chosen strategy

- Pressures on the gay scene to have sex outside the primary relationship, increasing the potential for slip-ups

- Unwillingness to wait long enough to go through a demanding testing procedure: unprotected sex may become the norm very quickly in a relationship as a signal that the relationship is intensifying

- Lapses in condom use before the HIV test window period is over.

Negotiation when testing uptake is low

A significant difference between the UK and Australia is the level of HIV testing within the gay population. In Australia nearly 90% of gay men are thought to have been tested at least once, but in the UK the proportion is closer to 50%. SIGMA Research has found that the proportion of gay men under 30 who have taken an HIV test is greater than the proportion of those over 35, and hence it may be reasonable to assume that this group may already be practising strategies of negotiated safety more frequently than their older counterparts (Weatherburn).

Yet it has also been reported that gay men over 35 are more likely to report unprotected sex with both regular partners and with casual partners (Coxon).

A consequence of the lower rates of HIV testing in the UK, in the view of some researchers, is the tendency of gay men to make assumptions about their own and their partner's HIV status. It should be noted that this `optimistic bias' is also likely to be a function of low HIV prevalence in comparison with the US and Australia. In such circumstances `negotiated safety' strategies need to be approached carefully in order that they do not promote more `guessing' about HIV status (based on the assumption that HIV testing is a community norm). This could occur if campaigns appear to communicate a primary message that unprotected sex within relationships is preferable to condom use, rather than focusing on the issue of how to make unprotected sex within a relationship as safe as possible.

Recent research in Edinburgh and Glasgow suggests that `negotiated safety' in the light of full knowledge about HIV status is still very rare. Research conducted in 1996 shows that only 16% of men questioned were having unprotected anal sex in a relationship were doing so in the light of knowledge about both partner's HIV status (Hart). This compares with around 60% in the Australian study discussed above.

Approaches to `negotiated safety' also need to take into account widespread psychological resistance to the suggestion that it is permissable for some gay men to stop condom use. The use of condoms has become inextricably linked with the idea of sex for many gay men, and it can seem threatening to suggest that 100% condom use is no longer necessary when some people have worked so hard to achieve it. For many, 100% condom use may be part of what constitutes being a good, responsible gay man.

Negotiated safety agreements are also used by HIV-negative couples to attempt to reduce the chance of HIV entering the relationship. In one study(Guzman, 2005) of 76 HIV-negative gay men with HIV-negative steady partners, 17% of the men did not practice anal sex and 22% maintained 100% condom use in all anal sex, inside or outside the relationship.

Another 11% had unprotected sex within and outside the relationship and had not negotiated any rules prohibiting it.

But 39 of the men (51%) had some sort of negotiated safety agreement in place in their relationship. Nineteen (25%) had unprotected sex with each other but had negotiated total monogamy. Three (four per cent) disallowed anal sex with partners outside the relationship but allowed other sex. And 16 (21%) allowed anal sex outside the relationship as long as it was always protected.

This left six (eight per cent) who had protected sex *within* the relationship but allowed unprotected sex outside it - a stance protecting their partner but not themselves.

However these negotiated safety agreements were often broken. Eleven (14% of the whole group, 29% of those who had an agreement) had broken it in the previous three months. However they were less likely to break it if there was a requirement that they `must always tell' if it had been broken; only 18% of those who had an agreement had broken it if the rule was always to say if they had.

Disclosure: an HIV-positive-controlled safer sex strategy?

There are two necessary conditions for any of these attempts to reduce HIV risk. Men have to know their HIV status. And disclosure (of HIV status, or in the case of the HIV-negative couples, HIV risk behaviour) has to happen.

The recent upsurge in studies of negotiated-safety behaviour has led to the asking of a question. In most of these situations the partner (or partners) with HIV are the ones in possession of the knowledge that makes a difference to behaviour.

Drives to get more high-risk people to test for HIV have been based on the assumption that, once they test positive, people will moderate their behaviour. In fact, as we have seen, HIV-positive people end up having *more* unprotected sex rather than less. This has led to anguished questioning among HIV prevention experts and a lot of hostile media coverage and intensified stigma against the perceived irresponsible behaviour of people with the virus.

If, however HIV-positive people are at least attempting to inform and protect their sexual partners, should more HIV prevention money be directed towards enabling them to do so? After all, HIV-positive people form 50% of any risky sexual encounter and 100% of those with the knowledge to reduce its risk.

An illustration of the paradoxes around disclosure and serosorting comes from the publicity surrounding a study of `Poz parties' in New York (Clatts).

Researchers interviewed 115 men attending an HIV-positive-only sex party in New York. The primary reasons cited by the men for attending were "Not having to worry about disclosing my HIV status (35% citing this as their primary reason) and "I like having uninhibited or unrestricted sex' (also 35%), with 14% citing `Not having to worry about infecting others'.

The majority of men indulged in unprotected anal sex: 59% receptive and 72% insertive. 47% and 50% respectively had receptive and insertive anal sex to ejaculation.

The men were on average relatively old (median 42) and relatively long-term diagnosed (nearly 10 years), though the youngest attendee was 20 and the most recently infected had been so for two months. A third of men said they had had an STI other than HIV diagnosed in the past year.

In contrast to concerns that the use of recreational drugs was fuelling unprotected sex among gay men, only a small number (nine out of 86) used `hard' drugs such as ecstasy, methamphetamine or ketamine, or sexual enhancers like *Viagra* or poppers.

Although the researchers acknowledged that the serosorting involved might be a public health benefit, they added that attendees had also had sex with status-unknown partners on other occasions.

They also cited the dangers of HIV superinfection, but as yet there is conflicting evidence as to exactly how often this happens or - more to the point - whether it often causes adverse clinical consequences.

Superinfection may turn out to be quite a frequent occurrence (see Smith 2004), but at present the cases that come to the attention of researchers do so *because* of adverse consequences, such as a person with wild type virus contracting resistant virus (see, for instance, Smith 2005). If superinfection is in fact common, one would also expect more evidence that it was damaging, though this evidence might be disguised as treatment failure attributed to other reasons.

However the choice of entitling the paper "An emerging HIV risk environment" may have been unfortunate in that it is easier to argue that on balance `poz parties' are a risk environment for every STI *except* HIV. Media outlets, however, mainly picked up on the `HIV risk' angle, with headlines such as "POZ parties may spread HIV superstrain" (Mitchell).

A similar controversy, though restricted to the HIV sector, arose in the UK around a London public-sex venue for gay men called Pigpitmen. This fortnightly sex club started off as an underground sex club in members' homes, but soon moved to an established gay venue.

Members are required to state (though not to prove) that they were HIV-positive to join. There was considerable debate in the HIV-positive press and websites as to whether the involvement of HIV prevention programmes in this club (some nights they set up stalls) was condoning behaviour destructive to the health of the participants or whether, being a space where HIV-positive men had their status 'predisclosed' for them, it was an HIV containment measure.

Such debates will continue to happen until it can be shown that disclosure and negotiated safety are actually helping to contain the spread of HIV among high-risk populations.

References

Bolding G et al. *Gay men who look for sex on the internet: is there more HIV/STI risk with online partners?* AIDS 19: 961-968, 2005.

Buchacz K et al. *Trends in primary and secondary syphilis and HIV seroincidence among men who have sex with men in San Francisco, 1998-2002.* 11th Conference on Retroviruses and Opportunistic Infections, San Francisco, 2004. Abstract 88.

Centers for Disease Control and Prevention HIV Prevalence, *Unrecognized infection, and HIV testing among men who have sex with men - five U.S. cities, June 2004-April 2005.* MMRW Weekly 54(24): 597-601, 2005.

Chiasson M A et al. *A comparison of on-line and offline risk among men who have sex with men.* 12th Retrovirus Conference, Boston, abstract 168, 2005.

Chinouya, M. & Davidson, O. *The Padare Project: assessing health-related knowledge, attitudes and behaviours of HIV-positive Africans accessing services in north central London.* African HIV Policy Network, February 2003.

Clatts MC et al. *An emerging HIV risk environment: a preliminary epidemiological profile of an MSM POZ party in New York City.* Sex Transm Infect 81:373-376. 2005.

Dodds JP et al. *Increasing risk behaviour and high levels of undiagnosed HIV infection in a community sample of homosexual men.* Sex Transm Infect 80:236-240. 2004.

Elford J et al. *High-risk sexual behaviour among London gay men: no longer increasing?* Eleventh Annual Conference of the British HIV Association, Dublin, oral presentation abstract O14, April 20 - 23, 2005.

Gisselquist D et al. *Let it be sexual: how health care transmission of AIDS in Africa was ignored.* Int J STD AIDS 14(3):148-61. 2003.

Golden M. *HIV serosorting among men who have sex with men: implications for prevention.* Thirteenth Conference on Retroviruses and Opportunistic Infections, Denver, abstract 163, 2006.

Goldhammer H et al. B*eliefs about viral load, sexual positioning and transmission risk among HIV+ men who have sex with men (MSM): Shaping a secondary prevention intervention.* 2005 National HIV Prevention Conference, Atlanta, USA, presentation W0-D1201.

Guzman R et al. *Negotiated safety relationships and sexual behaviour among a diverse sample of HIV-negative men who have sex with men.* JAIDS 38(1) 82-86. 2005.

Lightfoot M et al. *The Influence of partner type and risk status on the sexual behaviour of young men who have sex with me living with HIV/AIDS.* JAIDS 38(1), 61-68. 2005.

Mao L et al. *"Serosorting" in casual anal sex of HIV-negative gay men is noteworthy and is increasing in Sydney, Australia.* AIDS 20: 1204-1206, 2006.

Mitchell S. *POZ parties may spread HIV superstrain.* UPI release, 28 September 2005. See http://www.aidsmap.com/en/news/930CCABC-A29F-4CCC-B7A9-52D93402E765.asp

Russell S. *Decrease in new HIV infections smaller than expected.* San Francisco Chronicle, 31 March 2006.

Smith D et al. *Incidence of HIV Superinfection Following Primary Infection.* 11th CROI, San Francisco, abstract 21, 2004

Smith DM et al. *HIV drug resistance acquired through superinfection.* AIDS 19: 1251 - 1256, 2005

Van de Ven P et al. *Undetectable viral load is associated with sexual risk taking in HIV serodiscordant gay couples in Sydney.* AIDS 19(2): 179-184. 2005.

Weinhardt L et al. *HIV transmission risk behavior among men and women living with HIV in 4 cities in the United States.* JAIDS 36(5), 1057-1066. 2004.

E is for emergent prevention technologies

Common themes

Two illustrations

1. A vaccine against cervical cancer

On the 8th June 2006, the US Food and Drug Administration announced that it had given approval to *Gardasil*, a vaccine that had demonstrated 100% protection against four of the most common subtypes of the human papilloma virus (HPV), including the two most common types that cause cervical (and anal) cancer. Another cervical cancer vaccine, *Cervarix*, is expected to be licensed soon.

HPV is the most common sexually transmitted infection in the United States. The Centers for Disease Control and Prevention (CDC) estimates that about 6.2 million Americans become infected with genital HPV each year and that over half of all sexually active men and women become infected at some time in their lives. On average, there are 9,710 new cases of cervical cancer and 3,700 deaths attributed to it in the United States each year. Worldwide, cervical cancer is the second most common cancer in women; and is estimated to cause over 470,000 new cases and 233,000 deaths each year. Anal cancer, though rare, is 35 times more common in gay men and at least 70 times more common in people with HIV.

Shortly before licensing Alan Kaye, chairman of the National Cervical Cancer Coalition, had told the *New Republic* (Groopman): "I don't think anyone wants to stop a cancer vaccine."

However the vaccine did in fact cause unease among conservative groups. *The Chicago Tribune* reported that "conservative groups promoting abstinence say they will fight recommendations that children get shots," while the *Los Angeles Times* warned of a "clash between health advocates ... and social conservatives."

The HPV vaccines are not the first ever to be developed against a sexually transmitted disease: the first one was the hepatitis B vaccine. But whereas sexually transmitted hepatitis B mainly affects the same high-risk groups as HIV, HPV infection is so common that 60% of American women and gay men will have at least one strain after just five sexual encounters, and 80% of Americans eventually get infected (Jansen).

The vaccine would therefore have to be given to adolescents or, to be on the safe side, children (in whom it produced similar immune responses) before they start having sex.

It was this that worried the conservative groups. They were concerned that giving the vaccine would endorse promiscuity rather than their favoured method of STI (sexually transmitted infection) prevention, abstinence until marriage. "We feel people should have the choice of abstinence as a means to avoid HPV," a spokeswoman for Christian Medical & Dental Associations said. "Our concern is that this vaccine will be marketed to a segment of the population that should be getting a message about abstinence," sais the Family Research Council.

After meetings between the vaccine manufacturers and groups such as the Family Research Council, conservatives softened their outright opposition. However they still opposed the vaccine becoming mandatory. "Because parents have an inherent right to be the primary educator and decision maker regarding their children's health, we would oppose any measures to legally require the vaccination or to coerce parents into authorizing it," said the Family Research Council.

However for any vaccine against a common infection to be effective, it has to be as close to mandatory as it can be. The upsurge in measles cases in the UK when scare stories about the MMR vaccine caused a temporary drop in uptake is a case in point. In the USA this usually means adding the vaccine to the vaccinations that states require before students can enrol in school - a list that in the USA includes the hepatitis B vaccine.

HPV is transmissible through touch, so it can be caught through sexual activities other than intercourse. Even those who remain fully abstinent until marriage could contract it from their spouses. In short, HPV is a significant public health threat and the strongest possible steps should be taken to inoculate the entire population.

The Centers for Disease Control issues recommendations in the USA as to which vaccines should be distributed universally and added to regular immunisation schedules, and doctors follow guidelines closely. Even if conservative groups back such a recommendation, state governments would face a decision about whether to require that students be vaccinated - which public health advocates fear that Christian conservatives will oppose vigorously. At the time of writing, the widespread provision of the new vaccines remains in the balance.

2. Circumcision to prevent HIV infection

At the 2005 International AIDS Society Conference in Rio, the results of the first-ever randomised controlled trial (RCT) of the circumcision of adult men as a method of reducing the risk of HIV infection were announced (Auvert). They were conclusive. Circumcision reduced the risk of men contracting HIV through heterosexual intercourse by at least two-thirds and possibly by as much as three-quarters. Even in advance of two other RCTs whose results are expected in 2007 or 2008, men in high-prevalence countries like Swaziland heard the news and were reported to be besieging clinics asking for the operation.

At the Retrovirus Conference in Denver six months later, evidence was presented (Quinn) that circumcising men offered a smaller, but real, protective effect against HIV infection to the female partners of HIV-positive men too, reducing their risk of infection by about 30%.

In a best-case scenario, if 100% of men in a country were circumcised and circumcision prevented 70% of male infections, HIV incidence in the whole population would be reduced by one-third even if it had no protective effect on women. However if the protective effect on women was included, HIV incidence would fall by two-thirds if all men were circumcised and by 40% if half of them were.

However the presenter had a warning up his sleeve. If circumcision produced a perception in men that they were protected from HIV and could go back to having multiple partners, all benefits of the measure would be lost. Using the same projections, if the average number of partners circumcised men had increased by 50%, HIV prevalence would increase by 40%; if the average number of partners doubled, prevalence would more than double and would be higher than it is today.

International bodies like the World Health Organization (WHO) are waiting for the results of the two other RCTs before they make a decision on whether to recommend circumcision as a widespread HIV prevention measure. But confounders such as behaviour change may render predictions literally incalculable.

The need for better protection

While HIV treatment has been revolutionised, we essentially still have the same prevention tools that we had at the very start of the epidemic. Using condoms for sex and sterile needles for injecting: sexual abstinence or delay of sexual debut: reducing the number of sexual partners: and measures enabled by disclosure such as serosorting.

Behind these are strategies to ensure and support their wider use such as education for knowledge and skills; challenging or reinforcing traditional patterns of behaviour; and safer-sex promotion activities.

All of these measures have two features in common. Firstly, if they're to be effective they require the continued maintenance of the behaviour - lifelong in most cases - and a conscious effort of will. They are more like avoiding alcohol when driving than a car airbag.

Secondly, they're options which, for reasons to do with personal and social inequality, simply aren't available to a large proportion of the people most vulnerable to HIV in the world. This applies especially to women, and in particular married women. A married woman isn't expected to have sex using condoms and can't enforce their use: abstinence is an irrelevant concept for her: and, while she may be monogamous, she can't ensure that her partner or husband is.

These are the negative reasons why HIV prevention often doesn't work and why we need new answers. But there are positive ones too. Many people, and especially people in long-term relationships, don't want to spend their entire sex lives using barrier methods; condoms symbolise lack of closeness and trust; women (and men) want to have children. Current prevention methods all work by somehow blunting or modifying the experience of sex. The emergent prevention technologies hold out a promise of being either completely invisible and out-of-mind during the actual process of sex or, in the case of microbicides, even enhancing it. An HIV prevention intervention that actually made sex more fun and less anxiety-provoking might be extremely effective.

The unavailability, unenforceability and irrelevance of the traditional HIV prevention methods have led to increased calls for development of what are usually called New Prevention Technologies. Some of these, if developed, will be truly new such as an effective microbicide or vaccine. But some are ways of pressing older interventions into the service of HIV prevention. Circumcision is as old as history; antibody testing and the option of disclosure has existed since 1985; the possibility of post-exposure prophylaxis since the development of AZT soon afterwards.

For this reason, we prefer to call them Emergent Prevention Technologies, partly for alphabetical neatness, but also to make the point that many of these possible solutions to the continued spread of HIV were already out there.

The emergent technologies are a mixed bag of techniques and approaches that aim to answer one or both of the current deficits of prevention. Some, like circumcision and (hopefully) a vaccine are or would be one-off medical interventions that would involve no further effort of will on the part of the person concerned - they would decrease the person's vulnerability to HIV infection or its consequences to a specific degree and that would be that.

Others, like microbicides and PrEP, will require at least as much attention to 'adherence' as condoms do. But PrEP can be taken hours in advance of sex and in secret; microbicides, while they may be much more difficult to use without a partner's knowledge, are being touted as a prevention method that puts women firmly back in control of keeping themselves safe during sex. Even campaigners for post-exposure prophylaxis have stressed that making this 'backstop' option available will decrease anxiety of sex between sero-different people.

No magic bullet

However, as the above illustrations show, the development of new prevention technologies and the exploitation of existing ones are not unproblematic areas. There is no single intervention among them which *in itself* is likely to be able to turn round the course of the HIV epidemic. This is for a number of reasons:

1. Efficacy

None of the new prevention technologies outlined below is likely to match the 85-95% efficacy of properly and consistently used condoms in preventing HIV infection if used as the sole method of protection.

Universal HIV testing is contingent upon effective prevention support for people with HIV for its success. Circumcision, as outlined above, will still fail to stop one in four infections in men and will only have a small protective effect on women. Post-exposure prophylaxis will only ever be an emergency 'backstop' measure. For pre-exposure prophylaxis the scientific evidence for efficacy is highly contradictory, and we have no idea how to use it best. Even the most enthusiastic advocates of antiviral treatment to prevent sexual transmission would see it as a back-up to other methods for use in extreme circumstances, when condoms fail or to protect victims of sexual assault, or to cover limited periods in a person's life when they are at greatest risk of HIV infection.

Even optimistic microbicide researchers do not expect the first generation of products to have more than 65% efficacy and 'adherence' will be a crucial issue. The first generation of vaccines may not even prevent HIV infection but may work by slowing or preventing the development of AIDS in infected people; if they do prevent infection they may also only have partial efficacy.

This means that the evaluation of these technologies must always be undertaken alongside and in combination with existing approaches.

2. The safety problem

Any prevention intervention that involves administering a substance to people for internal or topical use must be rigorously tested for safety, and the safety barrier which the product must 'jump' in order to be approved needs to be higher than it is for treatments.

In a trial of a drug or other intervention for a disease, the risk/benefit calculation being made is whether the treatment will do more or less harm to the individual than the untreated disease. In a trial of a prophylaxis method, the risk/benefit calculation being made is whether using the intervention will do more or less harm than doing nothing. In the one case you are trying to fight an active process that is harming the individual and the more harmful the disease the more toxicity may be allowed in the treatments for it. In the second case you are trying to build in an additional layer of safety against a disease that might well have been avoided anyway. In the worst-case scenario you may even make people more vulnerable to infection with your prevention intervention. On an obvious level this happened in the COL-1492 trial of nonoxynol-9 as a candidate microbicide, where twice as many regular users of the intervention caught HIV as users of the placebo. On a more subtle level, your prevention intervention may do more net damage in the long run if its effect on behaviour change is not taken into account.

3. Behaviour change

Because none of these interventions are 100% effective, the risk behaviour of people who use them will be crucial for them to make a difference. If they create a false sense of security or cause people who would otherwise have refrained from sex or used condoms to have unprotected sex, their effect could be negative rather than positive. 'Condom migration', meaning the abandonment of condom use by people using alternative methods, is a continued concern of researchers into the new methods.

The effect of behaviour change depends sensitively on both the efficacy of the new intervention and the degree of use of old ones that might be abandoned. One of a number of mathematical models (Foss) developed to predict the effect of microbicides found that in situations where previous condom use was less than 50%, where condom efficacy when used was 95%, and where the microbicide was 50% effective then "any amount of migration can be tolerated if microbicides are used whenever condoms are not." The crucial part of that sentence is obviously the second half; for microbicides to succeed they will have to be both more available and more appealing than condoms.

Conversely, however, if condom use is already high then switching to a less effective microbicide would increase HIV incidence. This concern has been particularly expressed with regard to sex workers, who may have commercial incentives to find alternatives to condoms, but by doing so may put themselves in more danger. The same concerns have been expressed around PREP.

4. The statistics problem

Methods of preventing disease are inherently more difficult to research than methods of treating it. In a trial of a drug for an illness, the illness (whether fatal or not) will occur if you don't provide a treatment, or at least surrogate markers like immune dysfunction that predict that disease is going to occur will deteriorate. You are stopping something happening.

In a trial of a prevention method, there is no telling what would have happened on an individual level if you hadn't provided the intervention. Even in extremely high-risk populations, HIV incidence is in the order of 5-10% a year. Two per cent a year is the approximate HIV incidence in western urban gay men, and this is seen as large. You are trying to prevent something happen that on the balance of probabilities wouldn't have happened anyway to the majority of trial participants. HIV seroconversion will only happen to a minority of individuals with or without your intervention, so what you are hoping to find is usually the difference between a small percentage of individuals who are infected and an even smaller one. For your findings to reach statistical significance you need a large study group.

Then there is the ethical question of what you do for your control group. It is unethical to withhold existing prevention methods from them when available, and in a blinded RCT it is equally unethical to give the impression to the intervention group that your method *will* work. Existing methods of HIV prevention, such as free condoms and safer-sex advice, should therefore be given to all trial participants, and this may in fact be a better 'standard of care' than what is normally available - for instance, you may have to offer free condoms in countries where people normally buy them. This may further confound trial findings. The most extreme development of this problem was when community activists in Thailand objected to a trial of PREP among injecting drug users on the grounds that researchers should be offering all participants the best proven prevention, namely needle exchange, and that it was unethical to offer the choice between an unproven intervention or nothing when a proven one existed.

The problem was that needle exchange is illegal in Thailand, so participants would have been getting something denied to other drug users. Researchers countered that this would not only confound findings, it would be a possibly unethical incentive for people to join the trial.

Phase III trials of prevention methods therefore need to be much bigger - ten to 50 times bigger - than treatment trials. A lot of the argument (see below) about the trials of pre-exposure prophylaxis was to do with the choice of trial population. Researchers insisted that they could only do trials in populations where HIV incidence was sufficiently high for a feasibly-sized trial to produce a meaningful result. Community campaigners insisted that such groups did exist in the developed world.

Trials need to be bigger still if results are confounded by participants already using other prevention methods. For instance, in some microbicide trials, it already looks as if a meaningful result will be difficult to extract as the most consistent microbicide users are also the most consistent condom users. Then there is the question of what happens if a first-generation microbicide is partially but suboptimally effective. It will be unethical then to use an inert placebo in a trial of a hopefully more effective second-generation product; the partially effective microbicide should be used instead. But if this offers, say, 33% protective power then you are going to have to use a concomitantly larger number of trial subjects to detect any superiority in your new product.

The same effect applies between trials of different technologies, and concerns have been expressed that the introduction of new prevention methods (and of HIV treatment) may make it increasingly difficult to recruit 'pure' populations for vaccine trials.

5. The medicalisation of prevention

Prevention has always been talked about in the same breath as words like 'choice' and 'empowerment'. No one (except AIDS denialists of the garlic-will-cure-you variety) sees the treatment of HIV disease as the sole responsibility of the person with it; it is understood even at best as a collaboration between patients and medical professionals who have the drugs and the knowledge to relieve their condition, and at worst as the administration of medicine to an essentially passive sufferer.

Prevention has always operated from the opposite paradigm. Increased use of condoms, better choice of partner, decision-making ability about whether to have unprotected sex and with whom, will, it is assumed, only result from situations in which people have greater power and control over all areas of their lives. Because of this, along with preventing HIV and AIDS, much HIV prevention work has other goals. These may include changing gender relations, to increase boys' respect for girls and women and the confidence of girls and women in their ability to achieve their ambitions. Campaigners seek to increase the self-respect and social standing of people who have been marginalised in many societies, such as men who have sex with men and injecting drug users.

Some (though not all) of the emerging prevention technologies, however, are much more like treatments in that decisions as to availability may well be made by professionals in collaboration with, or instead of, members of affected communities. This is seen most starkly in the area of antiretroviral prophylaxis where the perception (whether real or not) that the medical profession is unwilling to provide PEP after sexual exposure has led to campaigns and legal action. The same will be doubly true in the case of PREP, which will not and should not be available 'over the counter'. Doctors or other health workers will be making decisions about who should and should not get it, and there are fears that these decisions may be clouded by prejudice, discrimination or ignorance. We have, after all, already seen this happen on a national scale in countries that refuse to provide needle exchange or substitution therapy for drug users.

The same may apply in the initial stages to microbicides, though it has always been the intention that formulations should in the end be commercially available or, in resource-poor settings, free, though then we run into the same problems and arguments about access as we do with HIV treatment. And the whole argument about the introduction of universal HIV testing in the USA has been about replacing a community-education and empowerment model of HIV prevention with a 'medicalised' one.

Proponents of emergent prevention technologies, however, would counter this by saying that in situations where people do *not* have power, whether because of cultural or institutional inequality or personal incapacity such as mental illness, then the only humane and compassionate thing to do is to medicalise HIV prevention and provide people with 'mechanical' methods of HIV prevention that will work regardless of whether they have personal choice or not. Individuals change their behaviour slowly and cultures change more slowly still; HIV infection can happen fast and we need interventions that will stop it no matter what the circumstances of vulnerable individuals.

6. Personal belief systems

In addition to, or masquerading as, the above rational concerns about the new prevention technologies, lie political, moral and religious belief systems that may cause people to prefer one prevention method over another. This is already so familiar in the case of the debate around abstinence programmes versus comprehensive strategies, including condom distribution, that there is no point in repeating it here, but these debates are bound to arise every time a new prevention method is suggested or becomes available, as in the case of the HPV vaccine above.

7. The importance of community consultation

The idea that new prevention technologies may negatively affect use of the strategies we already have may also occur to the communities among whom trials are done, and they may react negatively to what they see as a medicalised method that takes away their control over infection. We already have an example above with the PREP trial in Thailand.

The controversy that blew up so unexpectedly around trials of PREP in Cambodia, Cameroon and Thailand in 2004-5 was a salutary lesson to researchers that genuine consultation with trial subjects, members of their community, activists and advocates and other stakeholders such as political leaders was vital if large prevention trials were not to cause controversy.

There is a detailed list of the issues that arose in the section on PREP, but in brief what activists objected to was what they saw as undue pressure from researchers on candidate participants to join the trial, and the lack of provision for compensation and/or treatment in the case of trial failures (seroconversions) and side-effects.

Organising prevention research as a clinical trial opens the way to formal review by ethical committees, providing important safeguards to trial participants, and increasingly, those organising prevention trials have seen the need for and value of a Community Advisory Board. Most of the work that has been done on Community Advisory Boards has been in the context of preventive vaccine trials, and this is reflected in the UNAIDS ethical guidelines. Here, the main point to make is that the same considerations apply to all of the prevention research discussed here. Most of the ethical guidance set out by UNAIDS for vaccine trials is equally applicable to microbicide trials or trials of antiretrovirals used to prevent HIV infection.

One of the critical roles of the Community Advisory Board should be to decide on the nature of the HIV prevention efforts that should be directed at all trial participants, aside from the use of the product that is being evaluated. It is also vital that the standard of care to be provided to any trial participant who becomes HIV-positive should be discussed and agreed in advance of the trial.

However one lesson of the PREP trials is that the Community Advisory Board model is insufficient for truly comprehensive consultation as it begs the question: 'who is the community?' If a CAB consists of a group of self-appointed activists, or even more so in countries without a strong civil society tradition if it consists of paid NGO members, then there is no guarantee that the concerns expressed by the CAB are in any way representative of the concerns of all stakeholders or are uninfluenced by other considerations, or that the consultations with the CAB will be fed back accurately to the people they represent.

The PREP trials have therefore provided a sharp learning curve both in what truly comprehensive community consultation needs to look like and in the development of truly 'informed' consent in what may be highly marginalised and even illiterate people. An object lesson in how to do this is provided by the Peruvian PREP trial among gay men - see below.

Many questions may need to be asked. How do people understand the role of this new technology? How can they integrate it into their other strategies? Does it open up new strategies to them? Does it change the way they perceive the epidemic and their own and other people's relationship to it?

To answer such questions requires the active involvement of social researchers in evaluating new biomedical technologies. When it comes to HIV prevention, medicine is far too important to be left only to medical scientists.

Conclusion

So, all in all, there is no 'magic bullet' in prevention interventions which is likely to make as dramatic a difference to HIV infection as antiretrovirals have made to HIV disease.

However this is not in any way an argument that trials of new prevention methods should not be attempted. We already have a result in the shape of the circumcision trial, and demographic evidence from countries with high and low circumcision rates - which tend to match neatly up with whether they have high or low HIV rates - suggest it could possibly be a turning point in the worldwide prevention of HIV, even with all the above considerations taken into account. In practice, as more experience is gained with phase III trials of vaccines, PREP and microbicides, some concerns may disappear.

Even when a trial has a 'negative' result it should not be seen as an unqualified failure. The COL-1492 microbicide trial, discussed later on, was an impressive demonstration that it is possible to show the superiority of one product over another (even if it was the placebo that came out ahead), despite a successful campaign to promote increased condom use among trial participants.

Similarly, the VaxGen trials showed that it was possible to recruit, motivate and retain a large group of volunteers at continuing high risk of HIV without adding to their risk-taking. (Reported risk-taking behaviour declined during the course of the trial and HIV infection rates were stable.)

This highlights the importance of feasibility studies, to identify populations in which there is continuing HIV risk despite the wholehearted promotion of the best available means of HIV prevention.

It may also point to the need for multi-agency as well as multi-disciplinary projects, in which some or all of the prevention education can be provided independently of the researchers.

References

Auvert B et al. *Impact of male circumcision on the female-to-male transmission of HIV*. IAS Conference on HIV Pathogenesis and treatment, Rio de Janeiro, abstract TuOa0402, 2005

Foss AM et al. *Will shifts from condom to microbicide use increase HIV risk? Model projections*. International AIDS Conference, Barcelona, abstract no WeOrD1319, 2002.

Groopman S. *Conservative Christians and HPV: Blind Faith*. New Republic, 10 March 2006.

Jansen K. *Vaccine Protection against Human Papilloma viruses* (http://www.retroconference.org/2005/cd/Sessions/032.htm). Twelfth Conference on Retroviruses and Opportunistic Infections, Boston, abstract 126, 2005.

Quinn T. *Circumcision and HIV transmission: the cutting edge*. Plenary presentation, 13th Conference on Retroviruses and Opportunistic Infections, Denver, abstract #120, 2006.

The role of HIV testing in HIV prevention

It might seem strange to start with a section of HIV testing as a prevention method. After all, the role of HIV testing is to find out whether prevention has failed, isn't it?

This, however, is to ignore the contribution people with HIV can make to HIV prevention.

While there is very little evidence that HIV testing in itself leads to behaviour change in people who remain negative, there is abundant evidence that, once diagnosed, people with HIV reduce their risk behaviour. Maximising the uptake of HIV testing and detecting early infections should therefore, in theory, lead to a significant decline in HIV infections.

It has been known since the early 1990s that people diagnosed with HIV modify their risk behaviour. In previous years this fact tended to be obscured by researchers citing it as evidence that some people with HIV *continued* high-risk behaviour in studies whose primary aim was to quantify that figure so that prevention programmes could be directed at these people.

But it was eventually realised that the majority of people with HIV tended to reduce their risk behaviour and that because of this ensuring that as many people knew heir status as possible could be an effective prevention method.

To take a recent example: a study of recently-diagnosed gay men in the USA (Gorbach) interviewed 153 men an average of 4-6 weeks after diagnosis and then again three months later. It found that between the first and second interviews nearly a half (47%) of the 91% of men who remained sexually active men reported that they had reduced the number of sexual partners they had had in the previous three months, a third reported no change and

a fifth reported that they had increased their number of partners. The average number of partners within three months went down from 7.9 to 5.2, a 34% decrease.

Nonetheless, 54% of the newly-diagnosed HIV-positive men had unprotected anal intercourse (UAI) during the three months before the second interview. In the past this might have been regarded as a failure of prevention methods. However, the researchers found that, of the men who did have UAI, the majority switched to HIV-positive partners if they had unprotected sex. In other words, there was considerable evidence of serosorting.

At the baseline interview the men reported that nearly half (48%) of their UAI partners had been HIV-negative, a third of unknown status and less than a fifth (18%) HIV-positive.

Three months later the proportion of UAI partners who were negative had declined to 30% of the total (a 37% decline). The proportion who were positive had nearly tripled to 52% of the total (a 188% increase). And the proportion of unknown status had halved, to 18%. This is strong evidence both for disclosure (since fewer partners were of unknown status) and for serosorting.

These figures may underestimate the behaviour shift, since the first interview took place four to six weeks after diagnosis, and therefore during a third to a half of the preceding three months the men would already know they had HIV and might have already started to change their behaviour.

This evidence of behaviour change is nothing new. In a 1994 survey (Wenger) half of a group of HIV-positive men had UAI with HIV-positive partners but only a sixth with HIV-negative ones - exactly the same proportions as in the 2006 survey. The difference was that in this survey 41% had UAI with partners of unknown status, but that by 2006 this proportion had more than halved. Although obviously we are talking about two different groups of gay men who cannot be compared directly, this seems to provide some evidence of both increased knowledge of status and increased willingness to talk and ask about it.

The Centers for Disease Control in the USA (see CDC) has calculated that on average people with HIV once diagnosed reduce their risk behaviours (i.e. potentially serodiscordant unprotected sex and needle-sharing) by 70% by a year after diagnosis.

The difference HIV diagnosis may make could be even larger than this. The CDC used this figure and what it knew or suspected about the relative infectiousness of people with HIV and different disease stages to calculate that as many as a two-thirds of HIV infections could be transmitted by people unaware of their HIV status. This takes into account not only the behaviour change in people with HIV but the fact that because a proportion will be on treatment, their average infectiousness will decrease.

In 2004 Holtgrave and Anderson used these figures to claim that more than one in nine of people in the USA who don't know their HIV status pass on their virus in a year compared with only one in 58 of people who do know their status - over six times as many.

This may exaggerate the difference. A presentation at the 2006 thirteenth CROI Conference suggested that although people in acute HIV infection were on average 28 times more infectious than people in chronic infection, because the period of chronic infection was so much longer, transmission during acute infection only accounted for one in eight infections. However the fact remains that diagnosis allows people in both acute and chronic infection to reduce their risk behaviour, to seek treatment so they become less infectious, and to considerably reduce their chances of passing on their HIV infection.

Making HIV testing routine

Emboldened by this, the CDC in April 2003 announced its Advancing HIV Prevention Initiative (see MMWR). This was a strategic remodelling of prevention in which much more emphasis was to be laid on increasing HIV test uptake and diagnosing as many people as possible, and working with those who were diagnosed to reinforce safer sex messages. What was also implicit, though not declared, in the new policy was that federal funding for old-style community-based HIV awareness raising and prevention initiatives was to be downgraded.

Advancing HIV Prevention had four strategic aims:

- Make HIV testing a routine part of medical care
- Use new models for diagnosing HIV infection outside of traditional medical settings
- Prevent new infections by working with people diagnosed with HIV and their partners
- Continue to decrease perinatal HIV transmission

1. Make HIV testing a routine part of medical care

The CDC said that screening all persons in high-prevalence medical settings, regardless of what if any HIV risks are reported, made sense because testing based on reported or perceived risk alone was failing to identify many people with

HIV. Acceptance of HIV testing, as demonstrated among pregnant women, was greater when it was offered routinely than when it was based on risk assessments. Furthermore, routine HIV screening met the three generally accepted principles that apply to screening efforts:

- HIV infection is a serious disease that can be detected before symptoms occur using a reliable and inexpensive test.

- Treatment given before symptoms develop is more effective than waiting until after symptoms develop.

- The cost of screening is reasonable compared with the anticipated benefits.

2. Use new models for diagnosing HIV infection outside of traditional medical settings

The CDC said that HIV testing programmes outside of traditional medical settings were more likely to reach racial/ethnic minorities and 'people who report increased risk for HIV but do not have access to medical care', such as people without insurance and undocumented immigrants. It also said that evidence had shown that testing programmes conducted in some non-traditional settings produced higher rates of seropositivity. For instance, it was estimated that nearly a quarter of the HIV-positive people in trhe USA at some point passed through the prison system, but fewer than half of prisons routinely tested inmates on entry.

Recently approved rapid HIV tests could be done outside a traditional laboratory setting and could reduce the time it took to process tests from two weeks to 20 minutes. The availability of these tests meant that testing could be implemented in diverse settings and essential health information can be provided quickly in settings where people may be unlikely to return to receive test results.

3. Prevent new infections by working with people diagnosed with HIV and their partners

The CDC said that each person living with HIV who adopted safer behavior could prevent many potential transmissions of HIV infection. It cited the figure already quoted above, that people with HIV once diagnosed reduced their sexual risk behaviour by as much as 70%.

The CDC said: "Studies suggest that working with HIV-infected persons will result in greater reductions in risk behaviors and HIV transmission than working with HIV-negative persons."

It explicitly portrayed the specialised counselling of people who sought tests and turned out to be HIV-negative, however high risk their behaviour, as a waste of resources. It said that among persons testing negative for HIV, those receiving enhanced risk reduction counseling had only 18% fewer sexually transmitted infections at one year after testing compared with persons receiving standard counseling.

The CDC also said that it would "increase the emphasis on assisting HIV-infected persons in notifying partners of their recent exposure and ensure voluntary testing of partners," pointing out that when partners were referred, from 8% to 40% turned out to have previously undiagnosed HIV infection.

What help with preventing onward transmission would the newly diagnosed people get? The CDC said that prevention interventions included:

- ongoing case management

- focused risk-reduction counselling

- medical interventions (leaving these undefined)

- support for other psychosocial stressors (leaving these also undefined, though in another paper they specify as examples of stressors homelessness, and drink and drug problems).

4. Continue to decrease perinatal HIV transmission.

This speaks for itself; the CDC said it would continue to recommend that all pregnant women be screened for HIV in order to take advantage of medical interventions to reduce the risk of mother-to-baby transmission. It strongly supported an "opt-out" testing strategy for prenatal HIV screening, doing HIV tests as routinely as, and with the same consent forms, as other medical tests.

Reservations

This policy was received with suspicion by existing HIV prevention workers and advocates for people with HIV. Opinions were voiced that the main driver behind the new policy was the distaste that the Bush administration had for traditional community HIV prevention programmes, with their often bold and 'sex positive' campaigns and their explicit work with marginalised communities such as gay men of colour (or indeed any gay men) and sex workers.

Exactly a year after the CDC's policy was adopted Terje Anderson, Director of the National Association of People with AIDS (NAPWA), criticised its approach (Anderson). He said the narrow emphasis on testing and individualised counselling was inherently stigmatising:

The lack of any mention of anything that isn't an individual level intervention delivered behind closed doors in a doctor's or social worker's office - the lack of any mention of anything that happens in the community - lays individual responsibility for transmission on each person with HIV, lays no responsibility on their negative partners, makes possible no conversation about the social context that puts people at risk, and treats people with HIV as vectors of infection and not as full people.

In fact, the Expanding HIV Prevention initiative made surprisingly little difference to diagnosis rates in the USA. By 2002, an estimated 38-44% of people in the USA had been tested at least once for HIV; but despite this, the proportion of people with HIV who were unaware of their status stayed stubbornly at 25% of the total.

With the exception of routine testing for pregnant women, and despite repeated recommendations in support of routine risk-based testing in healthcare settings, the number of people at risk for HIV infection screened in acute-care settings remained low. In a survey (Fincher-Mergi) of 154 healthcare providers in ten hospital emergency departments, providers reported caring

for an average of 13 patients per week with suspected STIs, but only 10% encouraged these patients to be tested for HIV infection in the emergency department. Although 35% referred patients to confidential HIV testing sites in the community, such referrals had proved ineffective because patients did not turn up.

Reasons cited for not offering HIV testing in the emergency department included lack of established mechanisms to assure follow-up (51%), lack of the certification perceived as necessary to provide counselling (45%), and belief that the testing process was too-time consuming (19%).35

With routine HIV screening in some hospitals and emergency departments, the percentage of patients with positive tests (2% to 7%) often exceeded that observed nationally in publicly-funded HIV counselling and testing sites (1.5%) and STI clinics (2.0%) serving 'high-risk' people.

Should we test everyone for HIV?

In February 2005 the *New England Journal of Medicine* published two cost-effectiveness estimates (Paltiel, Sanders) of what would happen if there was universal screening for HIV - that is, at least one test performed on the entirety of selected populations ranging from high-risk people to the entire US population.

David Paltiel of Yale University divided the US population into a 'high risk' group (meaning an *undiagnosed* HIV prevalence of 3%, similar to gay men in London) and an annual incidence of 1.2%; a 'CDC threshold' group meaning populations the CDC had recommended for routine testing in its Advancing HIV Prevention strategy (undiagnosed prevalence of 1%, annual incidence of 0.12%); and the general US population (undiagnosed prevalence 0.1%, annual incidence 0.01%).

If everyone in 'high risk' populations (though how you discovered who was 'high risk' was a question left unaddressed) was given a routine one-off HIV test in addition to whatever voluntary HIV tests some of them may have, the average CD4 count at diagnosis would increase from 154 to 210, though there would be very little additional benefit in survival time.

Testing all these people at least once routinely would cost $36,000 per quality-adjusted life-year (QALY) gained, testing them every five years would cost $50,000 per QALY gained,and testing every three years would cost $63,000. One-off testing of the CDC Threshold group would cost not much more - about $38,000 per QALY gained. But if you tested the entire adult US population at least once, it would cost $113,000 per QALY gained.

Paltiel said his modelling showed that "in all but the lowest-risk populations, routine,voluntary screening for HIV once every three to five years is justified on both clinical and cost-effectiveness grounds." The threshold for what is regarded as a 'cost-effective' treatment is set at about £30,000 by the National Institute for Health and Clinical Excellence (NICE) in the UK, which translates to about $60,000 given the generally higher costs of health in the USA.

Gillian Sanders of Duke University found somewhat lower costs with her model than Paltiel. She found that one-off screening of the CDC threshold population would cost $15,078 per quality-adjusted life-year gained and that screening in any population with a prevalence of over 0.05% (a quarter of UK prevalence and one-twelfth of US prevalence) would cost less than $50,000 per quality-adjusted life-year. Screening the entire adult population every five years would cost $57,140 per QALY gained, "but was more attractive in settings with a high incidence of infection."

Sanders said her results were 'sensitive to the efficacy of behaviour modification', meaning that if the resultant newly-diagnosed people significantly reduced their risk behaviour, universal screening might be more cost-effective.

She concluded that "The cost-effectiveness of routine HIV screening in healthcare settings, even in relatively low-prevalence populations,is similar to that of commonly accepted interventions, and such programs should be expanded."

Encouraged by this, the CDC announced a much bolder move - they would push for a policy of universal screening. All adults in the USA should take at least one HIV test.

In a talk at the Thirteenth Retrovirus conference in early 2006, Timothy Mastro of the CDC quoted the startlingly high prevalence and incidence figures among gay men and particularly black gay men in cities other than San Francisco. In a large sample of gay men in five US cities 25% of gay men had had HIV and 48% were unaware of their infection; 46% of black gay men were positive and 67% did not know it. Late testing was also common: 45% of AIDS diagnoses were among people who had been diagnosed less than twelve months previously.

He said that HIV testing in the USA had not been increasing in recent years despite the launch of the Advancing HIV Prevention strategy in 2003.

He said that only about one in 500 visits to hospital emergency departments involved an HIV test despite the fact that, when tested, rates of previously undiagnosed HIV among A&E patients varied from 1.3% to 3.2%.

In Texas, which adopted opt-out testing in its STI clinics back in 1997, the proportion of STI patients tested for HIV increased by over 50% (from 78% to 97%) in one year and the number of positive tests had gone up 60% from 168 to 268. He showed a notice from a Dallas STI clinic which said that "All patients seen in this clinic will be tested for gonorrhoea, syphilis, Chlamydia and HIV."

He said that before opt-out testing had been adopted in pregnant women in the UK only 35% had tested because they feared it indicated high-risk behaviour whereas 88% accepted opt-out testing.

"We think the need for extensive pre-test counselling is less because it's 2006 and people now have a high level of knowledge about HIV," he said.

The CDC had therefore decided to revise its HIV screening guidelines and from June 2006 would be recommending routine, voluntary screening for all persons aged 13-64 in healthcare settings, *not* based on risk, and annual HIV testing for people with risk behaviour. Pre-test counselling would not be required.

'Healthcare settings' includes all hospital in-patient and out-patient departments and community clinics as well as STI clinics. An exception would be made of prisons, where it was recognised that receiving an HIV diagnosis created profound difficulties both for inmate and institution.

This is a radical proposal which would require revising a myriad of local regulations, including ones mandating pre-test counselling and written consent.

Mastro was faced with a battery of questions after his presentation by questioners with numerous concerns. Among them were:

- How would the CDC move from recommendation to implementation? It had recommended names-based reporting years ago but it had taken the threat of the removal of federal funds for states to move towards this.

- If the information given in pre-test counselling and discussion around informed consent is removed, where are patients going to get any option to talk about HIV and harm reduction?

- How real is the 'voluntary' nature of the testing when the photo he showed said 'You *will* be tested for HIV?'

- How is the opting-out process to work and how will it be recorded? Without adequate recording, patients could say they were tested without consent.

In an article on the universal test recommendation (Young), the *Atlanta Jounal-Constitution*, home-town newspaper of the CDC, pointed out that the CDC's ambitious plan was not backed by the force of law, and said that whether it would become reality remained a question.

It also pointed out that the guidelines conflicted with an influential federal task force's conclusion the previous year that widespread voluntary testing has no direct evidence of benefits. In July 2005, the US Preventive Services Task Force, the nation's leading independent panel of private-sector experts on prevention and primary care, issued its own findings on HIV testing. That group found there was not enough evidence to recommend for or against routine HIV screening.

Dr Bruce Calonge, task force chairman, said his group looked at the state of the scientific evidence to decide whether actions had documented benefits. They could not find documented benefits for universal screening.

The difference between the two recommendations, Calonge said, may point to the different missions of the task force and the CDC. The task force looks at benefits to the patient sitting in front of a clinician; the CDC is focused on public health and improving the overall health of a population.

The task force's recommendations are what the nation's health insurers generally look to when deciding coverage issues, and they are also influential with family physicians. The conflicting recommendations raise questions about whether universal testing will be adopted by family doctors and whether private and government health programmes will pay for the tests. In general, Medicare will not pay for routine screening tests unless specifically authorised by Congress.

Private insurers are studying the proposal, said Susan Pisano, spokeswoman for America's Health Insurance Plans, which represents them. "Generally speaking our member companies follow recommendations of the U.S. Preventive Services Task Force," she said.

Dr Carlos del Rio, chief of medicine at Grady Memorial Hospital in Atlanta, said he was concerned the new recommendations would go the way of the CDC's 1993 call for universal HIV screening of people going to hospitals in areas with high rates of HIV. He said that he and others had called it "the most ignored recommendation ever made by CDC."

Jeff Graham, senior director of advocacy and communications for the Atlanta-based AIDS Survival Project, said more testing is important. "However, the devil is in the details." He said his greatest concern was the plan to do away with pre-test counseling because it was one of the few opportunities for medical professionals to educate people on preventing HIV.

He said: "Our greater concern is not legal issues, but the personal sense of stigma."

At CROI, a presentation by Tom Coates of the University of California, San Francisco, had looked at drives to normalise HIV testing in Africa (where opt-out testing has been a policy in Bostwana since 2004 and where, in 2005, Lesotho announced a plan to HIV-test its entire population). His findings underscored these concerns. Africans were in general in agreement with normalising HIV testing (82% of Batswana, for instance, think that the routine testing introduced by their President Festus Mogae is 2004 was a good thing). However this contrasted with their individual distress at contemplating a positive result and the stigma and societal rejection it might bring.

In one qualitative survey, one said: "I have a dream of having children; if I test positive my dream will be shattered." Another said: "My father will chase me away from the house and call me Satan."

Despite these concerns, AIDS activists in the USA, who had previously been suspicious of recommendations for universal testing, broadly welcomed them. *Aidsmeds.com* founder Peter Staley, writing in the *New York Times*, said:

"AIDS groups should be screaming for expanded testing, and many of them are. But some are fighting any change, as though the epidemic hasn't evolved since the 1980s. In those days, there were important reasons to protect people getting tested for AIDS. There were no drugs to treat the disease. A positive test meant that you were just waiting to die.

"That's why AIDS groups argued that HIV. infection was very different from, for instance, diabetes, and that we needed to treat it differently. New York, along with other states, adopted policies that came to be known as 'HIV. exceptionalism.' The state passed laws to protect patients from unwanted testing.

"But today, treating HIV. can delay, sometimes indefinitely, the onset of AIDS. That has made HIV. testing - the first step toward dealing effectively with the disease - a lot more important. Testing itself has become less stressful as well. While older tests required patients to wait two weeks for results, new technology gives them an answer in 20 minutes.

The rigorous demands of HIV. exceptionalism are limiting the widespread availability of the HIV. test. And oddly enough, treating HIV. infection as a secret that must be kept at all costs makes it seem more shameful than other diseases. Right now, state legislation is "protecting" people so much that one in four HIV.-positive New Yorkers have to get sick to find out that they are ill. We can do better than that, and we should."

Staley quoted Dennis deLeon, president of the Latino Commission on AIDS, on his own change in attitude about testing. DeLeon said he had spoken with a pregnant woman who had no idea she was at risk for HIV - she had been married and monogamous, and had never used drugs. When her test came back positive, she was shocked.

"I had strongly opposed this testing program, but when I encountered this woman, I realised that I had been wrong," he said. "My activism may have served to deprive other women of knowing their status during pregnancy. That troubles me a lot."

An illustration of the difficulties the CDC policy may encounter came from San Francisco where Jeffrey Klausner, head of the San Francisco Public Health Department's HIV programme, introduced a policy saying that doctors no longer had to obtain written consent from patients taking an HIV test.

Klausner came under criticism for his efforts to make "a simple administrative change bringing some city [testing] facilities in line with what was already standard practice at most hospitals."

As a result of Klausner's actions on HIV testing reform, the San Francisco Board of Supervisors considered an emergency ordinance specifically mandating informed written consent as well as pre-test counselling at city-funded HIV testing sites. However, as the 'Bay Area Reporter' also pointed out, "...terms like 'informed consent' and 'counseling' rarely have a uniform statewide legal definition."

The position in the UK

Surveys in the UK have found that a large proportion of gay men and Africans who turn up at GUM for sexual health checkups and even with acute sexually transmitted infections were going away without being offered an HIV test.

For instance, the 2004 HIV Prevalence and Sexual Behaviour Survey among gay men in London, Brighton and Manchester (Dodds) found that, of the gay men who turned out to have HIV when tested anonymously, 44% in London had told the questionnaire they were HIV-negative or untested; 33% in Brighton; and 37% in Manchester.

The survey divided the men up into those who had had an STI checkup in the last year and those who had not. In London one in five GUM clinic attendees had HIV but 30% of those were unaware of it, implying that opportunities to test them had not been taken.

In contrast only seven per cent of London men who had *not* had an STI checkup turned out to have HIV.

In terms of Africans, during 2003, according to data from GUM clinics participating in the unlinked anonymous survey, the prevalence of previously undiagnosed HIV infection among heterosexuals born in sub-Saharan Africa was high, with 3.6% (137/3787) of those in London and 8.0% elsewhere in England, Wales and Northern Ireland, infected and unaware of their infection. This regional disparity probably reflects the recent dispersal of migrant populations to areas outside London, and highlights the increasing burden being placed on GUM clinics outside of London.

Current UK policy is to encourage STI clinics to make 'opt-out' HIV testing a routine part of care for anyone visiting a GUM clinic with an acute sexually transmitted infection.

The Sexual Health and HIV Strategy for Scotland says that "lead clinicians must develop a framework to ensure that HIV testing is offered to all GUM clinic attendees not known to be HIV-infected who present with a new STI.

"This offer should be made in the context of the HIV test being presented as a routine recommended test. Reasons for non-uptake should be recorded."

Although the Sexual Health and HIV Strategy for England and Wales was written before the greatly expanded use of HIV testing was being recommended as a strategy, the most recent guidance issued by the Department of Health says that "All GUM clinic attendees should be offered an HIV test on their first screening for sexually transmitted infections (and subsequently according to risk).

It adds: "Attenders at genitourinary medicine clinics are considered to be at increased risk of HIV infection because of their behaviour. Most clinics routinely offer an HIV test only to those in recognised high-risk groups, namely homosexual men, current/former injection drug users and people from or with close links to high prevalence countries (currently those in sub-Saharan Africa). We know from unlinked anonymous surveys of HIV infection carried out in a network of GUM clinics across the country that this selective strategy has not reached all those who have been at risk. A high proportion is still unaware that they have HIV infection after their visit."

Studies have shown that where opt-out testing is offered, the number of HIV tests taken immediately increases. One English clinic to do this early was the GUM clinic at the North Cumbria Hospital in Carlisle. In a paper in the *BMJ* in 2001 (Stanley), the clinic performed 154 syphilis tests in August 2001 and 70 'opt-in' HIV tests (i.e., patients had to specifically ask for an HIV test).

The clinic changed to 'opt-out' consent in September 2001. That month 148 syphilis tests were performed and 130 HIV tests - an 85% increase.

There were similar experiences in Scotland. At Glasgow's Sandyford Clinic opt-out testing was introduced at the start of 2004. Every person coming for an STI screen, whether symptomatic or not, would be offered an HIV test and consent would be taken verbally. Objections to the test would be recorded and patients would be told they had the option to return if they changed their minds.

In May to August 2003, from 400 to 470 HIV tests were performed a month at the clinic. During the same time period in 2004, 710-880 tests were performed a month, with an upward trend (the highest figure was the last recorded for the paper presented, in August 2004). This represents a 78-87% increase in HIV tests being performed from one year to the next.

Current UK policy on HIV testing has been established as a result of a number of factors:

- Desire to avoid compulsory testing

- Desire to avoid discrimination and stigmatisation

- Qualified medical support for widespread testing

- Lack of support from the voluntary sector for widespread testing.

Debates about HIV testing have tended to focus on the complex decision-making process which faces individuals who are considering whether or not to test. Many doctors and voluntary organisations continue to argue that HIV testing is an individual decision. The outcome of such a consensus is that the wider social consequences of not promoting HIV testing are never discussed because this would be seen to undermine individual choice.

However, it is important to discuss the negative consequences of not promoting HIV testing more aggressively. These include:

- Avoidable morbidity and mortality

- Avoidable mother-to-baby transmission

- Frequent incorrect assumptions about HIV status in sexual relationships

- Underestimates of the size of the infected population and of the costs of the AIDS epidemic.

Home testing

Home testing kits

Home testing for HIV antibodies became available in the United States in 1996. Two different testing kits - more accurately, home sampling kits, which enable people to send blood away for testing - have been approved for sale by pharmacists. There are no indications that such kits will become available in the UK in the near future, and strict regulations exist regarding who can perform HIV tests. Major AIDS organisations in the UK have consistently opposed the idea of any form of home testing, arguing that HIV testing should always be conducted with full pre- and post-test counselling.

However, US authorities decided that the potential benefits of home testing services outweighed the disadvantages, and that the systems proposed by the makers contained enough safeguards of confidentiality and the client's emotional reactions to the test result.

The home tests available in the USA

Neither of the testing kits available now in the US are true `home tests' in the way that pregnancy testing kits are understood to be. Both require individuals to send off a sample of blood to a laboratory and phone in for a result. Their chief advantages are anonymity and accessibility rather than speed.

The Confide testing kit

Confide is manufactured by Direct Access Diagnostics, a subsidiary of Johnson and Johnson. The testing kit is an over the counter product which consists of a blood specimen collection kit, pre-test counselling booklet and a personal ID number. The test kit can also be ordered by credit card phone line. They cost between $35 and $50 depending on point of sale.

The purchaser uses a retractable lancet to prick a fingertip and place few drops of blood on a paper test card. The card is then sent to the laboratory in a pre-paid envelope.

At the laboratory the sample is tested using a standard ELISA antibody test, with a confirmatory test using another form of test kit if the result is positive. False positives have not been reported in trials of this methodology, and the false negative rate is comparable with standard ELISA testing (5 in 1000).

Results are available in seven days by telephone. The caller gives their ID number to obtain the result. If the result is negative the caller has the option of speaking to a counsellor or recorded information. If the caller is positive or the result is indeterminate, he or she will be referred to a counsellor. Counsellors can refer to treatment centres and callers may use the telephone counselling service for up to two years after diagnosis. There is no way that the testing service can follow up callers if they opt out of the counselling process at any point.

The Home Access test

The Home Access kit is also available from pharmacies or by mail order, price ranging from $40 to $60. The test kit consists of a lancet and a filter paper circle which must be completely filled with blood. The sample is then sent to the laboratory, where it is tested by several ELISA kits. If a sample is positive by two ELISA tests, another test method will be used to confirm the result.

A trial has shown that the test method resulted in no false positive or false negative results when 756 individuals at high risk of HIV infection were tested. However, almost 7% of test kit users had problems providing the blood sample in such a way that it could be tested.

Results are available within three to seven days. Some people with negative results will be referred automatically to a counsellor. Others will be given the option. All callers with positive results are referred directly to a counsellor, who will give them referrals and post-test counselling. As with the Confide test, callers can opt out of the counselling process at any time.

Advantages and disadvantages

These testing kits offer a number of advantages over current methods of testing.

- Anonymity: many people may be put off attending HIV testing sites by embarrassment or the wish to remain anonymous

- Accessibility: testing sites may be inaccessible to some people either because they are too far away or because they are not open at convenient times.

However, there are several disadvantages:

- Lack of face-to-face counselling

- No guarantee that those who test positive will remain engaged with the counselling process once they have received a positive result

- Cost: those with very low incomes may be unable to afford the testing kits, and may continue to be underserved by free, anonymous testing sites.

However, it is generally agreed that the availability of such testing kits is likely to increase the level of HIV testing. It will be important to see the results of post-marketing studies into questions such as:

- Do a higher proportion of self-test kit users return for their results? In the US it has been reported that up to 50% of those tested do not return for their results at some conventional testing sites

- Does the system of referring people to physicians and treatment centres work?

- Is the quality of the advice people are getting about treatment options, safer sex and referrals up to scratch?

- What are the psychosocial consequences of receiving results in this way compared with conventional testing?

- What is the false positive and false negative rate in much larger sample group?

In the longer term home testing may be an important element in encouraging the early diagnosis of HIV infection. However, the introduction of such a system raises specific issues for the UK. For example, the UK has a very good system of GUM clinics which also function as HIV treatment centres and sexual health clinics. Home testing might damage the useful relationship between these services, which does not exist to the same extent in other countries.

Home testing also calls into question the right of British residents to free treatment and diagnosis under the NHS. It would be part of the creeping 'privatisation' of NHS services, and ought to be considered as part of the debate about how health services should be funded. Would it be a good thing if many people at lower risk of HIV infection ceased to use GUM services and took up home testing instead? Should people not at high-risk be charged for HIV testing anyway, as is the case in the Australian state of Victoria?

HIV testing has not been as widespread amongst gay men in the UK as it has in the United States. Would companies manufacturing the kits be permitted to market them in the same way as they do in the US, over the counter and backed up by advertising campaigns? Would this advertising be targeted at high risk groups or the general population? How would this affect health promotion activities targeted at gay men, who have much lower testing rates than injecting drug users (approx 50% of gay men vs 85% of IVDUs in contact with drugs services)?

Rapid self-testing

A further generation of home tests is likely to be offered in the next few years. These tests will use rapid, on the spot diagnostic techniques already developed for use in medical settings, testing saliva, urine or blood. These tests could be true *home tests*.

Such tests raise more difficult ethical issues. For example, how would people react to discovering a positive result without even having telephone support to talk about their diagnosis? Is there any guarantee that they would read or understand any counselling material supplied with the test kit?

There may also be a particular danger of false positive results with the technologies which could be employed for self-testing at home. This is especially problematic, since test kit users may not fully understand the need for confirmatory testing.

Home-testing may also be used in confused or even abusive ways. For instance, it may be used to test new sexual partners without a clear understanding of the potential window period. Partners or adolescent children may be forced to test, and it might be possible to test people surreptitiously with such test kits, particularly if they are based on a saliva or urine assay. This raises particular issues in the workplace, where compulsory drug testing is becoming increasingly frequent. If home testing became sufficiently routine, companies might be able to argue that the testing of employees did not constitute a discriminatory practice.

However, some doctors and policy makers in the US argue that self-testing would be good thing if it encouraged more people to come forward for HIV treatment earlier. They say that whilst it was appropriate for testing to be carried out on a restricted basis when treatment options were less promising, and the implications of a positive result very serious, it is now imperative that people are encouraged to test. However, this view pre-supposes that the resources will remain available to treat all the

newly diagnosed people. At present this appears unlikely, especially if home testing achieved what some of its proponents hope: a large increase in people from minority communities coming forward for treatment. It is this group of the US population which already has the poorest access to state of the art treatment, due to cuts in AIDS Drug Assistance Programmes, lack of health insurance, or restrictive health insurance.

A possible setback to extending HIV testing, especially home testing, happened in late 2005.

In November 2005 the FDA had met to give consideration to approving the oral *OraQuick* HIV test for over-the-counter sale in pharmacies. Currently the OraQuick test is only sold officially to doctors and nurses, although it has been unofficially available from Internet suppliers for some time.

Freya Spielberg, a researcher at the Centre for AIDS Research at the University of Washington, said the availability of a rapid, at-home HIV test "is the most powerful strategy we have to bring down HIV infections". She pointed out that about 8,000 people who test positive for HIV annually at health clinics in the USA never return to pick up their results.

The FDA was thought partly to be guided by the change of heart among HIV treatment activists. Two years ago Gay Men's Health Crisis (GMHC) in New York, the country's oldest HIV organisation, opposed home testing. But in November 2005 it said it supported it - with reservations.

"For people who don't have access to a clinic or make a decision not to go to a clinic, this is better than nothing," said GMHC's Gregg Gonsalves. "But it's not a magic bullet."

So-called 'home testing' kits have in fact been legal in the USA since 1996, but the two tests available until now, Confide® and the Home Access Test® have in fact been blood sampling kits where you take a fingertip blood sample with a lancet and send it off on a card for laboratory testing. However the OraQuick test has been unofficially available on the internet for some time.

However plans to make the test available over the counter were thrown into reverse after certain community centres using the OraQuick 20-minute HIV test reported ten times the expected number of false-positive test results.

A provision to direct the US Department of Health to purchase one million of the tests for distribution to pharmacies was unexpectedly stripped from a Senate Bill on 14 December 2005.

The problem first came to public attention when the Los Angeles Gay and Lesbian Center announced on the 8th of December that there had been a large number of false positive tests among people using OraQuick.

The centre said it performed 600 oral HIV tests a month and normally found about 20 people who tested positive. False positives were rare until November, when 13 people who had tested positive on the OraQuick test were later found to be negative on confirmatory testing.

Barbara Adler, the project's testing programme manager, said "It was excruciating for our clients and our staff to be getting these results, not knowing whether they were accurate." She said the project has gone back to using the pin-prick blood test it was previously using. Clinics in New York had also noticed an increase in false positives from 10 in October to 30 in November - about a quarter of all positive test results.

Dr Bernard Branson of the Division of HIV Prevention at the US Centers for Disease Control said he could offer no explanation for the rise in false positives in recent months. A CDC survey of 17,000 results found a false-positive rate of only 0.2% compared with over 2% experienced by the Los Angeles Gay Center.

In the UK selling HIV tests to anyone but medical professionals is illegal and likely to remain so for some time, even though a lower proportion of gay men test in the UK than in the US. In the last UK Gay Men's Sex Survey 56% of gay men had ever taken an HIV test.

UK activists have traditionally been more concerned by the ethical implications of the availability of home tests, not just in terms of whether people could face the shock of an unexpected positive result, but by whether repeat home testing could be used as a substitute for safer sex and even whether someone could surreptitiously test another family member for HIV without their knowledge.

References

CDC. *Advancing HIV prevention: new strategies for a changing epidemic --- United States, 2003.* Mortality and Morbidity Weekly Report (MMWR) 52(15): 329-332., April 2003.

CDC. *Advancing HIV prevention: the science behind the new initiative.* See http://www.cdc.gov/hiv/topics/prev_prog/AHP/resources/qa/AdvancingFS.pdf%20.%20 September%202003.

Dodds JP (http://www.ncbi.nlm.nih.gov/entrez/query.fcgi?db=pubmed&cmd=Search&itool=pubme d_Abstract&term=%22Dodds+JP%22%5BAuthor%5D) et al. *Increasing risk behaviour and high levels of undiagnosed HIV infection in a community sample of homosexual men.* Sex Transm Infect. (javascript:AL_get(this,%20'jour',%20'Sex%20Transm%20Infect.');)2004 Jun;80(3): 236-240.

Fincher-Mergi M, Cartone KJ, Mischler J, et al. *Assessment of emergency department professionals' behaviors regarding HIV testing and referral for patients with STDs.* AIDS Patient Care STDs 16: 549-553, 2002.

Gorbach PM. *Transmission behaviors of recently HIV-infected men who have sex with men.* JAIDS 42(1): 80-85, 2006.

Holtgrave DR and Anderson T. *Utilising HIV transmission rates to assist in prioritising HIV prevention services.* International Journal of STD & AIDS 15: 789-792, 2004.

Paltiel AD et al. *Expanded screening for HIV in the United States - an analysis of cost-effectiveness.* NEJM 352(6): 586-595, 2005.

Sanders GD et al. *Cost-effectiveness of screening for HIV in the era of highly active antiretroviral therapy.* NEJM 352(6): 570-585, 2005.

Staley P. Why It's Right to Test. *New York Times,* 02 June 2006.

Stanley R. *Uptake of HIV screening in genitourinary medicine after change to 'opt-out' consent.* BMJ 326: 1174, 2003.

Wenger NS et al. *Sexual behavior of individuals infected with the human immunodeficiency virus. The need for intervention.* Arch Intern Med. 154(16): 1849-1854, 1994.

Young A. *Routine testing for HIV advised.* Atlanta Journal-Constitution, 09 May 2006.

C is also for Circumcision

There is strong biological and epidemiological evidence that circumcised men are less vulnerable to HIV infection via heterosexual intercourse than uncircumcised men.

In Africa, the countries where less than 20% of the male population is circumcised form a broad swathe extending from the Central African Republic and southern Sudan in the north, through the former British colonies of east Africa, and down to Botswana, Zimbabwe, and Swaziland. (Halperin). The only country that has high (>10%) levels of HIV prevalence but also higher circumcision levels than 20% is South Africa, whose very mixed cultural, sexual and racial background may make it a special case.

Kenya is a special and more studied case. The general HIV prevalence in 1999 was estimated as 11% but prevalence in circumcised men was about 3%. In a study of Nyanza province on the shores of lake Victoria, prevalence in circumcised men was 2% and uncircumcised men 21%.

In countries where less than 20% of the male population is circumcised, HIV prevalence ranges from 25% in Zimbabwe to around 12% in Rwanda (these are figures from Halperin's 1999 paper and in some cases have been revised downwards now). In countries where male circumcision is under 20%, HIV prevalence ranges from 7.6% in Congo (Brazzaville) to 2% in west African countries like Guinea and Benin. Circumcision is probably not the whole explanation for these differences, but Halperin makes the case that countries with low circumcision also tend to have cultures where people have high-levels of non-commercial concurrent sexual partnerships. These two factors taken together, he says, are in themselves sufficient to explain differences in HIV prevalence.

Conversely, in many of the low circumcision countries such as Guinea and Ghana, non-primary-partner sex tends to be carried out with sex workers among whom HIV prevalence is very high, but where (except in certain cases such as the Ivory Coast) there has been little spread into the general population, possibly because circumcised sex-worker clients are at low risk of infection so do not carry HIV home to their wives as has been observed in other countries such as India where circumcision is less common.

Talking of HIV prevalence in Asia, the same pattern is observed there, though with HIV prevalences an order of magnitude lower. Countries where less than 20% of the male population is circumcised range from Cambodia (HIV prevalence 2.4%) to China (0.1%). Countries with more than 20% of men circumcised range from the Philippines (0.1%) down to Bangladesh (0.03%) and what HIV these countries do have tends to be concentrated among sex workers and injecting drug users. There is very little overlap between the countries. The near 100% circumcision rate in Muslim countries is one explanation why Middle Eastern countries still have low HIV prevalence.

Critics of the circumcision theory have suggested that Islamic prohibition of concurrent sexual partnerships may be the explanation of the difference, with circumcision a passive marker for being Muslim. As Halperin suggests, the two factors may work synergistically together but do not explain the situation in largely Christian countries like Ghana.

We have already, at the beginning of this article, outlined the findings from the randomised controlled trial of male circumcision in Orange Farm, South Africa, which found a 65%-75% protective effect for men who were circumcised. This trial of 3,500 men was only the first of three to report. Trials have also been going on in an urban area (Kisumu in Nyanza province, Kenya - 2,276 men) and a rural one (Rakai province in Uganda - 2,500 men). Both trials, though they started earlier than the South African trial, will not finish data collection until February 2007 in Kisumu and December 2007 in Rakai. The World Health Organization (WHO) has said it is awaiting the result of these trials before making a general recommendation that male circumcision should be used among high-prevalence countries as an HIV prevention intervention.

There are biological reasons why uncircumcised men may be more vulnerable to HIV. The mucosa that covers the inside of the foreskin contains more Langerhans cells than almost any other part of the body except the gut. This is a type of dendritic cell whose job is to ferry foreign particles to the lymph nodes for recognition by the immune system, and which HIV hijacks as part of its infection strategy. In ex-vivo explant models, foreskin mucosa was found to be nine times more vulnerable to HIV infection than cervical tissue.

Without waiting for the other two RCT results, some experts are already calling for the widespread adoption of circumcision in young men in Africa. After the Auvert trial results came out, Thomas Coates of the University of California San Francisco, writing in the *Johannesburg Star*, said: "It might be interesting if relatively small countries highly impacted by HIV, like Lesotho or Swaziland, might try male circumcision on a broad scale to see if they can reduce HIV infection among men and women by using male circumcision."

Would circumcision be accepted? Studies done between 2002 and 2005 in six African countries found that between 40% (Zimbabwe) and 65% (south Africa, Botswana, Kenya) of men said they would be willing to be circumcised if it protected them form HIV. In South Africa, Botswana and Kenya, parents were asked about their sons. South African fathers weren't sure: 50% said they would have their sons circumcised. But otherwise 70-75% of fathers and 75-85% of mothers said they'd be willing to have their sons circumcised.

It is crucial to circumcise young men under 20 as even in high-prevalence countries this group has generally not yet caught HIV; HIV prevalence in young men under 20 in Lesotho is only 2.5%, for instance; by the time they are 24 it will be 12%.

Some African men have heard the news and are not waiting for the WHO to say circumcision is a good idea. In an article in *Mortality and Morbidity Weekly Report* by the CDC on 28 February 2006, circumcision already appeared to have gained high regard in Swaziland. In the capital Mbabane, patients eager to undergo the procedure were reported to have almost rioted at an overbooked clinic where it was being performed.

References

Halperin D, Bailey R. *Male circumcision and HIV infection: 10 years and counting.* Lancet 354:1813-15. 1999.

Using antiretrovirals for HIV prevention

How can ARVs prevent HIV transmission?

Antiretrovirals (ARVs) can theoretically be used to prevent HIV transmission in two ways:

Firstly, when taken by people with HIV, they might suppress the virus in the person's body in a way that makes it harder to transmit to others.

Secondly, when taken by people who do not have HIV, they might prevent the virus from establishing itself in the body.

The first effect certainly exists. In one San Francisco study (Porco) it was estimated that, averaged over population of people with HIV, people on highly active antiretroviral therapy (HAART) were one-third as infectious as people not on treatment.

In one study of 415 members of the Rakai cohort in Uganda (Quinn), which is one of the most reliable guides we have to exactly how and how often transmission occurs (at least within heterosexual sex), no person transmitted HIV out of the 51 whose viral load was under 1500.

However it is usually thought unwise to rely on viral load as a means of HIV prevention. Why?

For one thing, viral load tests do not measure virus that is present inside cells. These can be transmitted through blood transfusions or through needle-sharing, and may be transmissible sexually, so an 'undetectable' viral load is not going to prevent transmission in this way.

Also, viral load in blood may not match that in semen or vaginal fluids, especially when a sexually transmitted infection or other reproductive tract infection is present. See **HIV transmission** for more on this. Some ARVs are more effective in suppressing viral load in seminal fluids than others. While some ARVs are concentrated in semen, others appear unable to enter it.

Even if viral load in the blood were an accurate guide, it would only be as good as the last viral load test. Any virus that is transmitted in the context of a rising viral load due to treatment failure may be drug-resistant.

There has already been a report of HIV transmission occurring to a steady sexual partner during a treatment interruption. Paradoxically, this does suggest that the treatment was previously a factor preventing HIV transmission (Tubiana).

One context in which further research on this effect is planned is in the provision of ARVs to women who are breastfeeding. The World Health Organization (WHO) has developed a protocol for international clinical trials that will seek to find out whether, and to what extent, ARV treatment for mothers can prevent breast milk transmission to their children. This could have major advantages in settings where formula feed is unsafe and unaffordable: in fact, the cost of ARVs for the mother is equivalent to the cost of formula feed for the baby and - it may be argued - could be a better use of limited resources.

The uncertainties about using viral load as a guide to whether a person is infectious or not has not stopped this being used 'informally' as a way for partners, predominantly gay men, to decide whether to risk unprotected sex or not.

Several recent studies have found that gay men are questioning each other about their HIV viral load in order to try and establish if they are infectious. "Are you undetectable?" is becoming as common a chatroom question as "are you poz?"

In a study from San Francisco (Goldhammer, 2005) 78% of 507 gay men questioned were familiar with the term `viral load` and one third (111 of the total sample) had discussed viral load with a partner of a different HIV status during the previous year in order to make decisions about which sexual practices to engage in.

Of those who had discussed viral load, more than half estimated that they used viral load disclosure to guide sexual decision-making in at least 70% of their sexual encounters.

In another study from Sydney(Van de Ven, 2005) researchers asked 119 men who were in an HIV-serodiscordant regular relationship about whether they used viral load as a basis for their decisions on condom use. Twice as many (39.4%) reported unprotected anal intercourse when the partner's HIV last viral load test was undetectable as when it was detectable (20.8%).

So it is possible to regard the provision of treatment to people with HIV as a preventative measure, and this is often factored into mathematical models of the likely future development of the epidemic.

However this is not what is generally thought of when we mention antiretrovirals in this context. In the vast majority of cases we are talking about:

- HIV drugs being given to HIV-negative people as emergency protection after a possible exposure event has already occurred (**post-exposure prophylaxis**or **PEP), or**

- HIV drugs being given to HIV-negative people as a general prophylactic regimen before any exposure occurs (**pre-exposure prophylaxis** or **PREP**).

The value of prophlyaxis being given to HIV-negative people to prevent HIV being established, is best illustrated in the case of two-dose nevirapine prophylaxis, used to prevent transmission from mothers to babies.

Here, the dose taken by the woman at the onset of labour does nothing to suppress her virus. The only way in which it can act is by reaching the baby across the placenta, from where it has been shown to reach levels sufficient to prevent HIV infection (a 'PREP' dose). A second dose of nevirapine, given to the baby 72 hours after birth, extends this protection long enough to ensure that any virus to which the baby was exposed during birth is unable to establish itself (a 'PEP' dose). This is discussed further in the context of preventing mother-to-child transmission.

References

Goldhammer H et al. Beliefs about viral load, sexual positioning and transmission risk among HIV+ men who have sex with men (MSM): Shaping a secondary prevention intervention. 2005 National HIV Prevention Conference, Atlanta, USA, presentation W0-D1201.

Porco TC et al. Decline in HIV infectivity following the introduction of highly active antiretroviral therapy. *AIDS* 18(1):81-8. 2004.

Quinn TC et al. Viral load and heterosexual transmission of human immunodeficiency virus type 1. Rakai Project Study Group. *N Engl J Med.* 342(13):921-9. 2000.

Tubiana R et al. Warning: Antiretroviral treatment interruption could lead to an increased risk of HIV transmission. AIDS 16(7):1083-1084, 2002.

Van de Ven P et al. Undetectable viral load is associated with sexual risk taking in HIV serodiscordant gay couples in Sydney. *AIDS* 19(2): 179-184. 2005.

Post-exposure prophylaxis

The case for providing antiviral treatment as 'post-exposure prophylaxis' after sexual exposure is an extension of the case for providing it in occupational settings. Much of the section on needlestick injuries in *HIV transmission* is relevant here.

PEP using AZT was in use by as early as 1988 in healthcare settings (Henderson and Gerberding).

The argument is based on a comparison of per-exposure risks. Estimates of these rates based on studies show that unprotected receptive anal sex with an HIV-positive partner is probably at least twice as risky in terms of the likelihood of infection from a single exposure as a needlestick injury, and may be ten times more risky if the partner has a high viral load. And although a single needlestick injury is probably three to four times riskier than a single act of receptive vaginal sex (unless the partner has a high viral load), factors such as trauma during rape may make this as risky too (Vittinghof - and see the table of per-exposure risks in **HIV transmission**).

It is obviously far more difficult to give prompt access to medical treatment when exposure occurs in the community than it is when accidents occur in a hospital. The usual occupational exposure target, of starting treatment within four hours of an exposure incident, is unlikely to be achieved.

A recent UK survey by the Health Protection Agency (Delpech) of PEP provision at ten London HIV clinics found that for people seeking post-exposure prophylaxis after non-occupational exposure, the average time elapsed between exposure and taking PEP was 23 hours, whereas for occupational exposure it was two hours.

It has not been possible, and may never be, to organise a randomised controlled trial of antiretroviral treatment to assess its effectiveness. The HPA survey above was originally designed as a case-control study but the control arm had to be abandoned because people who turn up for PEP are very unlikely to decline it. It is clearly unethical, when someone has just experienced what may have been a traumatic and worrying event, to allocate them to a control or placebo instead of giving them PEP.

Another reason is the comparative rarity of events that require PEP, so it is hard to predict in advance who will need it. One precondition for offering PEP is the widespread availability of HIV antibody testing, so that people at risk are aware of their own HIV-negative status. This would be especially important if the treatment option provided were inappropriate for treating HIV-positive people, for example, single dose nevirapine and/or short course *Combivir* (AZT and 3TC).

Finally, a large trial would be needed. Delpech estimated that 2.6 transmission events would occur in 300 people in the population studied in the HPA trial if PEP was not used. The study audited 1,500 cases in which PEP was given but was only able to find full details on 333 and had a 42% lost-to-follow-up rate, meaning that only 170 people could be traced later to see if there had been any seroconversions. A zero rate of seroconversions in a group this size would therefore have no statistical significance. In fact, there were two seroconversions among the 170 people who'd taken PEP. But both people had gone on to risk further exposures to HIV subsequent to taking PEP.

This underlines another of the big problems with assessing the effectiveness and desirability of PEP. No less than 27% of the whole group, and 34% of the gay men, had, after taking PEP, then gone on to risk further exposure within three months of taking it!

People are not necessarily rational about assessing the degree of risk they have been exposed to and may form very different estimates of the 'riskiness' of an incident even where the external circumstances are the same. The desire to seek PEP may also wax and wane according to several factors:

- whether the source partner is known to be positive;

- whether the source partner is judged to be a 'high risk' person if their serostatus is unknown;

- whether the source partner recommended PEP;

- whether the exposure was consensual or non-consensual or involved trauma;

- whether it occurred while the person was under the influence or drink or drugs;

- whether it occurred within a casual encounter or within a primary relationship;

- and psychological factors such as depression or fatalism among the person at risk.

All of these factors may influence the decision whether or not to seek PEP.

There is another unresolved question, whether treatments which are clearly inadequate for treating HIV may be perfectly adequate for preventing infection. Animal studies which used a form of tenofovir, and the mother-to-child prevention with two doses of nevirapine mentioned above, strongly suggest that this is the case. There are precedents from other diseases, such as tuberculosis and malaria, where single agents in relatively low doses are successfully used for prophylaxis whereas treatment requires much higher doses and/or combinations of effective drugs.

It is also argued that when antiviral drugs are given to people who are HIV-negative, the level of toxicity that can be tolerated is far lower than when drugs are used to treat a life-threatening illness.

The UK guidelines recommend 28 days of two nucleosides plus either nelfinavir or a boosted protease inhibitor. Didanosine (ddI) is excluded from the nucleosides for possible liver or pancreatic toxicity; abacavir and the NNRTI nevirapine are excluded because of the well-known risk of acute hypersensitivity reactions to these drugs; and efavirenz is excluded because it also causes rash and because it "causes short-term psychostimulation, which is possibly less well tolerated in anxious patients receiving PEP than in patients with established HIV infection." This leaves Either *Combivir* (AZT/3TC), *Truvada* (tenofovir/FTC), or d4t/3TC as the nucleosides plus either a protease inhibitor in the shape of nelfinavir, or a boosted PI such as *Kaletra* (lopinavir/r) or saquinavir/r.

The UK is one of the few countries in fact to recommend a three-drug regime. Many others continue to recommend two nucleosides except in very high-risk exposures or if there is evidence that the transmitted virus could be drug-resistant.

A poster at the thirteenth CROI Conference in 2006 (Rabaud) discussed the tolerability of PEP regimens given at nine hospitals in France. The regimens compared were AZT/3TC (*Combivir*) plus nelfinavir (*Viracept*); *Combivir* plus lopinavir/ritonavir (*Kaletra*); *Combivir* plus tenofovir (*Viread*); and tenofovir/3TC plus atazanavir/ritonavir.

The regimen containing nelfinavir was significantly less well tolerated, with 34.5% of patients discontinuing a 28-day course of PEP due to adverse events, compared with an average of 20% with the other regimens.

Commentators at the poster session said that they had found AZT-free regimens were better tolerated; questioned the usefulness of *Kaletra* due to its poor genital penetration; and aired the ever-controversial topic (in PEP terms) of whether to provide two or three drugs.

A survey of occupational antiretroviral post-exposure prophylaxis among health workers in Canada uncovered a major hidden cost. Time off work due to side- effects of the drugs cost the health service as much as providing the drugs for the treatment. This time off work appears to have doubled, from an average of 7.0 days to 15.8 days in the year 2000, when the protease inhibitor nelfinavir was added to the regimen, previously d4T plus 3TC (McLeod).

Experience to date with PEP

Large-scale prospective, placebo-controlled trials have not been carried out for PEP, and so a definitive answer regarding its effectiveness cannot be given at this time.

A much-cited 1997 case control study (Cardo) of healthcare workers from France, Italy, the UK, and the US came to the conclusion that PEP (in this case AZT monotherapy) reduced the risk of becoming infected with HIV by 81% (with a confidence interval of 48-94%.) This was equivalent to reducing the risk of infection from 1 in 200 to 1 in 10,000 risk. However, there are much less solid data on PEP's effectiveness after sexual exposure.

The San Francisco study

A 2005 study in San Francisco (Roland 2005) evaluated 702 subjects who took PEP for twelve weeks after their exposure. Seven subjects became HIV-positive despite PEP but in four of these there were either additional exposures to HIV after PEP had been initiated or HIV was found in blood specimens given at the start of PEP, meaning they either sought it too late or were already infected with HIV and did not know it. Three seroconverters reported having no exposures after PEP initiation and probably represented evidence of PEP failure.

Of course, given that the chance of getting HIV from a single occasion of receptive anal intercourse is in the region of one chance in 30 to one in 250, many of the men taking PEP would not have got HIV anyway. Because of this, among 702 men one would only expect about six infections if they only had one risky encounter each. But because only three who had definitely only had one encounter got infected, the study implies that PEP prevents at least one in two infections.

The average time delay between the sexual exposure and taking PEP was 32.5 hours, but among men who became HIV-positive it was 45.5 hours - nearly two days - indicating that initiating PEP within a day of exposure is probably necessary to ensure it has the best chance of working.

Researcher Michelle Roland from the University of California, San Francisco, said that the example of the four men who went on to have unsafe sex soon after taking PEP was a reminder that it could not be a stand-alone prevention method.

"It provides an important HIV prevention opportunity when exposed individuals may be especially receptive to assistance with reducing their HIV risk...but is only one part of that prevention activity," she said.

"Sexual exposures are usually not isolated, and helping people stay HIV-negative requires response to both the presenting exposure and attempts to reduce subsequent exposures."

The Brazil study

One of the more convincing studies was conducted in Brazil and reported at the nineth Retroviruses Conference in 2001 (Schechter). Here, 202 HIV-negative gay men were enrolled and followed for an average of two years. At the time of enrolment, 57% of the group reported "high-risk behaviour". PEP, consisting of four weeks of AZT/3TC, was used 100 times by 73 (36%) of the participants, 91% of whom completed the course. Most men took it just once or twice during the two years of the trial, but one man took it nine times.

There were eleven seroconversions among the group; however, only one occurred in someone who had taken PEP. Analysis of the strain of HIV that infected him despite using PEP showed that it harboured the *M184V* mutation which is likely to lead to high-level resistance to 3TC.

The researchers calculated that PEP reduced the seroconversion rate by 83%, from 4.1 cases per 100 patients a year to 0.7 cases.

However the study also found that although quite a high proportion of the study population took PEP, they were bad at evaluating risk and did not take PEP nearly often enough, or did not take it at the times it was really needed. As a result, there was almost no difference in the infection rate observed in the study population as a whole and what would have been expected if PEP had not been available.

During the trial eleven men (5.5%) became HIV-positive, representing 2.9 infections per 100 men a year. While the researchers were able to conclude that PEP, if used properly, could prevent at least 70% of sexual infections, the predicted rate of HIV infection among this group if they had not had PEP available was 3.1 infections per 100 men a year - meaning PEP had actually made almost no difference to the average HIV infection rate.

The reasons PEP was not taken were either that gay men mistakenly assumed their partner was faithful and HIV-negative, or that they caught HIV through routes they considered low risk, such as oral sex. This seems to bear out findings from the UK about gay men's estimation of risk.

The 2005 Gay Men's Sex Survey, *Risk and Reflexion*, found that gay men tend to see sexual risk in terms of risky actions rather than risky partners.

Sigma Research comment: "Overall, 89% of descriptions of risky sex given to the survey by respondents featured information about sexual acts or condoms, whereas only 15% mentioned the status of the partner or alluded to their potential sero-discordancy. The things that constitute risky sex give an insight into where men go wrong when they have sex they consider secure but which results in HIV transmission. The problems seem to be more with misreading the presence of HIV infection (exposure) than underestimating the potential for transmission when it is present."

When the reasons for not taking PEP were looked at in the ten Brazilian men who seroconverted, three thought they were at no risk from their partners. Two mistakenly assumed their boyfriend had been faithful, while another's partner had lied about his HIV status. One didn't want to be seen to be taking HIV drugs, and the reasons were unknown for one man.

This left five who considered their exposure low risk. This worryingly included three - nearly a third of the HIV infections - who said they had only had oral sex.

This study highlighted one of the central dilemmas of PEP. Unlike the other interventions considered in this section, its availability may be crucial to individuals who need it but, as an emergency measure only used by a minority of gay men, it is unlikely to make much difference to HIV incidence on a population level. This has led to controversy about exactly how much it should be promoted as a prevention method - see more below.

However because persons seeking PEP are highly motivated to avoid infection, they may be in a window period in which education and counselling will have significant influence.

Several other interesting findings came from this study. One was that "high-risk" behaviour declined during the study from 56% to 40%. Although it has been suggested from other studies that people reporting declines in risky behaviour may sometimes not be reporting the whole story due, possibly, to guilt at being a 'study failure', this finding may help allay fears that the widespread availability of PEP for sexual exposure will cause an increase in condomless intercourse.

Furthermore, 92% of the time, PEP was taken appropriately, i.e. after an exposure that researchers considered "high risk". This seems to offer a degree of assurance that PEP will not be abused by the 'worried well' concerned by very low-risk incidents.

Finally, the study issued people with 'starter packs' - ready-wrapped doses of AZT/3TC with instructions that participants should take them immediately following exposure. Other PEP schemes have relied on people reporting to A&E departments after weekend incidents. Since one of the key components to successful PEP is prompt treatment - ideally within 24 hours - this may explain some of the difference between the reported effectiveness rate of 83% in the Brazil

study and the 53% rate in the cost-effectiveness study detailed below (Pinkerton).

An earlier study in San Francisco has investigated the safety and acceptability of PEP after possible sexual or IDU exposure to HIV. Individuals who have experienced this type of exposure within the previous 72 hours are offered one month's treatment with AZT and 3TC in the form of one tablet twice a day (also known by the trade name *Combivir*). Other drugs (ddI and d4T) are being offered in cases where it is believed that a risk may exist of exposure to AZT and/or 3TC-resistant virus (Kahn).

The study collected data on the number of cases, the types of risk exposure, the uptake of PEP, side-effects, adherence, the development of drug-resistant HIV strains, and subsequent risk behaviour. The study is not large enough to provide statistically significant evidence of PEP's effectiveness, although it is collecting data on the number of seroconversions.

In total 401 requests for PEP were received between December 1997 and March 1999. A total of 91% of participants were men and the median age was 32 years.

375 of the 401 participants sought PEP because of sexual exposure and only 2% reported sharing of IDU equipment. Receptive anal intercourse was reported in 40% of the exposures.

PEP was supplied within 72 hours of exposure.

Certainty of source partner's HIV-positive status was expressed by 174 (43%) of participants. For the majority of participants exposed during sexual activity, the sexual exposure that prompted enrolment represented a lapse in safe sex practices rather than habitual high-risk behaviour.

In total 309 (48%) of participants completed four weeks of treatment. Complete adherence to medication in the four days before the clinic visit was reported by 84% to 78% of participants, despite high levels of self-reported side-effects, including; nausea (52%), fatigue (44%), headache (24%) and diarrhoea (15%).

This study is one of the first to provide data on the actual practice of providing PEP after sexual and IDU exposure. It demonstrated that people with sexual exposures will seek PEP. For the majority of individuals, the episode represented a lapse in safer sexual practices. The study demonstrated the feasibility of identifying persons with a sexual exposure to HIV as well as that exposed persons can be reliably and safely treated with a four-week course.

Completion rates were high at 78%. This was most likely due to several factors including, the provision of one-to-one medication adherence counselling, dispensing only a limited supply of medications at each visit which required individuals to make regular contact with staff and finally, the majority of participant took a dual nucleoside analogue regimen which was dosed twice daily. Such a regimen is associated with fewer side-effects and greater ease of use than triple combinations including a protease inhibitor.

The study was not designed to evaluate efficacy, though no individuals were observed to develop antibodies to HIV at six months after exposure.

Some other studies

In New York, seven patients were enrolled via a 24 hour telephone helpline to receive an individualised antiretroviral regimen. An NNRTI was given alongside AZT and 3TC, and those patients presenting between 48 and 72 hours after exposure were given nelfinavir. One patient discontinued nelfinavir due to elevated lipid levels, otherwise side-effects were limited to GI disturbances and did not require treatment modification or discontinuation. The researchers found that with adequate counselling and support, participants were able to demonstrate excellent adherence (Torres). This was the first non-occupational post-exposure prophylaxis (PEP) pilot program in New York City and aimed to enroll 120 participants over the first twelve months.

Several other preliminary studies have reported poor rates of adherence and follow-up; for example, only three out of eight sexually exposed patients completed a PEP course at the Chelsea and Westminster Hospital in London (Easterbrook), and only one out of eight returned for all follow-up visits. At St Vincent's Hospital in New York, none of the six individuals who received PEP after sexual assault returned for HIV testing when the course was completed (Opio). It is worth remembering that numbers in these studies are low.

The cost-effectiveness of PEP

A major concern about PEP is cost. It could be argued that offering everybody anti-HIV drugs as a preventative measure is a lot more expensive than offering condoms. However, it could also be argued that PEP is HIV treatment rather than HIV prevention, and should therefore be paid for out of treatment budgets. A universal policy of prescribing PEP for people who have experienced any significant HIV risk exposure could never be cost-effective, even though at around £750 the cost of a month's triple combination therapy PEP for a single individual seems to compares extremely favourably with the likely life-time costs of treating the same individual should he or she become infected with HIV. The cost-effectiveness of an intervention such as PEP can only be meaningfully calculated in terms of the amount of money that would need to be spent to prevent a single infection. On average, no more than about one out of every three hundred people who have a single episode of unprotected receptive anal sex with an HIV-positive person becomes infected as a result (Katz). So if all 300 came forward for PEP after their risk exposure, 299 would be treated 'unnecessarily', because they would not have become infected regardless of whether or not they received PEP. If doctors have to treat 300 people in order to prevent the one single infection, the cost of preventing that infection would be three hundred times £750, which makes £225,000. In blunt financial terms, this no longer compares so favourably with the life-time costs of medical care.

The cost-effectiveness of PEP could be improved by using fewer or cheaper drugs; for example, if only two nucleoside analogue drugs were used (or if an additional protease inhibitor was reserved only for specific cases of the greatest risk) the cost per course of PEP would be approximately halved. Moreover, PEP would also be more cost-effective if it were delivered only to people whose circumstances meant that they were most at risk of becoming infected (effectively reducing the proportion of recipients who are being treated 'unnecessarily').

Possible criteria for prioritisation might include limiting PEP to cases in which people had a risk encounter with someone who was known for sure to be HIV-positive - even though the US guidelines for occupational use do not carry such a restriction. PEP would also become more cost-effective if offered only to people whose risk had been substantial, such as unprotected receptive anal or vaginal sex or shared drug injecting equipment.

A study published in January 2004 (Pinkerton) attempted to calculate the cost-effectiveness of PEP. Here, Pinkerton and colleagues looked at 401 people who had sought PEP in San Francisco.

The group included men and women who sought PEP for incidents of unprotected anal and/or vaginal intercourse and needle-sharing. The researchers concluded that PEP reduced expected HIV infections by 53% by calculating that, according to types of risk reported by the study participants, an average of 2.36 HIV infections would have been expected: PEP reduced this to 1.1 infections.

This 53% reduction saved 11.74 quality adjusted life years (QALYs). This measurement, frequently used in cost-benefit calculations, means that, for those that used it successfully, PEP should lead to an extra 11.74 years of reasonable health. This in turn, it was calculated, would save a total of US$281,323 in future HIV-related medical costs. When all factors were taken into account, the cost of PEP per QALY saved was US$14,449 - approximately £9,500 at the time of the study or £7,950 now.

This may sound a lot, but in the US programmes costing $40,000 - $60,000 per QALY are seen as cost-effective. By comparison, similar cost-effectiveness studies (Freedberg) showed that HIV combination therapy resulted in a cost of US$23,000 per QALY saved. There is no official figure for the UK, but it is thought that the National Institute of Clinical Excellence (NICE), which guides Primary Care Trust spending, considers anything below £30,000 per QALY saved to be cost-effective.

By including a varied population with different risks, this study found that PEP, given to the general at-risk population, did work out to be much less cost-effective than other HIV prevention methods. One risk-reduction programme for at-risk women (Holtgrave 1996) attending an urban primary healthcare clinic was successful at increasing condom use and cost about US$260 per client or about US$2,000 per QALY. A similar programme for gay men, (Holtgrave 1997), although costing US$470 per client, was not only cost-effective but actually cost-saving: the cost of likely future treatment and care of those infected without the programme outweighed the cost of delivering the programme to the whole group. This compares with an average cost of US$8,607 per QALY saved for PEP for gay men as a whole, as reported by Pinkerton.

However, when it came to gay men who had been on the receiving end of unprotected anal sex (i.e. 'bottoms'), the Pinkerton study found that PEP was not merely cost-effective, but actually cost-saving. The cost per infection averted for this group was US$177,293 - which is less than the likely cost of their lifetime HIV treatment if they had not received successful PEP. On the other hand, PEP for gay men on the insertive end of unprotected anal sex (i.e. 'tops') was not considered cost-effective.

The variation seen in cost-effectiveness between subgroups of different populations is not surprising, given that you need to provide PEP to the people most at-risk for it to be cost-effective. The Health Protection Agency (HPA) estimates that gay men who are the passive partner in unprotected anal intercourse have a 1-in-33 risk of being infected with HIV if they are certain their partner is HIV-positive, but a 1-in-222 risk if they do not know the HIV status of their partner. They estimate that gay men who are the active partner in unprotected anal intercourse have a 1-in-555 risk of being infected with HIV if they are certain their partner is HIV-positive, but a 1-in-11,111 risk if they do not know the HIV status of their partner. However, other factors such as geographical location, STIs, viral load and bleeding may affect the risk estimate, so there is likely to be a range of risk of transmission rather than an exact value.

In short, if PEP in the UK is offered to gay men who have been the passive partner in unprotected anal intercourse and/or who have known HIV-positive partners, PEP could potentially save as much money as providing condoms and safer-sex education, as long as PEP is not routinely relied upon as a substitute for these other safer-sex practices.

Putting PEP into practice

The Australian policy on PEP for sexual exposure - the first of its kind - was first written in 1998, though a decision to actively promote PEP as a prevention tool was not taken until June 2000. The high-risk groups targeted initially were gay men and people in serodiscordant relationships; subsequently, IDUs and sex workers were also targeted.

A phoneline with the number 1-800-PEP-NOW was publicised, posters were placed in community press and information was issued in leaflets and on the web. There were 493 calls for the January-November 2001 duration of the helpline, of which 88% were direct requests for PEP. Sixty-one per cent met guidelines for PEP prescription; 28% did not because they were considered low risk, and 11% fell outside the 72-hour time limit.

Interestingly, and contrary to some other surveys, only 7.2% of callers were seeking PEP for exposure with regular partners.

In terms of community awareness of PEP, 64% of those polled in the target groups had not heard of PEP in February 2001. Six months later, 58.5% *had* heard of PEP. Triple combination therapy was prescribed at the start of the programme, but cost pressure meant that HAART was reduced to the dual nucleoside therapy, AZT/3TC.

Following on from the Australian experience, the Terrence Higgins Trust (THT) in the UK mounted an awareness raising campaign about PEP directed at gay men in 2004.

In the 2005 Gay Men's Sex survey (data collected 2004), when gay men were asked about what they considered 'risky' sex, no respondent mentioned anti-HIV treatments, viral load or post-exposure prophylaxis (PEP) as moderators of risk, suggesting these do not feature in men's perceptions of sexual risk and safety.

However, following the campaign, according to data released early from the 2006 National Gay Men's Sex Survey, gay men in the UK in 2005 were twice as likely to be aware of PEP than they were in 2003 - an increase from 22% to 39%. Awareness of PEP significantly increased in every demographic subgroup and in every area of the country, although the rise was greatest in London and Brighton, the cities most targeted by the THT's campaign.

The campaign also had a significant impact on the numbers of gay men seeking PEP, and the numbers of men being prescribed the drugs. In the UK, the proportion of gay men who had ever sought PEP increased significantly from 1.0% in 2003 to 1.4% in 2005, and the proportion who had ever actually taken PEP rose from 0.6% in 2003 to 1.2% in 2005.

Seeking PEP and taking PEP rose in all demographic groups and in all areas and remained highest in London and Brighton, among men with higher numbers of sexual partners and those with higher incomes.

Ford Hickson of Sigma Research, who conducted the research, said: "The proportion of those men who sought the treatment who went on to take it also rose significantly from 59% in 2003 to 74% in 2005, suggesting an on-going improvement in access to this service which is clearly necessary."

However, taking PEP is still very rare even among the group most at risk from HIV in the UK. Although 7.5% of men not tested HIV-positive said they thought they had been involved in sexual HIV exposure in the last year, only 1.2% of men, or 16% of those who thought they had definitely been at risk, had ever taken PEP.

Ethical and practical issues

Providing PEP after sexual or IDU exposures, then, presents different challenges than for occupational or perinatal exposures. Persons exposed to HIV from sexual or IDU activities often do not accurately assess their risk for infection and may delay seeking treatment.

Identifying a person's source partner and determining his or her HIV status after sexual exposure may be problematic.

Concerns have been raised that if PEP were provided for sexual or IDU exposure, individuals would experience unacceptable side-effects or would inadequately adhere to the treatment regimen or refuse to return for follow-up HIV testing.

Additionally, there is the concern that PEP would fail to fully suppress the virus and rapidly induce resistance to the drugs used. This risk is greatest, if people take it in the belief that they are HIV-negative when in fact they are already HIV-positive.

The point has been raised that the availability of PEP for sexual and IDU exposures might paradoxically increase risk behaviour. For this reason the San Francisco study described above included a number of sessions of risk reduction counselling.

In the study, only 10% of people seeking PEP reported an increase in risk behaviour following a PEP consultation. This compares with 74% reporting a decrease in risk behaviour and 16% no change. Health-related interventions such as PEP may therefore help capitalise on 'close calls' to motivate and sustain risk reduction.

A US survey of gay men in 1998 (Kalichman) attending a large Pride festival in Atlanta found that 3% of those surveyed had used PEP, 26% planned to use it, and 74% doubted if they would need to use PEP.

However, those planning to use PEP were more likely to have had unprotected receptive anal sex. They were also younger, less educated, more likely to have used recreational drugs and have a history of IDU.

This user profile could be seen either as a problem or as an opportunity. Does the availability of PEP mean that young, drug-using gay men have an 'excuse' not to try to maintain safer sex habits? Or, conversely, are they taking a realistic look at their behaviour and its likely risks and seizing upon a technology that may protect them?

There are also concerns about the potential cost (as opposed to cost-effectiveness) of PEP if taken up as a mass prevention measure. One of the implications of the San Francisco study is that if the entire annual US HIV prevention budget was used for PEP, it would fund 550,000 treatments and prevent a mere 880 new infections, or 2.2% of the estimated US annual incidence.

It will be difficult to define the boundary between cases of sexual risk which are high enough to justify offering PEP, and those in which the risk of infection is sufficiently low that the financial cost of PEP and the risk of drug side-effects is felt to be unjustifiable. For instance, the CDC guidelines indicate that combination therapy may be reasonable for healthcare workers who experience mucosal exposure to semen even where there are only grounds for suspicion, rather than certainty, that the source patient is HIV-positive. How does this differ from the situation of any gay man who has sex without a condom in a large city in the UK?

A 1998 review of ethical and clinical implications of PEP for non-occupational exposure concluded that it would be prudent to consider local HIV prevalence rather than relying on per-exposure risks calculated for very high prevalence cities when considering the likely need for PEP (Lurie).

How soon should PEP be used?

When used, PEP should be initiated promptly. Animal research suggests that PEP may be ineffective if started later than 24 to

36 hours after exposure. The animal study upon which this estimate is based comes from macaque monkeys given tenofovir as the sole PEP drug (Tsai 1998).

In this study, 24 macaque monkeys were divided into six groups of four. They were all given a dose of SIV (monkey HIV) ten times larger than the dose which would be expected to infect 50% of monkeys - a dose that should have infected all of them. They were then treated with tenofovir starting various times after infection and continued for various time periods. The results were as follows:

A Control group (treated only with saline, not tenofovir): 100% infected: all seroconverted by week four.

B Tenofovir started 24 hours after exposure and continued for 28 days: probably none infected (one monkey eventually showed antibodies to SIV after 32 weeks but free or cell-associated virus was not detected in any monkey).

C Tenofovir started 48 hours after exposure, continued for 28 days: all seroconverted to SIV by week 16, though virus was only detectable in 50% of monkeys.

D Tenofovir started 72 hours after exposure, continued for 28 days: all seroconverted by eight weeks, though virus only detectable in 50%.

E Tenofovir started 24 hours after exposure, continued for ten days: 50% eventually seroconverted, though virus only detectable in one (25%).

F Tenofovir started 24 hours after exposure, continued for three days: all seroconverted by eight weeks, virus detectable in 50%.

It is this study that is the basis for the recommendation that PEP should be started within 24 hours of exposure, though it may be 50% effective up to 72 hours after exposure.

A recent discussion of PEP for non-occupational risks recommends against initiating treatment more than 72 hours after the exposure (Katz), although the CDC guidelines argue that starting even one to two weeks post-exposure may be justified in cases of the highest risk. The protocol used at San Francisco General Hospital notes that "after an exposure, most healthcare workers are upset and find that decisions about treatment are very hard to make. We recommend that the exposed person start therapy. Therapy can be stopped later, after the exposed person has had a chance to talk with their clinician and loved ones. Once the immediate crisis has passed, it is usually easier to make the best decision." (San Francisco General Hospital Epi-Center). If PEP is ever to become a practical option for non-occupational exposure, a new system of 'rapid response' clinic services may be required to provide prompt access to treatment - as has indeed happened in San Francisco, where all patients seeking PEP are referred to one central clinic.

UK guidelines - the draft

In December 2004, HIV prevention experts and community activists met in London to discuss a draft of the BASHH guidelines at a round table session organised by Terrence Higgins Trust (THT).

The guidelines would cover, among other things:

- The scientific basis for recommending PEP
- A guide to calculating the risk of a given exposure
- The pros and cons of PEP as a prevention measure
- Recommended protocols
- Pathways for access
- An emphasis that PEP is only one strand in HIV prevention

The draft recommendations were as follows:

	Partner status HIV-positive	Partner status unknown
Receptive anal intercourse	Recommended	Recommended if partner high risk
Insertive anal intercourse	Recommended	Consider if partner high risk
Receptive vaginal intercourse	Recommended	Not recommended
Insertive vaginal intercourse	Recommended	Not recommended

Other factors to consider include whether either partner has a concurrent STI, the viral load in the HIV-positive partner, and whether there was sexual assault/trauma.

Draft recommendations for PEP regimens are:

	plus *either*	or
Combivir (zidovudine, AZT + lamivudine, 3TC) **or** *Zerit (stavudine, D4T) + Epivir* (lamivudine, 3TC) **or** *Truvada* (tenofovir, TDF + emtricitabine, FTC)	*Viracept* (nelfinavir)	*Kaletra* (lopinavir/ritonavir)

Although *Combivir* was suggested as one of the nucleoside components, this may be ruled out due to high rates of pre-existing HIV strains resistant to both drugs that are currently circulating within the UK. NNRTIs are not recommended because of the likelihood of short-term side-effects: central nervous system problems such as sleep disturbance and depression with efavirenz and liver toxicity with nevirapine.

Other draft recommendations included:

- 24-hour access and expertise via A&E
- Baseline HIV test mandatory
- Rapid GUM/HIV clinic referral
- Weekly follow-up during PEP period
- Three- and six-month HIV antibody test
- No limit on repeat requests, but an appointment with a psychologist or health advisor should be mandatory after several repeats.

This last recommendation contrasted with Australia's 'three strikes and you're out' policy. France and Spain allow a maximum of four and five repeats respectively.

Campaigns and controversy

The increased awareness of PEP did not go down well with some clinicians. An editorial in the journal *Sexually Transmitted Infections* in June 2005 by London HIV doctor John Richens opposed the idea of publicising PEP among gay men, saying it would increase sexual risk-taking. In the article, Dr Richens, from the London-based Centre for Sexual Health and HIV Research, said that promoting PEP could have the unintended consequence of encouraging gay men to take greater risks.

In the journal article, Dr Richens says: "There is a distinct danger that the promotion of PEP after sexual exposure could reinforce rising trends in risky sexual behaviour and might add to, rather than lessen, HIV transmission."

Richens also cites the cost of PEP as a reason to be concerned about its promotion.

Prescriptions of PEP after sexual exposure grew from 48 in 2003 to 119 in 2004 at one London clinic, the Mortimer Market Centre. Richens says that the projected drug cost to the clinic for PEP will be £180,000 at a time when sexual health clinics are already financially stretched. Dr Richens' views have been dismissed by another prominent HIV doctor, and lead author of the BASHH PEP guidelines (see below). Dr Martin Fisher of Brighton's HIV clinic said: "All available data suggest that the opposite behaviour occurs - high-risk sexual acts actually declined over time in the two studies that have examined behaviour after PEP."

He continued: "Clearly more work needs to be done on the possible effects of risk behaviour, though what work has been done to date suggests that there is not a deleterious effect."

However, Richens' views were soon to be contradicted from another quarter. In December 2005 it was announced that a groundbreaking legal action was to be launched. It accused the government of denying PEP tp people who had been sexually exposed to HIV.

A gay man (known by the pseudonym of Robert Jenkins) who firstly caught HIV from one partner and then inadvertently passed it on to another, was granted legal aid on public interest grounds to seek a Judicial Review to force the Department of Health to implement a national policy for PEP, and get the guidelines being written by BASHH to say that PEP should be available 24 hours a day at casualty departments and should be provided for all who have been at significant risk.

Jenkins said that widespread public ignorance of PEP for sexual exposure to HIV is leading unknown numbers to be unnecessarily infected with HIV. Jenkins passed on the virus to his partner after a condom split. Both were unaware of PEP and say that had they been, at least one and possibly both would not have been infected.

The BASHH Guidelines

In February 2006 the guidelines were eventually issued. They recommended that PEP should be provided on a 24-hour basis at casualty departments.

Any gay man presenting who was the passive partner in anal sex without a condom should be provided with PEP, they recommend, regardless of whether the partner is known to have HIV. The same would apply to heterosexuals having vaginal or anal sex who are from groups that have a high risk of having HIV, particularly people from sub-Saharan Africa.

Where the partner is known to have HIV, PEP should be provided for any sexual intercourse without condoms or where there has been a condom accident, whether the sex was anal or vaginal, active or passive, and PEP should also be 'considered' for oral sex where ejaculation into the mouth has occurred, again regardless of the partner's HIV status.

It is not recommended for oral sex without ejaculation, cunnilingus or any sex other than being the passive partner in anal sex where

the partner's status is unknown and they come from a group with low HIV prevalence, such as white UK heterosexuals.

Here is a summary of the full recommendations as they eventually appeared:

Source individual is known to be HIV-positive	
Receptive anal sex	Recommended
Insertive anal sex	Recommended
Receptive vaginal sex	Recommended
Insertive vaginal sex	Recommended
Fellatio with ejaculation	Considered
Splash of semen into eye	Considered
Fellation without ejaculation	Not recommended
Cunnilingus	Not recommended

Source individual is of unknown status and from a group or area of high HIV prevalence (>10%) *Attempt should be made, where possible, to establish the HIV status of the source individual (according to appropriate guidance on HIV testing and cosent) as early as possible.	
Receptive anal sex	Recommended
Insertive anal sex	Recommended
Receptive vaginal sex	Recommended
Insertive vaginal sex	Recommended
Fellatio with ejaculation	Considered

Source individual is not from the group of area of high HIV prevalence	
Receptive anal sex	Considered
Insertive anal sex	Not recommended
Receptive vaginal sex	Not recommended
Insertive vaginal sex	Not recommended
Fellatio with ejaculation	Not recommended

The drug regimens recommended were the same as in the draft guidelines, with the exception that boosted fosamprenavir (*Telzir*) or boosted saquinavir (*Invirase*) are added to the boosted-PI column alongside *Kaletra*.

PEP "is only recommended where the individual presents within 72 hours of exposure," the guidelines say, though they add that PEP "may be considered after this time if the exposure is 'high risk'". However, the efficacy of PEP is thought to diminuish very substantially more than 72 hours after exposure.

The importance of 24-hour access is underlined by the fact that the average time to giving PEP after an occupational exposure such as a needle-stick accident to a medical worker in the UK is only two hours, whereas in cases of sexual exposure it is 23 hours.

Studies in animals have shown that PEP can be up to 100% effective if it is given within 24 hours and a course of tablets is taken for four weeks. It failed half the time if it was taken three days after exposure or where the course was only for ten days.

HIV is found in the lymph nodes 2-3 days after transmission and in the blood after five days, which is generally seen as evidence of established infection.

People who visit casualty should be given 'starter packs' consisting of *Combivir* (AZT/3TC) or *Truvada* and nelfinavir or *Truvada* (tenofovir/FTC) to tide them over the first few days until a proper assessment can be made of their degree of risk, the guidelines say. All people coming forward for PEP must be tested for HIV in case of previous infection (and because giving PEP could cause drug resistance), and "strong efforts" should be made to establish the HIV status of the source partner if this is not known for certain.

The guidelines say that people who present repeatedly for PEP should not be penalised but should be "considered for repeat courses according to the risk of HIV acquisition at the time of presentation," particularly if their life situation means that they are exposed to a degree of regular risk (such as the negative partner of a positive person, a sex worker, or someone unable to get their partner to use condoms). However all repeat presenters should be encouraged to see a health advisor or psychologist, and people who present more than once a year "who do not otherwise have prevailing circumstances for doing so" should be told that PEP is conditional "on their attendance for discussions around future safer sex strategies"

The guidelines end by setting targets for PEP: at least 90% of prescriptions should be filled within 72 hours and should fall within the 'recommended' criteria; at least 75% of individuals should complete their four-week course; and at least 60% should get HIV tests done three and six months after presenting themselves.

PEP will never replace other HIV prevention strategies, the authors emphasise. They say: "It is crucial to consider PEP as only one strategy in preventing HIV infection and, as such, it should be considered as a last measure where conventional, and proven, methods of HIV prevention have failed."

The 2006 UK Guidelines for PEP after sexual exposure can be read at http://www.bashh.org/guidelines/2006/pepse_0206.pdf

It is a good idea for people seeking PEP to print them out and take them with them if they need to ask for PEP at a hospital A&E department, and they may help at some GUM Departments. When the GUM clinic is open, patients should tell reception they need to be seen immediately as an emergency appointment for PEP because of exposure to HIV. If the GUM clinic is not open, patients should go as soon as possible to the hospital's A&E department with the guidelines or take a piece of paper with the web address of the guidance.

THT Direct can advise patients who have problems getting PEP while they are still at the A&E or GUM. They can also ask the hospital worker to speak to THT Direct if this would help - 0845 12 21 200 [open Monday to Friday 10am - 10pm, Saturday and Sunday 12noon to 6pm].

Access is still difficult

About one in six gay men who seek PEP after an HIV risk may still be getting turned away 'inappropriately', according to Sigma Research (see Delpech for reference).

Sigma's Julie Dodds told the conference that five out of 30 PEP seekers Sigma interviewed about their experiences were turned away. Four of the five were denied it by A&E staff but a fifth was told flatly by a GUM clinic health advisor that 'There is no such thing as PEP'. Most interviewees had sought PEP in the six months previous to Dodds' presentation, so this was not an old phenomenon.

Altogether eight out of the 30 people Sigma interviewed in detail were turned away for PEP. In three cases, Dodds commented, the refusals were probably appropriate as the men had not understood that they were at low risk, and there were still cases of people getting PEP inappropriately too (for instance following oral sex without getting semen in the mouth).

However most gay men who sought PEP did so for good reasons. Four of the five who were turned away had had unsafe anal sex as the passive partner - in one case with someone known to be HIV-positive. In the fifth case the seeker was the active partner with a known positive person.

Even when given PEP, some men found the experience humiliating: "The GUM doctor said 'You know it costs a lot of money; if we give it to you this time, we won't give it to you again,'" said one person.

Three others had phoned the NHS Direct helpline to clarify their risk and were met with advisors who had never heard of PEP.

Kay Orton, head of HIV and Health Promotion Services at the Department of Health, was in the audience and said the training deficit at NHS Direct had already been addressed and that she hoped the publication of the BASHH guidelines would lead to better decision-making by casualty staff.

In general, however, both gay men's awareness of PEP and their success in getting it has improved.

Another survey suggested doctors in the USA were also prescribing PEP inappropriately or misunderstood their own guidelines. The Thirteenth Conference on Retroviruses and Opportunistic Infections (CROI) was told that the majority of calls to a helpline set up to advise doctors about non-occupational post-exposure prophylaxis (PEP) against HIV were made too late to offer much or any benefit to the person exposed.

Amy Kindrick of the National HIV/AIDS Clinicians' Consultation Centre reviewed all calls regarding sexual exposures made to the National Clinicians' PEP Hotline between January 2004 and September 2005. She said that 55% of calls were made more than 24 hours after the patient's exposure to HIV and that 28% of them were made more than 72 hours after exposure. Only 32% were definitely made within 24 hours of the exposure.

Altogether 918 calls concerning specific sexual exposures, excluding follow-up calls, were made to the helpline during the study period. Although the majority (58%) were made by doctors, most of these physicians were not experienced in giving PEP: only 12% had ever managed more than ten cases. Nearly a third of calls were made from A&E departments.

Clinicians did appear to assess exposure risk reasonably accurately. 54.6% of calls were made about exposures deemed by the investigators to be 'high risk' and only 4.8% were low risk. In 30.4% of cases the source partner was known to have HIV. The main types of sexual risk were receptive vaginal intercourse (38.7%) and receptive anal intercourse by a man (21.3%). However calls concerning oral sex (9.6%) were more common than ones concerning insertive anal intercourse (5.1%) even though this is probably more risky, and nearly as common as all calls concerning insertive sex (9.8%).

However it was the fact that only a third of calls were made within time to start PEP optimally that mainly concerned the investigators.

In a poster discussion on several studies concerning PEP and exposure counselling, chair Michelle Roland, author of the San Francisco study cited above, commented: "People still get the wrong message, which is: 'You have 72 hours to start PEP'. The message should be: 'You should start PEP as soon as possible'. You can always stop taking PEP if the risk is re-assessed; you can't 'have started' it."

PEP-related counselling

Michelle Roland (Roland 2006) discussed the sexual risk reduction counselling that accompanied PEP. She studied outcomes, in terms of reduction in unprotected sex acts twelve months after counselling compared with baseline, in 457 people given PEP in 2001-2002. Previous practice had been to offer five risk reduction counselling sessions during which clients were asked to discuss circumstances around the exposure, contrast it with times they had felt in control of their sexual safety, and determine what level of risk they were happy with.

Her study found that two sessions of counselling achieved a statistically significant reduction in risk exposures among 'lower risk' patients (defined as having had risky sex no more than four times before the request for PEP), but that it took five sessions to achieve a reduction in risk among patients who had had more exposures. Roland commented that despite very active outreach during the study period to high-risk environments such as sex parties and a documented increase in risky behaviour during that time, there was no increase in requests for or provision of PEP.

International guidelines

A review (Vitoria) of guidelines for the use of both occupational and non-occupational PEP from 41 countries, conducted by the World Health Organization., showed:

- All but one country had developed PEP guidelines, though 28% had only done so for occupational exposure. Forty-three countries had a national register of PEP use.

- Sixty per cent of countries recommended dual or triple regimens with only 40% recommending only triple ones.

- Fifteen per cent did not specify a four-week course as optimal and 10% did not specify a 'window' after exposure in which to prescribe PEP.

European guidelines

Guidelines for post-exposure prophylaxis (PEP) following non-occupational exposure were published by the European Project on Non-Occupational Post-exposure Prophylaxis in June 2004 (Almeda).

The guidelines recommend PEP following unprotected receptive anal sex and needle or syringe exchange when the source person is known to be HIV-positive or from a group with high HIV prevalence. They state that it should be considered after vaginal sex or insertive anal sex with someone known to be HIV-positive, as well as following receptive oral sex with ejaculation or a splash of semen into the eye from an HIV-positive source. However, following rape or other high-risk factors, such as bleeding, ulcers around the genitals or in the mouth or sexually transmitted infections, PEP should be used more readily.

Unlike British guidelines, the European guidelines state that any combination of drugs licensed for HIV-infected patients can be used, with the simplest and least toxic combinations being preferred. Triple-drug combinations are preferred, two drugs may be an option. They also recommend efavirenz (Sustiva) for people who are not pregnant, despite the drug's possible side-effects. However, if the source is known to be HIV-positive and treatment history can be obtained or a resistance test carried out, the results may be used to determine the best choice of drugs for PEP.

PEP should be started within 72 hours of exposure, starting as early as possible and lasting four weeks, with recipients receiving medical attention and counselling for at least six months.

United States guidelines

Unlike the United Kingdom guidelines, the guidelines from the United States state that any triple-drug antiretroviral regimen approved by the Department of Health and Human Services may be used. They also suggest that a dual nucleoside reverse transcriptase inhibitor (NRTI) regimen may be sufficient, as there is no evidence for the increased effectiveness of an extra drug, particularly in the face of increased risk of side-effects.

Preferred regimens include efavirenz (Sustiva) with 3TC (lamivudine, Epivir) or FTC (emtricitabine, Emtriva) and AZT (zidovudine, Retrovir) or tenofovir (Viread), and ritonavir-boosted lopinavir (Kaletra) with AZT and either 3TC

or FTC. This may be modified if details of the source patient's treatment history or resistance profile are available. The United States' guidelines recommend the avoidance of nevirapine and efavirenz in women of childbearing age.

As in other guidelines, the United States recommendations include care for patients for up to six months following exposure, to determine whether HIV infection has occurred, as well as tests for hepatitis B and C co-infection, sexually transmitted infections and pregnancy.

While European and United States' guidelines agree that treatment should be given for 28 days when the source is known to be HIV-positive, they differ when the source's HIV status is unknown. European guidelines recommend treatment following unprotected receptive anal sex or following unprotected anal, vaginal or oral sex with ejaculation with a person from a group or an area of high HIV prevalence (more than 15%). If the source is not from a group or an area with a high HIV prevalence, PEP is only recommended following unprotected receptive anal sex (Blackham). In contrast, the United States recommendations suggest deciding whether to administer PEP on a case-by-case basis.

References

The 2006 UK Guidelines for PEP after sexual exposure can be read at http://www.bashh.org/guidelines/2006/pepse_0206.pdf

Ackers ML et al. *Post-exposure prophylaxis among HIV-uninfected participants in a phase III HIV vaccine efficacy trial.* XIV International AIDS Conference, Barcelona, abstract WePpD2105, 2002.

Almeda J et al. *Proposed recommendations for the management of HIV post-exposure prophylaxis after sexual, injecting drug or other expsoures in Europe.* Euro Surveillance 9: 35-40, 2004.

Blackham J et al. *Differences between new United States recommendations and existing European guidelines on the use of postexposure prophylaxis (PEP) following non-occupational exposure,* Euro Surveillance 10: 3, 2005

Cardo DM et al. *A case-control study of HIV seroconversion in health care workers after precutaneous exposure to HIV-infected blood: clinical and public health implications.* N Engl J Med 337: 1485-1490, 1997

Delpech V. *PEP: the bigger picture.* Presentation at Nineth CHAPS Conference, Leeds, United Kingdom, 2006.

Dodds C et al. *PEPSeekers: Men's experiences of accessing PEP following sexual exposure.* Nineth CHAPS Conference, Leeds, United Kingdom, 2006.

Easterbrook P et al. *Post-exposure prophylaxis for occupational and sexual exposures to HIV: experience in a London hospital.* Twelfth World AIDS Conference, Geneva, abstract 33176, 1998.

Freedberg KA et al. *The cost effectiveness of combination antiretroviral therapy for HIV disease.* N Engl J Med 344: 824-831. 2001.

Henderson DK and Gerberding JL. *Prophylactic zidovudine after occupational exposure to the human immunodeficiency virus: an interim analysis.* J Infect Dis. 160(2): 321-327, 1989.

HIV Post Exposure Prophylaxis: Guidance from the UK Chief Medical Officers' Expert Advisory Group on AIDS. Department of Health, July 2000.

Holtgrave DR, Kelly JA. *Preventing HIV/AIDS among high-risk urban women: the cost-effectiveness of a behavioral group intervention.* Am J Public Health 86: 1442 -1445, 1996.

Holtgrave DR, Kelly JA. *The cost-effectiveness of an HIV prevention intervention for gay men.* AIDS Behav 1: 173 -180. 1997.

Jackson JB et al. *Nevirapine prophylaxis for prevention of sexual/blood HIV transmission in HIV uninfected subjects.* Fourteenth International AIDS Conference, Barcelona, abstract MoOrD1105, 2002.

Kalichman SC. *Post-exposure prophylaxis for HIV infection in gay and bisexual men: implications for the future of HIV prevention.* Am J Prev Med. 15(2): 120-127, 1998.

Kahn J et al. *Feasibility of post-exposure prophylaxis (PEP) against human immunodeficiency virus infection after sexual or injection drug use exposure: The San Francisco PEP study.* Journal of Infectious Diseases 183: 707-714, 2001.

Katz M et al. *Postexposure treatment of people exposed to the human immunodeficiency virus through sexual contact or injection-drug use.* New England Journal of Medicine 336: 1097-1100, 1997.

Kindrick A et al. *HIV post-exposure prophylaxis following sexual exposure is started too late for optimal benefit.* Thirteenth Conference on Retroviruses and Opportunistic Infections, Denver, abstract #906, 2006.

Lurie P et al. *Postexposure prophylaxis after nonoccupational HIV exposure: clinical, ethical and policy considerations.* Journal of the American Medical Association 280: 1769-1773, 1998.

Mauss S et al. *Rapid development of central adiposity after postexposure prophylaxis with antiretroviral drugs: a proof of principle?* AIDS 17: 944 - 955, 2003.

McLeod A et al. *Absenteeism adds significant cost to HIV needlestick prophylaxis.* Fourteenth International AIDS Conference, Barcelona, abstract TuPeE5167, 2002.

Opio G et al. *Post-sexual exposure prophylaxis with HAART after sexual assault.* Twelfth World AIDS Conference, Geneva, abstract 33174, 1998.

Pinkerton SD et al. *Cost-effectiveness of Postexposure Prophylaxis after Sexual or Injection-Drug Exposure to Human Immunodeficiency Virus.* Arch Intern Med 164: 46-54, 2004.

Rabaud C et al. *Post-exposure prophylaxis of HIV infection: comparison of tolerability of 4 PEP regimens.* Thirteenth Conference on Retroviruses and Opportunistic Infections, Denver, abstract #905, 2006.

Roland ME at al. *Seroconversion following nonoccupational postexposure prophylaxis against HIV.* Clin Infect Dis. 15: 41(10): 1507-1513, 2005.

Roland ME et al. *A randomized trial of standard versus enhanced risk reduction counseling for individuals receiving post-exposure prophylaxis following sexual exposure to HIV.* Thirteenth Conference on Retroviruses and Opportunistic Infections, Denver, abstract #902, 2006.

Sigma Research. *Risk and reflexion: findings from the United Kingdom Gay Men's Sex Survey 2004.* Sigma Research, 2005 (ISBN 1 872956 81 5).

Smith DK et al. *Antiretroviral postexposure prophylaxis after sexual, injection-drug use, or other nonoccupational exposure to HIV in the United States.* MMWR Recomm Rep 54: 1-20, 2005.

Stephenson J. *PEP talk: treating nonoccupational HIV exposure.* JAMA 289: 287-288, 2003.

Tsai, CC et al. *Prevention of SIV infection in macaques by (R)-9-(2-phosphonylmethoxypropyl)adenine.* Science 270: 1197-1199. 1995.

Tsai CC et al. *Effectiveness of postinoculation (R)-9-(2-phosphonylmethoxypropyl)adenine treatment for prevention of persistent simian immunodeficiency virus SIVmne infection depends critically on timing of initiation and duration of treatment.* J Virol 72: 4265-4273, 1998.

Torres R et al. *Preliminary report on nonoccupational post-exposure prophylaxis utilizing an NNRTI/NRTI regimen.* Thirteenth International AIDS Conference, Durban, abstract TuPeB3204, 2000.

Vitoria M et al. *Guidelines for post-exposure prophylaxis for HIV in developing countries.* Thirteenth Conference on Retroviruses and Opportunistic Infections, Denver, abstract #904, 2006.

Vittinghoff E et al. *Per-contact risk of human immunodeficiency virus transmission between male sexual partners.* American J of Epidemiology 150: 306-311, 1999.

Pre-exposure prophylaxis: the challenge

The most challenging option that is emerging is to use antiretrovirals (ARVs) to prevent sexual transmission, by giving them for extended periods to HIV-negative people at high risk.

In some populations, the risk of HIV infection may be so high that even with some of the current ARV drugs, people may choose to take the drug if it can prevent HIV transmission. PrEP is envisaged to be used solely by people who may be at frequent risk for HIV. This includes high-risk behaviour groups such as commercial sex workers, injecting drug users and people who have unsafe sex with a multiple partners.

As their names suggest, with post- and pre-exposure prophylaxis we are doing something very similar in both cases; using chemoprophylaxis to prevent an HIV infection establishing itself.

When Che-Chung Tsai did his original experiments using tenofovir to block HIV infections in monkeys, he gave his monkeys the drug at four different times relative to injecting them with SIV. He gave ten of them PEP five or 24 hours after infection. But he also gave 15 of them PrEP, 24 or 48 hours before infection.

Within these boundaries, the timing didn't greatly matter. In Tsai's initial experiments, all the macaques were protected.

And yet 'before' is a lot more controversial than 'after'. When we move from PEP to PrEP we are crossing a huge gulf in terms of how much we already know about whether the concept can work and about its eventual implications.

As we have seen, PEP itself is not an area lacking controversy. But it is the established, short-term emergency use of antiretrovirals by the already exposed that will probably never make more than a minor contribution to HIV prevention on a population scale. Also, as an emergency measure, PEP escapes some of the moral complexity that attends some other prevention methods; everyone can understand why someone might seek help to avoid the consequences of accidental exposure.

But to take expensive antiretrovirals *in anticipation* that you will indulge in risky behaviour? As Bill Gates said at the Seattle CROI Conference when first introduced to the concept in 2002, "Wouldn't it just be simpler if they used condoms?"

PrEP, which has never been properly tried except in an 'underground' way (see below), is an idea that even its advocates acknowledge is radical and fraught with potential difficulties. It would mean giving HIV-negative people potentially toxic antiretroviral drugs, not in order to prevent an infection they have been exposed to, but in order to prevent an infection they might *never* be exposed to - or which they could avoid by other means.

With vaccines we are talking about a one-off medical intervention (or, at worst, a series of shots that might need boosting now and then) which then requires no further 'adherence' by the subject in order to be effective.

With microbicides we are talking about something that will require adherence but which, it is intended, will be a benign substance that can be bought over the counter or given out. Even microbicides that contain antiretrovirals will be rigorously tested to make sure that they do not create any topical or systemic toxicity, and that they do not penetrate beyond that mucosa where they might cause resistance in a person who is already HIV-positive.

But with PrEP we are talking about a highly medicalised intervention, dispensed by a healthcare worker, that has the potential both to create systemic toxicity and HIV drug resistance and will therefore never (or should never) be sold over the counter.

It's also an obviously expensive prevention option (if you take it all the time).

This begs huge questions:

- Who would get it?

- Why not help people use other interventions instead, like condoms?

- Who would decide who gets it?

- How would it be distributed?

- What would be the consequences of a proportion (probably the most high-risk proportion) of the HIV-negative population being on antiretrovirals?

- Which drugs should we use?

- Do we currently have *any* antiretrovirals whose safety we are sufficiently comfortable with to allow them to be given to HIV-negative people as a preventative measure?

- What is the potential for drug resistance, given that it will be almost impossible to ensure that people who are seroconverting never take it?

- What are the cost implications, not just of the drugs but of things like viral load tests, which are implied in order to make sure we give PrEP to as few seroconverters as possible?

- As we have already explored, the usefulness of a New Prevention Technology will vanish if people abandon other proven, and possibly safer, measures such as condoms in favour of the new idea. If PrEP is not 100% effective, how do we explain to vulnerable populations?

- How do we do ethical trials of the concept?

The need for PrEP

And yet PrEP is also an obvious idea. What could be simpler - if it works - than popping a pill which could protect you against HIV? *If* such a measure was highly effective, *if* it was economically feasible, *if* it was safe and *if* the right people took it at the right time we might have something as effective as a vaccine, but here and now, in the shape of a pill you can hold in your hand.

There are historical precedents for the idea of PrEP. The classic one is the use of quinine against malaria.

Henry Hobhouse's book *The Seeds of Change* describes how six crucial plant products have shaped the history of colonialism. He gives pride of place to quinine, the anti-malaria drug which, as an ingredient of the 'tonic water' sipped by colonial Colonels, enabled the white man to conquer parts of the world where previously his life had been made impossible by malaria.

There would be a sense of historical justice if we could find a drug that could protect the developing world's native people from

a deadly disease that retards economic development as effectively as quinine protected its colonisers.

There are good reasons that testing PrEP as a concept should be an urgent priority.

The main reasons are those that also apply to microbicides. Condoms are frequently not used even by high-risk populations; women are unable to enforce condom use by men or may be unaware they are at risk. The most frequent number of sex partners young women under 20 in South Africa with HIV have had is just one. A recent survey from Andhra Pradesh in India showed that half of men who have sex with men had unprotected anal sex both with other men and with their wives.

PrEP has additional advantages. It involves using a pill that exists right now rather than developing new compounds and methods of application. It would be more discreet and user-controlled than either a condom or a microbicide. It could be taken well in advance of any sex or even afterwards.

In addition, the efficacy of the first generation of microbicides is forecast even by the most optimistic researchers to be no more than 60%.

There is a crucial kind of sex those candidate microbicides are not designed for - anal sex. Microbicides for rectal use pose considerably greater design, toxicity and testing challenges than vaginal ones. They are also an even less popular target for research funding. So far only a few small animal trials have tested the concept, and one acceptability trial, using a neutral gel, has taken place in gay men in Boston.

In addition, PrEP could maybe prevent transmission through needle sharing, which a microbicide could not.

There are, in short, populations who, like the intended users of microbicides, cannot or will not use condoms for social, economic or psychological reasons, but who are also unlikely to benefit from at least the first generation of microbicides, One argument for testing PrEP is that to do otherwise would be to disrespect the human rights of sexual and drug-injecting minorities who would get left behind if vaginal microbicide use becomes widespread.

'Doing a T' - underground PrEP

Some of the urgency around getting the concept of PrEP tested is fuelled by evidence that members of high-risk communities are already trying the concept out.

A study of gay men attending minority-ethnic gay pride events in four US cities (Kellerman), presented at the International AIDS Society Conference in Rio in 2005, found surprisingly high levels of HIV-negative gay men who've taken antiretrovirals in order to try and avoid HIV.

The researchers asked 1,046 people attending gay pride events in San Francisco, Oakland, Baltimore and Detroit: "Have you ever used AIDS medicines before engaging in risky behaviour because you thought it would reduce your chances of getting HIV?"

It also asked if they had heard of the PrEP concept at all.

The group questioned was quite mixed, with 7% being women, 18% saying they were heterosexual and 17% bisexual. Over 40% were black, reflecting the events where the research was done, with other ethnic groups represented evenly.

A quarter of those questioned had heard of PrEP and seven per cent had actually taken it (presumably 'borrowing' HIV-positive friends' pills).

The figures were higher in San Francisco and Baltimore, where nine per cent had taken PrEP, with only three per cent taking it in Oakland.

There was evidence that PrEP was an 'underground' phenomenon used by people who didn't believe everything they heard about HIV. People who'd taken it were more likely to believe that they had been tested for HIV without being told, or that HIV is a man-made virus. They were also less trusting of HIV information from official prevention agencies.

The researchers comment that the percentage of gay pride attendees who had taken PrEP was "surprising".

They add that further surveys should be done to find out "what medications are being taken, on what schedule they are being taken, from where they are obtained, and whether their use is associated with higher-risk sexual behaviours."

The Centers for Disease Control in the USA explicitly cited safety concerns around this practice as one of the reasons to mount the study of tenofovir PrEP in 400 gay men it is currently conducting in San Francisco and Atlanta (see below).

An article in the *Los Angeles Times* in December 2005 (Costello) reported that tenofovir was being sold in packets along with *Viagra* and ecstasy in gay dance clubs.

Costello interviewed one physician who already prescribed tenofovir to very high-risk patients. Marc Conant, an HIV doctor in San Francisco, said he recently began prescribing tenofovir to two uninfected men after they told him they were very sexually active and would not use condoms. Though troubled by the fact that the drug had not been proven effective for such a use and that his patients might be increasing their risky behavior while using it, he told the LA Times that using the drug was better than taking no precaution at all.

"What choice do I have? Forty-thousand people are still getting infected every year," he said. "Everyone knows condoms work, but they're not using them. All I am trying to do is reduce the risk that people harm themselves."

Part of the problem with this kind of use is that even if tenofovir is more effective than some animal studies might suggest, no trial so far has tested the efficacy of occasional use - so-called 'disco dosing' or 'taking a T'. While this might be advantageous in terms of reducing toxicity and the possibility of resistance, it is also as dependent as condom or microbicide use on patients' estimates of the risk they are running or likely to run - one of the factors continuous PrEP use was supposed to avoid.

The evidence so far

However, while it is crucial to start preparing answers for these questions now if we are to turn PrEP into a reality, we have to answer one question first. Does it work?

The answer is that we simply don't know. The few trials of the idea mounted so far have given contradictory results.

Back in 1994, the 15 (out of 35) macaques that were given tenofovir pre-exposure prophylaxis by Tsai were completely protected. This created strong initial hopes that it might be a very effective prevention measure indeed

Ten years later, at a study presented to the twelveth Retrovirus Conference (Subbarao), these hopes appeared to be dashed.

The US Centers for Disease Control gave 12 rhesus macaques either placebo, a daily dose of tenofovir, or a weekly dose.

However they also mimicked human anal sex more accurately than Tsai had done. He injected his macaques with a single massive dose of SIV. Subbarao introduced SIV repeatedly - as a weekly 'rectal inoculation'.

In this study, tenofovir delayed but did not stop infection in any monkey. Half the non-treated monkeys were infected after the first inoculation of SIV, whereas it took seven inoculations to infect half the treated monkeys. However, all the monkeys were infected after 15 inoculations, and all but one after 12.

The researchers put an optimistic spin on the results by saying that the study 'delayed infection by 85%'. But another way of saying it would be that it stopped zero per cent of infections.

Which study is more likely to reflect the effectiveness of PrEP in the real world? We don't know. There were about 400,000 SIV viral particles in each millilitre of the rectal inoculation. This is a 'viral load' three to five times higher than the maximum normally recorded in people who have acute HIV infection, when they are at their most infections, and 26-60 times higher than the usual viral load in chronic infection. We also don't know if the results would be the same for a vaginal sex model.

The following year at the Thirteenth Conference of Retroviruses and Opportunistic Infections (CROI), the pendulum swung back again. As with HIV treatment, there is a scientific rationale that using more than one drug may confer a higher level of protection than single-drug pre-exposure prophylaxis (PrEP). The benefits of this approach, often called 'combo-PrEP' have yet to be proven in humans.

A study (Garcia-Lerma) by the United States National Institutes of Health (NIH) tested daily intramuscular injections of high-doses of tenofovir (*Viread*) combined with the nucleoside reverse transcriptase inhibitor (NRTI) FTC (emtricitabine, *Emtriva*). All six macaques given tenofovir and FTC were protected following four rectal challenges with simian / human immunodeficiency virus (SHIV). Even after ten further exposures, all of the treated monkeys remained uninfected. In contrast, five of the six control monkeys, which received no treatment, seroconverted. This supported the effectiveness of the combo-PrEP used in this study.

Interestingly, when the experiment was repeated with FTC alone, two of the six monkeys became infected, demonstrating a weaker protective effect with FTC as monotherapy. It is important to remember that these animals were injected with treatment at higher doses than the normal oral therapeutic dose and so this finding is not directly analogous to the response that may be expected in humans. However, it is an important first study of the effectiveness of a combination of tenofovir and FTC in this monkey model. Trials in humans will be essential to validate these initial findings.

PrEP has, of course, been tried successfully on the most vulnerable of populations, new-born babies. As we point out above, in any single-dose nevirapine strategy, the drug is working not by suppressing HIV in the mother but by crossing the placental barrier and acting as prophylaxis in the foetus.

However among a large number of mother-to-child-transmission prevention studies have been some that included giving antiretrovirals to the baby after birth but not the mother. This effectively represents PrEP for infants against HIV transmission through breast milk.

The SIMBA trial in Southern Africa, for instance, gave AZT+ddI to the mothers from 36 weeks of pregnancy to one week after giving birth.

It then gave nevirapine or 3TC to the babies from birth until four weeks after weaning, with the mothers committing to breastfeed for only six months.

The 'late transmission rate' in babies (meaning infection from four weeks to six months after birth) was only one per cent, compared with a usual rate of around nine per cent, thus reflecting a PrEP efficacy in this case of around 80%.

Efficacy trials

So, so far, the evidence for PrEP has been very conflicting. As a result several US-based institutes - Family Health International, the Centers for Disease Control, and the National Institutes of Health - started trials of tenofovir as HIV prophylaxis in nine different countries - the USA and Peru (in gay men), Malawi (in 'high risk' men), Thailand (in injecting drug users), Botswana (young adults) and Cameroon, Nigeria, Ghana and Cambodia ('high risk' women including sex workers).

These nine trials between them would have involved 9,000 volunteers. This may sound a lot, but they are distributed among several risk groups (female sex workers, injecting drug users, and gay men) and none are as big as any of the phase III microbicide trials currently recruiting or about to start.

In fact some of these trials were halted prematurely, for reasons we explore below. What we have left at present are three studies of tenofovir as PrEP:

- A study of high-risk women in Ghana, sponsored by Family Health International and funded by the Bill & Melinda Gates Foundation (800 volunteers, expected to report 2007)

- A study of injection drug users in Thailand, sponsored by the United States Centers for Disease Control and Prevention (CDC) (1,600 volunteers, expected late 2007).

- A study of gay men in the United States, also sponsored by the CDC. This with 400 volunteers, is too small to produce a meaningful result as an efficacy study and is purely intended as a safety study.

Following recent promising data in monkeys, two other studies are being considered to test the combination of tenofovir and FTC (emtricitabine, *Emtriva*) to prevent HIV transmission. These include a CDC-funded study in Botswana focused particularly on sexual transmission in young adults, and a trial in Peru involving 1,400 gay men. These could be the first trials to test combination PrEP in humans.

It is hoped that these trials will help determine whether tenofovir, with or without FTC, is safe to use in uninfected individuals and whether it helps to prevent HIV. However, there is a risk that they may be too small to provide definitive answers, particularly since ethical considerations dictate that trial participants be counselled on how to reduce their risk of contracting HIV.

Trial problems

So we need more trials. But in fact, two trials have now been stopped permanently, two are not currently recruiting more volunteers (though it is following up those already recruited), and another has gone ahead in the teeth of bitter activist opposition.

Trials of tenofovir PrEP were prematurely halted at two sites, Cambodia and Cameroon, because activists were concerned that trial participants may not be offered antiretroviral therapy should they become infected during the study. Concerns were also raised about the provision of independent counselling on safer sex and injection practices and the availability of condoms and sterile needles.

Tenofovir trials at two further sites were stopped on different grounds. In Nigeria, the sites were not able to comply with the appropriate laboratory and clinical conditions needed for the safe conduct of the trial, while in Malawi, there were broader concerns regarding the ability of the government to implement PrEP if it were proven effective.

The first time the wider world became aware of trouble was when Womyn's Agenda for Change, an advocacy group for Cambodian sex workers, supported by the French activist group ACT-UP, demonstrated against the Cambodian trial at the Bangkok World AIDS Conference in 2004.

On 12 August 2004, after an intervention from the Cambodian Prime Minister, the trial was stopped.

On 31 January, a community meeting between Thai drug users and the researchers of the Thai study broke up after protests that people were being coerced to participate and that tenofovir was being offered as a second-best to needle exchange.

On 3 February 2005, after a French TV documentary questioning the ethics of the trial in Cameroon and demonstrations by ACT-UP had taken place in Paris outside the Cameroon embassy, this trial was suspended, with the country's health minister saying he was going to investigate the trial. On 22 February participant follow-up resumed, but no further recruitment was undertaken.

On 16 March Family Health International itself cancelled the Nigeria trial (leaving only the Malawi and Ghana arms of the trial intact) saying that local researchers had failed to meet "necessary scientific standards."

On March 30, the Centers for Disease Control announced that the Botswana and Bangkok trial was 'to start soon'

In April, the trial among drug users in Bangkok began recruiting. The small US trial in gay men (only 200 volunteers apiece in Atlanta and San Francisco) has been recruiting for some time. The Peru trial is yet to start.

The Malawi trial, among high-risk men, was due to start in September 2005 but was halted by the government very soon after recruitment started due to concerns that it would foster HIV resistance to tenofovir, which they are now using in second-line treatment.

Lessons learned

What happened here? Among accusations and counter-accusations, a number of issues stand out.

In some cases the scientific reservations that cause trials to be cancelled are valid. Tenofovir resistance, for instance, is a real concern.

Many studies have shown that tenofovir resistance is not easily transmitted and may decrease the capacity of the virus to replicate efficiently. More recent studies, however, have not been so positive. A study presented in 2006 found that four out of eleven monkeys dosed with high levels of tenofovir rapidly developed the K65R mutation within just one week. Another seven animals in the study developed resistance but over a longer period of six to nine weeks (Johnson).

Whether these results are significant for humans remains unclear: many of these studies involve infecting monkeys with extremely high levels of virus and administered through more efficient routes than might be expected in the normal course of sexual interaction in humans.

Although trial recruiters made great efforts to consult with 'the community', there is a difference between consulting with well-informed activists in NGOs and ensuring ethical treatment of actual trial participants. Nigerian activist Rolake Nwagwu said: "In Nigeria, sex work is illegal. These women have no human rights and are not organised, so I don't see how sex workers will be involved in any meaningful way."

In Cambodia, there was a political dimension to this. US government policies had resulted in the withdrawal of USAID funding from local sex worker support groups in 2003. They were unsurprisingly disinclined to co-operate when asked to help by the same people in 2004.

Stories were widespread about local recruiters misinforming participants in order to get them on the trials. A Cameroon participant and several Cambodian participants were quoted as saying that they thought that tenofovir was a 'vaccine' which would mean they 'no longer had to use condoms'. Karyn Kaplan of the Thai Drug Users' Network said: "The trial looked beautiful on paper, but there has been a lot of coercion by local staff who implemented it."

Whether these accounts are true or not they represent a failure to communicate the potential benefits and risks of the trials in a clear way. Recruiters have failed to correct an impression that PrEP is all about forcing a biomedical prevention tool on HIV-negative people in order to make profits for drug companies.

One complexity of a prevention trial is that in order to demonstrate the effectiveness of a new intervention (such as PrEP) older interventions (such as condoms) have to 'fail', and yet ethically researchers have to offer safer-sex advice and condoms. This can been seen as a conflict of interest on the part of researchers, who need to make it clear that they do not *want* participants to take risks, they just need evidence that risks get taken (in fact risk behaviour tends to fall during prevention studies).

It can also be seen as a distraction from campaigning for prevention measures that communities *do* want. In the case of the Bangkok trial, drug user activists saw tenofovir as a politically acceptable alternative to their own preferred prevention intervention, needle exchange. The ethical question then becomes: will more lives be saved by holding out for an intervention we know works, or will more be saved by accepting a trial of unknown effectiveness?

Activists in the four countries where trials have been suspended expressed frank disbelief that tenofovir would ever be made available to the local population. In Cambodia, Womyn's Agenda for Change said: "Obviously, there is a benefit to anyone whom tenofovir prevents from HIV infection, if it proves able to do that. But it is not likely that many Cambodians would be able to use it. It seems clear that tenofovir is being tested mainly in poor countries because that is cheaper than doing it in rich countries."

HIV prevention trials in general have focused attention on the issue of researchers' responsibility to care for people who are infected with HIV or suffer drug side-effects during the trial. There is a complex ethical debate around whether the standard of care offered for people infected with HIV should be the best possible, only that on offer in the host country, or something in between. There is also the issue of whether researchers have the ability or power to offer anti-retroviral treatment that might not be needed until ten years after the trial ends.

It is in the nature of trials that more people can be harmed than helped. The classic example of this in a prevention trial was the COL-1492 trial of the spermicide nonoxynol-9 in West Africa. This showed that using N-9, which killed HIV in the test tube, in fact doubled the rate of HIV transmission in frequent users because it disrupted the vaginal epithelium. While this trial proved that you could put on large, double-blinded placebo-controlled trials for a microbicide, it ended up causing more women to become HIV-positive than otherwise.

Given some of the above points, it is legitimate to ask why so far PrEP research in the developed world has been restricted to a small US trial in gay men. Talks are underway about a possible trial among gay men in Europe and Australia, but these are at a very early stage.

The Seattle consultation

A meeting between stakeholders involved in every current trial took place on 19-20 May 2005 in Seattle, convened by the International AIDS Society.

Participants included the Bill and Melinda Gates Foundation, which has sponsored the trials, the CDC, the NIH, and over 50 stakeholders representing participants in Botswana, Cameroon, Ghana, Malawi and Thailand.

The meeting's recommendations took note of a lot of the above points. Many country-specific recommendations were made, but broad ones that applied to all the trials included:

- An immediate review to ensure that the level of counselling participants receive is significantly improved;

- Ensure access to male and female condoms;

- Ensure that there are proper support mechanisms for individuals screened for enrolment in the trials who are found to be HIV-positive;

- Establish national guidelines to inform and improve civil society engagement - efforts so far were acknowledged to have been "at times ill-informed and inconsistent";

- Clear mechanisms for feedback and conflict resolution at trial sites.

This has now become part of an ongoing dialogue to ensure that future studies are properly planned and that they proceed with the support of the local and international communities. Since existing international ethical frameworks do not provide detailed guidance on the criteria for prevention research, this should empower and protect vulnerable populations, as well as ensure rigorous standards for the ethical design and conduct of future research.

Who is 'the community'?

At the 2005 IAS Conference in Rio, Renée Ridzon of the Bill and Melinda Gates Foundation expressed frustration at the opposition to the trials mounted by some activists.

She said: "The trials will not be all-answering. But PrEP can only be tested in humans, and the derailment of prevention trials and the loss of focus on the urgent need for prevention interventions show that 'the good can be the enemy of the perfect'. The definition of 'community' can be elusive, and we have heard many voices from the community on this issue, rather than one."

In an attempt to avoid the controversies excited by other trials, the researchers behind the trial of PrEP for gay men in Peru conducted a comprehensive community consultation process in 2004/5, the results of which were presented at the Thirteenth Conference on Retroviruses and Opportunistic Infections (CROI) in February 2006 (Goicochea).

The researchers conducted an informed consent review process with a community advisory board and an institutional advisory board. They conducted a series of open forums on the trial with HIV and non-HIV civil society activists and with academics. And they conducted 20 focus groups in the two cities that were trial sites with activists and with possible trial participants or people who would be interested. This included participants in existing HIV prevention trials, and three classes of men who have sex with men: 'buses', who are men who may or may not self-identify as gay but are mainly MSM who maintain a "straight" demeanour; 'deschavados', who are generally effeminate MSM who self-identify as gay; transvestites; male sex workers; and 'mostaceros', who are men who have sex with transvestites or deschavados but do not identify as gay.

They asked each group their opinion on five topics:

- How to obtain truly informed consent in vulnerable populations

- Adverse events and whether participants should be compensated for them

- Whether there should be financial compensation for trial participation and whether this would act as coercion to join the trial

- Whether the trial would lead to 'condom migration' or sexual disinhibition in participants

- Their general opinions on HIV prevention research and whether they might participate.

A wide range of opinions was expressed by the different stakeholders. For instance, while opinion leaders, academics and 'buses' expressed reservations about there being any financial compensation to participate and thought it would be coercive, activists wanted the allowance doubled, and sex workers wanted to be compensated for lost work time and opportunities. Academics and 'buses' were concerned that PrEP might lead to sexual disinhibition, while 'deschavados' recognised that high-risk behaviour already existed. Potential participants expressed a variety of unexpected concerns about the health implications of the trial. Would tenofovir interfere with female hormones taken by trangendered participants? Would the monthly blood sampling have a weakening effect? One opinion leader asked if compensation would extend as far as paying for dialysis if someone got renal toxicity from tenofovir.

The stakeholders' different comments were then used to write the final trial protocol. This exhaustive exercise delayed the start of the trial for nearly two years, but is probably an example of the kind of good practice in community consultation that prevention trials need to adopt in the future.

Designing second-generation trials

After the results presented in the 'combo-PrEP' trial, the trials in Botswana and Peru have now switched from using tenofovir to using *Truvada* (tenofovir/FTC).

Plans for second-generation trials into pre-exposure prophylaxis are already underway. A number of approaches are being considered, including the use of other antiretroviral agents such as protease inhibitors and entry inhibitors, which stop viral entry into cells. Since some of these drugs remain effective for a long time achieving high plasma or cellular concentrations, it may be possible to dose people at risk of infection less frequently. However, this remains hypothetical and no current studies are underway to evaluate less frequent dosing.

A further strategy may be to combine different types of drugs to prevent infection such as the use of topical microbicides together with oral drug treatment to prevent infection.

Access

Even if PREP proves safe and effective in human trials, distributing it in the community will face an enormous economic barrier. The US price of *Truvada* is about $10,000 per year, and of tenofovir $7,000. Both are made by Gilead Sciences, which supplies the drugs free of charge for the PREP trials but does not otherwise participate.

Gilead also has a "Global Access Program" that theoretically applies to 95 resource-poor countries, which offers to sell *Truvada* and tenofovir in these countries for $360 and $300 yearly, but which has been severely criticised by groups such as Médecins sans Frontières for slow progress, especially in tackling the licensing bureaucracy of some developing countries. In any case, if PrEP were to be adopted widely as a prevention strategy, $300-$400 a year would probably still be too high a price.

The answer lies probably in generic provision with a licensing fee paid to Gilead. But it throws up a second problem. PrEP should never be sold over-the-counter: the potential for misuse (for treatment as well as prevention) and resultant widespread HIV resistance is just too great.

But in that case, what would be the procedures for access and dispensing? We have seen in the example of PEP that some people seeking it have come across discriminatory attitudes from healthcare staff. Would the stigmatisation of marginalised, high-risk communities lead to PrEP being denied to the very people who need it most? These power inequalities and a comprehensive training programme for probable providers would have to be addressed in advance of any move to make PrEP widely available, regardless of other considerations.

Conclusion

As with many of the biomedical approaches being studied at this time, including vaccines and microbicides, we may have to anticipate that PrEP might not provide complete protection against HIV. PrEP may supplement condoms rather than supplanting them.

Generally, the PrEP trials have happened historically at a time when a stronger activist movement that is wary of further trials that provide no benefit to local people has started to develop in the host countries.

One example given was the AIDSVAX gp120 HIV vaccine trial in Thailand, which was widely criticised as pointless at the time by researchers as one compomnent of the vaccine had already proven ineffective. The Thai Drug Users' Network's comment was "At the time we weren't organised enough to resist the AIDSVAX trial. Now we are."

Researchers involved in all trials of new prevention technologies should take account of the above concerns and establish maximum clarity of communication with trial participants and their communities, without overstating the benefits or fluffing the risks of a trial.

If they do not, they could make prevention technology trials far more difficult to put on and delay or even prevent implementation of vitally needed new weapons against HIV.

- An excellent summary of the issues involved in the PrEP trials was published by the AIDS Vaccine Advocacy Coalition (AVAC) in March 2005. It can be found at http://avac.org/pdf/tenofovir.pdf

- The Community HIV and AIDS Mobilization Project (CHAMP) published a useful update on both PrEP and microbicides in May 2006. It can be found at http://www.champnetwork.org/media/HHSWatch0506.doc

References

Garcia-Lerma J et al. *Prevention of rectal SHIV transmission in macaques by tenofovir/FTC combination*. Thirteenth Conference on Retroviruses and Opportunistic Infections, Denver, abstract 609, 2006.

Goicochea P et al. *Finding the Community in "Community Consultation" to Prepare for Biomedical HIV Prevention Trials*. Thirteenth Conference on Retroviruses and Opportunistic Infections, Denver. abstract 898, 2006.

Johnson J et al. *Rapid emergence of drug-resistant SIV in tenofovir-treated macaques: implications for tenofovir chemoprophylaxis against HIV*. Thirteenth Conference on Retroviruses and Opportunistic Infections, Denver, abstract 609, 2006.

Kellerman S. *Knowledge and use of pre-exposure prophylaxis asmong attendees of minority gay pride events, 2004*. Third IAS Conference on HIV Pathogenesis and Treatment, Rio de Janeiro, abstract WePe10.3P03, 2005.

Subbaro S et al. *Tenofovir delays but does not prevent infection in rhesus macaques given repeated rectal challenges of SHIV*. Twelfth Conference on Retroviruses and Opportunistic Infections, San Francisco, abstract 41, 2003.

Tsai CC et al. *Prevention of SIV infection in macaques by (R)-9-(2-phosphonylmethoxypropyl) adenine*, Science 270: 1197-1199, 1995.

Microbicides

An introduction to microbicides

What is a microbicide?

Microbicides are any substances which protect people against infection by microbes, such as viruses or bacteria, on contact with those microbes. They might do this by directly killing microbes or physically preventing them from entering the body. The term 'microbicides' has replaced 'virucides' to embrace products that could be active against a wide range of infections, not just viruses.

Microbicides are still at a developmental stage, and no proven safe and effective products are currently available. However, the prospects are good for products with at least some efficacy and there is a growing body of opinion supporting their development. The main focus is on microbicides for vaginal use, which is seen as technically simpler than providing protection during anal sex. Ideally, microbicides are needed for anal sex to protect heterosexuals as well as gay men. However acceptability studies of rectal microbicides in humans and animal studies have taken place.

Microbicide research began by analogy with spermicides (contraceptives which kill sperm). Some microbicides may also be spermicidal. The big difference is that while spermicides only act to 'protect' women against sperm, a microbicide may be able to act in both directions. It could be used by HIV-positive women to protect uninfected men, as well as by HIV-negative women to protect themselves. Microbicide development advocates have called for sub-studies of microbicide effectiveness to prevent transmission as well as infection in the development of all candidate products.

Microbicides could take the form of a cream, pessary, film, sponge, foam or jelly. The first products to be tested are gels which closely resemble the lubricants used with condoms.

In reality, some products would have much broader activity than others, raising issues in public education. There is already a great deal of confusion around the meaning of 'safe' or 'safer' sex: safe from what? Pregnancy, HIV, other infections? Such questions must be answered as microbicides are evaluated and, it is hoped, made widely available.

A study commissioned by the Rockefeller Foundation has projected the impact of microbicides in four subpopulations in 73 lower income countries. In particular: sex workers and their clients; sexually active youth; injecting drug users and their sexual partners; women in regular partnerships. Numbers were estimated for those in each of these groups in contact with services that could distribute microbicides. Using conservative estimates of product efficacy (40-60% vs. HIV, 0-40% vs. STIs), coverage (10% of populations) and usage (50% of sexual acts), it was possible to show that over three years several million HIV infections could be averted (Watts).

Who supports microbicide development?

- The first advocacy group specifically for microbicides was formed at an eight-day consultation in 1993 when the International Women's Health Coalition, the Population Council and individuals held an 8-day consultation on microbicides in New York for women's health advocates;

Group decided to form the Women's Health Advocates on Microbicide (WHAM). This body organised a panel on microbicides at the 9th International Conference on HIV/AIDS in Berlin that year.

- An **International Working Group on Microbicides (IWGM)** was set up in 1994, which has sought to stimulate research and build consensus on future directions. IWGM is an inter-agency coordinating body which works to facilitate the development and approval of safe, effective, affordable and acceptable microbicides to prevent the sexual transmission of HIV and other STIs.

- The US **National Institutes of Health** have been major sponsors of microbicides research. The NIH issued its first grants in 1995, and at the Vancouver AIDS Conference in 1996, US health and Human Services Secretary Donna Shalala announced a $100 million initiative to support microbicide research.

- WHAM disbanded in 1997, to make way for two organisations, both founded in 1998, that have since driven the advocacy and research agenda:

- The **Alliance for Microbicide Development (AMD -http://www.microbicide.org/)** is a global, non-profit organisation whose sole mission is to speed the development of safe, effective, and affordable microbicides to prevent sexually transmitted infections, especially HIV. It maintains a database of current research and candidate products; monitors the progress of microbicide projects that are being pursued by research groups and biotech companies; and produces regular surveys of the state of the field. It also brings together those companies that are involved with interested scientists and activists, conducts conferences and meetings; builds alliances between developers; and advocates for funding.

- Advocacy has been pursued by the **Global Campaign for Microbicides (GCM - http://www.global-campaign.org/).** The Global Campaign for Microbicides is a broad-based, international effort to build support among policymakers, opinion leaders, and the general public for increased investment into microbicides and other user-controlled prevention methods. It raises awareness and mobilises political support for microbicide development, creates a supportive policy environment for the development, introduction and use of new prevention technologies, and ensures that as science proceeds, the rights and interests of trial participants, users, and communities are fully represented and respected.

- In 2000, CONRAD (Contraceptive Research and development - http://nam10/admin/components/asp/www.conrad.org) established the Global Microbicides Project (www.gmp.org) to help develop new microbicidal agents that specifically address the needs and perspectives of women. The main objective of this project is to develop vaginal methods that would protect women against sexually transmitted infections, including HIV/AIDS.

- Between the two of them, the AMD and the GCM helped to create a cohesive approach to the development of microbicides that avoided some of the fragmentation of the vaccines development field and some (though not all) of the controversies about trial ethics that have dogged the development of both PrEP and vaccines. However there was still frustration that microbicide development was underfunded in comparison with vaccines and that a truly coherent programme to research and deliver an effective microbicide was needed.

- So in 2002 **the International Partnership for Microbicides (IPM - http://www.ipm-microbicides.org/)** was established. Initial funding was provided by the Rockefeller Foundation which was also an early supporter of the International AIDS Vaccine Initiative. IPM, headed by Dr Zeda Rosenberg and based in the USA, is setting out to create public-private

partnerships to expand the pipeline of products in development, ultimately licensing them to industry in return for guarantees of access for users in developing countries. Similar in mission to IAVI, its goal is to deliver a safe and effective microbicide for women in developing countries as soon as possible. IPM both conducts its own research and works in partnership with other researchers. It identifies the most promising technologies and invests its resources to help develop them into usable products. Through its partnerships, IPM aims to accelerate and increase the efficiency of product development at every stage, including formulation and drug delivery research, clinical trials and manufacturing.

The need for a microbicide received powerful endorsement in the 2001 declaration issued by the UN General Assembly Special Session on AIDS.

There are many barriers to the development of a successful microbicide. To maximise access, a product would need to be sold cheaply or distributed widely without medical supervision. This militates against the involvement of major research-based pharmaceutical companies that are geared to developing prescription medicines. There has been even less private investment in microbicides than in vaccines.

Microbicide research has mainly been pursued by academic and charitable organisations, and a few small companies. The main funders have been the US National Institutes of Health (Reichelderfer) and private philanthropists, although increasing interest is being shown by other governments and the European Commission. The UK's Department for International Development and the Swedish International Development Agency have both funded work. Private funding has come from the Gates Foundation, the American Foundation for AIDS Research and the Rockefeller Foundation among others.

The microbicide development process

The earliest stages of microbicide development can be carried out in cell cultures and small animals. Increasingly elaborate models of the tissues that are exposed to HIV containing a mixture of different cell types, some vulnerable to HIV, are being constructed.

The Global Microbicides Project has collaborated on a screening system with investigators at the Pennsylvania State College of Medicine. This uses cell-cultures to test the ability of microbicides to interfere with binding by two distinct strains of HIV-1, one binding to CXCR4 and one to CCR5 receptors. It tests cell-free virus inhibition and cell-to-cell transfer of HIV. It also tests mammalian cell toxicity. Compounds that pass all of these tests are then assessed for their ability to protect human peripheral blood monocytes from clinical strains of HIV. It is then possible to use a wider range of tests to measure possible protection against other (non-HIV) pathogens, before taking products forwards into clinical trials (Claypool).

Mice are susceptible to herpes (HSV-2) and this can be used for studies of broad-spectrum microbicide candidates. Another mouse model has been developed, using immunodeficient animals implanted with human vaginal tissues and allowed to heal (Kish). Some studies have been carried out in female monkeys, using HIV-related virus strains developed for vaccine research.

The two basic questions throughout the process of development:

- Is it safe or does it damage healthy tissue?

- Can it prevent HIV or other microbes from entering the body?

Phase I and Phase II trials of microbicides address the first of these questions. Initially, a small number of low-risk women, abstaining from sex, are asked to volunteer to expose themselves to the substance and report any reactions they suspect may be related to it. Increasingly detailed protocols have been developed for vaginal and cervical examinations, including standardised systems for reporting injuries and inflammation.

Studies of the safety of microbicides for anal use may be justified at an early stage although for protection, it may be necessary to have entirely different formulations as the area of mucosal tissue at risk in the rectum is much larger and is open-ended rather than a closed space as in the vagina.

Can early clinical evaluation be accelerated? A three-day dosing schedule and a seven-day dosing schedule have been compared for C31G, a candidate microbicide that was compared to N-9 and found to be **more** irritating. Unfortunately, N-9 itself is now considered unacceptable, so any test which makes it look good is of limited value (Bax).

In the later stages of these trials, women who are sexually active with regular partners may be enrolled, along with their partners.

Discussion of efficacy trials for microbicides has emphasised their potential value in protecting HIV-negative women from infection by men, but the fact that they would be used by HIV-positive women must be considered in designing clinical trials. Involvement of HIV-positive people in these early tests of the safety of the product is therefore important.

While the COL-1492 study of nonoxynol-9 (see below) was greeted with dismay because it showed that nonoxynol-9, far from working, actually facilitated HIV transmission if used regularly, it did show admirably that these challenges can be met and paved the way for the current phase III trials.

There is a full review of the issues raised by such trials in Elias (see references).

For more on this issue, see **challenges to microbicide development** below.

References

Bax R et al. *Use of a rapid screening study to predict long term tolerance.* Fourteenth International AIDS Conference, Barcelona, abstract TuPeF5305, 2002.

Claypool LE et al. *Evaluating the in vitro anti-HIV-1 activity and cytotoxicity of compounds for potential use in topical microbicides: the CONRAD/GMP algorithm.* Fourteenth International AIDS Conference, Barcelona, abstract MoPeD3649, 2002.

Elias L et al. *Challenges for the development of female-controlled vaginal microbicides.* AIDS 8: 1-9, 1994.

Forbes AS. *Microbicide advocacy and mobilization: three models from the global north.* Fourteenth International AIDS Conference, Barcelona, abstract MoPeG4270, 2002.

Reichelderfer PS et al. *National Institutes of Health microbicide development.* Fourteenth International AIDS Conference, Barcelona, abstract TuPeF5304, 2002.

Watts C et al. *The public health and economic benefits of microbicide introduction: model projections.* Fourteenth International AIDS Conference, Barcelona, abstract TuPeF5307, 2002.

Do we already have a microbicide?

Natural defences against HIV infection

While breastfed infants can clearly be infected with HIV by mouth, the mucosal surfaces in the mouth do not seem to allow adult human infection so readily. It has been argued that the rarity of transmission of HIV through oral sex may be due in part to substances in saliva, which inhibit the growth of HIV (Baron).

Another key observation is that the per-exposure risk of HIV infection through vaginal sexual contact is generally low. Important exceptions apply where sexually transmitted infections (STIs) are present and possibly where girls are young and physically immature.

Natural human defences against HIV and other microbes, especially at mucosal surfaces, may therefore be important in preventing even more rapid HIV transmission. There is some evidence that these include local HIV-specific immune responses. In all microbicide research, it is necessary to be on guard against the possibility that a product will undermine natural protection -

or the protection gained from future vaccines - and so make the situation worse, not better. This is an area where microbicide and vaccine researchers can work together and are increasingly likely to need to exchange ideas and experimental results (Kaul).

Sexual lubricants as microbicides

Researchers at the University of Texas set out to assess all vaginal lubricants sold commercially in the USA for their ability to inhibit the growth of HIV in cell cultures, in the presence of seminal fluid. They also looked at the ability of these mixtures to protect against cell-free HIV. After excluding products containing nonoxynol-9 (N-9), and others thought most likely to cause irritation, they reached the conclusion that three of the 22 commercial products they examined could, indeed, greatly inhibit HIV. Specifically, *AstroGlide* (made by Biofilm of Vista, California), *Vagisil* (Combe, White Plains, New York), and *ViAmor* (WomenFirst Healthcare Inc). They have not, however, shown activity against other viruses or sexually transmitted infections (Baron).

Unfortunately, this does not automatically mean that these products can or should be promoted for HIV prevention. Experience with N-9 has shown that laboratory studies can be misleading.

The Global Campaign for Microbicides has observed that these products have not been evaluated for their effect on vaginal or rectal mucosa, especially when used regularly in the quantities that might be needed for microbicidal use. Their US licensing is only as cosmetics, not as medicines, which requires a lower level of safety testing.

The only way to assess the value of these or other products would be through conducting clinical trials specifically designed to assess their safety and efficacy. If their manufacturers are able to sponsor such trials, this may yet happen. Otherwise, the current consensus is that there are more scientifically interesting and promising candidates which should be evaluated first.

Some have asked if the 'placebos' used in microbicide trials are themselves protective (for example, in the COL-1492 trial discussed below, *Replens* was more effective than the N-9 formulation). Did that mean *Replens* had a neutral effect and N-9 a harmful one, of *Replens* actually had an actively microbicidal effect? Others argue that such products are clearly of only marginal value for HIV prevention and it is reasonable to demand that any microbicide shows a substantial improvement over them (Stein).

Two tales of possible microbicide candidates that turned out no be either useless of actively harmful serve as lessons that what may appear on the surface to be a promising microbicide may be nothing of the sort, and underline the crucial role of safety trials in these product: the use of lemon or lime juice as a 'natural' microbicide, and the tale of the spermicide nonoxynol-9.

Lesson one : lemon juice as a microbicide

A Melbourne-based researcher, Professor Roger Short, has called for consideration of lemon juice as a possible anti-HIV microbicide. The basic principle, that acids - such as lemon juice - can inactivate both sperm and HIV, has been known for some years.

Current microbicide research does include products - *BufferGel* and *Acidform* - based on the principle of keeping the pH of the vagina low during sex, though the goal has been described as 'acidifying the semen, not acidifying the vagina'. *BufferGel* is set for full-scale international clinical trials sponsored by the US National Institutes of Health through its HIV Prevention Trials Network. However, a study which combined *Acidform* and N-9 found that the acid increased the damage done by N-9 to an unacceptable level.

In an *in vitro* study by Roger Short of the University of Melbourne presented at a poster at the Fifteenth International AIDS Conference in Bangkok, a solution containing 20% lemon or lime juice was found to inactivate 90% of HIV reverse transcriptase activity within two minutes. A phase I safety study of using citrus juices as topical microbicides is now planned.

Obviously, finding that something as cheap and universally available as lemon juice could be an HIV preventative is an exciting idea, and Short mooted the idea of using it as a microbicide.

At the Bangkok Conference he explained to **aidsmap.com** that the idea had come to him during a conversation with Senator Mechai Viravaidya, Community Co-Chair of the Bangkok Conference and architect of Thailand's '100% Condom' campaign.

"I had been aware that women had used it as a folk contraceptive for centuries. And since then I have learned that sex workers in Nigeria and possibly other high-prevalence countries are using lemon and lime douches regularly as a post-coital contraceptive and anti-infective precaution. This means that we can design an ethical placebo-controlled study, whereas previously the possibility that the approach could cause damage would have made this very difficult."

Prevention researchers had urged considerable caution about Short's ideas, given the previous experience when the spermicide nonoxynol-9, which inactivates HIV in vitro, was found to actually facilitate HIV transmission in vivo because it damages the epithelial cells lining the vagina (and rectum).

However nonoxynol-9 is a surfactant, not an acid. Short said that the environment of the vagina is normally acid and that citric acid is a major component of semen. "The vagina is no stranger to an acidic environment," he said. One of the candidates in the efficacy studies of microbicides due to start in the second half of this year, *BufferGel*, uses the same principle.

Short's poster says that daily intravaginal administration of neat lime juice to macaque monkeys for one month caused no discernible epithelial damage.

Short then investigated the degree to which different dilutions of lime and lemon juice inactivated HIV replication and the viability of HIV-infected cells in a test-tube cell culture.

Short says he was optimistic "because if you can get the pH in ejaculate down to 4" (the lower the pH of a fluid, the higher its acidity) you can efficiently immobilise 100% of sperm cells within 30 seconds." The pH of neat lemon or lime juice is about 2.4.

Short exposed peripheral blood mononuclear cells (PBMCs) to different dilutions of lemon or lime juice. He them cultured HIV within the cells for two weeks and measured HIV replication by measuring reverse transcriptase activity.

A 5% lemon juice solution in culture halved HIV replication within an hour, while a 10% solution cut it by two thirds. Both of these were non-toxic to the PBMCs in culture. A 20% solution, while it reduced HIV replication by 90% within two minutes, also killed off 25% of the PBMCs, indicating possible toxicity limits to the approach.

However several studies presented in 2006 put paid to the hopes that lemon juice could be a good microbicide.

In one, conducted by Dr Anke Hemmerling, of the University of California, Berkeley, concluded that the practice was relatively safe - at lower concentrations.

In her trial, twenty-five women were randomly assigned to apply a tampon soaked either without juice or with a 10% or 20% concentration of lime juice for 14 consecutive days. Tests for genital infections, measurement for signs of inflammation and a colposcopy were performed before and after treatment.

None of the participants showed signs of severe vaginal irritation, although more than 70% of women in all groups reported minor and temporary side-effects such as dryness. No other significant problems were observed. However, in light of the preclinical activity studies, these concentrations would be unlikely to affect HIV transmission.

Dr Christine Mauck of CONRAD did a study enrolling 48 sexually abstinent women volunteers. She divided the women into four groups: those using 100% lime juice ("neat" juice with no water), 50% (half water, half juice), 25% (one part water, three parts juice) and one group using plain water.

Each group inserted their assigned test fluid twice daily for six consecutive days during two menstrual cycles. In one cycle, it was inserted via a douche and, in the other, via a modified tampon soaked in lime juice.

The result showed that some women got small but serious abrasions in the walls of their vaginas after using 50% and 100% lime juice. The women who used 25% juice or plain water didn't get these abrasions. So the juice had a dose-dependent effect, and the likelihood of damage increased as the concentration of juice increased. Among the women using 100% lime juice with no water, more than 65% experienced genital irritation, 50% experienced deep epithelial abrasions and more than 70% reported experiencing pain.

Carol Lackman-Smithof the Southern Research Institute did a laboratory study comparing the cytotoxicity (cell-damaging effect) and anti-HIV activity of lemon and lime juice to that of the spermicide nonoxynol-9 (N-9).

She tested these three substances on cervical explant tissue (human cells obtained from routine hysterectomies and kept alive in lab cultures) to find out what impact they might have on the same kinds of cells in the human body. She found the amount of cell damage caused by lemon and lime juice was similar to the damage caused by N-9.

Lackman-Smith also looked at how much lemon or lime juice was needed to stop HIV and found that it was the same concentration (50% or greater) that also caused cell damage. She concluded that, when the juice is diluted to a point where no cell damage occurred, it also had little or no effect on HIV.

This research suggests that, in real life use (in the vagina along with semen), a 50% concentration of lime juice is needed to stop HIV, but that this concentration is also likely to cause damage to the vagina - and possibly the penis. This damage could make it easier for HIV infection to occur.

As the *Economist* magazine wrote on 29 April, 2006, "as a microbicide, lime juice is safe when it is ineffective and effective when it is unsafe."

References

Baron S et al. *Practical prevention of vaginal and rectal transmission of HIV by adapting the oral defence: use of commercial lubricants.* AIDS Research and Human Retroviruses 17: 997-1002, 2001.

Economist, the: *Bitter fruit: another idea for stopping AIDS falls flat.* Print edition, 27th April 2006.

Hemmerling A et al. *The safety of lime juice used vaginally.* Microbicides 2006 Conference, Cape Town, abstract PB28, 2006.

Kaul R. Mucosal immunity and HIV-1 transmission. Microbicides 2002, Antwerp (http://www.itg.be/micro2002/downloads/presentations/3Tuesday_May_14_2002/Plenary_session/Rupert_Kaul.pdf), 2002.

Lackman-Smith C et al. *Preclinical evaluations of lemon and lime juice as microbicide candidates.* Microbicides 2006 Conference, Cape Town, abstract PA93, 2006.

Mauck C. *6-Day safety trial of intravaginal lime juice (in three concentrations) Vs. water, applied twice daily.* Microbicides 2006 Conference, Cape Town, abstract OB3, 2006.

Short RV et al. *Lemon and lime juice as potent natural microbicides.* Fifteenth International AIDS Conference, Bangkok, abstract TuPeB4668, 2004.

Stein Z et al. Appropriate controls in microbicide efficacy trials: the continuing search. XIV International AIDS Conference, Barcelona, abstract TuPeC4834, 2002.

Lesson two: nonoxynol-9

The most thoroughly studied candidate microbicides have been based on the spermicide nonoxynol-9, also known as N-9. This is a detergent which was chosen for research on the basis of laboratory findings that it disrupted HIV and other STIs, even at very low doses, and because it was already in widespread use, including in lubricants for condoms. Animal studies confirmed that N-9 protects female monkeys against challenge with HIV-related viruses (Miller, Weber). Unfortunately, N-9 causes damage to human tissue, leading to inflammation and ulceration, which is dose related (Niruthisard).

Research into N-9 as a rectal microbicide has been minimal and where it has occurred, has produced even more worrying results than in trials as a vaginal microbicide: the use of nonoxynol-9 caused the rectal lining to slough off in both mice and humans, prompting a warning about the popular use of N9-containing lubricants during anal sex. Far from protecting against HIV and other viral infections, N-9 leaves the rectum more susceptible to it (Phillips).

It was nonetheless hoped that low-dose N-9 products, used vaginally, might be able to protect against HIV without causing excess inflammation.

However, the results of the most extensive clinical trials carried out on any microbicide are clear-cut: N-9 increases HIV transmission to women who are at high risk of HIV when they use the product frequently, and appears to have no protective effect either against HIV or other STIs when used less frequently. There are better candidates available for evaluation, and the consensus is that future research should focus on those.

The most important evidence that nonoxynol-9 is ineffective - or has a negative value - as a microbicide came from a randomised, placebo-controlled trial of a low-dose nonoxynol-9 vaginal gel, COL-1492. (Van Damme).

This study enrolled 892 female sex workers in four countries: Benin, Cote d'Ivoire, South Africa and Thailand, all of whom were supplied with condoms and encouraged to use them, as well as having enhanced access to diagnosis and treatment of sexually transmitted infections. 765 women were included in the analysis of the results, of whom 376 were on N-9 and 389 on placebo. Among these women, a further distinction was made between frequent users and less frequent users, with a threshold mean value of 3.5 uses per day.

The N-9 product was made by Columbia Laboratories as *Advantage S* and the placebo, which was provided in identical packaging, was a vaginal lubricant called *Replens*. The women were asked to keep a diary of their activities (although this was replaced by interviews after some women were seen to complete their diaries in the clinic). All women were provided with condoms (free of N-9), which they were advised to urge their partners to use.

The findings were that among less frequent users, HIV rates were not significantly different between N-9 and placebo groups. However, among more frequent users, HIV rates among N-9 users were twice the rate among placebo users. There was no effect of N-9 on rates of gonorrhoea or chlamydia infection.

The Phase III study was double blinded, so neither the researchers nor the participants knew whether they were receiving *Advantage S* or placebo.

The researchers had anticipated that those receiving the placebo would have higher rates of infection than those who received *Advantage S*. Several safety studies carried out using this formulation before the start of the phase III trial failed to show any side-effects usually associated with N-9 such as genital sores and irritation.

The use of placebos as an alternative to active treatment (rather than to disguise which of two active treatments is being given) has become increasingly controversial in HIV clinical trials and is inappropriate as soon as a standard of treatment is established. Some commentators have extended this concern to argue that placebos should not be used in prevention trials either. However, until we have a microbicide of proven effectiveness, placebos must continue to be used. The COL-1492 researchers have drawn

attention, however, to the challenge this represents in explaining to trial volunteers precisely what placebo use means. (Ramjee).

Similarly, concerns that the promotion of condoms might prevent a valid finding of difference have not been borne out by these results. While condom use varied between the trial sites, it was clearly higher in the trial. This may help explain the finding that HIV infection rates among women receiving N9 were lower than in women who did not take part in the trial. But surely, this is what we should all want to see in every trial?

The most reasonable conclusion would seem to be, that N9 will not be the answer to the need for a microbicide but the trials show that other more promising candidates can and should be evaluated with the utmost urgency. There are many unanswered questions and the experience with N-9 has made microbicide researchers wary of premature adoption of untested products.

References

Miller C et al. *The effect of contraceptives containing nonoxynol-9 on the genital transmission of simian immunodeficiency virus in rhesus macaques.* Fertility and Sterility 57: 1126-1128, 1992.

Niruthisard S et al. *The effects of frequent nonoxynol-9 use on the vaginal and cervical mucosa.* Sexually Transmitted Diseases 18: 176-179, 1991.

Ramjee G et al. Challenges in the conduct of vaginal microbicide effectiveness trials in the developing world. AIDS 14: 2553-2557, 2000.

Van Damme L et al. *Effectiveness of COL-1492, a nonoxynol-9 vaginal gel, on HIV-1 transmission in female sex workers: a randomised controlled trial.* Lancet 360: 971-977, 2002.

Weber J et al. *'Chemical condoms' for the prevention of HIV infection: evaluation of novel agents against SHIV 89.6 PD in vitro and in vivo.* AIDS 15: 1563-1568, 2001.

Current microbicide efficacy trials

Three principles, multiple products

The candidate microbicides which are now closest to publicly funded full-scale clinical trials are based on three principles, two of which at least may end up being combined in a single product.

BufferGel (produced by Reprotect LLC) is based on the observation that vaginal fluids are naturally acid, whereas seminal fluids are alkaline. HIV and other sexually transmitted infections (and also human sperm) are inhibited by the natural acidity of the vagina, so the idea of *BufferGel* is to maintain this (below pH 5) even in the presence of seminal fluid.

Following successful US phase I trials (Mayer) the US National Institutes of Health has sponsored preliminary international clinical trials of this product (and also *PRO 2000*, see below) through its HIV Prevention Trials Network. These have shown that it is at least as well tolerated as dextrin 2 sulphate and other credible candidate microbicides.

PRO 2000 (originally made by Procept but sold to Interneuron), cellulose sulphate, and carrageenan (*CarraGuard* or PC515, backed by the New-York based Population Council) are three of the leading products in development, based on very large, stable polymers. Carrageenan is a natural product derived from seaweed; the others are also inherently easy and cheap to make.

These coat cell surfaces, preventing the binding of viruses or the entry of microbes into tissue. In addition, dextrin sulphate and *PRO 2000* are sulphonated polymers, whose sulphur-containing components have a great affinity for the receptor molecules on the surface of the cells HIV infects within the genital tract such as dendritic cells and preferentially latch on to them.

This activity has been confirmed in a range of laboratory studies using cell-cultures and there is evidence that *PRO 2000* and dextrin 2 sulphate can protect female monkeys from vaginal infection with large quantities of HIV-related viruses (Lewis, Weber).

None of these products has the inflammatory problems that go with N9; Phase I and II clinical trials have shown that these products are all very well tolerated.

Their molecular size makes them unlikely to be absorbed into the bloodstream, which increases confidence in their safety.

A third class of microbicides still being tried are the surfactants like nonoxynol-9, which disrupt cell and viral membranes. The only one still persisting into efficacy trials is C31G (*Savvy*), a compound found to be more cytotoxic than N-9 is previous trials. Two trials are continuing in Nigeria though one has been discontinued in Ghana, though not for reasons of toxicity - see below.

By the time of the 2006 Microbicides conference in Cape Town, eight large clinical efficacy studies of microbicides had begun. Although one was discontinued, mounting so many trials in such a brief period is a logistical triumph and testimony to the dedication of the researchers involved. The trials include:

- The *Carraguard* study is one of the furthest along in implementation. *Carraguard* contains a seaweed extract that acts as an HIV fusion or entry inhibitor. Formulated as a gel, the microbicide is being compared to placebo in a randomised controlled trial by the Population Council at three sites in South Africa (Cape Town, Durban and Limpopo). The study will be unblinded for final efficacy analysis in the second quarter of 2007.

- Cellulose Sulphate (CS) is another entry inhibitor formulated as a gel that is being compared to HEC gel (a non-active gel placebo) in two randomised controlled trials. Trial #1 is in Uganda, South Africa, India, Benin and Burkina Faso. The last follow-up in this study is expected be in July 2008, data analysis should occur in December 2008, with results in March 2009. Trial #2 is in Lagos, and Port Harcourt, Nigeria. The last follow-up in this study is expected to be in January 2008, with results due sometime later that year.

- HIV Prevention Trials Network (HPTN) study 035 is comparison of 0.5% *PRO 2000* and *BufferGel* versus two controls -- a placebo gel and open label no gel arm. The trial is looking at safety and efficacy against HIV and also bacterial vaginosis, a number of sexually transmitted infections and pregnancy at six sites in Malawi, South Africa, Zimbabwe, Zambia, and one site in the United States. The trial is currently still in a safety analysis phase, but will roll over uninterrupted into the efficacy phase in October this year, with primary effectiveness results expected by early 2009.

- Microbicides Development Programme (MDP) 301, is a study funded by United Kingdom's medical research council and DFID looking at two strengths of *PRO 2000* (0.5%, and 2.0%) versus placebo at six sites in South Africa, Uganda and Tanzania. The trial is expected to continue until March 2009 with results due later that year.

- Methods for Reproductive Health in Africa (MIRA) is conducting a study of the Ortho All-Flex diaphragm containing *Replens* gel (an acidifying buffer) in Harare, Zimbabwe, and in Soweto and Durban, South Africa. The study is fully enrolled, and final results are projected for the fall of 2007.

- Two trials of *Savvy*, a surface active agent formulated as a gel that provides a protective coating within the vagina, have begun: *Savvy* Nigeria, conducted in Lagos and Ibadan, Nigeria, began in October 2004 and is expected to continue until May 2007.

Savvy Ghana was discontinued when it was discovered that the HIV incidence among trial participants (in both placebo and microbicide arm) would be too low to reach any clear conclusion about the effectiveness (or lack of effect) of *Savvy*.

As the latter example attests, the fact that so many studies have begun is no guarantee that they will conclude successfully.

Researchers at the meeting discussed various challenges with conducting these trials, some anticipated and some not, including:

- Problems of study design and size - especially in light of lower than expected incidence rates.

- Recruitment of high risk women.

- How to provide a high standard of HIV care to women who test HIV-positive at screening or during these clinical trials?

- What to do when women in microbicide trials become pregnant?

- The benefits and challenges involved in measuring a microbicide's effect on other sexually transmitted infections.

- Poor adherence to the studies' experimental arms.

- Finally, if a somewhat effective microbicide is identified, approved and makes it to the market, how will this affect other ongoing or planned clinical trials?

References

Johansson E. *Population Council phase III study of the efficacy and safety of the microbicide Carraguard in preventing HIV seroconversion in women*. Microbicides 2006 Conference, Cape Town, panel discussion talk, 2006.

Karim SA. *HPTN 035 phase II/IIb safety and effectiveness study of the vaginal microbicides BufferGel and 0.5% Pro 2000/5 Gel for the prevention of HIV infection among women*. Microbicides 2006 Conference, Cape Town, panel discussion talk, 2006.

Van Damme L. *CONRAD Randomised controlled trial of 6% Cellulose Sulphate Gel and the effect on vaginal HIV transmission*. Microbicides 2006 Conference, Cape Town, panel discussion talk, 2006.

McCormack S. *MDP International multi-centre, randomised, double-blind, placebo controlled trial to evaluate the efficacy and safety of 0.5% and 2% Pro 2000/5 Gels for the prevention of vaginally acquired HIV infection*. Microbicides 2006 Conference, Cape Town, panel discussion talk, 2006.

Halpern V. *FHI Phase II/III study of cellulose sulfate in 2 Nigerian cities*. Microbicides 2006 Conference, Cape Town, panel discussion talk, 2006.

Padian N. *MIRA Latex diaphragm to prevent HIV acquisition among women: a female controlled, physical barrier of the cervix*. Microbicides 2006 Conference, Cape Town, panel discussion talk, 2006.

Feldblum P and Peterson L. *FHI Phase II/III study of C31G in 2 Nigerian cities and in Ghana*. Microbicides 2006 Conference, Cape Town, panel discussion talk, 2006.

Microbicides in development

At the Microbicides 2006 conference in Cape Town, professor Ian McGowan provided a summary of current human microbicide trials, showing that there were only five candidate substances in current efficacy trials, with a few more (some already discredited, and some where the exact formulation and mechanism of action is either unknown or a closely guarded commercial secret) in smaller safety and dose-ranging studies: (see table on page 7)

However he also provided another slide giving a much larger list of candidate compounds: (see table on page 7)

So although scientists have identified a great number of ways to disrupt HIV transmission, the near-term pipeline of microbicides ready to enter early clinical studies is fairly modest and needs to be expanded rapidly. The handful of microbicides that have advanced into large scale human trials have relatively low potency against HIV compared to antiretroviral drugs - and there is no guarantee that they will actually work in practice.

Fortunately, many ways to prevent HIV and other sexually transmitted diseases (STIs) in the vagina or rectum have been identified - each with its own set of strengths and challenges for development.

Surface active agents

Surface active agents (or membrane disruptive agents) could prevent HIV and STI transmission and pregnancy by forming a protective barrier in the vagina or rectum. Surface active agents are also cheap to make.

Microbicides in development

Phase	Membrane Disruption	Defence Enhancers	Entry Fusion Inhibitors	Replication Inhibitors
1		*Acidform* Lime Juice Lactobacillus	*VivaGel* Cellulose acetate	PC-815 UC-781 TMC-120
1/2	*Invisible Condom*			
2	(Praneem)			Tenofovir
2/2b	C31G	*BufferGel*	PRO-2000 (0.5% & 2%)	
3			*Carraguard* Cellulose Sulfate	

Preclinical microbicide candidates

Uncertain	Defence Enhancers	Entry/ Fusion Inhibitors	
Ciclopiroxolamine Praneem polyherbal	MucoCept HIV Lime Juice Acidform gel	Cellulose sulfate Cellulose acetate Carraguard VivaGel Dextrin-2 sulfate Cyanovirin-N C85FL K5-N, OS(H) SAMMA	C52L Tobacco-derived antibodies/ fusion proteins Anti-ICAM-1 Ab mAb B12, 2G 12 mAb 2F5, 4E10 CD4 IgG2 T20 T-1249
Membrane Disruption	**Replication Inhibitors**	Invisible Condom Novaflux Porphyrins PSC Rantes BMS-806 BMS-378806 CMP D167	SCH-C, D UK-427, 857 TAK779 AMD3100 SFD-1 Bicyclams Aptamers
Alkul sulfates Savvy (C31G) Beta cyclodextrin	Tenofovir TMC-120 UC-781 MIV-150 MC1220 C-731, 988		

Nonoxynol-9 (N-9) was an early surface active microbicide that has been abandoned because it was abrasive to mucosal tissue and actually increased transmission risks. Newer surface active products have been shown to have very low toxicity. However, such compounds are not specific for HIV and their effectiveness will depend on how thoroughly they coat the vagina or rectum, as well as how consistently they are used.

Furthermore, these products need to be applied shortly before coitus (and may not be on hand when intercourse has not been planned). If too closely linked to sex, products could be stigmatised in some cultures in the same way that condoms have been - although a study of 200 people in Nigeria presented at the Microbicides 2006 Conference suggested that this may not be a problem for the leading product, *Savvy*, and that acceptance of this microbicide was very high (90%). Even so, there were complaints about excessive wetness, and in other cultures where dry sex is the norm (such as parts of Southern Africa), men may insist that women not use such products.

USAID-sponsored efficacy trials of *Savvy* are ongoing - however, a major *Savvy* study in Ghana had to be discontinued when observed rates of HIV transmission were determined to be too low in both the *Savvy* and placebo-controlled arm for the study to reach a statistically significant conclusion. A related study in

Nigeria is still continuing, however, while a study comparing *Savvy* and tenofovir (*Viread*) gel vs. placebo is being planned.

Two other new surface active agents in development include cellulose acetate 1,2-benzenedicarboxylate (CAP), a polymer mixture, with a long history of safe use in humans as enteric coating for capsules and tablets, and octylglycerol (a naturally occurring antimicrobial lipid found in human breast milk). Preclinical studies in tissue models and macaques presented at the conference demonstrated that these products should be safe in the rectum (for octylglycerol) and vagina (for both products).

Acid/buffering agents

The environment of the vagina is on the acidic side, but semen contains strong alkalinising properties to protect sperm from the vagina's natural defences. Unfortunately, increasing the pH in the vagina also protects microbes such as HIV and increases the likelihood of their transmission. Acid or buffering agents, such as leading products, *BufferGel* (which has a pH of 3.9), and *Acidform* are sometimes called vaginal defence enhancers because they restore the vagina to its naturally acidic state. Buffering agents may also protect against both pregnancy and sexually transmitted infections by killing sperm and by inactivating acid-sensitive pathogens.

Many women try to restore their pH by using acidic washes (such as vinegar or juice), but as we have seen, are too toxic to use in effective concentrations. But the buffering agents in commercial development have low local toxicity and no systemic activity. They are active, in vitro, against bacterial vaginosis (BV) and several sexually transmitted infections. However, their potency is rather low, although it could be improved by combining them with other products such as cervical barrier delivery devices (see below).

A clinical efficacy study comparing *BufferGel* to *PRO 2000* (see below) and placebo is underway in Zimbabwe, Zambia, Malawi and South Africa.

Fusion/entry inhibitors

Most of the products in advanced clinical trials are simple entry or fusion inhibitors such as cellulose sulfate, *PRO 2000* and *Carraguard*. In test tube studies, the negatively charged active molecules in these gels have been shown to interfere with the binding of HIV, HSV-2 and other enveloped viruses to CD4 and other receptors on macrophages and dendritic cells.

Though these compounds are more directly microbicidal than surface active agents, they are fairly non-specific for HIV and may have a relatively low potency in the presence of seminal fluid and vaginal flora. While they may persist in the vagina longer than surface active agents, they are still generally formulated in gels which have to be applied (with plastic applicators) prior to sex.

But thus far they appear to be quite safe and have moved into large clinical efficacy studies. Researchers believe (Hillier) that if any of these products are shown to work in clinical trials, they are likely to only be "mildly" effective (reducing transmission by 30-40%) and may wind up being considered as secondary actives for combination products.

Antiretrovirals

One solution to the low potency potential of the previous microbicides would be to use antiretrovirals (ARVs), which already have proven efficacy as therapeutics. As we have seen, drugs such as oral tenofovir are being tested in advanced studies worldwide as pre-exposure prophylaxis (PrEP) to prevent HIV transmission, but tenofovir and many other ARVs can also be formulated as topical microbicides. Tenofovir gel is already moving forward into expanded phase 2 testing (HPTN 059).

One drawback of formulating ARVs into microbicides is that they only work against HIV (and, in the case of tenofovir, probably hepatitis B) - with no activity against other STIs or other benefits for vaginal health or contraception. Another potential weakness for ARV microbicides, at least for those containing only a single ARV compound, is drug resistance. For example, if a woman's partner has HIV which is resistant to the ARV in her microbicide, she may not be as protected as she thinks.

In the case of PrEP, if a woman who is unaware that she is HIV-infected takes a single drug like tenofovir, she could develop resistance to the drug and possibly limit her future treatment options. It is unclear, however, whether that would happen with a microbicide containing a single ARV that is not systemically absorbed. Drug levels would probably be too low to select for drug resistant virus - research is ongoing into this question.

Another issue is that the barrier to ARV resistance development may be lower for some subtypes of HIV. For example, in a presentation later during the conference, Professor Mark Wainberg, of Toronto, Canada, noted that the K65R mutation that confers resistance to tenofovir may be more common in people with HIV clade C. Prof. Wainberg conducted a laboratory study with HIV-1C isolates showing that resistance developed after only twelve weeks exposure to the drug (compared to more than a year for HIV-1B). If tenofovir becomes commonly used for treatment in southern Africa (and at present it is too expensive), its potential for microbicide use could be limited here.

One possible solution to the resistance problem would be to use combination ARVs in the microbicide.

Fortunately, there is a host of ARV compounds to choose from, including many whose clinical development as oral drugs was halted when they were found to have poor systemic absorption. Many of these ARVs have been licensed to the International Partnership for Microbicides (IPM). IPM identifies the most promising ARV candidates for microbicidal development, licenses them from the big pharmaceutical companies and handles their clinical development. If the microbicides are shown to be effective, IPM has the right to distribute the microbicides at affordable prices in the developing world while the originator pharmaceutical company retains the right to market the products in the western industrialised countries.

The first one, TMC120 (dapivirine), a non-nucleoside reverse transcriptase inhibitor (NNRTI), was licensed through an agreement with IPM and Tibotec's owners Johnson and Johnson (who also make sexual lubricants such as *KY* jelly) in 2004. Now a gel formulation of the product is slated to enter a very large (10,000+ participants) efficacy study in 2007. IPM is also studying a sustained release formulation of the drug (see below). A benefit of such delivery forms is that ARV-containing microbicides can be effective even when applied or delivered long before (or even shortly after) coitus.

CCR5 antagonists

CCR5 antagonists, including PSC-RANTES, aplaviroc, maraviroc and Merck-167, are a new class of highly potent ARVs that could be effective even when applied as topical microbicides days before coitus. CCR5 antagonists bind to CCR5 receptors and specifically block HIV fusion to cells for up to five days - and the virus finds it difficult to develop resistance to them.

Some CCR5 antagonists have had toxicity problems when used as therapeutic agents, but at the Microbicides 2006 conference Prof. Hillier said she thought that, since there are a number of these compounds to choose from, with careful preclinical selection, there is a good chance that a safe and effective product can be identified for further development as a topical microbicide.

None of these compounds are in human trials as topical microbicides yet. However, PSC-RANTES has been shown to protect against transmission in the macaque model and is being developed specifically for vaginal application. However, the formulation challenges are considerable because it is a rather large molecule and could be expensive to manufacture. Meanwhile, Merck 167 and two related molecules have recently been licensed for development by IPM.

gp120 binders

Although some microbicides in clinical development may block fusion by binding to gp120, a number of more sophisticated and potent HIV fusion inhibitors have been identified including cyanovirin-N, SPL, *VivaGel*, and a couple of Bristol Myers Squibb compounds that have now been licensed to IPM. Most are members of the molecular class called dendrimers - large, many-branched almost globular molecules that trap HIV and other viruses within their branches.

Cyanovirin, which is derived from blue-green algae may be difficult and expensive to formulate. However, it can be expressed in a number of different genetically altered organisms such as tobacco and potentially even in intestinal and vaginal flora (see below). The dendrimers SPL and *VivaGel*, which have also shown activity against herpes virus 2, are in phase 1 clinical trials and beginning studies for STI prevention.

Microbicide-expressing bacteria

The most radical idea in microbicide formulation is to genetically engineer naturally-occurring gut bacteria so that they manufacture microbicidal substances themselves.

Several researchers have investigated this possibility. Dean Hamer of the US National Institutes for Health described one approach at the third IAS Conference in 2005. He had devised a way of getting 'friendly' bacteria to colonise the gut and to produce bits of HIV proteins - which, in the test tube at least, have provoked enough of an immune response in gut-surface cells to stop HIV infecting them.

Hamer took a harmless but vigorous strain of the E. coli bacterium called Nissle 1917. This particular microbe has been used as a 'probiotic' in digestive supplements for over 50 years, so is known to be safe.

He spliced into it HIV genes that caused the bacterium to make HIV antigens - protein fragments of HIV that gut-surface immune cells 'recognise' and mount an immune reaction to that would repel a complete virus.

So far, in experiments in mice, the bacteria have colonised the gut and have out-competed other friendly bacteria without disturbing the digestive system. And in test-tube experiments the HIV fragments produced by the bacteria effectively stopped cells from being infected with HIV.

Once the E.coli bacterium was dosed, it colonised the mice's guts for weeks to months. So, in theory, a probiotic drink - or at least an enema - given every few weeks might provide enough protection against HIV.

At the 2006 Microbicides Conference Hamer gave a presentation on a strain of E. coli genetically engineered to secrete gp41 (which stably binds gp120) in the gut. Studies have demonstrated that it can colonise the rectum in mice following ampicillin treatment, and Dr Hamer presented new data showing that it effectively colonised the intestinal tract of rhesus macaques, protecting about half of them from rectal challenge with SIV.

Several other teams have shown that organisms that make up part of the normal vaginal or intestinal flora, such as *Lactobacillus* and *Escherichia coli*, can be genetically modified to continuously produce and release molecules with anti-HIV activity, such as soluble CD4, cyanovirin or gp41. A number of products have already been formulated including *MucoCept HIV*, a vaginal *Lactobacillus* which can secrete cyanovirin that is now being studied in pig-tailed macaques.

However there is a long way to go before we can find out if test-tube effects are reproduced in real live humans, and some researchers are sceptical that the bacteria will express enough viral protein to produce an immune response. Such vectors could also be delivered long before sexual activity, but it would be nearly impossible to ensure delivery of an effective dose. For one thing, the genetically modified organisms may not be as adaptable as the native flora, and it would be difficult to know whether successful and sustained colonisation had indeed occurred within an individual. Finally, the immune system may react against the organism or the protein which it is secreting.

The next step will be a trial in Rhesus monkeys and pig-tailed macaques to find out if this 'natural microbicide' can offer protection.

Combination and multi-purpose products

Combinations have a lower risk of breakthrough infections and have a proven therapeutic approach in a number of diseases. There are some challenges though because the complexity of formulating such products can be great. Furthermore, the regulatory approval process of combination products can be tortuous. For example, in the United States, the current Food and Drug Administration (FDA) regulatory pathway requires that combination products be evaluated in clinical trials with as many arms as there are individual drugs and combinations, plus placebo, creating daunting recruitment requirements. So a study of two new agents would have to be studies in an 'A versus B versus A+B versus placebo' design, unless one of the compounds was already shown to have limited efficacy as a microbicide, in which case it would be the standard of comparison. Clinical trials that are trying to measure small improvements (20 to 30%) in

an infrequent clinical marker (HIV seroconversion) can wind up being enormous and exorbitantly expensive - see *Challenges to microbicide development* below. Licensing issues can also be complex - the great hope here, though is IPM, which controls the rights to combine the products that they have licensed in any way they like.

Despite these difficulties, many researchers believe that combinations are the long-term future. In the nearer term future, if proven efficacious, combinations of cervical barriers and non-specific microbicides will be the first available. Combinations based on acid buffer gels plus a high potency active ingredient may be developed because they have lower regulatory barriers.

Given the difficulty in moving combination products through clinical trials and towards regulatory approval, it becomes all the more important to give early consideration of formulation and pharmacology challenges.

How will microbicides be delivered?

Most of the leading microbicides have been formulated as gels. To make certain that enough microbicide is delivered, plastic applicators have been developed prefilled with a set volume of gel that a woman must insert into her vagina. A number of studies at the Microbicides 2006 conference addressed the acceptance of these devices and the uptake of this process.

Cups or diaphragms that are used in contraception protect the cervix and could be adapted for use with different microbicides, concentrating the formulation on target cells in the cervix. A few of these are in development. Use of such cervical barriers is more common in industrialised nations and there is some question as to how well they will be as accepted in other cultures. According to one study from Brazil, diaphragms were the least popular of three delivery devices (comparing to plastic applicators and intravaginal rings). Some women complained of difficulty inserting them and of local or mechanical irritation. At US $0.25 per unit, they are also more expensive than standard plastic applicators.

Intravaginal rings are another commonly used device for contraception in industrialised countries that are relatively unknown in resource-limited settings. However, rings are a sustained release mechanism that could potentially deliver a variety of microbicides (with contraceptive, antibiotic, anti-STI or anti-HIV activity) over a long period of time. Rings increase compliance and acceptability because they can be inserted weeks before sex - and are usually undetectable to the male partner. The downside to this is that the woman is exposed to more drug so there is a greater potential for side-effects. Also, if a woman should seroconvert while using rings containing ARVs, this would be the optimal method for inducing ARV resistance. IPM has conducted phase I trials with rings containing TMC120 that have demonstrated good safety and tissue levels of drug. IPM is also looking at a variety of other new ring technologies which can deliver multiple drugs.

Perhaps the most innovative microbicide delivery research is being conducted by Dr Patrick Kiser and colleagues in Utah, who are looking at a number of technologies to optimise microbicide delivery in the vagina in the presence of semen. Polymers containing ARVs could be delivered in a long lasting gel that stays inert in the normal pH of the vagina. However, with exposure to semen, the gel turns into a liquid. Semen contains high levels of natural proteases that then free the ARVs (bound to a molecule which looks like the proteases' natural substrate or target). The ARVs are then immediately available to combat HIV present within the semen. This gets the drug exactly where it needs to go, when it is needed, and protects the woman from systemic effects of the drug when not having sex. Somewhat different gels could also be formulated for rectal deployment.

References

Primary reference

Hillier SL. *Microbicides: State of the Art and Its Evolution.* Microbicides 2006 Conference, Cape Town, Monday oral plenary, 2006.

Other references

Ballagh SA. *BufferGel® Duet: Safety and Acceptability Study of a Novel Product Combining a Mechanical and Chemical Barrier in the Vagina.* Microbicides 2006 Conference, Cape Town, abstract OB23, 2006.

Barnhart K T. *BufferGel® with diaphragm found to be an effective contraceptive in two Phase II/III trials.* Microbicides 2006 Conference, Cape Town, abstract OB22, 2006.

Cosgrove-Sweeney Y, Patton D. *Cellulose Acetate Phthalate (CAP): Vaginal Safety Evaluation in the Macaque Model.* Microbicides 2006 Conference, Cape Town, abstract PA57, 2006.

Hamer D. *Using live microbes as anti-HIV microbicides.* Third IAS Conference on HIV Pathogenesis and Treatment, Rio de Janeiro. Abstract MoPp0101. 2005.

Hamer D, Henry K. *Live Microbial Microbicides for HIV.* Microbicides 2006 Conference, Cape Town, abstract OA30, 2006.

Hardy E. *Devices for the administration of a vaginal microbicide: use difficulties, adherence to use and preferred device.* Microbicides 2006 Conference, Cape Town, abstract PC23, 2006.

Kilbourne-Brook M. *SILCS Diaphragm: acceptability of a single-size, reusable cervical barrier by couples in three countries.* Microbicides 2006 Conference, Cape Town, abstract PC33, 2006.

Kiser P. *Novel delivery systems for microbicides: semen triggered release and in situ gelling polymer carrier.* Microbicides 2006 Conference, Cape Town, abstract OA32, 2006.

Lagenaur L. *Vaginal lactobacilli for mucosal delivery of the anti-HIV microbicide, cyanovirin-N.* Microbicides 2006 Conference, Cape Town, abstract OA33, 2006.

Mosier D. *Lack of resistance to a candidate topical microbicide targeting CCR5.* Microbicides 2006 Conference, Cape Town, abstract OA8, 2006.

Oladele D et al. *Acceptability of savvy (C31G) gel in phase III randomised clinical trial in Lagos, Nigeria.* Microbicides 2006 Conference, Cape Town, abstract PC57, 2006.

Patton D, Cosgrove-Sweeney Y, Rohan L. *0.5% Octylglycerol Gel: Vaginal Safety Evaluation in the Macaque Model.* Microbicides 2006 Conference, Cape Town, abstract PA54, 2006.

Trifonova R, Pasicznyk J-M, Fichorova R. *Biocompatibility of solid dosage anti-HIV-1microbicides and vaginal products with the mucosal cytokine network.* Microbicides 2006 Conference, Cape Town, abstract OA35, 2006.

Wallace G. *HIV-1 nucleocapsid zinc finger inhibitors (zfi's) impede HIV-1 trans infection in cellular and explant models.* Microbicides 2006 Conference, Cape Town, abstract OA25, 2006.

Rectal microbicides

Rectal microbicides, it is realised by many researchers working in the field, are also an urgent priority for research and development, but for many reasons have lagged behind the development of vaginal microbicides.

HIV is transmitted about ten times as easily rectally as vaginally, with a frequency (from partners with chronic HIV infection) of about 0.8% per act of intercourse compared with 0.08% (Vittinghoff, Wawer). Obviously in many countries where the epidemic is concentrated among men who have sex with men it is the major route of transmission but both homosexual and heterosexual anal sex may also contribute disproportionately to infections in countries where heterosexual vaginal sex is presumed to be the main transmission route. The taboo nature of both homosexuality and anal sex makes if difficult to establish its exact contribution here.

HIV incidence among gay men is, at the very least, not decreasing in many countries and may be increasing.

One major concern of researchers and microbicide advocates is that once a vaginal microbicide is available it may well be used for anal sex too. Because the rectal mucosa is more delicate than the vaginal mucosa and cervix, this has alarming safety implications. A microbicide that is safe for vaginal but not rectal use could even hasten transmission.

It is also extremely important to realise that anal sex is not restricted to sex between men. In one study of women 'at high risk of HIV infection' (Gross), a third of the women had had anal sex. In another (Erickson) researchers conducted telephone interviews with sample of 3,545 California adults (undersampling those age 44 and older). Seven percent of the sexually active respondents, 8% of males, and 6% of females, reported having anal sex at least once a month during the year prior to the survey. Of these, most engaged in anal sex from one to five times per month, and about 60% reported never using condoms.

Because sexually active gay men probably form at most 3% of the population, this implies that anything from two to six times as many heterosexuals may have anal sex as gay men do - though of course they may not do so often, or with am many partners.

Rectal microbicides - the design challenge

Rectal microbicides need to pass more stringent safety tests than vaginal microbicides because of the fragility of the rectal mucosa. The vaginal mucosa is made up of a so-called 'stratified epithelium'' of cells arranged in layers some 10-12 cells deep. Infection through vaginal tissue is thought to take place only when dendritic cells patrolling the mucosal surface actively transport HIV into the body, or through tears and abrasions in the vaginal wall (the reason for nonoxynol-9's toxicity). The only area with a thinner mucosa than this is the cervix.

In contrast the rectal mucosa is made from a 'columnar epithelium' of just one layer of cuboidal cells. Infection is facilitated by several processes. As well as through tears and abrasions and transport by dendritic cells, HIV may travel passively through the cell in vacuoles (so-called transcytosis) or may actively infect cells which then discharge viral particles into the bloodstream. For all these reasons HIV finds it easier to get through - and microbicides may cause more damage. In addition, though this has yet to be proved, there may be more potential for antiretrovirals in a microbicide to get into the body systemically, with implications for resistance described above.

The other big challenge for rectal microbicides is that a much larger surface area has to be covered. Whereas the vagina is a closed pouch, the rectum is the bottom of an open-ended tube. Craig Hendrix of Johns Hopkins University has done some fascinating experiments subjecting volunteers to simulated sex (both vaginal and anal) within MRI scanning machines. In the case of rectal sex he found that four hours after simulated intercourse and ejaculation, the semen surrogate had travelled up the rectum and colon as far as the splenic flexure - where the colon takes a right-angled turn under the diaphragm to become transverse instead of descending, a distance of about half a metre.

This implies a rectal microbicide might need to have a very different formulation to a vaginal one - possibly in the form of an enema or douche - or at least might need greater volume

Exactly how much gay men were prepared to tolerate was measured by US researcher Alex Carballo-Diéguez in a study reported to the Third International AIDS Society Conference in Rio in 2005.

He got 18 gay men to insert measured amounts of a neutral gel rectally and then to say how much felt comfortable. He used a women's vaginal gel called *Femglide* similar to the placebo gels used in vaginal studies. The discomfort index was measured by how highly the men scored the gel on scales called 'leakage', 'bloating' and 'soiling'.

The upshot was that 20 millilitres (four teaspoons) was acceptable to all 18 men and 35ml to all but three. He then got 14 of the men to use the gel while having anal sex. This reduced the satisfaction scores so that only nine of the 14 found 35ml acceptable, though there was still a 100% acceptability rating for 20ml.

The question is, would this be enough gel to carry a microbicide and to get it everywhere it is needed? The answer is possibly not, given that it would have to get halfway up the colon. Microbicide-expressing gut bacteria may be a long-term solution, but this may never prove to be feasible.

Carballo-Diéguez is planning a second-line trial in 100 men to establish the acceptability of a thicker gel versus a suppository.

Commenting on his studies, Carballo-Diéguez said that part of the challenge of introducing gay men (or anyone) to a microbicide was that it introduced a new behaviour during sex - very much like persuading people to use condoms who hadn't done so before.

"You can't just put on a microbicide like a dab of lube," he said. "You have to put it right up the rectum with an applicator or it doesn't get to where it's needed."

He said the answer might be to put HIV-blocking substances into enemas devised for douching.

Before we can start testing microbicide candidates rectally, even for safety, we need to know about the safety of sexual lubricant gels when used rectally. Although gay men and others have been using these for decades, we know virtually nothing about their potential for cytotoxicity or irritation.

David Phillips of the Population Research Council assessed the safety of 17 different commercial 'lubes' in two studies he presented at Microbicides 2006. In the first study he compared five commercial lubricants (*Vagisil, Viamor, Astroglide, Delube,* and *KY-plus*) for cytotoxicity with a candidate microbicide, Carraguard and with the neutral gel methylcellulose both on rectal explants (cultivated pieces of rectal tissue) and by looking at the infectivity of herpes viruses delivered rectally to mice in the presence of the gels.

He found that two of the lubes (*Delube* and *KY-plus*) were very cytotoxic and all the others mildly so except for *Viamor*. In the case of KY-plus this is not surprising as it includes nonoxynol-9.

He extended his work for the Microbicides 2006 conference. Products assayed were *Forplay Gel-PLUS, Liquid Silk, Maximus, Wet Classic, Wet Platinum, Elbow Grease Light Gel, Eros Bodyglide, Probe Thick Rich, Slippery Stuff, Toys in Babeland, KY Jelly, O'My Natural.*

Methylcellulose and saline were used as the control.

None of the products tested proved to be safer or more protective than the controls. Overall the safest lubricants were found to be *Toys in Babeland, Elbow Grease, Slippery Stuff* and *O'my.* The least safe were *Probe, Anal Lube* and *ForplayGel Plus.* Results for *Maximus* showed that although it did not cause significant sloughing of rectal epithelial cells, it did enhance rectal infection by HSV-2 more than any of the other products.

Although Phillips' work may seem only tangentially connected with microbicides, it is essential to get an understanding of the effect of introducing *any* gel or lubricant into the rectum in order to have baseline criteria for the measurement of the performance of microbicides.

Animal studies

Nonetheless, rectal microbicides have shown evidence of efficacy in animal studies. The proof-of-concept study took place in 2003 when Che-Chung Tsai (who also did the pioneering animal studies in PEP and PrEP) used the dendrimer protein cyanovirin-N to inhibit HIV infection in male rhesus macaques challenged rectally with a 100% infectious dose of a virulent human/monkey chimeric virus, SHIV89.6P.

Four out of four untreated macaques and three out of three treated with a placebo gel were infected and experienced CD4+T cell depletion. In contrast, none of the ten macaques that received either 1% or 2% cyanovirin-N gel showed evidence of SHIV89.6P infection. The researchers reported that neither CV-N nor placebo gels produced any adverse effects in any macaque following the rectal application.

In a Microbicides 2006 Conference in Cape Town, a gel formulation of 1% tenofovir demonstrated protection in four out of six monkeys who were challenged with SIV rectally.

Rhesus macaques received 3ml of 1% tenofovir gel rectally and then 15 minutes or two hours later an infectious dose of SIV.

Infection in CD4 and CD8 cells in the blood was monitored for 20 weeks.

In four out of four untreated macaques and three out of four macaques given a placebo gel SIV virus was recovered at every time point tested from a week after infection.

In contrast, in only one out of six animals receiving tenofovir gel 15 minutes prior to virus challenge was virus recovered persistently and in this animal virus was not recovered until two weeks after challenge. In one other monkey, SIV was recovered only at weeks 2 and 6 and the other four animals appeared to be completely protected from overt infection.

Two out of three animals receiving the tenofovir two hours prior to virus challenge showed no evidence of circulating virus and in the third animal virus isolation was delayed until week 12.

Preparing for human studies

Although teams elsewhere, including the UK, are studying rectal microbicides, the strongest development pipeline for a rectal microbicide comes from the team led by Ian McGowan at the University of California, Los Angeles. The US National Institute of Health granted $16.5 million towards this research and other rectal microbicide research. McGowan's trials will work gradually towards the development of a microbicide whose active ingredient is the NNRTI antiretroviral drug UC-781 (thiocarboxanilide), a drug whose extreme non-bioavailability orally led to it being dropped as an anti-HIV treatment but which makes it ideal for a microbicide.

The first experiments, which are already underway, will compare the performance of gels containing UC-781, tenofovir and TMC120 on cell cultures, cell explants and in monkey challenge studies similar to the tenofovir one above. The second set of trials will research anal sex behaviour in women and men and do more acceptability studies.

Only if results from these are acceptable will McGowan move to a phase I safety study in human volunteers of the actual microbicide. If all goes to plan, this is due to start in HIV-negative subjects in mid-2007 and in HIV-positive subjects in mid-2008.

If safety proves to be acceptable, rectal microbicides could enter a phase II or even phase II/III study in 2010 - around the time the first generation of vaginal microbicides is expected to hit the market, if they prove efficacious.

Political unpopularity

The $16.5m granted for rectal microbicides is only 6% of the $280 million (£156.3m) spent on vaginal microbicides and only 1% on what has been spent on the search for an HIV vaccine.

Part of the problem is the stigma against anal sex and its extreme political unpopularity as a subject for research.

Dr Alex Carballo-Diéguez told a meeting of the US Rectal Microbicides campaign that he had had to call his study 'topical microbicide acceptability in high risk men'.

"We have to play this infantile game," he commented, "Avoiding all mention of words like 'gay', 'MSM' and 'rectal'. It gets past people who are hostile to gay men's work, but it means well-intentioned people trying to find out about rectal microbicide research can't find the paper."

Carballo-Diéguez criticised European funders for putting no money into microbicides for anal sex at all

A report issued at the 2006 Microbicides conference in Cape Town (Feuer) urged more investment into research for microbicides for use in anal sex.

It is estimated that to bring a vaginal microbicide to market, funders need to double the $140 million a year currently being invested in research.

But the report issued by the International Rectal Microbicides Working Group (IRMWG), the first one ever issued on this area of research, finds that this amount dwarfed what has been spent so far on research into rectal microbicides

Although some vaginal microbicide research will further the search for a rectal one, the report could only find $34 million that had ever been spent on rectal microbicide research, and that annual funding, after a promising start, was going down, not up.

In 2006 $7.1 million was granted for research, mainly by US public health bodies, but the US National institutes of Health, which fund the bulk of the research, estimated that only $5.5 million would be granted in 2007.

The IRMWG could find no European funding specifically directed at rectal microbicide research at all, though some is being done with general microbicide funding.

The group estimates that to develop even one rectal microbicide candidate over the next 10-15 years would cost $70 million and that to develop enough to find a really good one $350 million would be needed - meaning that 2006 funding would have to be multiplied fivefold.

Researchers are convinced that the underfunding of the area is due to political prejudices against gay men and the taboo area of anal sex.

Anna Forbes, of the Global Campaign for Microbicides, said: "A receptive sex partner is a receptive sex partner. We need rectal microbicides, just as we need vaginal microbicides, to help receptive sex partners save their own lives."

References

Carballo-Diéguez A. *Rectal microbicide acceptability: results of a volume escalation trial.* Third IAS Conference on HIV Pathogenesis and Treatment, Rio de Janeiro. Abstract MoPp0206. 2005.

Hendrix C et al. *Imaging the distribution of a rectal microbicide gel and semen surrogate in the lower GI tract.* Microbicides 2004 Conference, London, Abstract 02685.

Erickson PI et al. *Prevalence of anal sex among heterosexuals in California and its relationship to other AIDS risk behaviors.* AIDS Educ Prev. 7(6):477-93. 1995.

Feuer C. Rectal Microbicides: Investments and Advocacy. International Rectal Microbicides Working Group. 2006. Available from http://www.aidschicago.org/prevention/lifelube.php

Gross, M. et al. *Anal sex among HIV-seronegative women at high risk of HIV exposure.* JAIDS 24:393-398. 2000.

Patton D, Cosgrove-Sweeney Y, Hillier S. *Rectal Safety Studies Conducted in the Pigtailed Macaque.* Microbicides 2006 Conference, Cape Town, abstract PA59, 2006.

Shattock M. *Protection of macaques against rectal SIV challenge by mucosally-applied PMPA.* Microbicides 2006 Conference, Cape Town, abstract OA15, 2006.

Vittinghoff E. Per-contact risk of human immunodeficiency virus transmission between male sexual partners. *American Journal of Epidemiology* 150(3), 306-311. 1999.

Wawer M J et al. HIV-1 Transmission per coital act, by stage of HIV infection in the HIV+ index partner, in discordant couples, Rakai, Uganda. Tenth Conference on Retroviruses and Opportunistic Infections, Boston, abstract 40, 2003.

Challenges to microbicide development

Where microbicide trials differ from vaccine trials and even drug efficacy trials is that there is no obvious 'surrogate marker' for efficacy, in line with immune responses that can be measured for a vaccine or blood levels of a drug that can be compared with those that block the virus in cell cultures. While these may not translate into clinical benefit, candidate vaccines that do not produce such immune responses can be eliminated. With microbicides, there is no measure of success so far other than the incidence of HIV in the study population.

For this reason, microbicides need to progress relatively early to full-scale ('Phase III') trials of their effectiveness.

Phase III trials of microbicides (to test efficacy) are complex and expensive, and raise many of the same ethical issues as preventive vaccine trials. Microbicides must be provided alongside and in combination with other means of protection, including counselling, condom provision and medical treatment of infections.

For these reasons, studies have to be very large. Andrew Nunn of the Medical Research Council told the 2004 Microbicides Conference that a 12-month randomised study recruiting 2,000 women in a country with 5% annual HIV incidence (possibly high, even for Africa) would have a one in three chance of failing to detect a halving of the incidence.

This is because the actual difference in numbers between 50 and 25 women infected hovers very near the boundary of statistical significance. If the microbicide was 40% effective and the incidence 4%, no meaningful data could be generated, Nunn said.

The Carraguard study, for example, has enrolled 5,620 women so far, but there are plans to accrue 6,639 women to measure a 33% reduction in HIV incidence.

There are numerous behavioural problems that could confound the data. One of the most significant is adherence. Norman Hearst of UCSF pointed out that a theoretical efficacy of 98-99% for condoms had never been translated into a 'real world' actual effectiveness of more than 85-90%, due to the difficulty of maintaining 100% use. Given that an optimistic prediction for the efficacy of the first generation of microbicides is 60%, the actual proportion of infections prevented could be small enough to be undetectable except in the most high-powered studies.

Because adherence tends to weaken over time, opinion is turning away from huge trials lasting two to three years. If the aim of the first phase III trials is to demonstrate the efficacy of the compound under ideal conditions, more meaningful data would be generated by a group of very high-risk women receiving intensive monitoring for a shorter period. For this reason, a couple of the phase III trials changed their follow-up period from two years to one year or, in the case of the South African MDP trial of *PRO-2000* and dextran sulphate, nine months (this is also the biggest trial, with a planned recruitment of 12,600 women in six countries).

Microbicide trials are also a thorny ethical area. There is the problem of providing enough monitoring and support to participants to ensure adherence while not providing so much that condom use increases enough to make results meaningless.

Conversely, over-confidence by participants because they are using the microbicide could lead to 'condom migration'; and this could result in the trial producing more, rather than fewer, cases of HIV.

There is also the problem of placebo control. We may only have one 'go' at placebo-controlled microbicide trials, because if a compound produces marginally significant results it would not then be ethical to re-test it in a second placebo trial. It would have to be tested against another active compound and this would require an even larger trial.

Another area regarding the design of phase III trials that has caused great controversy, and not been properly resolved, is whether to include a no-treatment or 'condom-only' arm in trials. The US Food and Drug Agency has insisted on a three-arm design: a) microbicide plus condom b) placebo plus condom c) condom only.

A 'condom-only' arm is desirable, firstly because some placebo gels might have slight anti-HIV properties themselves and this can be measured against a condom-only arm; and secondly because it would then be possible to measure whether the microbicide/placebo becomes a disincentive to condom use.

But it is essentially adding an unblinded arm to a blinded trial. There is no guarantee that trials would not be biased by the fact that one group is receiving no compound changing their sexual behaviour. People in the microbicide and placebo arms could give trial compound to the no-treatment people (this has confounded results in trials of breast-milk substitutes before). And, of course, another arm either adds to the size of the trial by 50% or reduces its power by 33%.

It is thought that the HIV Prevention Treatment Network 035 trial of *Buffergel* and *PRO-2000*, which is regulated by the FDA, was delayed and had to be scaled down into a less powerful phase II/III trial (where safety is pre-assessed in a small preliminary study) because the FDA insist on a condom-only arm as a condition of any product receiving a licence.

Microbicide trials involve screening people for HIV, and in high-prevalence countries this results in a lot of women finding out they have HIV. Some presenters commented that this was leading to counsellor burnout and stretched support resources, particularly in rural areas with poor infrastructure.

Anal sex (a subject just beginning to be researched in Africa) could confound results, as could IV drug use and other high-risk activities. However, the exclusion of people who report these activities could simply lead to people concealing them in the 'coital diaries' that are a feature of many of the trials.

Finally there is the question of 'standard of care', which was the subject of a whole plenary. What are researchers' obligations to trial participants who become HIV-positive or suffer adverse events? Are researchers were obliged to offer the best possible care, the standard of care in the host country, or something in between?

A consensus arrived at the 2004 conference was that developed-world care standards were not realistic and that the best that could be hoped for was that the process of doing a trial would 'ratchet up' local skills and infrastructure enough to benefit the whole population as well as trial failures. However the increasing but patchy provision of antiretrovirals in trial countries means that these care standards have to be constantly recalculated rather than set in stone at the start of a trial that may last several years.

Estimates for the cost of bringing a successful microbicide or choice of microbicides to market from the current pipeline range from $750m to $1bn; and that is without accounting for unforeseen events like trial failures or new classes of compound.

At the 2006 Microbicides Conference in Cape Town, some of these concerns came into sharper focus.

Poor adherence to condoms means poor adherence to microbicides

Women randomised to microbicides in the phase III studies reported that they did not always use the products as consistently as they should, and in one study, adherence to the microbicides was lower without condoms than when condoms are being used.

Self-reported behaviour, particularly around microbicide and condom use (and sexual behaviour in general), is not always reliable but if these trends continue, it could make it more difficult for those studies to provide clear answers as to whether the products work or not. Numerous presentations at the Microbicides 2006 Conference focused on ways to improve acceptance, encourage longer-term adherence - and to verify whether the products are being used or not in the ongoing trials.

The investigators in the clinical efficacy trials of microbicides are in the awkward position of needing to encourage participants in their studies to use both the product to which they've been randomised (microbicide or placebo) *and* practice safer sex and use condoms - but the trials would have a better chance of reaching a clear conclusion about the effectiveness of the microbicide if people did not actually use the condoms.

According to Dr Elof Johansson of the Population Council, which is conducting the phase III trial of the microbicide, Carraguard, consistent condom use probably works better than the microbicide:

"For ethical reasons we have to promote condom use within the trial. In my 35 years of experience working with clinical trials, I've never been in such a difficult situation were you have to promote another treatment that will work **as good, and probably better,** than the product you are testing. So we have to rely on non-compliance on the condom side and compliance on the gel."

Yet just the reverse - better adherence to condoms than the microbicide - is being reported in some studies.

For example, in the cellulose sulfate trial in Nigeria, participants reported using a condom for 90% of sexual acts in the past week, but women reported using the microbicide less frequently for 83% of the sex acts in the past week. Reports from the *Savvy Nigeria* study are similar (88% using condoms, 78% using gel for sexual acts in the past week). Such high condom use rates, if true and sustained, would mean that very few women in the study may become infected - and that the trials may be too small to reach a clear conclusion.

And muddying the picture even further, women in HPTN 035, which compares *Pro 2000* and *BufferGel* to a gel placebo or no gel, are reporting that they use the microbicide less frequently when they don't use the condoms, which could confound the study's ability to measure the effect of the microbicide.

According to the study's protocol chair, Dr Salim Karim: "In many ways, we spend so much time within our trial promoting a highly efficacious prevention method in the form of condoms, and we have depended to some extent upon the fact that a condom will simply not be used on every occasion; and in those particular instances where condoms are not used, that we would have a high proportion of those women adhering to the gel. So in a way we are looking for two conflicting things, non-adherence to the condom and adherence to the gel and you can see the hazards and problems that that particularly poses." See table below.

Among participants assigned to gel, number of last vaginal sex acts reported by 422 participants

	With gel	Without gel	Total
With condom	82%	18%	70%
Without condom	57%	43%	30%
Total	74%	26%	100%

What if HIV incidence is too low?

Savvy is a surface active microbicide which entered into a phase III efficacy study in March 2004 at two sites in Ghana (Ampofo). The researchers estimated that there would be at least five infections per 100 person years in the placebo group, and that they would observe at least 66 incident infections.

However, halfway through the study, an interim analysis found that only 17 total seroconversions had occurred: nine on placebo and eight on *Savvy*.

This HIV incidence was dramatically lower than anyone anticipated, and the trial was closed on the recommendation of the Data Safety and Monitoring Board because HIV incidence in the study population was too low to demonstrate whether or not the microbicide had an effect.

"We cannot make any conclusion about product effectiveness using this protocol in the Ghana cohort," said Dr Leigh Peterson of FHI, who presented these results.

So what happened? No one is exactly sure but there are a number of theories.

- One is that the HIV epidemic in Ghana, or at least these parts of Ghana, has matured and that the incidence in the area is simply on the decline.

- Another is that the high rate of pregnancy - about four times as common as HIV seroconversion in this study - decreased the likelihood of the study to reach a result, because the women who were most likely to become infected simply became pregnant first, and then either dropped out of the study or changed their sexual risk taking behaviour for the sake of the pregnancy.

- A final possibility (that might be even more problematic for the conduct of these studies) is that simply participating in an ethical patient-centred prevention trial reduces the risk of HIV acquisition dramatically. It's important to remember that these women get the best available safer sex counselling and support, which is reinforced with every clinic visit. The stress of being repeatedly tested for HIV may be a fairly effective motivator to reduce one's risk taking behaviour.

In fact, self-reported condom use has increased significantly in several of the microbicide studies. For example, in *Savvy* Nigeria, participants reported that condoms were used for 66% of their last sex acts. After follow-up, however, participants reported that they now used condoms for 88% of their sex acts within the last seven days (gel use, however, was not as high). In the CS #2 study, self-reported condom use during the last week went up from 58% at screening, to 90% at follow-up.

There is also another answer, for "when a placebo is not a placebo?" When you receive free medical treatment to which you previously didn't have access, including treatment of sexually transmitted infections (STIs). Treatment of STIs directly impacts the likelihood of HIV acquisition.

If simply conducting a good HIV prevention study dramatically lowers HIV incidence, it would be a happy outcome for the trial participants, but many of these studies could find that they are underpowered.

Mess and awkwardness

The adherence issues in the MIRA study diaphragm study are even more complicated because the experimental arm has two components: the All-Flex diaphragm with *Replens* gel (a vaginal moisturiser). Overall, adherence in the study is lower than expected but if that weren't trouble enough, women often don't use the gel provided with the diaphragm. Participants in the trial reported using condoms at last sexual contact about 70% of the time (in both arms), while in the diaphragm and gel arm, only slightly more-76%-of the sex was covered by diaphragm, but the gel was only used in 50% of the last sex acts. Such low adherence could indicate that there is a problem with product acceptability in this setting, for both the diaphragm and for the gel.

More women in the study wanted to remove the diaphragm immediately after sex - but to be effective, diaphragms need to remain within the vagina for 6-24 hours after sex, depending upon the model. In another study from Madagascar,

Acceptability studies are usually conducted in the early stages of product development and clinical testing, in order to understand

Messiness or excessive wetness has frequently been cited as another drawback of some of the gels, and could be part of the problem with poor adherence in a number of the studies.

"Not surprisingly, gels increase lubrication" said the key note speaker on acceptability studies, Professor Joanne Mantell, a public health and social scientist from Columbia University, "but preferences regarding lubrication vary. Some studies show that women do not like a product that is too messy or drippy, although it is difficult to know what the underlying meaning is of excessive vaginal fluids."

In a Brazilian safety study (Hardy), participants said that would like to use a smaller amount each time, and that this gel should be less fluid to prevent excessive lubrication or messiness.

It should be pointed out that most of the various microbicides in advanced studies have specifically been designed to be less messy. Even so, the lubrication does not go unnoticed - including often, by the male partner.

While lubrication may be desirable for sex in Western society, in some African cultures, men prefer dry sex. Male partners may interpret too much lubrication, especially before sexual intercourse, as meaning that the woman is unfaithful, has a sexually transmitted infection or has poor vaginal hygiene. Several studies noted that regular male partners are occasionally problem for adherence in some studies - particularly if they were not informed of the woman's participation or involved in the study from early on.

But the acceptability or adherence problems in these studies could also simply be due to logistics, e.g., having access to and being able to insert the gel before sex occurs could be the issue. Several studies noted that storage and disposal of gel applicators and privacy needed to assemble the applicator and apply the gel in advance of sexual activity can be problematic in resource-limited settings.

Product adherence in clinical trials is generally higher than when products are on the market, so getting to the bottom of these problems is crucial in order to anticipate problems in up-take and adherence that could occur and actually be worse once an effective product goes to market.

Counselling messages

One of the reasons why there is usually higher product use is because of high levels of staff support and the desire to please staff. But another possibility is that the staff counselling participants in the studies could be communicating the mixed messages about using the microbicides.

Although there's only been a limited number of studies looking at the role of providers (from doctors to counsellors who are providing safe sex counselling), they have found that "providers say that they are reluctant to counsel people to use a 'half-safe method' especially when condoms offer a higher level of protection. The concept of harm reduction has not been incorporated into sexual risk reduction counselling in most settings, especially among family planning providers, who typically aim to promote the most effective contraceptive methods," Prof. Mantell said.

Preliminary indications are that this could at least be part of the problem. According to Dr Karem, in HPTN 035, "the team's initial exploration suggests that there may have been some misunderstanding of counselling messages among study staff and participants. So we're looking at how to address this challenge and refine the kinds of messages that might be used to improve adherence to gel. Over the weekend before the conference, the protocol team got together to develop enhanced adherence counselling messages and scripts for immediate use at all the sites."

Likewise, in the MIRA diaphragm study, they are focusing on the study staff, conducting in-person meetings trying to reinforce the importance of using the gel. They discuss how staff should respond to a patient who reports that either she or her partner does not want to use some/all products, stressing the importance of use for study results with role-playing and so on.

Such adaptability over the course of the study may overcome the adherence challenges faced in these studies - but in case it doesn't always work, performing on treatment or on-adherence analyses could salvage the ability of these studies to determine whether the microbicides are effective in the subset of women who actually use the products.

But since self-reports are not always reliable, some of the studies are looking for more concrete evidence that the products have been used. In the MDP301 study they are looking at gel returns after a pilot study found that, if asked, women will return virtually all their used and unused applicators. This practice also allows the pharmacy staff to flag the participants whose gel use is low, who then receive intensive counselling to achieve overall higher gel adherence.

Who will control microbicides?

The recurring motif of the Microbicides 2006 conference, represented everywhere on conference bags, programmes, and banners, was an illustration of a beautiful African woman in traditional dress, with hands outstretched as if receiving a gift - presumably, given the conference theme - of a way that she controls to protect herself from exposure to HIV. This is in contrast to condoms, which, although highly effective if used properly and consistently, require negotiation with her male partner - a negotiation that the woman is likely to lose in many situations in the developing world.

Microbicides have been billed as a female-controlled HIV prevention method; but even though most women like the idea that they could use such a product without informing their partners, most would nevertheless prefer to tell their regular partners if they are using a microbicide, according to studies presented at the Microbicide 2006 conference. Some want to disclose the use of microbicides to enhance intimacy while others believe that gel-based lubricants would be detectable to their partners - and fear negative consequences.

Such consequences have already been observed in some of the clinical efficacy studies as researchers reported that failure to involve men in the clinical trials of microbicides has sometimes contributed to poorer adherence to microbicide use and has even led to some women dropping out of the studies. As a result, researchers are increasingly looking at ways of involving regular male partners in the trials from early on.

"Microbicides are branded to be female-controlled or aimed at empowering women in sexual encounters which threatens the traditional gender roles and societal norms", Zoë Bakoko Bakoru, the Ugandan Minister for Gender, Labour and Social Development, told the conference.

"But the development of microbicides could be seen as a venture leading to taking power away from the men. And within your societies, you know who is in charge of sex and how it is played, and who enjoys it most and who doesn't." Minister Bakoru mentioned dry sex, a practice which increases women's vulnerability - and which could conflict with gel-based microbicides that increase lubrication. "Dry sex is not a pleasure for the women but for the man."

Even when the context of partnership and sex appears to be loving and trusting, women are at risk

"Ironically, trust and affection within marriage and other long-term relationships are sometimes part of the problem," said Minister Bakoru. "We have been preaching a lot about the use of condoms, but the use of condoms is also decided by the man. And research has also shown that when people have used condoms three or four times, then the question comes 'don't you trust me?' and the condom is thrown to the side." A number of studies suggest that the desire for love and trust within a relationship will lead to microbicide use being negotiated in much the same way as is condom use.

"The majority of studies show that women want to tell their partners about using a microbicide," said Professor Joanne Mantell, a public health and social scientist from Columbia University. "There are a number of reasons why. Communications

may enhance intimacy, and women want to share the responsibility for protection with their partners."

Even when women know better than to trust their regular partners, studies suggest it may not be easy to use a gel-based microbicide without him knowing.

"Covert use or the ability to use a prevention method without the explicit knowledge of male partners is one of the main reasons for developing microbicides," said Dr Hoffman. However, many participants in HPTN 050 (a US trial) felt that it would be difficult to keep using gel-based microbicides a secret. In the study, 86% of the women reported increased vaginal lubrication with the gel and some women were pretty sure that their regular partners would know. Other studies with gels also report increased vaginal lubrication. In one African study, even though HIV-positive men were supportive of their partner's microbicide use, the majority (51%) of the men reported that the women could not hide its use as they were able to feel the gel's wetness during sex.

Thus, since the use of a gel microbicide may be impossible to keep as a secret from their regular partners, studies show that some woman will disclose use to avert potential negative repercussions, such as preventing accusations of infidelity and avoiding the possibility of being abandoned by partners.

Future studies within the community at large will be essential to get the exact picture of how male involvement could affect microbicide use - and what sort of community-based marketing might be necessary to change attitudes. In the meantime, the job might be made easier if the microbicidal products that eventually go to the market have broader applications than simply being anti-HIV or anti-STI (sexually transmitted infections). Combination products that are seen being for female hygiene or contraception might raise fewer eyebrows and allow women more freedom to use a product without raising suspicion. Also, slow-release technologies such as intravaginal rings or even oral PrEP may better deliver on the promise of women-controlled devices.

Finally, Lori Heise of the GCM thinks that the development of microbicides present an opportunity to "begin the discussion about sex and power. But it can't end there. Successful microbicide introduction also requires working on the underlying gender power imbalances that condition women's risk.

"I think we need to embed our work on microbicides into women's protection strategies [which] also include the need for social power and economic opportunities, and if we don't [address these other factors], it's not going to matter if we have a safe and effective microbicide."

References

Ampofo W et al. *Randomized controlled trial of SAVVY and HIV in Ghana: operational challenges of the Accra site.* Microbicides 2006 Conference, Cape Town, abstract AB4, 2006.

Bakoru ZB. *Vaginas and applicators: expanding the national discourse on microbicides, sex and sexuality.* Microbicides 2006 Conference, Cape Town, Plenary talk, 2006.

Hardy E, Hebling EM, De Sousa MH. *Devices for the administration of a vaginal microbicide: use difficulties, adherence to use and preferred device.* Microbicides 2006 Conference, Cape Town, PC23, 2006.

Hebling EM, Hardy E, De Sousa MH. *Devices for the administration of a vaginal microbicide: suggestions on how to make three devices more attractive.* Microbicides 2006 Conference, Cape Town, OC6, 2006.

Heise L et al. *The WHO multi-country study on women's health and domestic violence: implications for microbicide development.* Microbicides 2006 Conference, Cape Town, OC12, 2006.

Kilbourne-Brook M et al. *SILCS Diaphragm: acceptability of a single-size, reusable cervical barrier by couples in three countries.* Microbicides 2006 Conference, Cape Town, PC33, 2006.

Manickum S et al. *Challenges in introducing vaginal diaphragm among women in a phase III HIV prevention clinical trial.* Microbicides 2006 Conference, Cape Town, PB44, 2006.

Mantell J. *Acceptability research: Outcomes & future direction.* Microbicides 2006 Conference, Cape Town, key note address #1, 2006.

Nunn A. *Criteria for advancing into phase III.* Microbicides 2004 Conference, London. Speaker presentation CT-03.

The search for an HIV vaccine

The day the discovery of the Human Immunodeficiency Virus was announced in 1984, the then US Health Secretary Margaret Heckler forecast that a vaccine against the newly-discovered virus should not be too difficult to develop. She said: "We hope to have such a vaccine ready for testing in approximately two years. Yet another terrible disease is about to yield to patience, persistence and outright genius".

We know an HIV vaccine must be possible. For example, on average ten years elapse from the time one is infected with HIV to when the virus has done enough damage to warrant AIDS diagnosis. This means that the immune system has some ability to control HIV, albeit temporarily. The role of a vaccine could be to boost these defences to where they can contain an HIV infection permanently.

Additionally, there are individuals who exhibit an exceptional ability to shrug off HIV infection, and analysing what is different about their immune systems yields ideas for vaccines. For example, some female sex workers and partners of gay men have remained uninfected, or infected but able to control infection so it is harmless, for many years, despite repeated sex without condoms. Researchers are building and testing vaccines designed to stimulate the immune cells that are believed to be responsible for these people's apparent acquired immunity to the virus.

Already experimental vaccines against SIV, a close cousin of HIV that infects monkeys, have been shown to prevent AIDS (Shiver). What works in animals does not always translate into humans; still this is an exciting proof of concept, and the results from these experiments have led to the development of only the second large

human trial of a candidate vaccine, the STEP trial of the Merck trivalent adenovirus-5 vaccine, which started in May 2006.

When Heckler made her original announcement, the listening experts already knew better than to expect a vaccine in a couple of years. Several scientists seated in the packed auditorium "blanched visibly" at Heckler's declaration, according to Randy Shilts' history of the early epidemic, *And the Band Played On*.

They were right to be cautious. After all, it had taken 105 years after the discovery of the typhoid bacterium to develop a vaccine for typhoid. For whooping cough (pertussis) it had taken 89 years; for polio and measles 47 and 42 years.

But the time lag was getting shorter. It had only taken 16 years from the discovery of the hepatitis B virus to the development of a vaccine against that disease. Margaret Heckler may have been naively optimistic, but surely HIV, probably the most intensively-researched pathogen of all time, would yield to an effective vaccine within a decade or two?

Far from it. Twenty-two years after the discovery of HIV, we appear nowhere near the development of a truly preventative HIV vaccine. About the furthest we have got are experiments in which some monkeys given a vaccine and then challenged with SIV, though still infected, showed signs of not progressing to AIDS: they maintained their CD4 counts and had lower-than-average viral loads

Even researchers previously optimistic about a vaccine have tempered their optimism in the last few years.

At the Barcelona World AIDS Conference in 2002, for instance, Jose Esparza, then of the WHO Vaccine Initiative, advised caution about the then much-publicised first-ever large efficacy trial of an HIV vaccine, the AIDSVAX trial. (he was right to be: six months later it was found to be ineffective). Nonetheless, he predicted that at least one phase III trial of a workable vaccine would be underway within the next three years - and that there should be at least one effective HIV vaccine available by 2009.

Two years later at the Bangkok World AIDS Conference, Esparza, by this time seconded to the Bill and Melinda Gates Foundation, was much less optimistic.

He said: "When HIV was discovered we all expected that an HIV vaccine would be very quickly developed. And we were wrong because this virus proved to be much more complex than we had thought at that time." Developing an HIV vaccine, he added, was "one of the most difficult scientific challenges that biomedical science is confronting."

Esparza pointed out that the search for a **first generation** of HIV vaccines - ones that elicit antibodies to neutralize HIV (see below) - was started soon after HIV was discovered in 1984. It appeared to have finally run into the ground 20 years later in February 2003 when the first-ever (and still effectively the only) large phase III efficacy trial of an HIV vaccine ended in failure, demonstrating that the AIDSVAX gp120 vaccine was ineffective.

He said that the search for the **second generation** - vaccines that elicit a cellular immune response and stimulate anti-HIV CD8 cells - started in around 1990. The first study that stands a chance of showing whether a CD8 vaccine offers significant protection to humans, the STEP study of the Merck adenovirus-5 trivalent vaccine, started in 2006 and may produce results by 2011/12. It may therefore take at least two decades to find out if this approach yields an effective vaccine.

There are many reasons to suspect it won't, or that it will only produce a vaccine that moderates the course of infection rather than prevents it.

Esparza therefore advocated for the development of a **third generation** of HIV vaccines, ones that include both a CD8-stimulating component but which also stimulate elusive 'broadly neutralising' antibodies that will act against fleetingly-exposed 'conserved' parts of HIV that cannot evade immune control.

The first serious experiments describing these broadly neutralising antibodies took place in 2000/1 (see Stiegler).

Given the time taken to show proof-of-concept (or lack of it) for the previous two generations of vaccine candidates, therefore, Esparza forecast that an effective HIV vaccine might now not be available until 2017-2021.

Why had Esparza's estimate of the time for the arrival of a vaccine jumped ten years forward in the space of two years? To answer that question we will have to look at what an HIV vaccine would have to do in order to work.

What an HIV vaccine would have to do

A vaccine is essentially a 'fake infection'. It is a way of priming the body by getting it to mount an immune response to essentially harmless microbes - or to parts of microbes called antigens - so that these immune responses also work against a similar but disease-causing microbe later on. The principle is essentially unchanged since Robert Jenner observed that dairymaids exposed to the relatively harmless cowpox virus were later immune to the ravages of the smallpox virus.

Vaccines set in motion an immune response the body would mount against the dangerous pathogen (disease-causing organism) anyway.

The reason most diseases kill is not that the body mounts no fight against them but because there is always a timelag between an invasion by a previously-unknown infection and the immune system learning how to fight it.

In a few cases the invader will win and kill or cripple - either by directly causing damage before the immune system can stop it, or by generating an immune response so extreme that it starts to damage the body's own cells (this is what is thought to happen in illnesses like SARS and bird flu, and it is also the cause of the liver damage in chronic hepatitis B infection).

In most cases the immune system will eventually win and the invader will be driven out. Vaccine, with most diseases, primes the immune system to invaders so that when it eventually arrives, it is already 'known' to the immune system and there is a much shorter timelag between infection and the generation of an effective immune response.

Vaccines do this in the same way that infections do. Once an antigen of any sort - a bacterium, a virus, a parasite, a vaccine, even chemical, drugs and dust - enters the body for the first time, the immune system sets about devising an immune response that will, in future, defeat this invader. It does this in several ways - with **innate** immunity (a set of chemicals that non-specifically attack invaders), with **humoral** immunity (a set of free-floating proteins called antibodies that either chemically neutralise invaders or tag them for destruction) or with **cellular** immunity (a set of roving cells that destroy infected cells).

In the latter two cases, the initial attack leaves behind a few **memory** cells. These are cells that have 'learned' the signature of the invaders to that when the same one (or apparently the same one) turns up again, the immune system can spring into action far faster and contain an infection before it has any time to do damage.

It is this memory effect that vaccines exploit, and the goal of an HIV vaccine would be to produce enough broadly-effective memory B-cells (which make antibodies) and T-cells (which direct and operate the cell-killing mechanism) to recognise any strain of HIV when it arrives and quickly neutralise it.

Vaccination happens all the time naturally, in the spirit of Nietzsche's saying "That which does not kill us, makes us stronger."

Malaria, for instance, is a particularly tricky infection because, like HIV, it constantly changes its shape in order to fool the immune system. However children in Africa who do not die of repeated malaria infections within their first three years will eventually develop a broad enough immune response to malaria to either repel further infections or develop only mild symptoms.

One theory as to why allergies like asthma are so much more common in the modern world is the so-called 'hygiene hypothesis'. This states that children these days are not exposed to *enough* allergens and germs when they are young. As a result, their immune system does not 'learn' to respond appropriately to certain foreign substances and mounts a disproportionate response when it finally encounters them.

This provides the clue as to why it has proven so difficult to develop a vaccine against HIV. The body *does* mount an immune response to HIV - indeed, without one, the virus would destroy the average person's immune system within weeks rather than years.

However in the case of HIV infection the immune response is sufficient neither to prevent infection in the first place nor to prevent the virus circumventing the body's immune defences in the long run.

An HIV vaccine, therefore, would have to do 'better than nature' - and that is why is has proven so difficult to develop.

An HIV vaccine would have to do one of three things.

Humoral immunity

It could prevent infection in the first place by generating so-called 'sterilising immunity'.

Sterilising immunity, broadly speaking, happens when the body mounts an antibody or humoral response to the infection. Antibodies are extremely variable Y-shaped protein molecules that are produced in huge quantities by the B-cells of the immune system. They either destroy invading microbes themselves or tag them for destruction by other components of the immune system. If the invader is one the body already recognises, an antibody response can be generated so fast that an infection never becomes established. If it is not recognised, it may take some time for enough antibodies that 'fit' the invader to be generated.

Some vaccinations, so-called **passive** ones, actually consist of antibodies rather than of antigens that generate an antibody response. Passive inoculation with anti-hepatitis B antibodies, for instance, is used to strengthen the immune response and augment the regular vaccine, especially in cases where exposure may have already happened as in a needlestick injury. However passive inoculation is similar to using a drug - the antibodies quickly disappear from the body and no permanent immunity is generated.

Antibodies generally only recognise the surface molecules of bacteria, viruses, parasites etc. The first generation of candidate HIV vaccines, therefore, used this principle. They consisted of parts of HIV's envelope - the outer viral covering. In particular, they used the gp120 protein that forms the 'knobs' on the surface of HIV that are the virus's mechanism for entering cells.

Hope that an envelope vaccine might work died when the AIDSVAX vaccine trial (see below) proved ineffective in February 2003 (rgp120 HIV Vaccine Study Group), and were finally buried when the second AIDSVAX trial in Thailand (Pitisutithum) proved equally ineffective two years later.

Why did they not work? The answer lies in the hyper-variability of the HIV envelope.

The gp120 protein, and in particular the part of the molecule called the V3 loop that actually makes contact with cellular receptors, is the most variable part of the HIV virus. Not only is the antibody sequence that makes up the core chain of the protein more variable than any other part of HIV, but it is also heavily 'glycosylated'. This means that HIV, as it evolves, coats its envelope protein with an immensely variable 'fuzz' of sugar molecules that frustrate the attempts of antibodies to latch on to it.

What this means, essentially, is that an HIV envelope vaccine would produce an antibody response - but only one that worked against the *exact* strain of virus that the vaccine was developed from, or imitated. The first generation of vaccines did not work because they were uselessly specific.

Cellular immunity

The other thing a vaccine could do is to delay or halt the damage that an established infection can do.

It would do this by stimulating the other branch of the immune system - the **cellular** immunity.

The prime movers in the cellular immune system are the cytotoxic T-lymphocytes, otherwise known as the CD8 cells. This branch of the immune system developed to deal with the problem that once a virus is inside a cell, it essentially becomes invisible to the humoral immune system.

However cells have a mechanism whereby they 'advertise' their contents by displaying tiny fragments of their internal constituents, called epitopes, on their surface. This is the way the body distinguishes between self and not-self - and between healthy cells and ones subverted into virus-making factories.

Cells infected by viruses and other pathogens display tiny pieces of the viral proteins on their surface. When the immune system senses the presence of foreign epitopes, a cascade of immune activation is generated which ends with the CD8 cells destroying the infected cell.

The advantage of this kind of immunity is that the cell displays protein fragments from all parts of the invading virus and not just its envelope. In the case of HIV, this means that an immune response can be generated against deeper, more 'conserved' parts of HIV that cannot afford to vary so much genetically if the virus is to work.

The disadvantage of the cellular immune response is that it does not prevent an infection, but acts against already-infected cells.

In most illnesses, this does not matter; the cellular immune response rids body of sick cells and the disease is gone. Serious damage only occurs if so many cells are infected that the immune response itself becomes harmful.

However in the case of retroviruses like HIV and the HTLV viruses, the virus becomes incorporated into the cell's genetic code itself - as proviral DNA.

By the time this has happened, the virus has essentially lost its identity as an independent entity and become so much part of the cell that it is not recognised as foreign. It is only when the cell is activated and starts producing new viruses that the immune system can recognise it as infected.

For this reason, a vaccine that generated cellular immunity could have immensely variable effects depending on whether it acts in time to prevent the incorporation of HIV's genes into the human cells' DNA.

At best, it might be able to turn people into 'exposed seronegatives'. The majority of exposed seronegatives remain little-studied and we don't know how many there are and why they did not develop HIV infections. They are people who remain HIV antibody-negative but in whom extremely sensitive tests detect signs of a historical infection by HIV - one that remains so well-contained that not enough virus is ever present to trip the humoral immune response and induce antibodies to HIV.

Even though exposed seronegatives do not have antibodies to HIV, immune experiments showed that their T-cells 'recognise' HIV in the test tube - so they must have seen it before (see Shearer). The types of cellular responses detected included both CD4 and CD8 cell responses to HIV and the production of immune-activating cytokines in response to HIV. These CD4 and CD8 responses have been reported in sexual partners of HIV-infected individuals, as well as in seronegative healthcare workers who were accidentally exposed to HIV-infected blood via a needle stick.

At the time of the above study, no HIV was detectable within these people by PCR viral load testing. Subsequent extremely sensitive PCR testing, however, has found that many exposed seronegatives may have extremely small viral loads - in the order of 0.05 copies This means that they do have some cells that have been infected by HIV and contain proviral DNA.

What appears to be the case with most of them, however, is that by good luck, good genes or good timing, their immune system developed a CD8 response against actively-infected cells so efficient that it nips any productive viral infection in the bud.

One fascinating example of this phenomenon was a study by Tuofu Zhu presented at the Bangkok International AIDS Conference. Zhu was studying long-term exposed seronegative partners of HIV-positive gay men. The group consisted of the HIV-negative partners of HIV-positive men who had been diagnosed between 1994 and 1998.

Out of 94 HIV-negative regular partners of positive men, he found 14 who had in fact become HIV-positive - a rate of only 15%, despite regular unprotected sex with their partners over a period of years.

Two of the partners appeared to have caught HIV from their partners early on in their relationship, but to have mounted a successful immune response to it. They had no antibodies to HIV and therefore did not test HIV-positive. The fact that they had HIV at all could only be detected by hypersensitive viral-load testing, which picked up HIV in their blood at a count of 0.05 copies - one thousandth of the amount usually called "undetectable" by standard "ultrasensitive" tests.

The ultimate goal of a CD8 vaccine, therefore, would be to turn people into 'fake' exposed seronegatives.

However no CD8 vaccine has come anywhere near producing such an effective immune response, and the exposed seronegatives - or at least the ones that have been studied, who are mainly multiply-exposed people that somehow do not become HIV-positive - remain with their immunity secrets tantalisingly elusive (it appears now that they may also generate broadly neutralising antibodies - see below).

What CD8 vaccines have done up until now, at least in animal studies, is to blunt HIV infection. Though the vaccine-generated immune response may not be able to stop people becoming HIV-positive, it may be enough to slow down viral production by interfering with the chain-reaction of viral infection and reproduction. A vaccine of this kind might not be able to prevent people becoming HIV-positive (and in many cases would actually generate a 'false positive' result itself). But it might be able to contain HIV reproduction and enable people to develop a much lower viral load; so low, possibly, that progression to AIDS might never happen.

This kind of vaccine essentially blurs the distinction between a **preventative** vaccine and a **therapeutic** one. The latter are not the subject of this chapter as they are a treatment. But the object of scientists who are trying to develop therapeutic vaccines is essentially identical: by manipulating parts of the immune system of people with HIV in such a way that their anti-HIV CD8 responses are amplified, they are aiming to contain HIV infection to the point where it becomes non-pathogenic.

The other very important thing therapeutic or cellular vaccines could do would be to do what HIV treatment can also do - they would act to prevent onward HIV infection by lowering the average viral load in the infected population.

Mucosal immunity

There is a third kind of immunity a vaccine might be able to generate, but it's not one that previous vaccines have attempted to stimulate. This refers to humoral or cellular immune responses that are concentrated at the mucosal surfaces where most HIV transmission takes place, such as the vagina and rectum. Vaccines may be able to induce immune responses acting only at these surfaces, to prevent HIV transmission through sex or breast milk. They would not work against infection by injection, but since the majority of HIV in the world is spread through sex or from mother to baby, they would potentially contain the epidemic.

What would a mucosal vaccine look like? It might look a lot more like a microbicide than a vaccine, though it would be one that generated an immune response. It does not take a big leap of science to move from the idea of a microbicide that would work by getting genetically-altered versions of natural gut and genital bacteria to develop microbicidal substances like cyanovirin-N to getting genetically-altered bacteria to develop bits of HIV proteins that would then generate an immune response.

Such an approach has indeed been developed by Dean Hamer of the US National Institutes of Health. Because its method of delivery is more like a microbicide than a vaccine, it is described under **microbicide-expressing bacteria** in the **Microbicides** section.

In December 2005 one of the leading exponents of both microbicide and vaccine technology, Dr Robin Shattock of St

George's Hospital, London, told a vaccines meeting organised by the National AIDS Trust that the first effective HIV 'vaccine' to be developed might indeed look more like a microbicide or a long-acting contraceptive device than a standard injection. He said that the first vaccines might also only work for months at a time, and his talk was a useful summary of the challenges HIV throws at vaccine developers and why this might be so.

"With an HIV vaccine we are trying to do something science has never done before," he said. "Most vaccines mimic the successful immunity the body mounts against an actual infection. With HIV this response does not work, so we have to do better than nature.

"And most vaccines work for years against a virus that changes very little over time. But HIV changes rapidly. In an untreated person a billion subtly different copies of HIV are produced every day.

"There is more genetic diversity in the HIV in a single patient than there is for influenza over the entire world."

Shattock added that most diseases for which a successful vaccine had been developed got into the body via the lungs or the digestive system. Apart from hepatitis B we had little experience of a vaccine against something that usually gets in through the genital tract. He said that the direction his own research was taking might not be a truly preventative vaccine, but one that blunts the huge surge in viral load people get when they are first infected with HIV (within the first six weeks). It is estimated that because people are so much more infectious at this time, anything from 30-60% of all HIV is transmitted by people who have just got it themselves.

He said: "If we could do this it might give infected individuals a better prognosis - and it would have a major impact on transmission within the community."

However he warned that it might require "regular and repeated vaginal [or rectal] exposure" to have an effect.

So he was looking at technologies like intravaginal rings and caps that could deliver a sustained-release dose of a substance that would stimulate HIV-specific immunity. Such devices might reinforce or potentiate the effect of a more conventional injected vaccine.

Shattock said he was not pessimistic about the eventual discovery of a vaccine against HIV. "We have found out that conventional approaches don't work against HIV, but we only know that because of 20 years of intensive research," he said.

Broadly neutralising antibodies

As we said above, exposed seronegative people have also been found who have antibodies that are broadly effective against a wide range of different strains of HIV infection rather than just very specific ones.

Researchers such as Robert Gallo (see below) have argued that CD8 vaccines will not prove to be enough to prevent HIV and that a completely new 'third generation' approach to an HIV vaccine should be developed using a combination of CD8 stimulation and broadly neutralising antibodies.

Broadly neutralising antibodies are extremely rare and so far only a few have been isolated from the blood of exposed seronegative individuals. A study in 2004 (Binley) found that just one antibody, 4E10, neutralised every one of a panel of 90 HIV viruses with moderate potency. One called 2F5 neutralised 67% of isolates, but none from clade C of HIV, the most common type in Africa. An antibody called b12 neutralised 50% of viruses, including some from almost every clade, while one called 2G12 neutralised 41% of the viruses, but none from clades C or E.

Experiments with these antibodies have so far mainly involved using then as passive inoculations and studying how they are eliminated in the body. Here they act more like potential long-lasting anti-HIV drugs, as they are eliminated from the body over a timescale of one to three weeks. Some artificially-created antibodies such as the experimental drug TNX-355 use the same principle.

Developing a vaccine which induces the body to generate them will be much more difficult. The reason these antibodies work against so many types of HIV appears to be because they act against highly 'conserved' parts of HIV that have to retain the same configuration in order to infect cells. In the main these are parts of the viral infection mechanism that are only exposed for a fraction of a second during the intricate unfolding and insertion process that happens during the infection of a cell. It is therefore challenging to establish which epitopes elicit the antibodies.

Vaccines against viral proteins

Vaccines can be made against toxins that bacteria and viruses produce as well as against parts of the mature virus. An example is the tetanus toxoid vaccine. It is an inactivated version of the bacterial toxin the tetanus bacterium produces, and it induces antibodies against the toxin itself.

HIV produces several harmful proteins that could be vaccine targets. The most promising so far is the tat protein, which is produced early on in the viral lifecycle and stimulates the host cell's genes to become active.

The tat protein is so important to HIV that it is highly conserved. A small trial involving 47 volunteers in Italy ending in 2006 produced a strong immune response in 80% of subjects given it. The Italian team studying it is trying to get funding for a large African trial scheduled to end in 2011.

The hurdles to climb

In a paper in the Lancet in November 2005, Robert Gallo summarised the barriers to developing a vaccine and made recommendations as to future directions for research.

He said HIV vaccine development was difficult because of the following factors:

- **An HIV vaccine cannot consist of attenuated, actively replicating (live) HIV** (as the measles vaccine does). See below for more on live attenuated vaccines: although the best vaccines for other viral diseases have usually used live viruses, there is an inherent danger that attenuated HIV could cause AIDS.

- **Killed whole virus** (like the polio vaccine) might also be dangerous because one could not be sure one has killed all viral particles and it had worked poorly in animal tests.

- **HIV vaccines therefore had to use subunits** of HIV. There are successful vaccines that use subunits of viruses such as individual proteins: an example is the hepatitis B vaccine. However medical science was less experienced with them.

- There is **no truly useful small animal model for studying HIV infection.** Vaccines have to be developed using SIV or the artificial monkey/human virus SHIV in monkeys. SIV infection tends to follow a different path in monkeys and they are, says Gallo, "both expensive and available to very few investigators."

- **We do not know with certainty which immune response will provide protection.** This is a major problem. Pre-efficacy studies of vaccines in monkeys and humans use correlates of immunogenicity such as CD8 cell response, and in particular use the production of cytokines. The most rigorously evaluated approach is the ELISpot assay, which counts the number of T cells making the cytokine interferon-gamma. However at the 2004 AIDS Vaccine Conference in Lausanne, Switzerland, studies found that immune-stimulated cells might respond by producing other cytokines such as interleukin-2: and whatever they produce, we do not know enough about whether this immune response will translate into a protective one.

- **HIV is extremely variable** and as we have already seen with the broadly neutralising antibodies, a vaccine may not work for all subtypes of HIV. Because of this, bodies such as IAVI are supporting the development of vaccines against different subtypes.

- **HIV is a retrovirus** and we have never before attempted to develop a vaccine against a retroviral infection. This, Gallo believes, is the most important obstacle of all. As detailed above, it means that a vaccine has a small 'window' of opportunity in which to prevent infection and will have to be extremely effective if it is to prevent viral DNA from being integrated into the host genome and establishing a permanent infection.

- **HIV produces viral proteins** such as tat that actively interfere with the immune response of both infected and uninfected cells They may do with a cellular vaccine response too. For this reason, Gallo believes that an effective vaccine would have to include an anti-tat component.

- **CD8 cellular vaccines** do not block infection because they act at too late a stage. They are therefore acting against a continued infection rather than stopping one happening. Because of this, in some monkey studies, the virus mutated and acquired immunity to the CD8 cellular response. In other words, HIV may become 'vaccine-resistant' in the same way it becomes drug-resistant. CD8 vaccines, if they work, largely do so by reducing the viral load in chronic infection, but would not necessarily do much to reduce the peak level of viremia in the early burst of viral reproduction that occurs in acute infection, so they might not do much to control infections transmitted by people in acute infection.

Gallo concludes by saying that "Instead of focusing on finding the elusive correlate [of effective immunity], obtaining or approaching sterilising immunity should be the goal; both conceptually and experimentally we know of only one practical way to accomplish this, namely - by eliciting neutralising antibodies that are broadly reactive against various HIV strains and that are expressed for long periods."

He therefore makes a plea that much more research should be aimed at developing vaccines that stimulate broadly neutralising antibodies, and that include an anti-tat component.

Gallo has been a notable sceptic about more conventional approaches to HIV vaccines, but has proven right in his predictions that the first generation of antibody-eliciting vaccines would be ineffective. Despite his scepticism, however, research into the second generation of cellular-immunity vaccines continues apace, with some indications that they may be more effective than the previous generation. What methods are being used?

Types of HIV vaccines

To date, over 40 different HIV vaccines have been tested in several thousand volunteers. Most of this research has consisted of early safety and efficacy studies of recombinant proteins, produced in a variety of different systems. Despite some encouraging evidence of immune responses in people, it is unclear whether many of these would prevent HIV infection.

Typically, vaccines are administered to large numbers of people at high risk of infection. After a certain time, the vaccinated participants' experiences are compared to those of people who received a placebo. This may involve assessing the antibodies present in their blood, or the response of their CD8 T-cells to HIV in the test tube, or looking for HIV seroconversions in the trial participants.

Researchers have explored a number of strategies that they hope will produce protective immune responses. These include:

- Live attenuated vaccines
- Inactivated vaccines
- Recombinant vectored vaccines
- Recombinant sub-unit vaccines
- DNA vaccines and replicons

Several studies have examined the use of combination or 'prime and boost' vaccines, in which two or more different vaccines to broaden or intensify immune responses. Examples include a vector virus to prime a T-cell response with a subunit booster to produce antibodies, or two different vector viruses expressing the same gene sequence.

Live attenuated vaccines

One of the most powerful ways to create vaccines is by weakening or 'attenuating' the pathogen. These defective viruses are harmless to people, but stimulate the body to produce an immune response. Creating live attenuated vaccines normally involves deleting genes that protect the virus against the immune system, but which are not essential for its reproduction. The measles vaccine is an example.

Live attenuated HIV vaccines are considered unsafe, after research in monkeys indicated that can a live attenuated vaccine, made by deleting the nef gene, protected monkeys against SIV, but caused AIDS, albeit more slowly than the normal virus (Baba, Daniel)

Inactivated vaccines

Creating vaccines based on inactivated or 'killed' viruses is another classic technique, which was used in creating the world's first successful polio vaccine. However, the technique is considered risky, as vaccine recipients could easily be infected with HIV if the inactivation process should fail. There have been no claims of a significant level of success with these types of vaccine for HIV, although some, such as Remune, an HIV preparation with envelope protein gp120 removed, are being pursued as therapeutic vaccines for people already infected with HIV.

Recombinant vectored vaccines

Recombinant vectored vaccines are made by incorporating fragments of HIV into established vaccines made from harmless viruses, such as the canarypox viruses or adenovirus. These vaccines aim to stimulate the immune system to recognise the fragments of HIV, protecting the vaccinated host from future infection. Vector vaccines have been shown to produce HIV-specific cytotoxic T-cell responses in animals and humans. Adenovirus vectors appear to be among the best of those tested so far, but the first and most widely used strain, Ad5, has problems because of widespread natural immunity to the virus.

Adenovirus vaccines

Adenovirus is a relatively harmless and common human virus associated with cold-like illnesses. Despite two large companies developing HIV vaccines based on adenovirus, a problem is that adenovirus 5 (Ad5) is widely distributed across the world and a substantial proportion of the population are naturally exposed to

it, leading to high levels of natural immunity. This renders Ad5-based vaccine useless, as all they can do is re-awaken natural immunity to Ad5 (Isaacs).

However, recent research results have indicated that Ad5-based vaccines may in fact generate immune responses even in people with pre-existing immunity to the virus. Merck & Co. is currently running a large phase II trial, the STEP trial (see above), of an Ad5-based vaccine that contains the HIV genes gag, pol and nef.

Pox virus vaccines

The most advanced vectors used for HIV vaccines are pox viruses, using relatives of the smallpox virus. One attraction of these is that they induce strong cytotoxic T-lymphocyte (CTL) immune responses. Researchers are working on the bird viruses fowlpox and canarypox, and bird-adapted strains of vaccinia, such as NYVAC and modified vaccinia Ankara (MVA).

Canarypox

Canarypox is known to be safe since it is already the basis of a commercial rabies vaccine. Aventis Pasteur has developed a range of canarypox vaccines in their ALVAC range. The first ALVAC product, vCP125, consisted of gp160 inserted in the vector, while a second product, vCP205, which also contains env, gag and protease appear to generate greater cell-mediated immune responses.

The most extensively tested candidate is vCP1452, which incorporates sequences from the env, gag, nef and pol genes. Unfortunately, however, since the cellular immune responses seen with canarypox constructs appear to be weak, transient and only seen in a minority of trial volunteers, little research is currently being carried out into their use alone.

However, they are being tested in prime-boost strategies with subunit vaccines. The controversial RV144 phase III trial, which at the time of writing is still ongoing in Thailand and which is due to finish in 2008 (see below), uses the ALVAC vCP1521 vaccine as the prime and the AIDSVAX gp120 envelope subunit vaccine as the boost.

Modified vaccinia Ankara

MVA was given safely to tens of thousands of people in the 1970s. MVA has long been studied in animals, but its first clinical use as the basis for an HIV vaccine is as a booster in a 'prime-boost' strategy. Other MVA-based vaccines are being developed and tested in further trials.

Other vectors

Other viral vectors currently being studied with HIV or simian immunodeficiency virus (SIV) in animals include rabies, measles, poliovirus, herpes simplex, human rhinovirus, influenza and pertussis.

Measles is of particular interest because the live attenuated measles vaccine in common use is extremely effective in generating long-lasting immune responses when given to infants. This might be ideal to protect young people in countries where HIV is widespread.

The recombinant rabies virus vaccine potentially has a number of advantages, since few people are vaccinated against rabies, the attenuated rabies virus infects most human cells but does no damage and it may produce ongoing exposure to HIV antigens in the body. Research in mice has found that a rabies-based HIV vaccine produced HIV-specific neutralising antibodies and cytotoxic T-cells that targeted HIV-infected cells (Schnell).

Recombinant sub-unit vaccines

Recombinant sub-unit vaccines stimulate antibodies to HIV by mimicking proteins on the surface of HIV. A range of HIV proteins has been produced as potential vaccines for HIV. Initially, the main targets for vaccine developers were the viral envelope protein gp120, and its precursor gp160, in the hope that they would prevent HIV entering human cells. More recently, vaccine developers have experimented with other HIV proteins, including regulatory proteins such as Tat, which may modify the course of disease in monkeys.

Envelope proteins

The first HIV vaccine to enter full-scale efficacy testing was the AIDSVAX gp120-based vaccine. This was designed to induce neutralising antibodies in the hope of preventing or aborting infection with HIV.

One AIDSVAX version, based on two different isolates of subtype B viruses, was tested among 5400 people at risk of sexual transmission of HIV in a randomised placebo-controlled trial in the United States, Canada, Puerto Rico and the Netherlands. The trial produced no evidence of protection among the trial volunteers as a whole, although the vaccine did elicit HIV antibodies (rgp120 HIV Vaccine Study Group). A second trial, of an AIDSVAX formulation based on Thai subtype E and subtype B viruses, began in March 1999. This study recruited 2500 injecting drug users in Thailand, but found absolutely no evidence of protection (Pitisutithum).

Modified envelopes

Other strategies for stimulating the immune system to produce antibodies have stemmed from better understanding of the way HIV's proteins interact with the cells they infect. For example, HIV's proteins are often hidden from the immune system by a coating of sugar molecules: removing some of these molecules from the protein's surface may lead to neutralising antibodies that can act against the virus Secondly, there are 'variable loop' regions within the virus's proteins. In these regions, mutations and changes in the protein's structure have no effect on the virus's ability to replicate and cause disease, but they enable it to escape from immune responses directed against those regions by acting as 'decoys'. Studies have shown that removing parts these loops produces stronger antibody responses. For more, see **broadly neutralising antibodies** above.

Regulatory proteins

Several groups of researchers have been investigating the use of HIV proteins other than the envelope proteins in vaccines, such as the regulatory proteins Tat and Nef.

Tat we have looked at above: nef is also of interest, despite the fact that some HIV strains can infect and cause disease without it. If cellular immune responses target cells expressing Nef, they could select for less virulent viruses.

More recently, researchers have reported animal studies using a vaccine consisting of an envelope protein plus a Nef-Tat fusion protein. The combination of these two elements was able to protect monkeys against disease, though not against infection, after challenge with a highly pathogenic simian / human immunodeficiency virus (SHIV). This vaccine is now being evaluated in clinical trials in the United States and Belgium.

Peptide vaccines

Instead of vaccinating with a whole protein, another approach is to use a fragment of a protein, called a peptide, which consists of a few amino acids. A vaccine containing the V3 sequences from several strains of HIV has been used in animals and produced antibodies able to neutralise several laboratory-adapted virus strains. Peptide vaccines have been tested in HIV-positive patients, with some antibody and cellular immune responses against HIV (Pinto, Kran). Whether these will be translated into protection in HIV-negative people, however, remains to be established.

Linking a peptide to a lipid has also been explored as an HIV vaccine technique. The lipid carries the peptide directly into cell membranes where it can be presented to the immune system with maximum efficiency. A number of preliminary clinical trials of such vaccines have been carried out and a phase II trial using lipopeptides as boosters for canarypox vaccines is planned.

DNA vaccines

DNA vaccines are small pieces of DNA containing genes from HIV, which can be grown in bacteria. After injection, the animal's cells effectively make the vaccine themselves by expressing the HIV genes. Although they work well in mice, it has been more difficult to get DNA vaccines to work in primates, including humans, as it is difficult to get enough DNA into each injection. There are also safety considerations inherent in the design of DNA vaccines, since the genetic material of HIV could effectively result in infection with the virus.

A further problem is that a single mutation in HIV's genetic material can be sufficient to undermine the protection of an HIV vaccine. In one study, in which eight monkeys were vaccinated and challenged with the virus, one monkey became sick and died within six months of initial infection after its virus mutated to be resistant to the vaccine (Barouch). Although a range of DNA vaccines could be used, this would result in even larger doses of DNA being needed. DNA vaccines that trigger the production of cytokines have also been tested. Experiments in monkeys show that this approach works surprisingly well, but this has been less successful in human studies (Boyer).

Replicons

Replicons may be a better way of getting HIV's genes into cells, by using a carrier virus to transport the vaccine genes. Replicons have the same physical properties as viruses, including the ability to enter cells of specific kinds, but they have the advantage of not reproducing after entering the human cell, so there is little or no immune response to the carrier virus. Thus, one replicon system could be used repeatedly in the same person, to deliver a series of different vaccines or gene therapies.

The three leading replicon systems for HIV vaccines are based on Venezuelan equine encephalitis (VEE), Semliki forest virus (SFV), and adeno-associated virus (AAV). All three have shown some success in animal studies. Papillomaviruses have also been developed as the basis for replicons, which appear to offer the possibility of mucosal immunity to HIV antigens following oral immunisation in mice (Zhang). However, it remains to be seen if this can be translated into comparable effects in monkeys or people.

Prime-boost vaccination strategies

A number of trials into prime-boost strategies for HIV vaccination have been attempted. In general, these use two different vaccines, in order to strengthen the immune response to a single vaccine, or to complement an antibody response with a cell-based immune response.

Vaccines - a summary of the issues

So, more than twenty years after the discovery of HIV there is still no preventive vaccine against AIDS. However, while the first vaccine to complete a full-scale clinical trial has so far failed to show any convincing evidence of protection, and despite all the obstacles to developing one, other more credible candidate vaccines are entering trials in increasing numbers. Progress has been made by showing that vaccines can alter the course of HIV-like disease in monkeys and the identification of antibodies that can protect against infection with a wide range of HIV strains.

HIV has focused attention on the need for new vaccine technologies (discussed in the *HIV & AIDS Treatments Directory*) and these in turn raise questions about how an HIV vaccine can be evaluated and, if effective, made available to those who need it.

Preventive vaccines against HIV and AIDS are actively being pursued by governments and inter-governmental agencies, the pharmaceutical industry and non-governmental organisations. Progress towards this important but challenging goal requires a long-term commitment to partnerships across sectors, with the active involvement of communities affected by HIV.

The need for a vaccine

Historically, vaccination is the only strategy that has ever led to the elimination of a viral disease, namely smallpox, in poor countries as well as in wealthy ones, for women and children as well as for men. While the biology of HIV is less favourable than smallpox to vaccine development, some experimental vaccines do, to varying degrees, protect animals against related viruses.

An ideal vaccine would be cheap to produce, stable at room temperature, easy to transport and administer without special equipment, completely safe, and would need only one dose to provide complete lifelong protection against all routes of transmission and all variants of HIV. All current vaccine candidates are likely to fall short of these criteria, although even an imperfect vaccine could deliver public health benefits and provide further insights for prevention and treatment strategies.

To achieve this, we need to think in terms of a series of vaccines to be developed and tested, in parallel and then against each other, possibly in combinations, and successively improved over many years. This process will require extended collaborations between countries with the technical resources to develop the vaccines and those with the largest populations affected by HIV. It will require private sector expertise in manufacturing and production of vaccines, underpinned by public financial and legal guarantees where market mechanisms fail to secure the investment to take products forwards. It will need community education and mobilisation to enable evaluation to proceed in an ethically acceptable way, with backing from governments and international institutions.

For the communities worst affected by HIV and AIDS, whose members must be involved in any programme to evaluate preventive vaccines, there are increasingly complex medical and social issues to be addressed. At a community level, any vaccine will need to be evaluated and used in combination with other treatment and prevention strategies. It is essential that this happens in ways that reinforce those other strategies and do not undermine them.

Preventing infection

Firstly, a vaccine might prevent a person becoming infected with HIV (sterilising immunity). Measuring this effect is simple in principle. A population of individuals at risk is recruited into a clinical trial, and a proportion is vaccinated. After follow-up for a number of months or years, the number of new infections in the vaccinated group is compared to the number in a control group. If there are fewer infections in the vaccinated group, this may be evidence for the efficacy of the vaccine.

The prototype for a trial to measure this was the VaxGen Phase III trial discussed below, where the primary endpoint was the number of people who became HIV-positive in the vaccine recipient group compared to the placebo recipient group.

Delaying illness

Secondly, a vaccine might delay or prevent the progression of illness, despite HIV infection. This effect is likely to depend on a cellular immune response directed against HIV-infected cells. There is evidence from animal studies that such effects can be achieved. In a clinical trial they would be detected using viral load tests, comparing individuals who had received a vaccine and then went on to be infected to others who became infected without first having received the vaccine.

Extracting the true protective effect of a vaccine that delays infection is obviously more difficult. However a statistician working for the US HIV Vaccine Trials Network has argued that an initial trial might still randomise people individually, in a similar design to the AIDSVAX trials, to receive vaccine or

placebo. In a population with a 2% risk of HIV infection every year, it should be possible to get answers from a trial that recruited 5,000 people over twelve months and followed them for another four years. This would show if the vaccine did, in fact, have an impact on HIV infection rates - and would be large enough to tell the difference between a vaccine that was 30% effective and one that was 60% effective.

With no protection against infection, this trial design would also make it possible to compare two groups of people with HIV for an average follow-up of around 18 months. This might be long enough to look at some markers of progression (viral load and falling CD4 counts) although this could be obscured by treatment. As follow-up increased, the likelihood of treatment obscuring any effect of the vaccine could become greater (Self). (It might also be reduced, if treatment is driven by CD4 counts, since better control of the virus should lead to deferred treatment.)

If it were possible to show that the need for antiviral treatment was delayed through vaccination, hopefully by years, at least this would provide a clear cost-benefit rationale for providing such a vaccine to populations at risk.

A vaccine in this category might also, in principle, be directed at making HIV disease easier to treat, for example, by specifically blocking the development of drug-resistant viruses. It might also be possible to direct the immune response against specific parts of the virus that are responsible for its virulence, so that viruses which escape from the vaccine-induced response cause less damage than would otherwise be the case.

Blocking transmission

Thirdly, a vaccine might **reduce the chance of onward HIV transmission**. For example, from a mother to her baby, or through sexual transmission. This, like the second effect, would be likely to follow from a reduced viral load seen in vaccinated individuals compared to those who had not been vaccinated.

The greatest benefit from a vaccine would be if it reduced viral load in vaccinees in the period immediately after infection and before antibodies were produced. If so, this should be reflected relatively rapidly in lower rates of new HIV diagnoses over the course of the study, in communities that have received the vaccine compared to those which have not.

The greatest value of a vaccine with this as its main effect would be seen at a population level. The ideal way to test it would therefore be to compare populations in which a vaccine is available with those in which it is not (Self). It would be necessary to ensure a continuing high uptake of HIV testing, which is likely to depend on excellent and expanding access to treatment. The proper comparison would then be between populations, all of which had high levels of access to treatment, some of which were also provided with a vaccine and in which the majority of the HIV-negative population were persuaded to take that vaccine.

The success of a clinical trial based on this principle would depend on identifying and randomising populations which were large enough for most sexual contact to be taking place within them but small enough for the trial to be feasible.

This proposed trial design sets up a number of challenges. Results could vary, as for different STI control strategies, depending on the maturity of the epidemic. The size of the communities compared, the actual level of vaccine coverage achieved, and the extent to which community membership and patterns of sexual mixing remain stable over the period of the study, may all be issues. So, too, is the question of how and from whom consent should be sought for such a study.

Nonetheless, this proposal would eliminate the conflict sometimes perceived between treatment and care, including access to antiretrovirals, and prevention, including vaccines. It could also strengthen the case for providing HIV/AIDS treatment and care in smaller and more rural communities, where such trials would be most likely to give clear results.

In practice, this would probably need to follow on after a trial which had demonstrated a reduced early viral load in people infected with the virus, and in which lower levels of the virus in semen and/or vaginal fluids can be linked to vaccination.

Regardless of whether such trials can be carried out, this proposal rightly draws attention to the ultimate test of the value of such a vaccine. This must be whether it reduces the burden both of disease and of its treatment, in populations where it is made available as compared to those where it is not.

Preventive trials: Phase I, II, III

HIV preventive vaccine trials are generally discussed in terms of three phases, I, II and III.

Phase I involves low-risk volunteers, usually from 20 to 80 in number, who receive a candidate vaccine, or perhaps just a component of such a vaccine, and are monitored for between six months and two years to assess immune response and safety. More than forty different vaccine candidates have now undergone Phase I clinical trials. Most have proven to be at least as safe as any other vaccine and most have induced some immune responses.

Phase II trials would include high-risk volunteers, drawn from populations in which efficacy trials might later be carried out. These look at how to maximise immune response in terms of dosage and methods of administration. They would normally be larger than Phase I trials, possibly running into hundreds of volunteers.

Both Phase I and Phase II trials may be placebo-controlled in order to distinguish adverse effects linked to the vaccine from those which are not. The experience of running trials in high-risk seronegative populations has been that many 'adverse events' are reported, most of which have nothing to do with vaccination.

The aim of a Phase III trial might be to assess whether a candidate vaccine is able to prevent infection, or to prevent disease in the presence of infection, or to prevent onward transmission of the virus. In other words, to discover whether a potential vaccine works. Through giving the vaccine to larger numbers of people, it is also possible to identify rarer side-effects and problems.

In practice, the design of Phase III trials has been dominated by the first objective - preventing HIV infection - although the first such trials also include a follow-up phase aimed at evaluating the second objective - delaying disease. In future trials, the emphasis is likely to shift.

Phase III trials are costly and have an impact on all other aspects of the response to HIV and AIDS. This is because they must recruit populations at high risk of HIV transmission, deliver vaccines and placebos in combination with other prevention interventions, and evaluate the outcomes.

A 'successful' Phase III trial would be enough to get a vaccine licensed, at least in the country or region where it is carried out, but the real work of getting vaccines into proper use is then only beginning.

By 2006, only one type of vaccine had entered Phase III trials, as described below.

Logistical issues in Phase III trials

The size and length of follow-up for a Phase III (efficacy) trial will depend on:

- the incidence of HIV in the population where the trial is taking place

- the likely efficacy of the vaccine

- volunteer drop-out and non-response rates

- the trial design, and the outcome(s) being assessed (as previously discussed).

If a trial is too small, runs for too short a period, and the vaccine has a limited effect, then it may be inconclusive. Alternatively, if a trial is too big, it could waste resources.

Once a vaccine has been identified which is at least partially effective, it would become necessary to compare that vaccine with other potential vaccines. These trials might be looking for simpler vaccination schedules giving at least the same level of protection, longer duration of protection, and/or reductions in new HIV cases from a lower baseline. All of this implies that trial size and/or duration needs to increase as soon as a partially effective vaccine is identified.

As of June 2006, there were 31 trials taking place of HIV candidate vaccines worldwide. See the IAVI database of AIDS vaccines in human trials for a continuously-updated list at http://www.iavireport.org/specials/OngoingTrialsofPreventiveHIV Vaccines.pdf

- There was one phase III efficacy trial taking place in Thailand. This is the controversial RV144 prime-boost trial using the ALVAC vCP1521 canarypox vector vaccine as prime and the AIDSVAX gp120 envelope clade B/AE subunit vaccine as boost. There are about 7,000 volunteers enrolled. This started in October 2003 and is due to continue until at least 2008.

There were three phase II trials.

- The largest is the STEP trial of the Merck clade B adenovirus-5 trivalent vector vaccine. This will recruit about 3,000 volunteers worldwide. This started in September 2004

- The second is the HVTN204 prime-boost clades A, B and C trial of a naked DNA vaccine (VRC-HIVDNA016) as prime and the adenovirus VRC-HIVADV014-00-VP vector vaccine as boost. This started in September 2005, is taking place in the USA and Latin America, and will recruit 480 volunteers.

- The third is the IAVI A002 trial of the tgAAC09 clade C adeno-associated virus replicon vaccine, taking place in South Africa, Uganda and Zambia. This started in November 2005 and has so far recruited 78 volunteers in South Africa.

All the others are small phase I or phase IIa trials in low-risk populations.

Mobilising support worldwide

On 18 May 1997, US President Bill Clinton challenged the US research community to find an effective vaccine within the next ten years and set this as a national goal. That year's summit of the G8 countries, held in Denver, also recognised the need for an HIV vaccine; subsequent G8 summits have reiterated this commitment. The Commonwealth Heads of Government Meeting held in Durban, South Africa, in 1999, included a paragraph personally committing the leaders to advancing the response to HIV and AIDS including vaccine development. (For further information, see www.para55.org.)

Such commitments underpin the support for vaccine and microbicide development included in the final statement of the UN General Assembly Special Session on AIDS held in New York in June 2001.

Researchers in the United States, Australia, Britain, Cuba, France, Germany, Japan and South Africa among others have developed vaccine candidates. Clinical trials for HIV vaccines are ongoing or have taken place in the past in the United States, Thailand, various European countries including Britain, France and the Netherlands, Brazil, China, Cuba, Haiti, Kenya, Trinidad, Uganda. Other countries in which trials are planned, or are under serious discussion, some of them with vaccine research programmes, include Argentina, Botswana, Cote d'Ivoire, Honduras, India, Nigeria, Peru, Russia, South Africa and Tanzania.

The International AIDS Vaccine Initiative

IAVI was constituted in 1995 in the USA as a non-governmental organisation sponsored by various US foundations and donors and is headed by Dr Seth Berkley.

IAVI was founded out of a judgement that the global effort towards a preventive vaccine was in trouble, following a 1994 decision not to proceed with US efficacy trials for gp120 vaccines. It has lobbied the US government, other G8 countries, intergovernmental organisations including the World Bank and UN agencies and entered into working agreements with the European Union, South Africa, India, China, Brazil and other countries. It has equally sought to engage with corporations and community organisations, with formal partnerships agreed between IAVI and agencies in a number of countries including Britain's National AIDS Trust.

One key idea that it has promoted is the creation of a guaranteed and credible market for vaccines, by securing the promise of major loans to buy any proven vaccine on behalf of governments of countries that are in the greatest need. Such loans could be repaid from future savings on humanitarian aid and need not add to the debts of the countries worst affected by HIV.

IAVI funds research specifically directed at vaccines which would be appropriate for countries where the need is greatest and the resources most limited.

By 2001 it had funds and pledges totalling more than US $230 million towards a fundraising target of US $550 million needed to fund vaccine development work plan through to the year 2007, following its *Scientific Blueprint: 2000*. The largest single funder so far has been the Bill and Melinda Gates Foundation. Other major supporters include the Rockefeller, Sloan and Starr Foundations, UNAIDS the World Bank, and a number of governments. These include the UK (through the Department for International Development), Canada, Ireland, the Netherlands, Norway, Sweden and the USA (through USAID).

IAVI publishes a scientific newsletter, *IAVI Report*, and makes its publications freely available through its website, http://www.iavi.org/.

The Global HIV Vaccine Enterprise (GHVE)

The GHVE is a new organisation set up in 2004 after a position paper in *Science* journal argued that an AIDS vaccine is one of the most difficult challenges facing biomedical science today, and while important progress has been made, there is a critical limitation in the way vaccine R&D is currently conducted.

Most of the work is undertaken by small groups of investigators - academic laboratories and biotechnology companies - who typically operate independently of each other, and the scale of their projects is often too small to adequately address major scientific questions. The pace of progress could be increased through greater cooperation and collaboration and more funding targeted to large projects that tackle major questions.

Enterprise members agree to reach consensus on scientific priorities, voluntarily divide responsibility for addressing them and establish joint ventures that pool expertise, infrastructure and resources. They agree to iteratively apply each other's advances so that the best science emerges as quickly as possible and unnecessary duplication is avoided.

The GHVE lists its six aims as

- Reaching a scientific consensus on the most promising research directions in HIV vaccine science, explicitly noting that vaccines that elicit both cellular and humoral immunity will be necessary.

- Standardising assays that measure correlates of immune protection.

- Developing a vaccine manufacturing process that makes consistent batches over time.

- Supporting greater capacity to mount large clinical trials through on-site manufacturing capacity, enhancing research infrastructure, including trial sites and laboratories, training and supporting qualified staff and educating the public about vaccine trials to help with recruitment of informed study participants.

- Standardising regulatory systems for clinical trials, especially in developing countries, which often lack expertise and well-defined processes for reviewing and approving clinical trials and assessing results.

- Agreeing on intellectual property arrangements that balance the need to incentivise and protect individual researchers or companies, and the need to promote greater and more rapid sharing of information among scientists that can lead to potential breakthroughs in HIV vaccine research.

Enterprise members will develop systems for more openly exchanging information as well as share research protocols so that the work of one group is compatible with others. In these ways, the Enterprise is patterned after the Human Genome Project, a scientific alliance that is widely credited with speeding the successful identification of all of the genes in human DNA.

The *Science* paper argued for additional resources, given that total global spending to develop a vaccine is just a fraction of spending to combat the epidemic, and more resources would better position vaccine efforts for success. Enterprise members will mobilize new resources and see that they are targeted to priority areas. The Enterprise received the endorsement of leaders of G8 nations at their summit in 2004, and the G8 pledged to take up the issue of additional resources for vaccine R&D at future summits.

In September 2005 the first Chief Executive of the GHVE was appointed - Dr Adel Mahmoud, former president of Merck Vaccines.

The AIDS Vaccine Advocacy Coalition (AVAC)

AVAC is a community and consumer based organisation, founded in December 1995 to accelerate the ethical development and global delivery of vaccines against HIV/AIDS. It provides independent analysis, policy advocacy, public education and mobilisation to enhance AIDS vaccine research and development.

AVAC publishes the AIDS Vaccine Handbook, a comprehensive (404 page) introduction to AIDS vaccine science, ethics and community advocacy. It can be downloaded from http://www.avac.org/primer2.htm . AVAC also issues reports of various aspects of the development of vaccines and the other new prevention technologies.

In the introduction, Executive Director Mitchell Warren says:

An effective AIDS vaccine remains the world's best chance to contain this relentless epidemic. But the search for an AIDS vaccine must not come at the expense of our immediate response. And it doesn't have to. Testing vaccines requires that we do all the other key things anyway: delivering the best-possible risk-reduction and counselling tools; ensuring confidential, voluntary counselling and testing; providing referral to comprehensive treatment.

The handbook covers:

- The basics of AIDS vaccine science

- Clinical trials including being a volunteer; the ethics of trials, including making sure that trials leave communities better rather than worse off; ensuring community participation and readiness; and how to work with trials that 'fail' as in the AIDSVAX trial

- The experience and ethics of doing vaccine trials with different vulnerable communities

- Global advocacy and political leadership

- Personal accounts of involvement with trials.

AVAC has also set up a small-grants fund that will function as a small-scale "emergency fund" to assist needy clinical sites that require immediate help with purchases such as additional medical or lab supplies not covered by grants or contracts for vaccine research.

The Global Alliance for Vaccines and Immunization (GAVI)

GAVI is not an HIV vaccine development organisation, but may become important if an effective vaccine is found. It was founded amid concern that existing financing mechanisms were not enabling vaccination programmes in the developing world to be sustained. Founded in 2000, it is a global alliance of Governments in industrialised and developing countries, UNICEF, WHO, the World Bank, the Bill & Melinda Gates Foundation, non-governmental organisations, vaccine manufacturers from industrialised and developing countries, and public health and research institutions.

GAVI has been financed by ten governments to date - Canada, Denmark, France, Ireland, Luxembourg, the Netherlands, Norway, Sweden, the United Kingdom, and the United States - as well as the European Union, private contributors, and the Bill & Melinda Gates Foundation.

GAVI's aim is to help strengthen health and immunization systems in the developing world, accelerate access to selected vaccines and new vaccine technologies, especially vaccines that are new or underused, and improve injection safety.

It provides multi-year grants to more than 70 of the world's poorest countries to enable them to put on vaccination programmes, especially in children.

Ethical issues in trial design

The general ethical principles that govern all clinical research apply to vaccine trials, and there are a number of international statements on medical ethics that apply. It is fundamental that participation in trials must be voluntary and based on individual informed consent.

The principal difference between preventive vaccine trials and HIV therapeutic trials is that because participants might otherwise have a normal life expectancy and a low level of disability, the level of potentially acceptable risk is much lower.

In the case of HIV preventive vaccines, much of the discussion of ethics of trials has been driven by perceived and actual disparities of power between those at high risk of HIV and those carrying out the research, and between Western countries and multinational companies and communities in developing countries. There is an obvious danger of exploitation, if benefits and risks from research are not evenly shared. There is also a danger that if governments and international agencies are over-protective, the effort will be stalled.

UNAIDS' guidelines

In 1997-99, UNAIDS sponsored a series of consultations leading to the publication of a detailed eighteen-point guidance document in May 2000. The following section outlines and comments on this guidance, which can be read in full on the UNAIDS website (http://www.unaids.org/).

HIV vaccines development (point 1)

UNAIDS begins with the need to develop vaccines and make them available: 'it is imperative that they benefit the population at greatest risk of infection.' It distinguishes between 'investigators', 'host countries' where trials might be held and 'communities' from which volunteers would be drawn, 'donors and international agencies' and 'sponsor countries' acknowledging that vaccines are being developed in public-private partnerships rather than on a purely commercial basis.

Vaccine availability (point 2)

Issues of availability including but not limited to availability in the country and population where a vaccine is tested need to be addressed throughout the process of vaccine development. 'The discussions should include decisions regarding payments, royalties, subsidies, technology and intellectual property, as well as distribution costs, channels and modalities, including vaccination strategies, target populations, and number of doses.'

Capacity building (point 3)

A recurring theme, with the goal of enabling host countries and communities to participate as equal partners in the process.

Research protocols and study populations (point 4)

Any study must be scientifically sound and have the potential to benefit the population recruited into the study. An ethical trial must be capable of answering the questions it sets out to answer, using the most efficient and humane means of addressing scientific uncertainty, e.g. to show whether a candidate vaccine is immunogenic, safe and/or effective. The relevance of this point is greater for populations at high risk in host countries than for populations at low risk in sponsor countries, where exploitation is seen as less of a danger.

Community participation (point 5)

'Community representatives should be involved in an early and sustained manner in the design, development, implementation, and distribution of results of HIV vaccine research.' The guidance identifies categories of interested people who should be consulted in the course of setting up arrangements for community participation, including those eligible to volunteer for a specific study as well as care-givers and people living with HIV.

Scientific and ethical review (point 6)

Host countries must be capable of independent scientific and ethical review of research proposals, an area in which capacity building by agencies independent of vaccine developers may be needed.

Vulnerable populations (point 7)

This refers to the need to recognise and take steps to overcome social factors that may make research participants vulnerable to exploitation. This vulnerability is not solely economic, and may derive from inadequate respect for human rights on a variety of grounds.

Clinical trial phases (point 8)

This breaks with past guidance on international clinical research, which has required that early phase trials should be confined to the country in which a product is first developed. UNAIDS acknowledges that any country may legitimately decide to conduct phase I trials, provided there is sufficiently strong scientific, clinical, and ethical review infrastructure to protect the volunteers. The case for doing this is enhanced when a vaccine candidate is based on isolates of the virus from a particular community, country or region where trials will be carried out.

Potential harms (point 9)

Likely harms need to be identified in research protocols, and fully explained to trial volunteers in the informed consent process, including an explanation of how people will receive treatment and compensation if needed.

'HIV infection acquired during participation in an HIV preventive vaccine trial should not be considered an injury subject to compensation unless it is directly attributable to the vaccine itself, or to direct contamination through research-related activities. In addition to compensation for biological/medical injuries, appropriate consideration should be given to compensation for social or economic harms, e.g. job loss as a result of testing positive following vaccine administration.'

A distinction is made here between the need for compensation for HIV infection and the need for access to treatment and care, which is addressed separately. It would seem better to prevent social or economic harms rather than merely to plan for compensation. This is why 'consideration should also be given to setting up an ombudsperson who can intervene with outside parties, if necessary and requested, on behalf of participants, as well as to providing documentation to participants that they can use to show that their false positive is due to their participation in research.'

Benefits (point 10)

Potential benefits to trial volunteers from participation should be clearly explained to them, without presenting them in such a way as to unduly influence the decision to join a trial.

Control group (point 11)

'As long as there is no known effective HIV preventive vaccine, a placebo control arm should be considered ethically acceptable in a phase III HIV preventive vaccine trial. However, where it is ethically and scientifically acceptable, consideration should be given to the use in the control arm of a vaccine to prevent a relevant condition apart from HIV.' (The examples given are hepatitis B and tetanus.) The guidance might have pointed out that the failure to provide for a blinded control group in any trial involving high-risk volunteers might lead volunteers to assume that a vaccine protects them when it does not and increase their HIV risk, leading to real harm. If volunteers are to take part in a blinded trial they must remain ignorant for the duration of the trial of whether they have received an HIV vaccine, without losing the ability to check their own HIV status.

Informed consent (point 12)

This is a 'strategy and process' arising from a 'process of consultation between community representatives, researchers, sponsor(s) and regulatory bodies.' Individuals must be free to decide for themselves whether to take part, on the basis of 'complete, accurate, and appropriately conveyed and understood information.' Furthermore, 'efforts should be taken to ensure throughout the trial that participants continue to understand and to participate freely as the trial progresses.' Informed consent is needed separately for HIV tests before, during or after the trial.

The guidance observes that in any preventive vaccine trial it must be possible to distinguish the effects of the vaccine from those of natural infection. The costs and feasibility of doing this will vary between different vaccines. Vaccines based on the fullest possible range of viral components may need special and costly provision.

The most obvious test of remaining virus-free is failure to isolate the virus from a blood sample. However, even with a well-equipped laboratory it can still be difficult to isolate HIV from some people who are clearly infected with it, so a negative result on this test may not be convincing. Alternatives like p24 antigen tests (moderately expensive) and PCR tests (more expensive) would not be triggered by most likely vaccines. Some vaccine designers have deliberately excluded the HIV protein gp41 from vaccine systems so that commercially available ELISA tests for antibodies to gp41 may be used for this purpose (Corey, 1996; Yao, 1996).

Informed consent special measures (point 13)

This lists categories of people whose ability to consent freely on their own account may be limited by their social, legal, economic or gender status, for whom additional protective measures may be needed.

Risk-reduction interventions (point 14)

'Appropriate risk-reduction counselling and access to prevention methods should be provided to all vaccine trial participants, with new methods being added as they are discovered and validated.'

One issue, which has much exercised people, is a supposed conflict of interest between trial volunteers, who surely want to stay uninfected at all costs, and researchers 'needing' some people to become infected to prove that others those vaccinated are genuinely protected. In practice, this conflict can be resolved by implementing prevention programmes that in theory and practice reduce the HIV risk of trial volunteers, whether or not they receive a vaccine.

Monitoring informed consent and interventions (point 15)

This needs to be provided for, with plans made before the trial begins.

Care and treatment (point 16)

'Sponsors need to ensure care and treatment for participants who become HIV-infected during the course of the trial.' This does not imply an obligation for sponsors to provide care and treatment for everyone in a community where a trial is taking place, nor for everyone identified as HIV-positive during the course of screening trial volunteers. UNAIDS found during its consultations that there was no consensus as to what level of care and treatment needs to be provided during a vaccine trial. As this issue has been one of the most contentious, it is worth quoting the guidance point in full:

'Care and treatment for HIV/AIDS and its associated complications should be provided to participants in HIV preventive vaccine trials, with the ideal being to provide the best proven therapy, and the minimum to provide the highest level of care attainable in the host country in light of the circumstances listed below. A comprehensive care package should be agreed upon through a host/community/sponsor dialogue which reaches consensus prior to initiation of a trial, taking into consideration the following:

- level of care and treatment available in the sponsor country

- highest level of care available in the host country

- highest level of treatment available in the host country, including the availability of antiretroviral therapy outside the research context in the host country

- availability of infrastructure to provide care and treatment in the context of research

- potential duration and sustainability of care and treatment for the trial participant.

Women (point 17)

This observes that as women including those who are potentially pregnant, are pregnant, or are breastfeeding, should receive future preventive HIV vaccines, women should be included in clinical trials. The implication is that there should not be an absolute exclusion of pregnant or breastfeeding women from the later stages of HIV vaccine trials, although the need to warn women of potential risks to their children as part of the informed consent process is clearly set out.

Children (point 18)

This states, 'children should be included in clinical trials' and discusses the circumstances in which adolescents need to give individual informed consent, noting that the requirement for additional consent by parents or guardians will vary between countries depending on their legal provisions. In the case of breastfed infants, the requirement would be for consent by a parent on behalf of the child, or both parents if required by national legislation.

Trials that 'fail'

It is still possible to get a lot of information from a trial that is a failure in the sense of not showing efficacy and there is an ethical obligation to plan any trial to make the most of that information.

UNAIDS makes the point that the sponsors of a trial in a developing country should always aim to enhance the capacity of the country and community where a trial takes place, to deliver treatment and care and to engage in future research.

It is equally reasonable to expect that a community where a full-scale vaccine trial takes place will gain from the extra effort that is made to deliver effective HIV counselling and prevention to volunteers, and the empowerment of volunteers and those who represent the community through the trial process. Put simply, 'it should be a better place than if the trial hadn't happened.'

It has been argued that Phase III trials should go ahead for HIV vaccines even without strong evidence from Phase II trials that they will work, on account of what can be learned even from a partially effective vaccine. That said, some evidence suggesting that a vaccine will work is very desirable before proceeding to a Phase III trial. Investors would certainly want this, as mass-production of a commercial product should begin before a trial starts, so there would be no question of differences between the vaccine used in the trial and the one subsequently put on the market.

Vaxgen's trials

The leading example of a biotech company developing an HIV preventive vaccine is VaxGen with its *AIDSVAX* products. VaxGen is a company spun-off from Genentech (a biotech company now largely owned by Roche) to develop Genentech's gp120 recombinant vaccine after the US government refusal to support Phase III trials of a prototype in 1994. VaxGen succeeded in raising private funds to run Phase III trials in the USA, Canada, the Netherlands, Puerto Rico and Thailand. It is greatly to their credit that they completed the trials despite many expert opinions to the effect that it would be impossible to recruit or retain volunteers. In fact, trial volunteer retention was higher than predicted in all settings and higher in Thailand than in North America.

The first VaxGen trial

The first VaxGen trial recruited 5,417 volunteers at risk of HIV infection from sexual transmission, around 90% of whom were gay men. One third of the volunteers were randomised in a double-blind trial to receive placebo injections and two thirds a 'bivalent' vaccine based on a genetically engineered version of the gp120 surface protein from two different HIV-1 subtype B isolates.

The protocol for the trial involved seven injections over thirty months (0, 1, 6, 12, 18, 24 and 30 months) with follow-up visits for blood tests two weeks after each injection and six months after the last injection. All volunteers were given prevention advice and counselling.

All volunteers who became HIV-positive during the study are due to be followed up every four months for 24 months. There is no restriction on the treatments HIV-positive volunteers may receive, although treatments are not provided directly as part of the study. Social harms experienced by volunteers, including self-reported risk behaviour, were closely monitored.

5,009 volunteers received at least three of the seven scheduled injections and were included in 'on treatment' analysis which did not, in the event, differ substantially from the 'intent to treat analysis' which included all volunteers for whom an outcome was known.

VaxGen's results: no overall protection

The results of the first phase III HIV vaccine study released in February 2003 showed that Vaxgen's AIDSVAX offered no significant protection against HIV infection in the study population as a whole.

The annual study infection rate 2.7% which was not significantly different between placebo and vaccine recipients. Among all volunteers the level of apparent 'protection' was just 3.8% (p-value = 0.76; confidence interval: -23% to 24%). In other words, it was 95% certain that the **upper limit** for protection was below 25%. The trial had been designed in the hope that if the **lower limit** was above 30%, the vaccine could still be licensed for use in the USA.

The second VaxGen Phase III trial commenced in Thailand during 1999, using a gp120 vaccine based on 'subtype E' (now classified as a 'circulating recombinant form') and subtype B isolates of the virus. This recruited 2,500 volunteers from drug treatment centres around Bangkok, to evaluate protection from direct blood exposure, with an equal number of placebo recipients and vaccine recipients. The annual infection rate was exactly the same in vaccine and placebo recipients: 3.4% a year for both arms, or a vaccine efficacy of exactly zero.

The ongoing VaxGen/ALVAC trial: incrementalists versus serendipists

As we have said above, the AIDSVAX gp120 vaccine continues to be used as the 'boost' in the RV144 phase III trial in combination with the ALVAC vCP1521 canarypox vector as prime. This, the only current phase III trial has attracted fierce criticism form scientists and activists alike. In 2004, 22 researchers wrote to *Science* stating that the US government was wasting its resources on funding a trial of a vaccine combination where there is no evidence that either component works well on its own.

Other researchers said that the addition of the gp120 boost would only muddy the results and make it difficult to establish if the ALVAC vaccine had any immune stimulating effect. "There is no credible scientific justification for the inclusion of gp120 in the trial," said the article's co-author John Moore. "It's an expensive, inert component that complicates any analysis of the final outcome."

The trial's sponsors, NIAID, defended the decision to proceed with the trial. NIAID's Margaret Johnston said that, although the results are arguably modest, early studies showed that the combination augments immune responses relative to each vaccine alone, and that the combination vaccine induced CD8 responses in 25%-45% of individuals. However the critics said the enhanced responses seen could be just as well studied in a smaller trial and is was a waste not only of money but of human resources - in the shape of human volunteers who would probably ben excluded from a future vaccine trial.

The central dilemma in AIDS vaccine research seems to be embodied by the RV144 trial. The field is split between researchers who say that vaccine development is incremental and that 'more immune protection than the last one' is sufficient reason for a trial to move ahead. People arguing this point of view say that the only 'failed' vaccine trial is one that produces no information and that even the numerous candidate vaccines that have produced little immune response or, if they have, have yet to show that that translates into efficacy, are part of an immense scientific project that is teaching us huge lessons about virology and immunology.

Researchers sympathetic to the opposite point of view say that, historically, successful vaccines have not been developed incrementally, but have usually come out of the serendipitous success of an often new approach. Like Robert Gallo, they argue that we are at too early a stage in HIV vaccine development to start incrementally developing anything; the incremental stage comes when we have strong candidates that will provide real efficacy. It is a waste of human and financial resources to put on large trials of products that are suspected not to be efficacious and it may be unethical if it provides volunteers with a false sense of security against HIV infection.

Ethical implications for people with HIV

People with and without HIV, living in the same HIV-affected community, may have very different perspectives on all aspects of life, with major implications for HIV prevention programmes. In particular, gay and bisexual men are both united and divided in responding to AIDS, with one of the major divisions being on the basis of HIV status. It is therefore essential in planning any primary prevention programme, including vaccine research, to consider its impact on people with HIV as well as on those without.

For people with HIV, the call for vaccine research has sometimes been perceived as a kind of abandonment and as a potential diversion of funds away from therapeutic research.

Some of these concerns are realistic: large-scale vaccine trials would certainly be expensive. There can be no absolute guarantee that funding for any particular kind of AIDS research will be maintained, since this depends on political will and judgements, including scientific judgements, of the strength of competing priorities.

Some of the concerns, as has been argued in this chapter, may now be outdated. Insights from preventive vaccine research are likely to be of genuine value to people living with HIV. If therapeutic vaccines prove feasible, these will be of direct value to people with HIV. The line between what is a therapeutic and what is a preventative vaccine is likely to grow ever more blurred over time, as argued by Robin Shattock.

In any case, many people with HIV passionately want to see an end to the epidemic, since they have lost more than anyone else and can see preventive vaccines as a part of the answer.

Since some of the stigma of being HIV-positive arises from fear of infection, a vaccine which offers genuine protection is also a potential remedy for social stigma.

Arguably the biggest obstacle to participation in vaccine research is that it means people facing up to the risks that they are running. At a practical level, it means taking an antibody test and acknowledging the possibility of being HIV-positive. How to ensure treatment programmes are in place in resource-poor settings for the not inconsiderable number of people who test positive during screening for a trial remains one of the thorniest issues in trial design, community liaison and funding.

Ethical implications for HIV-negative people

What of those who are HIV-negative and at risk? Many will want to participate, for obvious reasons, but some will not.

It might mean identification as a person at particular risk of HIV, and so being linked to people from whom you would prefer to keep a psychological and social distance. A small-scale interview study of gay men in France who declined to take part in vaccine trials found this to be their dominant problem. This contrasted, however, with Brazilian studies where the dominant reasons for not participating were given as concerns about side-effects and lack of credibility of a vaccine product (Silva).

However, one of the fundamental problems with being HIV-negative and at risk is that being HIV-negative is a 'non-status'. Like virginity, it cannot be aspired to, only lost. Prevention of HIV by methods other than vaccination never succeeds for longer than 'the time being'. For people who are HIV-negative, vaccines

offer the possibility of acquiring a status as a 'protected person' which they could work towards for themselves or for others.

There are particular ethical implications for people who volunteer for vaccine trials, many of them common to all trials of new prevention technologies:

- Will participation in the trial provide a false sense of security and/or change behaviour so that people are more rather than less at risk of HIV infection?

- How can we ensure fully informed consent when working with communities of people who may be stigmatised, vulnerable to incentives to take part in unethical trials, illiterate and innumerate or at least not educated about the science of HIV and vaccines?

- How do we ensure the fairest and most comprehensive treatment for those who seroconvert in the course of a trial?

- Some CD8 vaccines will induce the production of antibodies that will mean that vaccine recipients test 'HIV-positive', at least on an ELISA test. How do we educate these people about the meaning of their antibody response, and how do we monitor them in the future for HIV infection?

Securing global access

If a successful vaccine is developed, large-scale investment will be needed to make it available on a global scale. IAVI has made five recommendations to secure that investment and general access, especially if any reliance is placed on private sector involvement in the process. (IAVI, 2000a):

- Effective pricing and global financing mechanisms must be developed to ensure that vaccines are promptly available for use where they are needed.

- Mechanisms must be developed to make reliable estimates of demand for specific vaccines and to ensure creation of production capacity to permit accelerated worldwide access.

- Appropriate delivery systems, policies, and procedures must be developed for adolescents, sexually active adults and other at-risk populations.

- National regulations and international guidelines governing vaccine approval and use must be harmonised.

- To demonstrate global commitment to effective worldwide deployment of important vaccines, immediate efforts should be undertaken . building on existing mechanisms, such as the Global Alliance for Vaccines and Immunization (GAVI) and the Global Fund for Children's Vaccines (GFCV) - to achieve maximum use in developing countries of one or more currently under-utilised non-AIDS vaccines.

Tiered or 'equity' pricing - where prices reflect what countries can afford - will be needed from the moment an HIV vaccine is launched. This implies safeguards, including political support in wealthier countries, against the international trading of cheaper vaccines from developing countries into wealthier countries.

The traditional pattern is that new products are introduced first into wealthy countries, sold at premium prices which enable the manufacturers to recoup their costs in developing the vaccine. Fifteen or more years later, when development costs have been written off and patents have expired, prices can be reduced sufficiently for international agencies to purchase them for use in developing countries. IAVI is saying that this traditional pattern is unacceptable for HIV, and in fact should be unacceptable for any vaccine or treatment.

There are encouraging signs that this thinking is now being adopted by some of the larger companies in the field, in respect of a range of new vaccines that are being developed against diseases that are either confined to countries with limited resources or present far greater public health problems in those countries than in wealthier, industrialised countries.

Financing refers to the need for both 'push' and 'pull' mechanisms to overcome the perception that there are no profits in making vaccines. Direct public investment in vaccine development by private companies is one form that 'push' mechanisms can take. The French and American governments, and the European Commission, are already doing this. Purchase funds, underwritten by international development agencies such as the World Bank, or by individual governments committing themselves to purchase future vaccines meeting set criteria, are examples of 'pull' mechanisms. Many years ago, the State of California enacted specific legislation limiting liability and guaranteeing purchase of any effective vaccine, and this seems to have helped Californian biotechnology companies (Chiron and Genentech, later VaxGen) take an early lead in this area.

It may never be possible to make an accurate assessment of the demand for any HIV vaccine until it is in widespread use. Nonetheless, it is important to realise that companies will be unlikely to risk large sums of money building manufacturing facilities on a global scale, unless there is some assurance for them that their money will not be wasted.

To produce a potential vaccine on a small scale, to test out an idea in a very few animals, is well within the capability of a well-equipped academic laboratory. However, to produce a vaccine in bulk, to the high industrial standards required by regulatory bodies for any product given to humans, is a very different matter. Expertise in this area is almost entirely located in the pharmaceutical industry, and indeed four large companies produce most of the world's commercial vaccines. These are Merck, Aventis Pasteur, American Home Products (Wyeth Lederle), and GlaxoSmithKline, all of which have had some level of involvement in HIV vaccine development.

A new and interesting model that is emerging in the UK is represented by Cobra Pharmaceuticals, a company that makes vaccines on behalf of developers, owning some of the delivery technology (in particular, for DNA vaccines) but not seeking to produce or market vaccines for end-users. While they currently make vaccines primarily on a pilot scale, they plan to expand facilities to produce in larger quantities. Such facilities might be developed in public-private partnerships, with public investment to enhance the scale of multi-purpose manufacturing facilities.

Delivery systems to administer vaccines to adults are not widespread. Most vaccines are given to young children, and in many countries it would require new systems of medical records and administrative measures to identify and invite adults or even adolescents to be vaccinated.

There is a need to standardise procedures and criteria across different countries' regulatory agencies. Within Europe, there is now a system which provides both for mutual recognition of decisions to license pharmaceutical products and for Europe-wide registration through the European Medicines Evaluation Agency (EMEA). However, drug regulation is more variable in other countries: South Africa has a professional regulatory agency, but many others do not. A related issue is the absence of any fast-tracking procedure for vaccines, to prioritise those where the safety concerns are minimal and the disease against which they are directed is most serious as a public health problem.

Liability issues may be real. Vaccines are given to people who are well, including young children, often at an age or in circumstances where they may, perhaps coincidentally, be diagnosed with other conditions. In the United States, lawsuits about such cases led most pharmaceutical companies to stop manufacturing vaccines, until legislation was passed setting a ceiling on such liabilities. However, the damage had been done.

As vaccines succeed in eradicating a feared disease, the real adverse effects of the vaccines may match or outweigh the immediate threat to individuals from the disease itself. Public health authorities have not always been effective in dealing with this issue, with an ever-present temptation to deny that these effects occur and to resist compensating those who suffer for a very real public benefit.

The UK government's Policy and Innovation Unit, part of the Cabinet Office, recently published a detailed review of incentives for private investment in meeting global public health needs, with particular reference to HIV, TB and malaria.

An evolving programme

It is unlikely that there will only ever be one vaccine or one clinical trial. The first candidate vaccines will probably have limited efficacy and will certainly be cumbersome to deliver. Most require multiple injections over an extended period. This means that a series of extended clinical trials will prove necessary, over the next fifteen or twenty years.

It has been argued mathematically (Anderson and Garnett) that even a low-efficacy vaccine targeted at high-risk populations could have a major impact on the course of an HIV epidemic, provided that limited effect was long-lasting. Such a vaccine would obviously have to be offered in the context of a wider prevention campaign.

It may be that very different vaccines, eliciting entirely different immune responses, prove equally capable of preventing HIV disease.

It may be that sexual transmission (in the general population, including gay men and injecting drug users) and blood-borne transmission (injecting drug users, healthcare workers and others exposed to blood) ultimately require different vaccines.

If there will be no single magic bullet in the foreseeable future, then it follows:

- that vaccine research must be multidisciplinary and integrated with other prevention research

- that we must find ways to test and later to deploy vaccines in ways that complement and reinforce other prevention methods, and vice versa.

Conclusions

The mobilisation and renewal of effort which has begun at a global level with the launch of the International AIDS Vaccine Initiative needs to be matched and extended at national and community levels.

Vaccine research needs to be constructed as a partnership, including volunteer participants and their communities, researchers, governments and other funding agencies, public research teams and private companies producing vaccines.

The UK and other European governments and institutions could help by clarifying what they want to achieve through vaccine research, and how they propose to advance it. They could work to remove obstacles and create incentives for private sector involvement in vaccine development, following the lead of the US state of California which enacted laws ten years ago, limiting liability for vaccine-related injuries and committing funds for the purchase of any vaccine proven to be effective.

Community leaders and activists can help by informing themselves and those they are working with on the issues surrounding vaccine research and development, and by passing that information to policy makers in government and industry.

There is no certainty that this effort will succeed, although there is good reason to believe that it can. It is, however, completely certain that without sustained efforts now, we could easily be in the very same position in ten years' time.

The experience with hepatitis B, where technically successful vaccines have been on the market for more than two decades, yet new infections continue to occur even in wealthy countries, shows that it takes more than a vaccine to stop an epidemic.

'An ideal HIV vaccine would be oral, inexpensive, safe, and heat stable; it would require only a single dose, last a lifetime, and be effective against all strains of the virus and all routes of exposure. Short of this ideal, practical limitation will constrain the efficacy of any vaccine ... Reaching those at greatest risk for HIV infection promises to be as complex with vaccination as it has been with behavioural interventions. Even a successful vaccine will be only one component of a broad prevention strategy aimed at reducing the number of new infections by diminishing the incidences of exposure to HIV, through reduction of risk behaviour and other means.' (Stryker)

Nonetheless, the impact of demonstrating an effective vaccine, even an imperfect one, would be immensely positive for the global response to AIDS. It would open up a real possibility of working towards the elimination of HIV, rather than the temporary and partial control of it. Money spent on controlling and treating HIV in the meantime would become a supporting investment towards an achievable and finite end, rather than a potentially unending drain on resources. The mobilising and energising effect this could have across the whole range of HIV-related needs should not be underestimated.

Websites

- AIDS Vaccine Advocacy Coalition, www.avac.org

- Bill and Melinda Gates Foundation, http://www.gatesfoundation.org/

- Global Alliance for Vaccines and Immunisation (GAVI),

- Global HIV Vaccines Enterprise, www.hivvaccineenterprise.org/

- HIV Vaccine Trials network, www.hvtn.org/

- International AIDS Vaccine Initiative, http://www.iavi.org/

- IAVI database of AIDS vaccines in human trials, http://www.iavireport.org/specials/OngoingTrialsofPreventive HIVVaccines.pdf

- International Council of AIDS Service Organisations, www.icaso.org

- UNAIDS, www.unaids.org

- US National Institutes of Health AIDS Vaccine Research Working Group. www.niaid.nih.gov/daids/vaccine/avrc.htm

- WHO-UNAIDS HIV Vaccine Initiative, www.who.int/vaccine_research/diseases/hiv/en/

References

Baba TW et al. *Pathogenicity of live, attenuated SIV after mucosal infection of neonatal macaques.* Science 267: 1820-1825, 1995

Barouch DH et al. E*ventual AIDS vaccine failure in a rhesus monkey by viral escape from cytotoxic T lymphocytes.* Nature 415: 335-339, 2002

Boyer JD et al. *Vaccination of seronegative volunteers with a human immunodeficiency virus type 1 env/rev DNA vaccine induces antigen-specific proliferation and lymphocyte production of beta-chemokines.* J Infect Dis 181: 476-483, 2000

Daniel MD et al. *Protective effects of a live attenuated SIV vaccine with a deletion in the nef gene.* Science 258: 1938-1941, 1992

Esparza J. Vaccines: *State-of-the-art and future directions.* Fifteenth International AIDS Conference, Bangkok. Plenary address, abstract ThPl15, 2004.

Gallo RB. *The end or the beginning of the drive to an HIV-preventive vaccine: a view from over 20 years.* Lancet. 366(9500):1894-1898, 2005.

Isaacs R. *Impact of pre-existing immunity on the immunogenicity of Ad5-based vaccines.* AIDS Vaccine 04, Lausanne, abstract 69, 2004

Kran AMB et al. *HLA- and dose-dependent immunogenicity of a peptide-based HIV-1 immunotherapy candidate (Vacc 4x).* AIDS 18: 1875-1883, 2004

Pinto LA et al. *HIV-specific immunity following immunization with HIV synthetic envelope peptides in asymptomatic HIV-infected patients.* AIDS 13: 335-339, 2002

Pitisutithum P. *Efficacy of AIDSVAX B/E vaccines in injecting drug use.* Eleventh Conference on Retroviruses and Opportunistic Infections, San Francisco, abstract 107, 2004

rgp120 HIV Vaccine Study Group. *Placebo-controlled phase 3 trial of a recombinant glycoprotein 120 vaccine to prevent HIV-1 infection. rgp120 Vaccine Study Group.* J Infect Dis 191: 654-665, 2005

Schnell MJ et al. *Recombinant rabies virus as potential live-viral vaccines for HIV-1.* Proc Natl Acad Sci U S A 97: 3544-3549, 2000

Shearer GM. *HIV-specific T-cell immunity in exposed-seronegatives.* Third Conference on Retroviruses and Opportunistic Infections, abstract S42, 1996.

Shiver JW et al. *Replication-incompetent adenoviral vaccine vector elicits effective anti-immunodeficiency-virus immunity.* Nature 415(6869): 272-273.

Stiegler G et al. *A potent cross-clade neutralizing human monoclonal antibody against a novel epitope on gp41 of human immunodeficiency virus type 1.* AIDS Res Hum Retroviruses 17(18): 1757-1765, 2001.

Zhang H et al. *Human immunodeficiency virus type 1 Gag-specific mucosal immunity after oral immunization with papillomavirus pseudoviruses encoding Gag,* J Virol 78: 10249-10257, 2004.

Zhu T et al. *Breakthrough HIV-1 infection in long-term exposed seronegative individuals.* Fifteenth International AIDS Conference, Bangkok, abstract TuOrA1141, 2004.

HIV prevention: which methods work?

Evidence-based HIV prevention

This chapter is intended to provide a practical introduction to the evidence regarding the effectiveness of HIV prevention methods.

After two decades of AIDS and HIV prevention activities, there are increasing demands amongst funders and practitioners for evidence that HIV prevention methods work. The phrase 'evidence-based prevention' has been coined to describe the need for HIV prevention activities to be developed in line with evidence regarding risk factors and outcomes. The notion of an `evidence-based' approach follows calls in NHS clinical practice for greater standardisation of patient care through the adoption of `best practice' which is backed up by evidence from sound clinical trials.

The call for evidence-based prevention is only part of a wider demand that health promotion activities, psychotherapy and counselling, and other non-drug-based interventions are subjected to the same kind of scrutiny as drug treatments.

With drug treatments (and surgical procedures, a surprisingly high proportion of which have never been scientifically evaluated) the potential for harming patients with untested treatments is obvious.

But prevention done the wrong way can be harmful too. To take one of the most prominent examples, the COL-1492 study evaluating the use of nonoxynol-9 as a possible microbicide in 765 women in west Africa resulted in frequent users of N-9 having twice the rate of HIV infection as users of a placebo.

Behavioural interventions can have negative results too. In a recent meta-analysis of adherence interventions, for instance (Amico), most interventions were positive or neutral in their effect. But a trial in which 40 participants wrote about an optimistic future in which they would only take one medication a day had a significantly negative effect, with nearly 60% worse adherence in the intervention group.

In the big meta-review cited below (Albarracin), programmes that used threat-inducing arguments to encourage condom use (such as the fear of pregnancy) and normative arguments ('everyone else does it, you should too') had significantly negative effects across participants as a whole, though there were exceptions (for instance, people under 21 responded positively to normative arguments).

It is therefore scientifically important to review the effectiveness of prevention programmes as to do otherwise would not only waste public money but might significantly increase HIV infection.

This chapter reviews:

- The evidence provided by a couple of large meta-reviews of HIV prevention programmes

- The underlying philosophies of HIV prevention, and how and why people change their behaviour

- How and why do we know that HIV prevention efforts have worked, and issues in measuring effectiveness

- Some more research evidence regarding effective interventions.

How do we know HIV prevention efforts have worked?

Effectiveness reviews

In recent years HIV prevention workers, researchers and funders have become increasingly concerned with identifying how best to spend limited funds. This requires a better understanding of which HIV prevention initiatives have been most effective, and which ones are least effective.

A study funded by the UK Health Education Authority (now part of the National Institute for Health and Clinical Excellence) attempted to identify examples of effective interventions, using criteria developed in other healthcare fields (Oakley). These criteria demanded that studies reporting on the effectiveness of prevention interventions should ideally display the following characteristics:

- A clear definition of aims

- A description of the intervention package and design sufficiently detailed to allow replication

- A randomly allocated control group or matched comparison group*

- Data on numbers of participants recruited to the experimental and control groups

- Baseline (pre-intervention) data for both groups*

- Post-intervention data for both groups*

- Drop-out rates for both groups

- Findings for each outcome measure as defined in the aims of the study.*

However, the review used only four of these characteristics (those marked with an asterisk) when defining studies with a 'sound' methodology. Paradoxically, for a review intended to develop awareness of effective interventions, replicability (point 2) wasn't amongst these criteria!

The study found that just 18 out of 68 outcome evaluations could be described as methodologically 'sound'. Just nine of these studies were conducted with adults in high risk groups. These studies are amongst those discussed in more detail in *What is known about the effectiveness of interventions?* later in this chapter. A number of other studies published since this article appeared are also discussed below.

Another review discusses the question of sound methodology in more detailed terms. A review funded by the US National Institutes of Mental Health and the US Centers for Disease Control proposes a series of standard reporting requirements in HIV and STI prevention behavioural interventions which will allow comparisons between effectiveness studies.

- Describe recruitment and sampling methods: In order for any study to be replicated it is essential that the description of the methodology is as full as possible. It is also important for the reader to be able to judge whether any aspects of the methodology could have biased the results. For example, was the sample a volunteer group or random sampling? How were they selected?

- What proportion of potential participants were recruited into the study?

- What was the refusal rate? What differences exist between participants and non-participants?

- Define the sample size required to produce statistical significance. When a study is designed, statistical methods should be used to define how large a sample will be required in order to detect a certain magnitude of effect on a behavioural or biological outcome. For example, researchers might predict that in order to detect a 20% reduction in syringe sharing, they would need to recruit 100 people into a study in order to be certain that a 20% reduction wasn't due to chance, but to the effects of the intervention. This is called statistical power

- Was there a control group, and if so, how were people randomised? A control group can guard against the effects of being studied (such as people telling researchers what they think they want to hear)

- Report length of follow-up. This allows readers to judge whether there is evidence of a sustained effect

- Describe the theory of behaviour change and education underlying the intervention. This allows the reader to judge whether the design of the intervention is likely to test the theoretical assumptions underlying the intervention

- Describe the intervention. Too many study reports fail to describe the intervention in sufficient detail. What were the messages communicated to participants? How many sessions/exposures were there?

- Describe outcome measurements used. A more detailed discussion of outcome measures follows later in this chapter

- Report results of mediation analysis. Mediators are the elements of an intervention which mediate between the intervention itself and the behaviour change. "Mediators are generally conceptual variables designed to be addressed by the intervention because they are believed to cause behaviour change, such as perceived social norms, skills, self-efficacy or perceptions of risk. Mediation analysis involves demonstrating that the intervention changed the mediator as well as the behavioural outcome" and that controlling the mediator also affects levels of risk behaviour. If this relationship cannot be proven, then another factor is responsible for behaviour change, and the theoretical relationship between the mediator and the behaviour targeted for intervention is unproven.

References

Oakley A et al. Behavioural interventions for HIV/AIDS prevention, AIDS 9: 479-486, 1995.

O'Leary A, DiClemente R et al. Reflections on the design and reporting of STD/HIV behavioural intervention research, AIDS Education and Research, 9 Supp A, 1997.

What works? Two meta-reviews

1. Dolores Albarracin et al. 2005

The largest ever meta-review (study of studies) of HIV prevention interventions (Albarracin) reviewed the effects of 354 HIV prevention interventions and compared their effect with the results for 99 control groups within 33 countries over a 17-year span (though three-quarters of studies were US-based).

Altogether 104,054 people took part in the HIV prevention programmes while another 34,751 were included in control groups (the number in control groups was smaller because many studies compared the effect with matched cohorts or historical controls).

About 45% of participants were men (allowing for a few studies in which gender was not identified); their average age was 26; 34% were white, 47% Afro-American or African and 13% Latino. Only 36% of participants had completed high school.

Many studies did not record which risk groups participants belonged to but 11% were designed specifically for gay men, 15% for injecting drug users, 17% for multiple-partner heterosexuals, 14% for recreational drug users, and 8.5% for sex workers (programmes could target more than one risk group). Fifty-five per cent of participants reported multiple partners.

Of note, very few studies recorded the HIV status of participants, possibly because of a presumption that participants were negative, although in studies where serostatus was recorded, it was 20%.

Baseline condom use was poor - before the interventions 64% of participants 'never or almost never' used condoms, 34% 'sometimes' used them and only 2.3% 'always or almost always' used them. The total proportion of acts of intercourse in which condoms were used was 32.3%.

The size of the meta-review allowed Albarracin and colleagues to calculate the effectiveness of prevention interventions for particular groups of people, both in terms of demographic characteristics like gender, age and race, and in terms of risk category.

It also enabled them to calculate the effectiveness of *specific* kinds of intervention well enough to provide a set of 'decision trees' at the end of the study to help prevention workers decide on the best kind of intervention for a specific group in future.

There was one important limitation to Albarracin's survey. She only used condom use as her primary endpoint. She therefore did not include studies which had other aims such as abstinence, sexual delay or reduction in the number of partners, nor did she look at the ultimate effect, HIV incidence.

However the size of the study did allow her to also calculate the effectiveness of programmes on *intervening* effects between the intervention and the condom use.

This is important because it is an aid to theoretical rigour of design. An intervention may be based on one of the theories outlined below and produce a positive result; but without measuring how participants' psychological attitudes have changed, it leaves open the possibility that the change in condom use is due to other factors such as the introduction of treatment. Or it could find out that the intervention did indeed produce the desired psychological effect - but that this change had a negative effect. This was what happened with threat-inducing arguments, where presumably the heightened perception of increased threat ("I will catch HIV unless I use condoms") led to a feeling of helplessness rather than the thing behavioural studies are looking to increase, namely *self-efficacy*.

Self-efficacy is very different from general self-confidence. It is the self-confidence that one can perform a specific task. Neglecting the importance of tying the increased confidence to a task can also result in negative effects. For instance, programmes that taught interpersonal skills such as assertiveness training also had negative effects in some groups. This may be because the increased interpersonal skills were not tied specifically enough to a particular behaviour and may even have been used negatively - as in improving participants' abilities to pick up partners or persuade them not to use condoms.

Albarracin analysed interventions according to the following categories (many studies would use more than one method):

- 'Attitudinal': containing arguments designed to induce a positive attitude about using condoms - 48% of programmes

- 'Normative': containing arguments designed to increase social responsibility or increased perceived peer-group or societal pressure to use condoms - 15% of programmes

- 'Behavioural': containing verbal training or arguments designed to improve participants' condom-using behaviours - 20% of programmes

- 'Behavioural skills': containing training getting participants to practise behavioural skills - 22% of programmes

- 'Threat': containing 'persuasive arguments designed to increase perceptions of threat [of HIV infection or poor sexual health] among recipients' - 47% of programmes

- Most programmes (94%) provided information about HIV

- Twenty-two per cent of programmes distributed condoms to intervention groups and 7% to control groups

- Eighteen per cent of programmes administered an HIV test

- Forty-nine per cent included 'active' interventions such as HIV counselling and testing and behavioural skills training.

- Two-thirds of interventions (where it was recorded) were delivered to groups, 20% to individuals and 8% to both

- Thirty per cent were delivered in clinics, 31% in schools, 21% in community venues such the street, community centres or gay bars, and just 3% consisted of a mass communication.

Results

As stated above, Albarracin's bottom-line finding was that 'active' intervention programmes that required participants to practise a skill or do something else health-enhancing like produced an average 38% increase in occasions of sex in which condoms were used, relative to baseline. Activities include role-playing safer-sex negotiation situations and practising putting on condoms. They also included programmes that involved the taking of an HIV test. Because baseline condom use was 32.3%, this resulted in an absolute increase in condom use of 7.8%.

These are the increases in the proportion of sex acts in which condoms were used. In addition, the baseline proportion of people sometimes using condoms 'at least sometimes' implies that 17% more people would start to use condoms at least sometimes.

'Passive' programmes were ones in which participants merely received a communication such as reading or being taught information, or seeing a video. These produced on average a 13% increase in condom use, relative to baseline, or a 4.2% absolute increase.

Of note, there was also a condom use increase of 8%, relative to baseline, in the control groups. This is probably due to the well-known effect in which inclusion of participants the control group of a study tends to improve their results, not so because of a 'placebo effect' in this case - how can you have a placebo that looks like an intervention? - but because control groups were generally provided with some intervention, such as leaflets, or were on the waiting list for interventions, and were therefore an already motivated group.

The effect of active interventions was therefore to increase condom use by 30% over control groups, and of passive interventions by 5%.

The only exception to this difference between passive and active interventions was in condom provision where - unsurprisingly - simply providing participants with condoms worked better than requiring them to actively ask for them to be provided.

Most types of intervention were effective to some degree, though ones that taught behavioural skills and which induced positive attitudes towards condom use worked best.

The effects observed were strongest for interventions that took place in clinical settings (which, in Albarracin's definition, also included HIV voluntary organisations that offered some sort of clinically-relevant service.) The effects of most types of intervention did not reach significance for interventions conducted in schools or in community settings, though condom provision had a significantly positive effect in community settings.

What may be the most significant single finding of the meta-review was that interventions that increased participants' sense of the threat of HIV or of related outcomes, such as sexually transmitted infections or pregnancy, had a consistently negative effect, across all categories of recipients.

Put simply, if you frightened people about HIV they used condoms *less*, not more. Remember that nearly half of all programmes included some element of threat arguments.

Normative arguments didn't work either, except with young people under 21. Otherwise, in fact, young people were rather a resistant audience, showing much less tendency to use more condoms after interventions.

Men responded particularly badly to threat arguments (fear) and women to normative arguments (guilt) though both sexes responded equally well to behavioural-skills training.

Africans responded badly to both threats and normative arguments though they did respond well to general training in interpersonal skills as well as specific skills, unlike whites and Latinos. All groups responded well to teaching behavioural skills, not just in condom use but to management skills such as safer-sex negotiation.

High-risk groups (including gay men) generally did not respond as well as low-risk groups, but this may have been a statistical effect whereby groups that already had relatively high levels of condom use did not increase their use as much as groups that initially had low levels. They responded particularly badly to normative and attitudinal arguments. But they responded well to condom provision and condom use training.

Albarracin acknowledges that if she had used sexual abstinence or partner reduction as the outcome measure, threat arguments might be found to work. Scaring people is a legitimate tactic in health promotion if you want to stop people doing something, such as smoking cigarettes or drink-driving. It's much less likely to get people to take positive self-protective steps such as using condoms.

One finding was the striking paucity of trials of programmes for HIV prevention for people with HIV. Seroprevalence data among trial groups were only available in 22 of the 354 trials, which, comments Albarracin, "severely limited the possibility of analysing the different intervention components." Albarracin was able to show that the higher the HIV prevalence was in groups of participants where it was reported, the more positive the behaviour change which, as she comments, "indicates that HIV-positive people generally increase their condom use," a finding backed up by other studies.

However the lack of statistical power meant that only attitudinal arguments encouraging condom use, fear-inducing arguments about the consequences of not using them, and condom provision could have their effectiveness measured. Fear-inducing arguments and condom provision had a neutral impact. But attitudinal arguments actually had a negative impact on people with HIV: programmes that *didn't* try and get HIV-positive people to have a more favourable attitude towards condoms worked better than ones that did (p=<.001).

Albarracin's finding than just 3% of papers addressed mass-media campaigns also underlines the paucity of research into the effectiveness of this kind of intervention. See **Mass Media Campaigns** below for more on this.

We'll return to Albarracin's meta-review when we look at the theories of behaviour change that underlie the planning of prevention programmes.

2. Wayne Johnson et al. 2002

We take this as an example of a smaller meta-review of HIV prevention interventions targeting a specific population - in this case, gay men. There are so many HIV intervention studies conducted that an attempt to review all meta-reviews - to study the studies of studies - is beyond the scope of this section. However Johnson's is interesting partly because it is about the

group that still has the highest HIV incidence in the USA and the UK, and partly because it supports a number of Albarracin's conclusions, but equally interestingly does not support others.

Johnson sifted through 99 HIV prevention studies conducted in the USA to find nine that targeted specifically gay men (and comments on the fact that the highest-incidence group in the USA only had 10% of studies devoted to it). The date of studies ranged from 1989 to 1998 and Hamilton comments that he would have had at least twice the data to work with if he had included later studies. Altogether 2,270 gay men participated in the interventions.

The bottom-line effect of the interventions was a reduction of 26% in instances of unprotected anal sex relative to baseline. Because only 32% of gay men reported unprotected sex before the interventions (a big contrast to Albarracin's populations, where only 32% *did* use condoms) this represents an absolute decrease in unprotected sex acts of 8.5%.

Many of Johnson's findings mirror Albarracin's. He divided up his interventions in a slightly different way thus (with some interventions using a number of methods):

- Training in *interpersonal* skills such as safer-sex negotiation, disclosure and communication

- Training in *personal* skills such as self-management, decision-making and stress management

- Programmes designed to enhance *self-esteem* or community pride

- Programmes designed to increase the *social acceptability* of condom use by means such as peer leader endorsement and outreach by peer volunteers (similar to Albarracin's 'normative' studies)

- Programmes designed to enhance *responsibility* by the use of means such as behaviour contracts and agreements.

Like Albarracin, Johnson found that interventions that included interpersonal skills training produced the most clearly favourable effects. Behaviour contracts and responsibility agreements produced the weakest effects.

In contrast to Albarracin, Johnson found that the three interventions that took place in the community worked better that ones that involved small-group training, though these worked too. Two of these were similarly-designed studies which recruited community 'opinion leaders' as disseminators of information and advice about safer sex in gay bars and clubs. See **Community mobilisation** below for more detail on these studies.

The success of these programmes may be culturally-specific, as when the same concept was tried in Glasgow, Scotland it did not work. It may also, be a statistical artefact; the participants in the gay-venue studies had higher levels of unprotected sex, which is concordant with Albarracin's finding that the lower the baseline level of condom use, the greater the improvement interventions tend to produce.

Also in contrast to Albarracin, interventions generally worked better on younger people, and significantly worse in men over 33. Johnson comments that this may also be because older men tended to have baseline higher levels of condom use. It may also be because the majority of interventions that targeted young people in Albarracin's meta-review took place in schools - and it has proved particularly difficult to deliver sex education programmes of proven efficacy in schools, as witnessed recently by the failure of a particularly well-designed programme in Mexican schools (Walker).

One of Johnson's most important findings was to identify significant 'antagonisms' between particular methods. For instance, studies that included personal skills training and self-esteem boosting were effective as long as they did *not* also include arguments for the acceptability of condom use or safer sex. Similarly, programmes for young people worked particularly well if they had low baseline levels of condom use as long as they did *not* include behavioural contracts. This is valuable preliminary work towards finding out what components of an ideal HIV prevention programme work well together, and which don't.

Do Johnson's findings apply to programmes for other risk groups? Well, in the same supplement issue of the *Journal of Acquired Immune Deficiency Syndromes* there are meta-reviews of prevention programmes for safer-sex among drug users (Semaan), for sexually-experienced adolescents (Mullen), and for heterosexual adults (Neumann). Their results are pretty comparable:

- Johnson found a significantly protective effect for interventions with gay men (Odds Ratio 0.69, equivalent to a 26% reduction of instances of unprotected anal sex.)

- Semaan's meta-review of 33 HIV prevention interventions on the sexual risk behaviours of drug users in the USA found a significantly protective effect for this group (Odds Ratio 0.61, equivalent to the proportion of drug users who reduced sexual risk being 12.6% higher in intervention groups than control groups).

- Mullen's review of 16 behavioural interventions in sexually experienced adolescents found that they had a significant effect in reducing instances of unprotected sex (Odds Ratio 0.66) but not in the number of partners (OR 0.89) or STIs (OR 1.18).

- Neumann's meta-review of 14 behavioral and social interventions for heterosexual adults found statistically significant effects in reducing unprotected sex (Odds Ratio 0.69 and in reducing STIs (OR 0.74).

HIV prevention programmes show a remarkable consistency of effect across different groups. However there was less information in the above studies than there was in Albarracin's big review as to which methods work best.

Summary

- Averaged over all interventions and all risk groups, HIV prevention programmes show a remarkable consistency of success, with increases in safer sex/condom use in the order of 25%.

- 'Active' programmes that get people to practise behavioural skills work about three times better than passive programmes that just deliver information.

- Programmes that encourage positive behaviours and develop self-efficacy work better than normative programmes (appeals to social responsibility), though the latter work well for young people.

- Programmes that use 'scare tactics' and the threat of AIDS have significantly *negative* effects (except possibly for people with HIV: see below).

- There has been very little randomised controlled research into the efficacy of mass-media HIV prevention initiatives.

- Similarly, there has been little in the effect of HIV prevention interventions on people with HIV (but see Positive Prevention below).

- Programmes work best if delivered by experts in clinical settings or by organisations that already offer services to people with HIV.

3. And the UK?

A 2003 meta-review (Ellis) by the Health Development Agency (HDA - now part of NICE, the National Institute for Health and Clinical Excellence) of reviews assessing the effectiveness of interventions in the UK came up with a considerably slimmer body of evidence than the largely US-based meta-reviews above.

It found no research in the UK on which specific modifying factors produced better outcomes: no studies of cost-effectiveness and no studies of whether theory-based interventions were more effective.

Among its list of 'key evidence gaps', it found:

- Very little review-level evidence relevant to UK gay men

- Very little review-level evidence relevant to UK commercial sex workers

- No review-level evidence relevant to UK African communities

- No review-level evidence about interventions with people with HIV

- And, crucially, very little review-level evidence about the vast majority of interventions. None on condom distribution schemes, small media (leaflets) and community development work.

and this is not a comprehensive list. So what *did* it find?

- It found that cognitive-behavioural group work interventions that concentrate on role-playing, communication skills and sexual negotiation can be effective for gay men; it also found that community-level interventions involving peers and popular opinion leaders could be effective in influencing gay men's sexual risk behaviour.

- It found that community level, especially peer led, interventions can be effective in influencing the sexual risk behaviour of commercial sex workers.

- It found that small group interventions delivered at the community level can be effective in influencing the sexual risk behaviour of black and minority ethnic women.

- And it found that a positive HIV diagnosis positively influenced sexual risk behaviour, but no evidence that a negative one did.

This was the total amount of statistically significant evidence it was able to cull from UK HIV prevention studies.

The HDA was at pains to point out that, for the many different HIV prevention programmes that have been carried out in the UK since the beginning of the epidemic, lack of evidence of effectiveness was not the same as evidence of lack of effectiveness. However the lack of scientifically-rigorous research into HIV prevention in the UK, especially into the difference in effectiveness between methods, does not serve as a good foundation for future programmes.

References

Albarracin D et al. *A test of major assumptions about behaviour change: a comprehensive look at the effects of passive and active HIV-prevention interventions since the beginning of the epidemic.* Psychological Bulletin 131(6): 856-897, 2005.

Ellis S et al. *HIV Prevention: a review of reviews assessing the effectiveness of interventions to reduce the risk of sexual Ttansmission.* Health Development Agency, 2003. This report may be downloaded from http://www.nice.org.uk/page.aspx?o=502571

Johnson WD et al. *HIV prevention research for men who have sex with men: a systematic review and meta-analysis.* JAIDS 30: Supplement 1, S118-S129, 2002.

Mullen PD et al. *Meta-analysis of the effects of behavioral HIV prevention interventions on the sexual risk behavior of sexually experienced adolescents in controlled studies in the United States.* JAIDS 30 Supplement 1: S94-S105, 2002.

Neumann MS et al. *Review and meta-analysis of HIV prevention intervention research for heterosexual adult populations in the United States.*

Semaan S et al.*A Meta-analysis of the effect of HIV prevention interventions on the sex behaviors of drug users in the United States.* JAIDS 30 Supplement 1: S73-S93, 2002.

Van Damme L et al. *Effectiveness of COL-1492, a nonoxynol-9 vaginal gel, on HIV-1 transmission in female sex workers: a randomised controlled trial.* Lancet 360: 971-977, 2002.

Walker D et al. *HIV prevention in Mexican schools: prospective randomised evaluation of intervention.* BMJ 332: 1189-1194, 2006.

The theory and philosophy of HIV prevention

1. Theoretical models of behaviour change

Many of the programmes Albarracin surveyed will have been devised with a particular theory in mind about how people change their behaviour, and programmes that are theory-based have been shown in general to work better. Programmes devised without a consistent theory of behaviour change may offer subtly contradictory or antagonistic messages, as Wayne Johnson tentatively shows.

In another paper (Durantini) from Dolores Albarracin's team at the University of Florida which used the same data as her previous one, experts trained in the theory and technique of at least one method of behaviour change produced better results when they led interventions than did briefly-trained peer educators; the one exception was that peer educators worked at least as well with younger people under 21 as long as the educator was of the same gender and/or ethnicity as the group trained.

The theoretical models discussed here have been developed and tested by researchers working within the fields of medical sociology and psychology to account for the effects of a wide range of health promotion activities. This section discusses the main theoretical models and their relevance to HIV prevention, and relates research literature on HIV prevention to these models.

HIV prevention is always based on a set of assumptions about the ways in which people make decisions about risks, and how they respond to attempts to persuade them to change their behaviour. Sometimes these assumptions are broadly correct, but sometimes researchers have discovered significant problems with such assumptions when they are tested.

The core difference between these theories is that they postulate different *routes* people travel in the process of changing their

behaviour. Or, to put it another way, they give different weight to different drivers of behaviour, usually seeing one particular one as primary. These may be divided roughly into theories that see *information* about the health threat to be avoided as the main driver; ones that see the learning of *behavioural and interpersonal skills* as the main driver; and ones that see *social pressure and personal self-efficacy* as the most powerful influences.

This is summarised in a diagram from the Durantini paper, which is shown below.

Reference

Durantini MR et al. Conceptualizing the Influence of Social Agents of Behavior Change: a Meta-Analysis of the Effectiveness of HIV-Prevention Interventionists for Different Groups. *Psychological Bulletin* 132(2) 212-248. 2006.

The health beliefs model

This model (and the similar protection-motivation model) attempt to explain how individuals will take action to avoid ill health. First, individuals must recognise that they are susceptible to a particular condition (at risk), and must perceive that the severity of the condition is such that it is worth avoiding.

They must also perceive that the benefits of avoidance are worth surmounting any barriers to changing their behaviour, and that they have the self-efficacy (in terms of skills, assertiveness etc) to change their behaviour. Cues to action are considered important in assisting all stages of change in this model. A cue for action could be a poster, a face-to-face encounter with an outreach worker or a conversation with a friend.

Rosenstock argues that *programs to deal with a health problem should be based in part on knowledge of how many and which members of a target population feel susceptible to AIDS, believe it to constitute a serious health problem and believe that the threat could be reduced by changing their behaviour at an acceptable psychological cost.*

The attractions of this model are obvious, especially because responses to cues to action at each of the theorised stages are easily measurable by surveys of knowledge and attitudes and of self-reported behaviour.

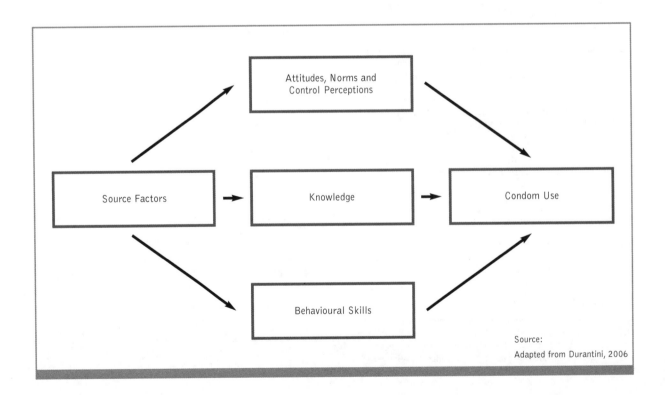

Source:
Adapted from Durantini, 2006

But the model does not offer much insight into long-term sustenance of behaviour change, and allows sexual and drug-using behaviour to be framed in terms of `relapse' if it does not conform to the model of behaviour change offered to the target audience. The notion of relapse assumes that behaviour change is a once-and-for-all event rather than an evolution which requires `sustenance' and support, and does not take into account new situations in which previous learning will be inappropriate. An example might be the decision to abandon condom use in a relationship, which can be more fully explained by the `reasoned action' model discussed below.

The model does offer some useful tools for questioning assumptions embedded in HIV prevention. For example, it can often come as a surprise to those involved in HIV prevention to discover that members of the target audience consider the consequences of HIV infection to be less serious than other outcomes (such as demonstrating a lack of trust in a partner or a loss of sexual pleasure from condom use). Rosenstock argues that behaviour change is most likely to occur in circumstances where severity and susceptibility are rated highly by individuals, and as Dowsett argues, gay and bisexual men in particular have come to very uneven perceptions of risk as a consequence of their experiences after almost 20 years of warnings about AIDS.

The health beliefs model of individual behaviour change has been widely criticised for its lack of reference to the social and interactive context in which individuals come to judge their susceptibility to risks. In particular, critics have argued that it makes no reference to the pressures from peers or partners which may encourage risky behaviour. This is ironic given the emphasis placed on 'self-efficacy' by some proponents of the model, who have developed educational programmes which focus on the development of skills designed to deal with precisely such pressures. The social learning model discussed immediately below grew out of the Health Beliefs model during the 1970s and 1980s as educators began to appreciate its limitations for explaining how and why people change their behaviour, and the need for concentrating on the development of skills or cognitive techniques.

One earlier meta-analysis (Gerrard) found that there was no association between a person's perceived vulnerability to HIV and the care they took to have safer sex. And, as seen above, interventions that attempted to reinforce the threat of AIDS were generally counter-productive.

Albarracin says:

The health beliefs model and the [similar] *protection motivation theory both suggest that inducing perceptions of threat concerning HIV should increase condom use. Communications designed on this basis typically use highly emotional scare tactics in the hope that negative affect will stimulate condom use. For example, one campaign presented an image of the Grim Reaper as the source of an HIV-prevention message. Other, less extreme communications based on the dame assumptions may describe the consequences of the disease, provide data on infection rates, or conduct a detailed interview about HIV risk behaviour to sensitise participants to risk. As noted, however, these strategies may be counterproductive for proactive target behaviours like condom use.*

However, there are some suggestions that interventions that stress the negative consequences of HIV transmission may work well for one particular audience: people who already have HIV.

Rothman and Salovey (1997) proposed and demonstrated that threatening (*loss-framed*) persuasive messages are effective only when the target behaviour consists of avoiding a risk factor (such as avoiding lung cancer). The same messages, however, are presumably detrimental when one wishes to promote a proactive measure (such as signing on to a smoking cessation course). HIV-positive people may be motivated much more by the negative consequences of infecting others (which can be as severe as criminal prosecution) than the relatively meagre reward of behaving responsibly.

Albarracin found that interventions stressing the threat of HIV transmission at least had a neutral, rather than negative, impact on people who already had HIV in contrast to their negative impact on seronegative people. At the 2006 Retrovirus Conference, Jean Richardson of the University of Southern California demonstrated conclusively that 'loss framed' messages work better in people with HIV than 'gain-framed' ones.

She divided a group of 585 people with HIV (86% males, 74% gay, with men and women represented equally among the heterosexuals) into three groups that received HIV counselling.

The counsellors were asked to fame their messages with a particular slant. The control group talked neutrally with their clients about everyday concerns such as medication adherence. The 'gain frame' counsellors put in positive messages about safer sex into their discourse with clients: you will protect your partner if you use condoms, you'll stay free of STIs, you will feel in control of your behaviour, and so on. The 'loss frame' counsellors gave essentially the same messages the opposite slant: if you *don't* use condoms you will expose your partners to HIV, you are more likely to get STIs, you will feel out of control, and so on.

The findings were highly statistically significant. 'Gain framed' messages produced no significant change in behaviour relative to control. But 'loss framed' messages produced a reduction in instances of unprotected sex of 12.5% in people with one regular partner and 38% in people with two or more partners.

Richardson commented that she had 'hoped' there would be no difference in the results of the framing of the messages - possibly because loss-framed messages sound punitive. But it does look as if, when working with people with HIV and *only* with them, the emotional weight of negative messages may work better than positive ones do.

References

Catania J et al. *Towards an understanding of risk behaviour: An AIDS risk reduction model,* Health Education Quarterly 17, 53-72, 1990.

Dowsett G. *Practicing desire: homosexual sex in the era of AIDS,* Stanford University Press, 1996.

Richardson J. *Prevention in HIV clinical settings.* Thirteenth Conference on Retroviruses and Opportunistic Infections, Denver, abstract 165, 2006.

Rosenstock IM et al. *The Health belief model and HIV risk behaviour change in Preventing AIDS: theories and models of behavioural interventions* DiClemente RJ & Peterson JL (Eds), Plenum Press, New York, 1996.

Rothman AJ and Salovey P. *Shaping perceptions to motivate healthy behaviour: The role of message framing.* Psychological Bulletin 121(1), 3-19, 1997.

Social-cognitive and information-motivation-behavioural skills models

Bandura's social-cognitive learning theory is a general theory of self-regulatory agency, which proposes that *perceived self-efficacy* lies at the center of human behavior. According to this model, effective self-regulation of behaviour and personal change requires that people believe in their efficacy to control their motivation, thoughts, affective states, and behaviours. In other words, people are unlikely to change unless they want to, believe they can, feel they will, and have the behavioural skills to actually change.

People develop the social and self-regulatory skills required to translate their concerns regarding this information into preventive action (e.g. negotiating safer sex and condom use). This model also proposes that people will require practice and feedback in order to develop self-efficacy in taking preventive action (e.g. learning how to use condoms), and social supports for the desired personal changes will be essential.

The environment in which social learning takes place is created by the interaction between three forces: personal factors such as gender, biological attributes; interactive aspects such as negotiation and the nature of the emotional interaction (is this anonymous sex; what does it mean to refuse to share a needle with a sexual partner?); and social/cultural setting (for example the meanings attached to sex between men).

This model does not offer a strong theoretical explanation for why people choose to change, but as Bandura argues, "the major problem is not teaching people safer sex guidelines, which is easily achievable, but equipping them with skills and self-beliefs that enable them to put the guidelines into action consistently in the face of counteracting pressures".

A refinement of the social-cognitive learning theory is the information-motivation-behavioural skills model (Fisher and Fisher). This also assumes that information, motivation, and behavioural skills underlie behavioral change. The information-motivation- behavioral skills model, however, is a feedback-loop model: it also assumes that the three components exert potentiating effects on each other.

To this extent, the finding by Albarracin that information has positive influences on behavior *only* when accompanied with active, behavioral strategies can be taken as evidence that the confluence of strategies is as important as the selection of each individual approach.

Examples of successful programmes which improved self-efficacy include controlled programmes with gay men and with African-American youth in the US. In both programmes groups identified to be at high risk were taught how to negotiate safer sex in high risk situations through role play with feedback. Both programmes used control groups. In the gay men's programme the control group received no intervention, whilst in the African-American youth programme, the control group received an information-only intervention.

Recipients of the self-efficacy programmes reported lower levels of unprotected sex with partners over extended periods of follow-up, although it is impossible to control for lying in studies with self-reported outcome measures (see below). Nevertheless, especially noteworthy is the fact that the African-American youth study was carried out first in young men and then replicated in young women in another neighbourhood with the same positive outcome (Jemmott).

One programme, not especially with HIV prevention as its main aim, which uses the development of self-efficacy as its core strategy is the Positive Self-Management Programme (PSMP). See the **Self-Management of Life with HIV** section in the **Mental health and quality of life** chapter of the *AIDS Reference Manual* for more.

References

Bandura A. *Social cognitive theory and exercise of control over HIV infection in Preventing AIDS: theories and models of behavioural interventions* DiClemente RJ & Peterson JL Eds, Plenum Press, New York, 1994.

Fisher JD and Fisher WA. *Theoretical approaches to individual-level change in HIV risk behaviour.* In JL Peterson and CC diClemente (eds.), Handbook of HIV Prevention, 3-55. New York: Springer. ISBN 0-306-46223-0.

Jemmott JB et al. *Reductions in HIV risk associated sexual behaviours among black male adolescents: Effects of an AIDS prevention intervention* Am J Pub Health 82: 372-377, 1992.

Jemmott JB et al. *Increasing condom use intentions amongst sexually active black adolescent women,* Nursing Research 41: 273-278, 1992.

Kelly JA et al. *Behavioural intervention to reduce AIDS risk activities* J Consult Clin Psychology 57: 56-67, 1989.

Reasoned action model

The reasoned action model (Fishbein) assumes that most forms of human behaviour are a matter of choice. Thus the most immediate determinant of any given behaviour is an individual's intention whether or not to perform that behaviour. This in turn is influenced by the degree to which the person has a positive attitude towards the behaviour, and the degree to which they expect that important others will think that they should perform the behaviour. It therefore combines elements of self-efficacy with elements of social norm-forming. Changing these underlying beliefs about the desirability of an action is what will produce the greatest long-term changes in behaviour. For example, if someone is told not to do something by someone they respect, they are more likely to act on that warning, according to the reasoned action model.

This model is strongly biased towards explaining the success of information giving, and measuring its impact through knowledge and attitudes surveys. It is also strongly biased towards changing subjective beliefs, but doesn't prescribe a particular methodology for doing so.

Research in this area has investigated the cognitive structures which underlie sexual decision-making rather less. There are very few reports of tests of methodologies used to alter beliefs and intentions amongst people at risk of HIV infection, despite the strength of association demonstrated between intention and behaviour in such areas as smoking control, alcoholism treatment, contraceptive behaviour and weight loss.

Albarracin's meta-analysis teased apart the attitudinal and normative parts of the reasoned-action model. It confirmed that programmes that attempted to help participants develop a more positive attitude towards condom use generally worked. However it found that normative arguments only worked in young people under 21.

Albarracin explains this finding thus:

This result does not imply that younger individuals are normatively driven whereas older ones are not. Instead, it appears to suggest that younger individuals do not perceive that making decisions based on social consensus is undesirable, whereas adults are more prone to try to act independently even when they cannot escape being influenced by norms - even if the influence ends up being a reaction against the norms.

One study which has looked at the cognitive structures underlying decision-making about safer sex is research conducted by Australian psychologist Ron Gold. He looked at the underlying justifications which gay men used to explain to themselves why it was permissible to have unprotected sex with partners.

These justifications were overwhelmingly clustered in three themes:

- assumptions about partners' HIV status

- feelings of invulnerability

- desire for intimacy.

Another study by the same research team looked at cues which subjects used to judge the HIV status of a partner. Gold interviewed 66 men with an average age of 26 who had reported unprotected sex in the previous six months. Participants were asked to make judgements about the likely HIV status of potential partners based on written descriptions. Gold found that participants were more likely to rate men with attributes of intelligence, well-adjusted personality and a healthy appearance as potentially `safe' partners, while men rated highly attractive were more likely to be judged `unsafe'.

Another study which looked at the cognitive basis for sexual decision-making was Sigma Research's review of the rationales underlying unprotected sex. Hickson argues that the strongest influence upon the decision to abandon condom use is assumptions made about self and partner's HIV status.

References

Fishbein M. *Using information to change STD-related behaviours in Preventing AIDS: theories and models of behavioural interventions* DiClemente RJ & Peterson JL Eds, Plenum Press, New York, 1994.

Gold R et al. *On the need to mind the gap: on-line versus offline cognitions underlying sexual risk-taking,* in D Terry et al, The theory of reasoned action: its applications to AIDS preventive behaviour, Pergamon, Oxford, 1993.

Gold R et al. *Desire for unprotected intercourse preceding its occurrence: the case of young gay men with an anonymous partner,* Int J of STD and AIDS 4: 326-329, 1993.

Gold R et al. *Situational factors and thought processes associated with unprotected intercourse in gay men,* Psychology and Health 5: 259-278, 1991.

Hickson F et al. *Perceptions of own and partner's HIV status and unprotected anal intercourse among gay men,* Second Conference on Biopsychosocial Aspects of AIDS, 1994.

Stages of behaviour change models

The behaviour-change-stage model (Prochaska) offers an explanation of the stages through which an individual will progress during a change in health behaviour. This model is particularly associated with notions of `relapse' behaviour, and has been used widely in the treatment of alcoholism and smoking. It divides behaviour change into the following stages:

1. **Pre-contemplation:** lack of awareness of risk or no intention to change risk behaviour

2. **Contemplation:** beginning to consider behaviour change without commitment to do anything immediately

3. **Preparation:** a definite intention to take preventive action in the near future

4. **Action**: modification of behaviour, environment or cognitive experience to overcome the problem

5. **Maintenance**: the stabilisation of the new behaviour and avoidance of relapse.

This model was used as the basis for the US AIDS Community Demonstration Projects, which targeted five at-risk populations in five US cities. Messages were developed from the experiences of community members to model behaviour change steps to target people considered to be at each of these five stages.

A similar model is the AIDS Risk Reduction Model of Catania, which divides behavioural change into three stages, each with several influencing factors:

1   Recognition and labeling of one's behaviour as high risk

- *Influences:*
  - knowledge of sexual activities associated with HIV transmission;
  - believing that one is personally susceptible to contracting HIV;
  - believing that having AIDS is undesirable;
  - social norms and networking.

2   Making a commitment to reduce high-risk sexual contacts and to increase low-risk activities

- *Influences:*
  - cost and benefits;
  - enjoyment (e.g., will the changes affect my enjoyment of sex?);
  - response efficacy (e.g., will the changes successfully reduce my risk of HIV infection?);
  - self-efficacy;
  - knowledge of the health utility and enjoyability of a sexual practice
  - social factors (group norms and social support)

3   Taking action. This stage is broken down into three phases:

- information seeking;
- obtaining remedies;
- enacting solutions.

Depending on the individual, phases may occur concurrently or phases may be skipped.

- *Influences:*
  - social networks and problem-solving choices (self-help, informal and formal help);
  - prior experiences with problems and solutions;
  - level of self-esteem;
  - resource requirements of acquiring help;
  - ability to communicate verbally with sexual partner;
  - sexual partner's beliefs and behaviours.

Both theories, then, attempt to define a sequence of stages that go from behaviour initiation to adoption to maintenance. Successful interventions should be the ones that focus on the particular stage of change the individual is experiencing and facilitate forward progression.

Presumably, knowledge of HIV/AIDS or more general risk perceptions may serve to prompt change when people are not yet performing the behaviour, but may not elicit movement beyond the initial stage. Similarly, inducing favourable attitudes may be important at the very initial stages but not when people are already performing the behaviour and are aware of its outcomes. People who have already adopted the idea of change and begun to perform the behaviour may then need *new* skills to foster complete success.

Albarracin's meta-analysis suggests that, consistent with these theories, behavioural and self-management skills training are more important later than earlier in the change process. On the other hand, contrary to expectation, attitudinal and informational arguments were equally important for both inconsistent and more consistent condom users.

Albarracin comments: "From this point of view, our data suggest that *everything* might be more effective when people have previously engaged in condom use, rather than supporting the specific predictions made by Prochaska and colleagues." In other words: it gets easier the more you practice, but you still need the most basic kind of backup and reinforcement in terms of getting information and keeping attitudes positive if you're not to relapse. People are engaged on a kind of 'Continuous Professional Development' course when it comes to the maintenance of safer sex.

This finding should give some cheer to the developers of mass-media and prevention information campaigns. They imply that although behavioural-skills training is generally a necessary part of an effective HIV-prevention programme, the provision of information, though it does not effect change in itself, can prompt people to *think* about changing and can help them maintain safer behaviour when they have done.

Reference

Catania JA et al. *Towards an Understanding of Risk Behaviour: and AIDS Risk Reduction Model (ARRM)*. Health Education Quarterly17, 53-72, 1990.

Prochaska JO et al. *In search of how people change: applications to addictive behaviours*, Am Psychol 47: 1102-1114, 1992.

Social diffusion model

Innovations are diffused through social networks over time by well-established rules; health-related behaviours are no exception.

A body of social theory called social diffusion theory has studied the diffusion of innovations in fields such agriculture, international development and marketing. More than 4,500 studies have been published on the diffusion of innovations.

Diffusion of innovations theory has been adopted for the study of the adoption of behaviour intended to avoid HIV infection. Diffusion theorists argue that a behaviour or innovation will be adopted if it is judged to have a high degree of utility, and if it is compatible with how individuals already think and act.

However, an innovation will only be considered if it is known about, and one of the major problems facing HIV educators is the difficulty of frank communication about HIV risk and how best to protect oneself and one's partners. The taboo status of much discussion about HIV makes it difficult for individuals to judge the utility of an innovation such as condom use, because frank discussion of condom use is impossible on television.

Diffusion research has also observed that innovations tend to be adopted in a population according to a distribution that follows an S-shaped curve: that is, few at first, then an increasing proportion, and a few late adopters. Diffusion researchers have been very interested to define the characteristics of who adopts early, and who influences those who adopt an innovation later.

They discovered that rates of adoption varied according to the homogeneity of the group, with innovations diffusing more rapidly in groups which were relatively homogenous. `Change agents' who modelled a new innovation or disseminated information about it were most likely to be successful if they came from that group. The decentralisation of diffusion is also judged to be important. If many different individuals are diffusing an innovation, it is likely to be diffused more quickly.

Two other factors cited as important in the diffusion of innovations have particular relevance to HIV prevention. `Testability' - opportunities for individuals to experiment with an innovation - and visibility - the knowledge that others are already doing it - are crucial steps in the diffusion process.

One of the earliest successes in reducing HIV incidence comes from Uganda, where HIV incidence went into a sharp decline in the late 1980s. It was accompanied, and probably caused, by an equally sharp reduction, unique among African countries at the time, in the average number of sexual partners people had (see **B is for being faithful and behaviour change** for more on this.)

This decline appears to be evidence that it was not merely the ending of war and the restoring of civil order on the accession of President Yoweri Museveni in 1986, which would involve men returning from the army and militias to their families, which created this change in behaviour patterns.

According to Low-Beer, Stoneburner and colleagues:

Ugandans are relatively more likely to receive AIDS information through friendship and other personal networks than through mass media or other sources, and are significantly more likely to know of a friend or relative with AIDS. Social communication elements, as suggested by these kinds of indicators, may be necessary to bridge the motivational gap between AIDS prevention activities and behavior change sufficient to affect HIV incidence.

In other words, Low-Beer is arguing that the social diffusion model in which there is (a) a wide personal acquaintance with HIV/AIDS in the population and (b) the encouragement and willingness to speak about it and pass knowledge on in informal social networks is the method that has worked best to influence behaviour change. Similar changes now appear to be taking place in other countries, including the highest-prevalence ones such as Zimbabwe.

A wide personal acquaintance with HIV/AIDS is the inevitable consequence of a developing untreated epidemic: the encouragement and willingness to speak about it, however, can be influenced by political leadership and widespread awareness-raising work. Such work was, supporters say, initiated by Museveni when he started his AIDS awareness campaign in 1986, which included his famous `Zero Grazing' policy, which urged monogamy on all Ugandans.

It is easy to see how this model applies to the development of safer sex and safer drug use in the 1980s, but what does it have to offer HIV prevention workers once the initial lessons have been learnt? It's reasonable to argue that ongoing HIV prevention work is a process of continual innovation as interventions are refined.

Dearing describes how the innovation of bleach as a decontaminant of syringes was successfully diffused in San Francisco in the 1980s. Bleach was adopted because it interfered very little with the process of drug injecting, and because it was viewed as a highly effective decontaminant by drugs workers and by drug injectors. It was successfully diffused by outreach teams which took bleach to the places where injecting drugs users scored drugs or injected. Watters notes that seroprevalence amongst IDUs in San Francisco began to level off after bleach was introduced, whereas other cities which did not adopt the innovation saw a continued rise in prevalence in the following years. Several other projects which relied upon a social diffusion model are discussed under *Community mobilisation* below.

References

Dearing JW et al. *Diffusion theory and HIV risk behaviour change in Preventing AIDS: theories and models of behavioural interventions* DiClemente RJ & Peterson JL Eds, Plenum Press, New York, 1994.

Low-Beer D, Stoneburner R. *Behaviour and communication change in reducing HIV: is Uganda unique?* African Journal of AIDS Research 2(1): 9-21, 2003.

Watters JK. *Epidemiology and prevention of HIV in intravenous drug users in San Francisco 1986-1990*, Sixth International Conference on AIDS, abstract No.FC 106, 1990.

Social/environmental change

The final model assumes that social or environmental changes are necessary in order to change individual behaviour, and that influencing group norms, social policy, sexual mixing patterns and the social and medical infrastructure are the key routes to achieving this change. This model proposes the necessity of working with social groups, not individuals, and underlies such notions as peer education and community mobilisation. But it is also the theoretical underpinning for activism, advocacy and political lobbying.

Friedman and Des Jarlais argue that it is only by reference to social factors that we can understand differences in HIV prevalence amongst different ethnic groups of injecting drug users in the US. many other examples of social determinants of HIV risk are discussed elsewhere in this volume (see *Understanding the epidemic*), and the social change model is extremely influential in setting the agenda for HIV prevention. However, an overemphasis on the social/environmental change model can lead to the downgrading of individual behavioural and cognitive techniques which are of proven efficacy.

Probably the best way to use social change models with individuals is to develop `community pride' programmes which lead to the development of greater self-efficacy and the reduction of isolation among participants. In Wayne Johnson's meta-review, for instance, two of the nine programmes (Choi and Peterson) were for gay men of specific ethnicity: Asians and Pacific Islanders, and African Americans, respectively.

The Choi workshop consisted of a single three-hour session of group councelling, which, among other things, aimesd to help gay Asians and Pacific Islanders "develop positive self-identity and mutual social support". Similarly, the Peterson intervention, which consisted of three weekly three-hour sessions, as well as teaching things like self-management, also used" attempts to develop self-identity and social support among African-American MSM."

References

Choi KH et al. *The efficacy of brief group counselling in HIV risk reduction among homosexual Asian and Pacific Islander men.* AIDS 10: 81-87, 1996.

Friedman S & Des Jarlais D. *Social models for changing health-relevant behaviour*, in DIClemente R & Peterson JL (Eds): Preventing AIDS: Theories and methods of behavioural interventions, Plenum Press, New York, 1994.

Peterson JL et al. *Evaluation on an HIV risk reduction intervention among African-American homosexual and bisexual men.* AIDS 10: 319-325, 1996.

Differing philosophies of HIV prevention

A: Harm reduction or risk elimination?

Since the beginning of the epidemic we have been faced with two competing philosophies about the relationship between acceptable levels of risk and sustainable degrees of behaviour change and public health measures.

One model, that of harm reduction, has sought to demonstrate that the risks of HIV transmission are identifiable and that proven methods of protection against infection exist. These include:

- Avoidance of serodiscordant unprotected sex

- Avoidance of needle-sharing, and provision of sterilised needles and oral substitution drugs such as methadone or buprenorphine

- Use of condoms in penetrative sex, and provision of them

- Screening of the blood supply

- Heat treatment of Factor VIII or provision or safe recombinant clotting factor

- Avoidance of breastfeeding where feasible and necessary

- Adoption of universal precautions in medical settings where invasive procedures take place.

Thus HIV prevention based on a harm reduction philosophy involves substituting less harmful activities for those which pose the greatest risk. For example, the promotion of needle exchanges is a form of risk or harm reduction; it does not eliminate the potentially harmful activity of injecting drugs, but it does offer a means of reducing the risk of HIV infection.

Similarly, the promotion of condoms to gay men for anal sex is seen as preferable to a policy of discouraging gay men from having anal sex altogether. It offers gay men a choice of ways in which to reduce their level of risk, and offers substitutes which are proven to be of lower risk, e.g. oral sex instead of unprotected anal sex. Exactly the same strategy has been employed with workers in the sex industry in many countries.

The majority of debates around the New Prevention Technologies such as pre-exposure prophylaxis, microbicides and mass circumcision are about whether these harm reduction methods actually *will* reduce harm. Indeed, the whole debate about programmes that promote abstinence versus ones that promote condoms hinges on whether, if you take the danger out of sex, you will 'encourage' people to take risks they would otherwise not have done.

Risk elimination

Risk elimination, on the other hand, depends on the belief that protecting both public health and the health of the individual requires the elimination of risk. Risk elimination approaches take two forms:

- The promotion of abstinence over condoms and needle exchanges. This approach questions the efficacy of 'safer sex' as it is commonly conceived, and suggests that injecting drug use is just as harmful as the sharing of injecting equipment.

- The highlighting of very low risks as unacceptable risks.

The previous edition of the AIDS Reference Manual argued strongly against risk elimination. But in the real world, things are not so simple, and it is possible to at least make a case that, by providing harm-reduction methods, HIV prevention workers may at times potentially facilitate sexual contacts that would not otherwise have happened.

In one 2005 study from Uganda (Kajubi) researchers from Makerere University randomised 378 young men aged 18-30 from two urban communities near Kampala into two groups.

The intervention group attended a three-hour workshop teaching them about how condoms stopped HIV and STIs, how to put on a condom, strategies for negotiating condom use with partners and talking about barriers to having safer sex. They were then given vouchers to redeem for free condoms provided by young people in their local community.

The control group was just given a general lecture on the HIV situation in Uganda and given the free vouchers but no condom tuition.

The men taught how to use condoms certainly used (a lot) more - 110 per man in the six-month period after the study compared with 13 per man in the control group. However the public health benefit of this was offset by the fact that they had an increased number of partners. In contrast, the control group reduced their partners.

Men taught condom use increased their average number of partners from 2.13 to 2.44 in the six months whereas the control group decreased their number of partners from 2.20 to 2.03. This was highly statistically significant ($P = 0.004$)

The control group had fewer partners whether regular or casual. In contrast, the intervention group, while reducing their number of casual partners slightly, had considerably more regular partners.

This would not matter if condom use was consistent. But while the amount of unprotected sex in control group had declined with both regular and casual partners, the condom group only reduced unprotected sex with all partners slightly - and actually slightly increased the amount of unprotected sex they had with casual partners.

After adjusting for the fact that men in the condom group were on the whole somewhat older and more likely to be married, the researchers calculated that providing the men with condom lessons actually led to them having 48% more unprotected sex than the ones without lessons.

The researchers commented: "Prevention interventions in generalised HIV epidemics need to promote all aspects of sexual risk reduction to slow HIV transmission."

However, it will be noted, Kabuji and colleagues do not therefore propose risk elimination methods instead - such as the probably fruitless task of telling young male Ugandans to be sexually abstinent. They simply advocate for a comprehensive programme of HIV prevention rather than relying on one single intervention.

In other situations, worrying about very low risks can have the paradoxical consequence of inducing fatalism about past sexual practices and reducing adherence to current tried and tested safer sex guidelines, as a 1992 Dutch study showed amongst gay men. Those who became worried that oral sex was risky were most likely to abandon the use of condoms in anal sex, believing themselves to be already exposed to the virus through oral sex.

Another example are the costly and anxiety-provoking 'lookback' exercises that have been conducted by hospitals when a healthcare professional who has performed exposure-prone procedures has been found to have HIV. These have been done to address public (and professional) anxiety about the tiny risk of infection through an invasive procedure (there have only ever been four documented cases of HIV transmission from a healthcare worker to a patient). However it may be argued that they do more to provoke anxiety than contain it, and draw attention away from the need for universal precautions to be employed in all invasive procedures. This undermines confidence in such precautions, misinforms the public about the risk of HIV infection, and in some cases has resulted in harassment and exposure of the healthcare worker.

These lookbacks have become less frequent since 2001, when the Department of Health altered its guidance so that patient notification only happens where an injury to the infected healthcare worker has happened.

Of course, we have to make allowance for what we do not know and err on the side of caution in predicting the risks of the developing epidemics. Worst-case predictions are intended to be treated as such precisely in order to prevent such scenarios from coming about. However, when such scenarios interfere with demonstrably effective health education, they become almost as dangerous as denial of any risk whatsoever.

A further principle associated with risk reduction is that of minimal disruption. Changes in behaviour are thought to be more sustainable if they involve the least possible change in behaviour required to protect oneself. This is why for many people, cutting down the amount of fat one eats is likely to be a far more realistic, if minimal, form of risk reduction than giving it up altogether. Advice of this sort works with the grain of long established and pleasurable behaviour, rather than against it. Sexual habits are deeply rooted in everyone's lives, and require rather more than will-power to change.

Those who advocate risk elimination argue that the public have the right to be aware of all the risks associated with HIV infection, and to make up their own minds on the basis of such information. Such an argument presupposes:

- That everyone makes up their mind about potential risks on the basis of all the available facts

- That taking steps to reduce certain risks automatically makes it more likely that some people who would previously have avoided that risk will now decide to take it

- That perceptions of risk in the community are all formed by the same factors, leading to an even perception of risk. An example might be sexually transmitted diseases: some people regard these as more disastrous because they have less sex, or because they interfere with an existing relationship, or because the consequences of a sexually transmitted disease might be more serious for a woman than a man

- That the facts are presented neutrally

- That information about AIDS and HIV is not received by people in the light of previous prejudice, misinformation or blaming

- That the information is presented in such a way as to be easily understood

- That everyone is equally capable of acting upon that information to protect themselves

- That there are unlimited resources to present information about even the tiniest theoretical risks. An example of this might be the choice between educating gay men about the dangers of unprotected anal intercourse and the much smaller danger from oral sex.

Realistic risk reduction advice

Following on from the criticisms of risk elimination, it is important that risk reduction advice should be:

- Evidence-based. We have already seen evidence above that messages that aim to instil fear of infection may be counter-productive, as they make people feel helpless

- Easily understood by those it is intended to reach

- Implementable. In other words, people have to be willing and able to take the suggested precautions. To suggest that all sex is risky is to invite denial of any risk attached to sexual activity

- Persuasive, not punitive

- Not more disruptive than absolutely necessary.

For further discussion of these issues see *Safer sex* and *Drug use* in the *AIDS Reference Manual*.

Reference

Kabuji P et al. *Increasing condom use without reducing HIV risk: Results of a controlled community trial in Uganda.* JAIDS 40(1): 77-82. 2005.

2. HIV prevention or sexual health promotion?

The Government's strategy on the promotion of health in England for the 1990s, entitled *The Health of the Nation* (HMSO, 1991), has been the most influential publication in the UK to use the term sexual health promotion. Subsequent strategy documents have emphasised the importance of sexual health promotion, and in 1998 the Department of Health set targets for reducing the number of teenage pregnancies as one of the key planks of sexual health promotion.

The publication in July 2001 of the National Strategy for Sexual Health and HIV, which was subtitled "Better Prevention, Better Services, Better Sexual Health," only set this tendency in stone. The intention had originally been to write a long-overdue HIV strategy for the UK but this was changed to encompass a broader sexual health strategy.

There is a reduced emphasis on HIV prevention compared with the 1980s, despite the fact that the rate of new infections within the UK continues at approximately nearly 3,000 per year.

In this context sexual health promotion covers prevention activity focused on different topics, but mainly referring to contraception and sexually transmitted diseases including HIV infection. This gradual policy shift forced many HIV prevention workers to reorientate their work to fit within this wider framework; to coordinate more closely with other prevention activity; to take a more positive health promotion approach, or simply to use different terminology to ensure continued funding. Being aware of this change in emphasis is all the more important because of the likelihood of HIV-specific funding being removed in the near future and, following the NHS reforms, the new contractual requirements of purchasing authorities.

HIV prevention

Traditionally, prevention is described as being at three levels: primary, secondary and tertiary:

- Primary HIV prevention refers to activity focused on preventing uninfected people becoming infected and on preventing infected people transmitting HIV (e.g. through sex education; condom promotional campaigns; needle exchange schemes)

- Secondary HIV prevention refers to activity aimed at enabling people with HIV to stay well (e.g. HIV antibody testing to allow people to know their status; welfare rights advice; lifestyle behaviour change programmes; anti-discriminatory lobbying)

- Tertiary HIV prevention aims to minimise the effects of ill-health experienced by someone who is symptomatic with HIV disease (e.g. the prophylactic use of drugs and complementary therapies; welfare rights advice to maximise benefits; immuno-supportive educational programmes; disability lobbying).

However, such a distinction of activity has been neither so wide nor so obvious in practice; in general terms HIV prevention has implicitly referred only to primary prevention with the additional recognition that people with HIV are themselves involved in ensuring that they do not pass the infection on and that the primary prevention of other STIs is in itself important secondary HIV prevention for them. In this way, HIV prevention has mainly focused upon elements of sex education (safer sex promotion) irrespective of HIV status.

This division hasn't been helped by the existence of a rival set or categories which defines 'primary prevention' purely as activity focused on preventing uninfected people becoming infected, and 'secondary prevention' as being prevention measures targeted at people who already have HIV. This distinction is still sometimes made in the USA.

However it has been pointed out (not least by people with HIV and their advocates) that HIV prevention whether for people with or without HIV involves the same set of changed behaviours and that some of the same ways of changing them may work. It also implies a hierarchy of importance when it comes to targeting people for prevention programmes - a hierarchy that some advocates for the targeting of people with HIV for prevention activities feel is the wrong way round.

However findings such as the fact that HIV-positive people modify their sexual risk behaviour after diagnosis and there is little evidence that negative people do (see **Counselling and HIV antibody testing** below), or that people with HIV respond positively to 'loss framed' messages that HIV-negative people find disempowering, may indicate that interventions to help stop people *transmitting* HIV may need to be based on different theories of change and involve different methodology and content than prevention to stop people *acquiring* HIV.

Sexual health promotion

However, both groups of people have the same set of needs if a wider sexual health promotion attitude is taken. If HIV is viewed as just one of a number of acute and chronic conditions that impact on sexual health (albeit one of the most serious and expensive ones), 'positive prevention' may legitimately be seen as a specialised division or primary **sexual health promotion**.

Sexual health promotion can be used to mean a wide variety of things and justify both prescriptive and more liberal approaches.

For example, there have been fears voiced that this term could be used to return to an era of medicalisation as far as the topic of sex is concerned - focusing on disease and the mechanics of sexual behaviour at the expense of sexual pleasure, desire and identity.

This is most obvious in situations where sexual health promotion refers to clinic-based contraception and sexually transmitted disease services. However, this need not be the case even where the focus is on medical services; sexual health promotion can be used to widen the approach of such services to include a social dimension and an example of this is given below (see French & George, 1994).

Advocates of new prevention technologies, however, would counter this by saying that it is precisely medicalised prevention interventions that we badly need. Since prevention measures focused on teaching behavioural skills, social responsibility or better communication can only prevent a certain proportion of infections, the most humane, proactive and cost-effective thing to do is to campaign for interventions that do not require people to change their behaviour or psychological attitudes, but prevent HIV infection physically.

Circumcising a heterosexual man, for instance, is safe when done under medical supervision; is a one-off operation; and it may protect him from 65% to 75% of future HIV infections. Side-effects, such as loss of sexual pleasure, occur, but they are relatively rare (see **C is also for circumcision** under **developing prevention technologies**). Circumcision may therefore protect the health of this person and of his community better than prevention workshops which offer only 26% efficacy and whose impact tends to wear off over time (in Johnson's meta-analysis, condom-use rates were already becoming lower when they were investigated six months after the end of interventions, in comparison to ones that were evaluated only one or two months after the intervention).

The crucial aspect of sexual health promotion is obviously choice, and making sure that even 'medicalised' interventions are consciously chosen and consented to as part of a person's general determination to reduce the risk to their sexual health.

In the USA, the Centers for Disease Control (CDC) are putting into action a plan to test every adult between 15 and 65 for HIV at least once, in the knowledge that diagnosed people tend to reduce their sexual risk behaviour by at least 50% (and also so that people can be treated before presenting so late that they have AIDS).

However the CDC was also responding to political disapproval of community HIV prevention programmes. On 15 April 2003 they initiated what they called the Serostatus Approach to Fighting the Epidemic (SAFE). This involved a refocusing and reallocation of HIV prevention resources on to people with HIV.

Henceforward, the CDC announced, it would focus on a drive to maximise the number of people tested for HIV. Once people had tested HIV-positive they would be managed by "ongoing case management, medical interventions, and support for other psychosocial stressors."

There is some justification for laying a very strong emphasis on testing as a key element in HIV prevention. According to the

CDC's own statistics, there are over 900,000 people with HIV in the USA. About 700,000 know their status. The annual incidence rate is about five per cent a year. But HIV incidence in people infected by people who know their status is less than two per cent (1.73%). Conversely, HIV incidence in partners of HIV-positive people who do *not* know their status is nearly 11% a year (10.79%) (Holtgrave and Anderson).

But HIV prevention for positive people cannot consist solely of testing. There has not been the same effort put into developing prevention advice and programmes for people who *are* diagnosed as part of this screening drive.

In other words, CDC's strategy was to test HIV-positive people, tell them not to pass their infection on, blame them if they did, and possibly treat 'stressors' such as depression and drug use, but not necessarily to provide people living with HIV with any training in how to minimise the risk of transmission themselves.

So sexual health promotion can be used positively to facilitate discussion about sex and encourage the growth of educational and personal development opportunities (e.g. in youth work, with targeted groups). However, they can also be used in a restrictive, medicalised way to allow only the presentation of biology and treating HIV transmission with preventative medicine as if it was possible to do so in the same way that statins are used to prevent heart disease. There was also an unspoken set of questions about how exactly contact tracing would be performed under the new testing regime.

Sexual health promotion could also refer to activities which enable people who identify collectively to express their own needs. Such community-based activity spans a wide range and can be thought of in terms of the amount of real power people have in determining the allocation of resources to meeting needs. The terms community mobilisation and community development have both been used to describe aspects of this kind of work.

Finally, sexual health promotion can also embrace the role of policy makers and opinion formers in creating a local or national climate which itself promotes sexual health. This can cover anything from liberal or prescriptive mass-media messages, enabling or restrictive legal frameworks or policies and guidelines (e.g. sex education guidelines in schools; age of consent laws; improving the availability of sexually explicit material for 'health' reasons; allowing condom advertising on TV).

References

Anderson T. *Expanding the boundaries of positive prevention programs.* Fourth Annual Center for AIDS Prevention Studies Conference, San Francisco. Plenary two. See http://hivinsite.ucsf.edu/InSite?page=cfcaps2004-01&ss=xsl%2Fconf-t2 . 2004.

Department of Health: *The health of the nation,* June 1991, HMSO.

Department of Health: *HIV/AIDS and sexual health: the health of the nation key area handbook,* 1992, HMSO.

Department of Health: *National strategy for sexual health and HIV,* July 2001. May be downloaded from http://www.dh.gov.uk/assetRoot/04/05/89/45/04058945.pdf

Holtgrave DR, Anderson T. *Utilizing HIV transmission rates to assist in prioritizing HIV prevention services.* Int J STD AIDS 15(12): 789-972, 2004.

The limitations of the evidence-based approach

Are randomised, controlled trials appropriate in HIV prevention?

There has been considerable debate amongst health promotion professionals and researchers over what constitutes evidence of effectiveness in health promotion. One of the chief disagreements has arisen over the question of the research methodology that should be used to measure effectiveness. Oakley and colleagues have argued that the gold standard measure for effectiveness is a randomised controlled trial (RCT). However, this view has been criticised as a relic of biomedical research which isn't appropriate for the assessment of behavioural interventions (Fraser).

An obvious parallel can be drawn with HIV treatment research. In a treatment environment where there is just one new drug available and little previous treatment experience, it's easy to recruit and randomise people and judge the effects of the drug, providing you have an agreed endpoint, or outcome measure. But when you have disagreements about the endpoint's validity, even this form of simple study becomes difficult to interpret.

The situation becomes much more complex when the standard of care has improved greatly, and many drugs can now be combined to treat a disease. It becomes a lot more difficult to find people who have never been exposed to anti-HIV drugs. It's unethical to give people just one drug. It must be added to the standard of care, and the study can't last very long because of the medical and commercial urgency of proving that new drugs work. So we don't know whether the drugs produce long-term changes, or whether the regimens will need to be changed frequently.

Substitute HIV prevention intervention for drugs in this scenario and it's easy to understand why randomised controlled trials are inappropriate in some circumstances (although the circumstances in which they may be appropriate are discussed in *Outcome measures* below).

Researchers are adapting to the new virology and the new treatment environment by designing new sorts of trials and being much more flexible about the kinds of evidence that will be needed to license drugs and develop effective treatment strategies. There is no reason why the HIV prevention field needs to ignore these lessons or to adopt a methodology simply because it is a medical orthodoxy. In reality, one of the big attractions of the randomised controlled trial in a conservative culture may be its capacity to slow down the diffusion of innovations and reduce spending on experimental approaches. It contributes to the rationing of scarce resources, but it may not be the best way of determining how prevention money should be spent.

Stifling innovation

There is also a danger that researchers and practitioners will be unwilling to draw inferences from study results, and will persist in advocating conservative solutions to prevention problems rather than following paths which are plausible. This is exactly what happened in the field of HIV treatment, where some researchers and purchasing authorities have insisted on obtaining evidence from one or several clinical endpoint trials in order to validate particular treatment strategies, rather than being prepared to extrapolate from existing evidence as to which treatment strategies might be biologically plausible.

Yet the history of HIV treatment shows that since the advent of antiretroviral therapy, it is those who have advocated biologically plausible therapy who have tended to get things right. For instance, triple combination therapy was advocated on the basis of biological plausibility over two years before clinical trials proved that it was superior to dual therapy or monotherapy.

Inadequate service provision

This leads us to another danger of the evidence-based approach as it is currently being pioneered. This is the possibility that health authorities will only choose to fund the approaches which are validated by randomised controlled trials or the effectiveness reviews cited above. Lucas has argued that the approaches cited as most effective by such reviews should only be seen as the minimum contents of a package of prevention measures. They should not become a prescription for purchasing.

Nor do such reviews give any guidance on the allocation of resources between different types of programme. This isn't possible without some concomitant analysis of outcome measures. Whilst a programme which increases people's ability to talk about safer sex may have been proven by an RCT, how effective is the intervention at changing infection rates? Ultimately, resource allocation must be judged according to the

capacity of different elements of a prevention programme to exert the best possible effect on new infections.

With meta-reviews we are beginning to collect data that can allow us to judge which measures will have the most effect on this outcome. However these reviews of reviews are only as powerful evidentially as the studies whose findings they analyse. While many studies use outcome measure like condom use and unprotected sex acts, fewer use change in partner numbers or STI incidence.

Still fewer use the ultimate endpoint of HIV prevention interventions - change in HIV incidence. This is largely because even in a high-risk population, incidence, at a few per cent a year, is usually too small for anything other than a huge trial to be sufficiently powered to produce a statistically significant result. The same incidence problem has bedevilled studies of the New Prevention Technologies, especially as control groups recruited into the trials often modify their behaviour positively as well.

Currently available effectiveness reviews have another weakness. They don't tell commissioners or providers what sort of agency is best suited to carry out particular types of interventions. Of course, you can make a guess, and evidence is beginning to seep through. For instance, a number of meta-reviews have found that prevention programmes conducted at clinics often have a statistical edge.

But it helps if you understand the models of behaviour change which underlie a particular intervention package. For example, a community mobilisation approach proposed by a local health promotion agency needs to be considered as an example of a social diffusion intervention. What does social diffusion theory in general tell us about the likely nature of the agents best placed to bring about change in a community or group? Is a local health promotion agency best placed to develop this type of programme effectively? Is the community mobilisation approach likely to be the best method of allocating scarce resources, or might other methods of diffusion have a higher contact rate (and a speedier diffusion process)?

In summary, the current limitations of effectiveness reviews suggest the need for better efforts to define the aims and objectives of prevention efforts. A more outcome-focussed set of aims and objectives would allow purchasers and providers to think through the implications of different interventions with more attention to establishing realistic measures of efficacy.

For example, take a town with a large gay population which has a very limited range of prevention activities. This town is not close to any other major gay centre, so it's realistic to use several inter-related outcome measures to measure the overall effectiveness of prevention activities. These might be gonorrhoea reports as short-term indicator, and if possible over the longer-term, HIV incidence in a cohort recruited from the local gay population.

The aim of local prevention activities would be to effect a reduction in both these indicators within a given budget. But what should the package of local prevention activities consist of? To define this package a purchaser could take one of several approaches:

- Fund several different outcomes: number of condoms distributed; number of gay men attending counselling sessions for partners having unprotected sex; number of workshop sessions provided for men having risky sex; number of peer educators/volunteers trained according to the overall aims of the local HIV prevention strategy.

Evaluation of projects funded under this strategy would follow two tracks: process investigation of service delivery, and self-reported behavioural and cognitive changes amongst a sample of gay men recruited from users of these services. Waiting list control groups for some of these interventions could also be required as additional back-up.

This strategy takes account of several different models of the ways in which people change their behaviour, and seeks to deploy these in a mesh of prevention activities to be targeted at the local gay community

- However, it doesn't help purchasers judge where they will get the most value for money. What is the factor leading to most new infections in the locality? Is it unprotected sex in relationships? Is it unprotected sex in saunas and sex clubs? Or are gay men reporting a large number of unprotected contacts whilst using recreational drugs? Whilst these factors can be extrapolated from the research literature, local action research and ethnography will be a vital precursor to funding a cost-effective local strategy. The other vital element during this phase of commissioning is the maintenance of existing levels of service.

Local needs assessment need not reproduce national behavioural data, but it can often give an idea of particular local factors which are facilitating new infections - or more likely, local opportunities for exploiting social networks. For example, a local needs assessment need not investigate what sort of risk-taking activity is going on amongst local men, but it will need to map local gay networks.

The role of research in commissioning and project design

A conference, *Building Bridges*, held in the mid 1990s indicated the extent to which the processes of effectiveness research, needs assessment, service provision and commissioning remain separated.

A number of issues were identified by presentations at the conference:

- Action research ought to be embedded into HIV prevention activities.

- Greater education amongst all involved in project design and management regarding assumptions about behaviour change, risk behaviour and valid outcome measures in relation to the above.

- Avoiding hoodwinking of commissioners and providers by researchers.

- Avoiding research in the interest of researchers rather than providers or commissioners.

- Greater involvement in the research process for those who will be responsible for implementing changes proposed as a consequence of research.

- Better dissemination of findings to those stakeholders/change agents.

All these issues are discussed in the *Building Bridges* conference report, and in particular, in presentations by Graham Hart and by Nicola Woodward.

References

Deverell K (Ed). *Building bridges: linking research and primary HIV prevention* (Conference report), NAM, 1996.

Fraser, E. *How effective are effectiveness reviews?* Health Education Journal 55: 359-362, 1996.

Lucas G. *Effectiveness reviews*, Current HIV Education Research, Spring 1997, HEA.

Oakley A et al. *Behavioural interventions for HIV/AIDS prevention*, AIDS 9: 479-486, 1995.

Measuring effectiveness

Outcome measures

Researchers and prevention workers have attempted to assess the effectiveness of interventions by using a number of measures:

- Changes in knowledge and attitudes.

- Numbers of persons reached.

- Changes in uptake of condoms or injecting equipment.

- Changes in reported behaviour amongst a cohort.

- Changes in reports of sexually transmitted infections.

- Changes in HIV incidence or prevalence in the population.

- Changes in HIV incidence or prevalence in a cohort.

This section looks at the value of these measurements, with reference to recent examples from international research, and then goes on to summarise what is known about effective interventions. This list of measurements covers those used in process evaluations and those used in outcome evaluations.

A couple of papers in *AIDS* journal have reviewed what indicators ideally ought to be measured in the evaluation of national HIV prevention programmes, and in the case of the State of California (Page-Shafer), which indicators could and could not be measured.

References

Mertens T et al. *Prevention indicators for evaluating the progress of national AIDS programmes*. AIDS 8(10): 1359-1369, 1994.

Page-Shafer K. *Evaluating national HIV prevention indicators: a case study in San Francisco*. AIDS 14(13): 2015-2026, 2000.

Knowledge and attitudes

Investigation of the effects of HIV prevention campaigns on the knowledge and attitudes of the target population was one of the first measurements of effectiveness to be adopted by researchers. It was considered to be a crucial first step in determining whether or not information about HIV and AIDS had been received and understood by the target population.

During the 1980s knowledge and attitudes surveys carried out in the UK showed wide and rapid dissemination of messages about HIV infection and AIDS, but also showed alarming levels of miscomprehension of these basic messages. These surveys tended to investigate the impact of basic HIV awareness campaigns, and provided useful baseline data.

Such surveys are of limited usefulness today except in situations where new concepts are being introduced to a population. For example, knowledge and attitudes surveys amongst gay and bisexual men in the UK over the past eight to ten years have repeatedly demonstrated high and unvarying levels of knowledge about AIDS, HIV, modes of transmission and safer sex. There is also no automatic relationship between levels of knowledge and behaviour.

Hickson et al. note that whilst UK samples of gay men consistently demonstrate very high levels of knowledge about HIV risks, a significant proportion practice unprotected anal intercourse with regular partners.

In some studies an *inverse* relationship has been observed between knowledge and risk behaviour. Older gay men who are well-educated about HIV risks are having the most unsafe sex, either because knowledge can be used at the service of rationalising risks (as in decisions to have unprotected sex based on a person's viral load - see **Disclosure, Serosorting and negotiated Safety**) or because people worry less about long-term threats to the health as they get older.

Another form of 'knowledge and attitudes' research which may be more relevant is the evaluation of skills acquisition, although this can be difficult to measure realistically. The skills acquired might be condom use or the ability to raise the topic of safer sex with prospective partners, and skill acquisition must be measured by self-report.

The final form of attitudinal research is investigation of responses to published materials, media campaigns or particular issues identified as important to the design of prevention initiatives. Examples include evaluation of leaflets by focus groups or assessment of comprehension of core messages by questionnaire or focus group.

Such investigations may be necessary in order to establish the acceptability of a certain type of intervention for a target group, or to test an assumption about methods of communication or influence. However, information derived from qualitative evaluations of this sort tends to be much more ambiguous than quantitative data, and contrary to the traditional view that 'you can use statistics to prove anything', it is arguable that you can use qualitative research to prove anything you want it to prove, depending on the interpretation. Qualitative research of this nature is better thought of as useful because it teases out and articulates behaviours that can then be the subjects of quantitative research.

Numbers of people reached

Numbers reached by an intervention are a very basic measure of its success, but a high contact rate does not lead automatically to large measurable effects on behaviour or incidence. A project which reaches a relatively small number of people may have a much greater long-term effect on behaviour and incidence, especially if those people are either opinion leaders themselves or the section of a particular community that demonstrates the highest risk behaviour. Measures of quantity are not very useful unless they are accompanied by measures of quality.

It is also useful to focus on demographic groups such as women or young people if research evidence suggests that these groups are at particular risk of HIV infection. For example, there is some evidence that younger injecting drug users are at greatest risk of HIV infection, and it may be appropriate to set targets for contacts with this group as a surrogate or mediator for an effective intervention to reduce HIV transmission amongst injecting drug users.

However, there is no clear evidence that young gay men are at greater risk of HIV infection than those over 30 (rather the reverse), or that black or Asian men are at intrinsically greater risk purely as a consequence of demographic factors, so a demographic target for this group would be inappropriate as one of the mediators for reduced HIV transmission.

Changes in uptake of condoms or injecting equipment

One way of measuring whether an intervention is working is to look at changes in the uptake of condoms or injecting equipment over time. This form of measurement is relatively easy to carry out, since it only involves monitoring the output of a project. However, there is no guarantee that the output of a project can be related to changes in behaviour or incidence.

For example, whilst a project may experience a 25% increase in demand for condoms over the course of a year, there may be no change in the incidence of gonorrhoea in the locality. This might be due to the fact that individuals are ceasing to obtain condoms from any other source, and relying on a project to provide for their total needs. Or the increase might be explained by an increasing uptake of condoms by those who travel in from other districts and who use sexual health services in other districts. Interventions targeted at gay men carried out by individual London health authorities which are measured locally are a good example of this problem (Kelley). The problem might even be that the provision of condoms contributes to greater risk behaviour, as seen in the Ugandan study above (Kabuji).

A variant of uptake measurements is the assessment of returns of injecting equipment to syringe exchange projects.

Reference
Kelley P et al. *How far will you go? A survey of London gay men's migration and mobility,* Gay Men Fighting AIDS, 1997.

Changes in addiction and treatment patternsThere is substantial evidence that addiction to heroin and drug treatment are strong predictors of HIV risk and risk reduction respectively (Rhodes). Measurements of changes in the time that elapses between the onset of addiction and the first demand for treatment, and of changes in drop out rates from treatment programmes are likely to be important indicators of prevention efforts with injecting drug users. However, it is important to be aware that certain types of treatment programme are in themselves likely to be more successful. Programmes which permit long-term maintenance rather than graduated reduction in dosage were most likely to be successful.

Reference
Rhodes T. *Risk, behaviour and change,* Health Education Authority, 1994.

Changes in self-reported behaviour amongst a cohort or sample

Much of the evidence regarding the effectiveness of HIV prevention measures comes from studies of prospective cohorts. These groups of people are recruited at the beginning of an intervention and followed through the study period to assess changes in behaviour. Such studies are reliant on the self-reported sexual or drug-using behaviour of participants, and also carry the risk that participants will be lost to follow-up, thus biasing the results towards the more co-operative or compliant participants.

However, a range of techniques have been developed by behavioural researchers to reduce these potential biases.

For example, Project Sigma, a UK investigation of gay men's sexual behaviour, used two methods to elicit information about reported sexual behaviour. One was the standard questionnaire method; the other was the process of keeping a sexual diary over the period of a month. Significant discrepancies in self-reporting were noted when the two accounts were compared by researchers (Coxon).

An example of a study in which changes in self-reported behaviour were the measured outcome is the investigation of community diffusion amongst gay men in three small US towns by Kelly et al. This study, described in more detail in *Community mobilisation,* used measures such as frequency of condom use and instances of anal intercourse.

References
Coxon T. *Between the sheets: gay men's sexual diaries,* Cassell, 1995.

Changes in reports of sexually transmitted infections

Gonorrhoea incidence has been used as a surrogate marker for unprotected sex by a wide range of researchers. Gonorrhoea incidence is a very responsive marker of changes in sexual behaviour because of the short incubation period of the infection. Active gonorrhoea is also implicated as one of the factors which increases the risk of HIV transmission, so it is reasonable to assume that a fall in gonorrhoea incidence will influence HIV incidence too. A 1994 study in Tanzania demonstrated a strong association between reduced gonorrhoea incidence and reduced HIV incidence by dividing a district into two and pursuing an aggressive screening and treatment programme for STIs in one area, whilst continuing standard HIV prevention activities in the other (Grosskurth).

Between 1993 and 1995 the US state of Louisiana distributed 21 million free condoms in communities defined as high risk (those with highest HIV prevalence and gonorrhoea incidence). Gonorrhoea reports declined 22% statewide during the programme, and researchers noted a strong association between the highest density of free condom outlets, numbers of condoms distributed and greatest decline in gonorrhoea reports when they assessed trends on a district by district basis (Cohen).

This programme was accompanied by a cohort study (n = 620) which compared changes in self-reported condom use between intervention and non-intervention districts. Condom use rose by 14% in intervention districts and 7% in non-intervention districts. The study was not designed to test either the validity of self-reports (for example by cross-checking with partners), or to distinguish between levels of condom use amongst those with many sexual partners and those with few sexual partners.

Nevertheless, at a population level this study offers proof of the concept that social marketing/free distribution of condoms has a significant impact on sexual health which may contribute to HIV prevention.

However, in recent years studies have started to notice a 'disconnection' between HIV incidence rates and the rates of STIs in gonorrhoea. Increases in STIs, especially syphilis, in gay men, has not led to a concomitant increase in HIV infections. This has shaken the assumption that increases in STI rates can be used as surrogate markers or predictors of increases in HIV. In the US, or instance, huge increases in syphilis in gay men have not coincided with equally big increases in HIV. Serosorting may be one reason why an increase in STIs in gay men, especially syphilis, has not led to a concomitant increase in HIV infections.

Conversely, in certain African countries like Zimbabwe, STI rates have gone down while HIV incidence has not, because more HIV infections are now occurring within marriages and fewer within casual encounters. For more on this see *Disclosure, serosorting and negotiated safety*.

References

Cohen D et al. *Operation Protect: a statewide condom social marketing program*, Eleventh International Conference on AIDS, abstract ThC4379, 1996.

Grosskurth P et al. *Impact of improved treatment of sexually transmitted diseases on HIV infection in rural Tanzania: randomised controlled trial*, Lancet: 530-536, 1995.

Changes in HIV incidence or prevalence in the population

HIV prevention workers and researchers have often pointed to changes in HIV incidence or prevalence as evidence that HIV prevention efforts are succeeding or failing.

However, one should be very cautious when drawing on such data.

For example, it is extremely difficult to tease apart the range of factors which may be responsible for changes in **incidence** over time. The most controversial example is the question of whether changes in HIV incidence amongst gay men during the 1980s were a consequence of changes in behaviour or an inevitable feature of the normal pattern of an epidemic.

Whilst it is clear from international data that early safer sex education coincided with rapid falls in sexually transmitted infections, and that HIV incidence peaked in gay communities in 1983/84, it has been argued that the subsequent decline in HIV incidence may be attributable to a declining number of men in the primary phase of infection capable of transmitting HIV easily to their partners.

According to this model, a slight reduction in the transmission rate at a relatively early stage in the epidemic would have a disproportionate effect on the multiplication rate of the epidemic. For example, if the average number of partners per month amongst a group with 10% HIV incidence per annum fell by 50% (from eight per month to four per month), the chance of encountering an individual recently infected with HIV would fall by a correspondingly greater multiple.

Thus relatively minor and short-term interventions - such as closing bathhouses - may have had a much greater long-term effect than the widespread adoption of safer sex, providing that they occurred relatively early in the course of the epidemic.

This model also depends on the assumption that infectivity is very high during primary infection (assumed to last for three to fpur months after exposure), and much lower thereafter. One of the justifications for universal testing has been that it will catch a higher proportion of people in primary infection, when they are much more infectious. Estimates of the proportion of HIV

infections attributable to someone in primary infection have been as high as 50-60%.

Recent mathematical studies by Professor Roy Anderson's team at Imperial College (Fraser) have suggested that people in primary infection are indeed very infectious - but that in most situations the majority of infections are transmitted by people with chronic, asymptomatic infection, because the time during which people are in this state is in the order of 30-40 times longer, even in the absence of antiretroviral treatment.

An analysis of infections in the Rakai cohort in Uganda showed that people in primary infection were on average 28 times more infectious than people in chronic symptomatic infection. But because the period of chronic infection was so much longer, it actually contributed a much higher proportion of infections.

Fraser's models indicated that transmission during primary infection accounted for no more than 12% of infections; that transmission on chronic infection accounted for 71%; and that transmission from people with symptomatic AIDS, when viral loads were generally higher, accounted for the other 17%.

The kind of intervention needed therefore depends on the stage of epidemic a particular community has reached. Behaviour skills training may work better in mature epidemics where the majority of people are in chronic infection: but much more interventionist measures such as early HIV testing including RNA testing may be needed in situations where there is a rapidly proliferating chain of HIV infection happening among a community.

Changes in **prevalence** amongst some segments of the population may indicate that HIV prevention efforts are succeeding in a broad sense, or may give indications of increasing transmission rates. However, it takes a leap of faith to correlate such changes with prevention programmes unless a long time span is being used.

For example, it is reasonable to argue that a fall in HIV prevalence amongst Ugandan women attending antenatal clinics for the birth of their first child suggests that prevention efforts have reduced HIV prevalence in that country, since this group of women are likely to have become sexually active since the beginning of the AIDS epidemic (Asiimwe-Okiror). But a fall in HIV prevalence in the course of one or two years in a much smaller locality cannot be attributed to the efforts of prevention activities in that locality.

For example, a fall in HIV prevalence was noted amongst gay men attending GUM clinics in London by the unlinked anonymised HIV prevalence survey (UA) between 1990 and 1995. However, researchers noted that it would be wrong to assume that this reflected a fall in incidence amongst gay men in the capital. The fall in prevalence could be explained by a change in policy at one of the GUM clinics participating in the survey; diagnosed HIV-positive men were no longer treated in the same GUM clinic sessions as undiagnosed gay men, and would not be routinely tested for HIV as part of the UA survey.

Changes in HIV diagnoses are a similarly unreliable guide to the success of prevention efforts, although presentation for a voluntary HIV test appears to be remarkably responsive to media coverage.

References

Asiimwe-Okiror G. *Declines in HIV prevalence in Ugandan pregnant women and its relationship to HIV incidence and risk reduction*, Eleventh International Conference on AIDS, abstract MoC905, 1996.

Fraser C. *Quantifying the impact of primary infection on HIV transmission and control*. Thirteenth Conference on Retroviruses and Opportunistic Infections, Denver, USA. abstract 162, 2006.

Koopman J. *Core groups cause primary infection to dominate HIV transmission even when more than 90% of virus is excreted during later stages of infection*, Eleventh International Conference on AIDS, abstract MoC570, 1996.

Changes in incidence amongst a cohort

A crude measure of the generalised effect of prevention efforts over time is HIV incidence in a prospective cohort. Two examples of such cohorts are the Sigma gay men's cohort in the UK, and cohorts of injecting drug users recruited by researchers monitoring the success of city-wide needle exchange projects in North America. Data derived from these cohorts demonstrate the strengths and weaknesses of this measure.

The Sigma cohort reported an increase in HIV incidence amongst its sample in 1990-1991 following relatively stable incidence since the cohort began testing in 1987. However, it is important to note that the Sigma cohort was a 'decaying' cohort, with a high drop out rate. Such incidence trends become indicative rather than authoritative in cohorts over long periods of time.

Syringe exchange incidence studies have generally demonstrated a decline in incidence. However, a study in Montreal, Canada, demonstrated a greater risk of seroconversion amongst syringe exchange users than non-users during a mean follow-up period of 15 months (33% versus13%) (Bruneau).

However, another study of all needle exchanges in the Canadian city of Vancouver showed that needle exchanges tended to attract those injecting drug users already identified by other studies as those at highest risk - unstable, high frequency injectors with multiple risks including sex work, unprotected sex with other IDUs, polydrug use and high frequency of sharing with strangers. Injecting drug users who used syringe exchanges less frequently (less than once a week) were less likely to share these characteristics (Archibald). These two studies of syringe exchange illustrate the danger of jumping to unwarranted conclusions solely on the basis of incidence data.

References

Archibald C et al. Needle exchange program attracts high risk injection drug users, Eleventh International Conference on AIDS, abstract TuC.320, 1996.

Bruneau J et al. Increased HIV seroprevalence and seroincidence associated with participation in needle exchange program, Eleventh International Conference on AIDS, abstract TuC.323, 1996.

Summary

This review of efficacy measures is intended to highlight the huge difficulties in applying simple measurements to the evaluation of HIV prevention programmes. From the examples cited above, it should be evident that the more robust measures of effectiveness are those which form part of an inter-linked sequence of measurements which test the various assumptions underlying a programme. For example, it would be desirable in assessing the success of a nationwide HIV prevention programme targeted at a gay men to include the following measurements as performance indicators:

- measures of awareness of particular interventions

- measures of understanding of messages

- process efficiency measures of numbers reached

- baseline incidence

- a large cohort to measure changes in incidence over time

- a qualitative research project which looked at the sexual behaviour of cohort seroconverters, such as self-reported reasons for unprotected sex

- proof of concept or mediator studies which tested assumptions such as: increased availability of condoms translates into increased use of condoms by people who would otherwise have engaged in unprotected anal intercourse; or, knowledge of own or partner's HIV status influences condom use.

Can randomised, controlled trials be used in HIV prevention research?

A number of the proof of concept studies identified above appear to demand controlled study. It has been argued in the past that randomised controlled studies in HIV prevention are extremely difficult, particularly if HIV incidence is the outcome measure used. However, there is no reason why studies which examine particular elements of a prevention strategy, and which use carefully chosen outcome measures, should not be conducted successfully.

The major difficulty in using such studies as 'proof of concept' investigations lies not so much in the element of randomisation or the selection of a valid control group, but in the resources needed to mount such studies. Relatively large studies will be needed to draw valid conclusions, and national research networks do not yet exist in the genitourinary setting to mirror those developed by the Medical Research Council for its anti-retroviral studies. Such a network could be developed alongside efforts to establish a national gay men's vaccine cohort (See *Developing prevention technologies: HIV & AIDS vaccines*).

Further reading

Outcome measures are also discussed in:

- *Risk, intervention and change*, by Tim Rhodes, HEA, 1994.

- *Outcomes in HIV prevention* by Chris Bonell, HIV Project, 1996 and *Using outcomes in HIV prevention: a how-to guide* by Chris Bonell and Paul Devlin, HIV Project, 1997.

What is known about the effectiveness of interventions?

Methodology or message: which is more important?

A fundamental confusion often arises in discussions of effectiveness regarding the relative importance of methodologies and messages. Two points need to be made at the outset of this effectiveness review:

- Most controlled research into the effectiveness of methods has concentrated on methodology. Implicit within this has been the assumption that there is a 'core curriculum' of HIV information and skills which need to be taught. There is no discussion in the literature of the detailed content of programmes, so we have no way of comparing whether some programmes proven to be effective actually say contradictory things

- All controlled research which demonstrates effectiveness has relied on the adaptation of the 'core curriculum' of skills and information to the culture and needs of the target group. Nevertheless, similar outcomes have been seen in all controlled studies - the intervention, whatever it is, has a greater impact than doing nothing.

Further investigation of the methodology versus message question is needed in HIV prevention research before it is possible to argue either that 'doing something is better than doing nothing', or that 'doing nothing may sometimes be a better use of resources than doing something'. For example, investigation of the relative impact of campaigns which promote undifferentiated safer sex messages to negative and positive men versus campaigns which promote negotiated safety would be a useful way of testing this question.

Research on the effectiveness of interventions for specific communities

A lack of research on interventions for African communities

This review largely covers interventions with gay men, students and injecting drug users because little or no research has been conducted in the UK on interventions targeted at African communities.

A detailed preliminary evaluation of a number of UK projects targeted at African communities (Maharaj) had been published by the Health and Education Research Unit of the University of London Institute of Education in 1996.

However by 2005, when the Medical Research Council published its own review (Prost) of research among black African communities affected by HIV in the UK and Europe, it could still find no randomised controlled trials on HIV prevention interventions among Africans, though there have been significant surveys of treatment and social needs (Project NASAH), sexual attitudes and lifestyles (the Padare Project) and HIV prevalence and testing (the Mayisha Projects).

The review included 129 studies, of any kind, of which 29 were published in peer-reviewed journals.

Twenty-four of these were descriptive quantitative studies, and five were qualitative studies. A total of 100 'grey literature' publications (mainly reports and online publications) encompassing quantitative and qualitative data were also included.

There were no studies in peer-reviewed journals describing HIV prevention interventions with people of sub-Saharan African origin. However, information on existing interventions was available through 'grey literature', and details of 31 interventions were thus obtained, 22 in the UK and nine in other European countries.

Only one of these actually attempted to measure its own efficacy in terms of public health indicators. This consisted of two King's Fund-financed seminars for 40 people, with four follow-up workshops, offering information and advice on HIV and sexual health to Swahili-speaking young people in Islington. It measured, and found, a significant reduction in the number of unwanted sexual health outcomes (unwanted pregnancies and STIs) among seminar attendees. This is the only prevention study among UK (or European) Africans that had as an outcome measure anything other than a measurement of the busy-ness of the project itself such as leaflets distributed, phone calls made, or clients contacted.

References

Maharaj, K et al. An assessment of HIV prevention interventions with refugees and asylum seekers. Health and Education Research Unit of the University of London Institute of Education, 1996.

Prost, A. A Review of Research among Black African Communities Affected by HIV in the UK and Europe. Medical Research Council, 2005.

Research on interventions for injecting drug users

This section does not attempt to duplicate an excellent and lengthy summary which has already been published by the Health Education Authority, and a book by the same authors:

- Tim Rhodes. *Risk, Intervention and Change: HIV prevention and drug use*. HEA, 80 pages. 1994. ISBN 0-752-10121-8.
- Richard Hartnoll and Tim Rhodes. *AIDS, Drugs and Prevention*. Routledge, 260 pages, 1996. ISBN 0-415-10204-9

Research on interventions with gay and bisexual men

Excellent summaries of psychosocial factors involved in HIV risk reduction and the success of interventions can be found in:

- Ralph DiClemente and John Peterson. *Preventing AIDS: Theories and methods of behavioural interventions*, edited by, Springer, New York, 1994. See especially Chapter Fourteen. ISBN 0-306-44606-5
- Jeffrey A Kelly. *Changing HIV Risk Behavior: Practical Strategies.* The Guilford Press, New York, 195 pages, 1995. ISBN 1-572-30009-4.

What is known about the effectiveness of specific approaches

Mass media campaigns

The success of mass media campaigns in increasing awareness of HIV and risk behaviours has been well reported elsewhere, and research suggests that the content of mass media messages is a crucial determinant of the success of advertising and media campaigns. The UK 'Iceberg and Tombstone' campaign of the 1980s is widely credited with raising public awareness of AIDS at an early enough stage to keep the UK a low-prevalence country relative to the USA and some other European countries - much as its content was criticised at the time. The African 'ABC' campaign that has covered much of an entire continent in roadside posters is also seen as an essential component of prevention activities in the region.

In Switzerland (Lehmann) a booklet about AIDS was mailed to every Swiss household in March 1986. Of the population aged 20-69, to whom the book was sent, 56% read the booklet. For those who read the booklet compared with those who did not the results showed an improvement in knowledge and a better understanding of the risks of specific behaviours and of exposed groups and thus less fear of becoming infected through daily activities. The Swiss campaign was the subject of a number of qualitative and qualitative studies which are still ongoing (Dubois-Arber).

However subsequent, smaller campaigns have not been evaluated properly in terms of actual behavioural change, and most research into mass media campaigns dates from the early days of the epidemic, or at least the pre-HAART era. There has been very little rigorous evaluation of mass media campaigns in the last ten years. Dolores Albarracin reports that only 3% of the 354 HIV interventions she reviewed were evaluations of the efficacy of mass media campaigns.

The difficulty with mass-market interventions such as posters, leaflets, websites and social-marketing campaigns is partly due to the problem of finding a satisfactory control group who have not seen the intervention. As a result, a lot of 'research' into the effectiveness of mass media campaigns stops short of obtaining efficacy evidence and only conducts focus-group-style research into the degree of penetration and recognition of campaigns and qualitative data on whether consumers thought they were effective.

However, it's important to emphasise that absence of evidence as to the effectiveness of mass-market campaigns does not mean evidence of absence.

References

Dubois-Arber F et al. *Long term global evaluation of a national AIDS prevention strategy: the case of Switzerland.* AIDS 13(18): 2571-2582, 1999.

Lehmann P et al. *Campaign against AIDS in Switzerland: evaluation of a nationwide educational programme.* BMJ 295: 1118-1120, 1987.

Moatti JP et al. *Impact on the general public of media campaigns against AIDS: a French evaluation,* Health Policy 21: 233-247, 1992.

Small media

Small media refers to interventions such as leaflets, posters and advertising in small circulation or community publications.

The primary evaluative tools which have been used to assess the impact of these interventions have been investigations of numbers who have seen the leaflet or advert, its comprehensibility and its relevance to the target audience. Small media interventions may be measured for other impacts if they are part of a specific campaign with a defined set of aims and objectives. An example of this might be a leaflet or advertising campaign which seeks to introduce messages about 'negotiated safety' or assumptions about HIV status. It would be possible to measure the impact compared with baseline in awareness of the ideas communicated in the leaflets or adverts, but would it be possible to correlate this awareness with changes in behaviour? Is this a reasonable expectation?

If an intervention's aims and objectives are correlated with a particular set of assumptions about how behaviour changes in response to informational cues (see *Models of behaviour change* above), some researchers argue that it is reasonable to assume that changes in behaviour have occurred in response to informational interventions. However, research needs to be designed in such a way as to prove that it was exposure to the leaflet or poster which was an essential component of the intervention, rather than other factors such as participation in the study which influenced behaviour.

An Australian study has shown that small media in the form of posters have little or no impact on behaviour amongst those already exposed to a message by other means. Men who had reported unprotected sex were randomised either to a cognitive behavioural intervention, to receive copies once a month of posters judged by the researchers to be good examples of gay men's safer sex promotion, or to a control group which received no intervention.

Participants were asked to record their reactions to the material, and also their sexual behaviour during the follow-up period. Those randomised to the poster group reported that they found the posters attractive and that the posters put across the safer sex message effectively, yet reported little or no change in levels of unprotected sex during the follow-up period in comparison with the no-intervention control group. In contrast, the cognitive intervention group reported a much lower rate of unprotected sex (Gold).

Such findings are problematic because of the resources allocated to the development of small media interventions. They are seen as the core of AIDS education because they are low-budget and because they can slot into many other programmes of work, such as outreach or peer education.

An effective small media intervention is likely to have the following characteristics:

- Cultural sensitivity to the idioms and styles of the target audience

- Visual impact, attractiveness

- Tailored to the educational level of the target audience

- The target audience has repeated exposures to the intervention.

Given these characteristics, it is amazing how many small media interventions in the HIV prevention field ignore fundamental

rules of marketing and advertising, and how rarely professionals in the fields of copywriting and marketing are employed to develop such materials. This is not a consequence of budgetary restrictions, by and large, but of a failure to appreciate that health communications are no different from other forms of marketing or PR. This is not an argument for turning HIV prevention over to advertising agencies, but for allowing the finished product to be created by communications professionals rather than a committee.

References

Gold R: *AIDS education: has it gone wrong?* National AIDS Bulletin, March 1996.

Counselling and HIV antibody testing

Evidence of the effectiveness of HIV antibody testing and counselling in altering behaviour is contradictory. A major review published in 1991 concluded that no reliable, controlled data existed to confirm the value of HIV testing as a prevention measure.

This was the case, at least, where the result of the test was a negative one. HIV testing *has* been found to have a significant impact on the risk behaviour of people who test positive - see **positive prevention** below.

Only amongst heterosexual couples was there any clear evidence that counselling and testing had any impact on the practice of safer sex. Amongst injecting drug users in contact with methadone maintenance programmes, HIV testing and counselling were associated with reductions in needle sharing, but there were no differences between those who tested positive or negative, suggesting that knowledge of HIV status was not the critical factor in encouraging safer behaviour (Higgins).

Amongst gay men there is no strong evidence that knowledge of HIV status in itself predisposes to safer sexual behaviour, although this has been inferred from a number of studies (Kippax).

All studies which have reported on the effects of testing and counselling have been uncontrolled, and it has been suggested that the self-selecting nature of such studies may bias the results, because those who come forward for testing may be more motivated to change their behaviour. However, testing may speed the process of behaviour change in the view of some commentators, and may act as a reinforcer of intentions regarding behaviour change, particularly if the practice of HIV testing receives social or peer support (Cohen).

It is important to tease apart the impact of the knowledge of serostatus from the impact of any pre- or post-test counselling.

In the latter case, even if testing was proven to have a significant impact on subsequent behaviour, it is still questionable whether a successful counselling intervention that reinforced the general impact of serostatus could be replicated by others. This is due to the subjective nature of the counselling encounter, which relies on the skills of the counsellor, the information content of the counselling session and the number of 'doses'.

Sigma Research has shown wide variation in the content of counselling sessions and in their impact on individuals in the South-East of England, and there may be variations even within a counselling team. Recent research at the Chelsea and Westminster GUM clinic in London showed that significant divergences existed amongst both counsellors and clinicians regarding definitions of high, low and medium risk sex acts.

There is no guarantee that counselling interventions, even if they are standardised, will be received in similar ways by all clients. Critics of the Health Beliefs and Reasoned Action models of behaviour change have pointed out that social and peer pressures may act against 'rational' assessment of information provided by counsellors, and that using HIV testing as a means of changing people's behaviour presupposes that people will act on the risk reduction information they are given (Beardsell).

References

Beardsell S et al. *Should wider HIV testing be encouraged on the grounds of HIV prevention?* AIDS Care 6:1,1994

Cohen M. *Changing to safer sex: personality, logic and habit*, in Aggleton P et al Eds: AIDS: Responses, interventions and care Falmer Press, London, 1991.

Higgins DL et al. *Evidence for the effects of HIV antibody testing and counselling on risk behaviours*, JAMA 226: 2419-2429, 1991.

Peer education

Peer education has been one of the most important methods by which information about HIV and behaviour change has been transmitted. Peer education models have been especially common amongst students, ethnic minorities and gay men. However, it is difficult to separate peer education from other components of HIV prevention activity in research reports. See *Community mobilisation* and *Group cognitive interventions* below for further discussion of the role of peer education.

Workshops

There is little or no evaluation of workshops as an intervention despite the increasing frequency with which they are offered. It is also difficult to define whether workshops constitute a group cognitive intervention (attempting to reframe people's thinking about their sexual behaviour), a behavioural intervention (attempting to offer techniques for avoiding situations, negotiating condom use etc.) or whether they are a purely informational intervention. Most workshop programmes appear to offer a combination of these approaches, and any evaluation needs to make clear the balance of aims and objectives, and to define outcomes suitable for measuring each of these objectives.

An informal insight in the role of workshops within community mobilisation was offered by Tom Coates, a researcher on the US-based Men's Network research project, at the Berlin AIDS conference in 1993. Coates observed that whilst exposure to safer sex messages through events such as parties and discos was associated with a reduction in unprotected sex, workshops organised by the group tended only to attract those who had a high commitment to safer sex at baseline. In other words, they may be a technique for maintaining safer behaviour, but may be a less attractive change agent for those who are having risky unprotected sex (Coates). However, it is also worth considering ways in which workshops have been marketed to the target audience when their success is being evaluated. Are the organisers using methods likely to recruit people who are most likely to demonstrate post-intervention changes in behaviour, or are they preaching to the converted? Evaluation of any workshop programme should include pre-testing of the recruitment materials to ensure that they will attract people at higher risk of HIV infection or of having unprotected sex.

References

Coates T et al. *Prevention in developed countries*, abstract RT-08, Ninth International Conference on AIDS, 1993.

Outreach work

Outreach work has developed in a number of settings thought to expose individuals to high risk of HIV infection. These include public sex environments (PSEs), commercial sex premises (saunas, massage parlours) and gay clubs. Outreach work has also occurred on the streets amongst injecting drug users, homeless youth and commercial sex workers.

The attraction of outreach work is that it can bring individuals into contact with services and messages they might not have received otherwise (e.g. 'Bleach and teach' in San Francisco, see *Social diffusion* below). It also reaches people at earlier stages in their drug using careers, although there is no clear evidence that it is a superior method for reaching men who are just becoming homosexually active.

Outreach work is highly labour intensive when professionalised, and difficult to regulate when performed by volunteers. There is a considerable literature on outreach projects with injecting drug users (e.g. Rhodes 1991), which have been evaluated more thoroughly than work in cottages and cruising areas (PSEs). Rhodes et al found that existing outreach methods among injecting drug users had a number of limitations:

- They only reached those who were relatively easy to reach drug users.

- Outreach tends to target individuals rather than the social networks in which they use drugs or have sex, despite the fact that community-wide norms influence behaviours.

- Drug users had a variety of other needs which took precedence over receiving advice about HIV risk. They wanted housing, money and treatment.

Nevertheless, Rhodes concluded that outreach had an important role to play in HIV prevention work with injecting drug users, a view endorsed by the Department of Health and NHS Executive in its 1997 guidance on purchasing effective treatment and care for drug misusers. However, the guidance also recommended that providers should collect data including statistics on 'the effect of contact', without a clear discussion of how purchasers might judge when the aims and objectives of an outreach project were either realistic or being met effectively in terms of behaviour change. Specific outcome measures for assessing behaviour change and project efficacy amongst IDUs are discussed in *Risk behaviour: injecting drug users* below.

Outreach work with gay and bisexual men in public sex environments has been one of the preferred models of intervention with this group, based on a number of assumptions:

- A significant population of hard to reach gay and bisexual men exists who can only be

- Cottages and cruising areas are a significant locus of unsafe sexual activity.

Evidence from research in the UK tends to contradict both these assumptions. Many cruising areas are heavily used by gay men who also frequent the commercial gay scene, as the Sigma Research Pride surveys have demonstrated. Weatherburn has also shown that men who do not use the commercial gay scene with a high degree of frequency and who may not identify as gay, nevertheless have a high level of knowledge about HIV. Other researchers have shown that unprotected sex is less likely to occur in cottages than at home.

However, research by GMFA on the sexual behaviour and condom use of men using London's largest cruising area, Hampstead Heath, indicates that:

- A large proportion of men who use that location to meet sex partners will have anal sex with those partners, either on the Heath or later, at home.

- Condoms distributed by GMFA were used on the Heath.

- A large proportion of men did not bring condoms to the Heath.

- A large proportion of those who did bring condoms did not bring lubricant, or brought condoms which may be unsuitable for anal sex.

- The population reached on the Heath was not disproportionately different from that identified by another GMFA survey (Kelley, 1997) as regular users of the commercial gay scene.

This research suggests that outreach which concentrates on face-to-face contacts will be less cost-effective than outreach targeted at sites where a high volume of sexual contacts takes place, and where many opportunities exist to supply appropriate condoms and lubricant.

References

Kelley P, et al. *How far will you go?*, GMFA, 1997.

Rhodes T, et al. *Hard to reach or out of reach: an evaluation of an innovative model of HIV outreach education*, Tufnell Press, London, 1991.

Rhodes T, et al. *Out of the agency and onto the streets: a review of HIV outreach health education in Europe and the United States* , ISDD, 1991.

Rhodes T *Outreach work with drug users: principles and practice*, Council of Europe, 1996.

Weatherburn P, et al. *No aggregate change in homosexual HIV risk behaviour change among gay men attending the Gay Pride festivals, 1993-1996*, AIDS 10: 771-774, 1996.

Weatherburn P, et al: *Behaviourally bisexual men*, HEA, 1996.

Group cognitive/skills interventions

A number of group cognitive interventions have been tested in well-controlled studies. They draw from different models of behaviour change, but all involve the development of skills and cognitive frameworks to help people sustain safer behaviour. Some methods are more labour intensive than others, and some could be adapted to other media. All have been proven to work with particular populations.

The first is a twelve-session AIDS risk reduction programme targeted at gay men during the late 1980s in the US state of Mississippi. The programme recruited 104 men at high risk for HIV infection and randomised them into two groups: immediate intervention versus a four-month delay. The delay group served as a short term control group.

Baseline data showed that participants in both groups used condoms in approximately 23% of all instances of anal intercourse. However, the study report does not differentiate between anal intercourse with regular partners and casual partners.

Programme participants were then exposed to a series of workshops on safer sex, assertiveness training, how to deal with risky sexual situations, how to avoid sex when intoxicated, how to raise the topic of safer sex and how to deal with safer sex within relationships.

Four months after the intervention participants had used condoms in 66% of all instances of anal intercourse, whilst members of the control group had used condoms in just 19% of all instances of anal intercourse. This rate of condom use was sustained during over two years of follow-up, and 60% of subjects completely refrained from unprotected anal intercourse during the follow-up period (Kelly).

Despite the short period of controlled study, it is reasonable to argue that this intervention had a significant effect on behaviour, but it raises the question of whether or not the success of the intervention was dose-related i.e. would a similar effect have been seen with six or even one workshop instead of twelve?

A US study shows that such methods can be translated to other population groups. A study of 197 African-American and Hispanic women with sexual histories suggesting HIV risk were invited to participate in a programme based at a Milwaukee primary healthcare clinic. They were randomised to two groups. One received a five session HIV risk reduction programme led by female group leaders. Women in the control group attended five sessions on unrelated health topics.

The HIV risk reduction programme included skills training in condom use, sexual assertiveness, examination of the circumstances which triggered risky behaviour for individuals and peer support for efforts to change behaviour. All skills training was developed with the assistance of a focus group to ensure that it was culturally appropriate.

Three months after the conclusion of the programme women in the intervention group reported condom use in 56% of sexual encounters involving vaginal intercourse. This was up from baseline of 26%. The number who used condoms at any time during the preceding three months rose from 43% to 66%. Participants also reported using condoms with a larger proportion of their male partners than at baseline. In contrast no changes in any of these variables were reported in the control group. Moreover, the women in the intervention group tended to have a more complete understanding of HIV risks, to have a more accurate personal estimation of their risk, and to view themselves as more personally vulnerable to HIV infection (Kelly 1992).

The study evaluation also looked at the quality of the skills developed by women to see whether the skills training component might have contributed to behaviour change. After three months women who had received skills training were rated by blinded evaluators as significantly more effective in resisting pressure to have sex without a condom, and in persuading a partner to postpone sex until a condom could be obtained.

Another US study piloted an intervention aimed at pregnant women that used a novel measure of efficacy: the use of credit cards which could be redeemed at local pharmacies to obtain condoms or spermicide. The programme enrolled 206 young single pregnant women in Akron and randomised them to one of three groups: HIV prevention, general health promotion and no intervention.

Women in the HIV prevention group were exposed to four small group sessions of one to two hours, which began after the fourteenth week of pregnancy. The group sessions focussed on the development of a sound 'health action' plan. To enhance cross-group consistency, sessions were built around the use of culturally relevant health videos. The thematic content of the health promotion and HIV prevention was linked, but specific content differed. For example, if participants were invited to focus on activities which might have a negative impact on the foetus, the health promotion group would be directed to discuss the impact of smoking and drinking, whilst the HIV groups would look at mother-to-baby transmission of HIV. Skills development included negotiation and assertiveness skills, role playing, problem solving and aversive conditioning (imagining adverse consequences of behaviour).

All study participants were also given credit cards that could be used only at local pharmacies to obtain either condoms or spermicide. The uptake of condoms and spermicide was used to measure the impact of the workshops. Interestingly there was no significant difference in the uptake of condoms or spermicide between the HIV prevention and health promotion groups, but there was a difference in behaviour: women in the HIV prevention group were more likely to use condoms or spermicide with their partners, and had a stronger intention to do so, after three and six months of follow-up. However, the benefits obtained from the HIV prevention intervention were only moderately greater than those obtained from the health promotion group (Hobfoll). Both groups did better on all scores (HIV-related knowledge, safer sex intentions and behaviours, discussion of HIV risk with partners and condom usage) than the no-intervention control group.

This study seems to suggest that free condom availability needs to be supported by educational activity and skills training if it is to be translated into safer behaviour.

A number of other US programmes have also provided controlled evidence of the effectiveness of multiple session workshop programmes focussing on the development of knowledge and skills. These include a study of HIV prevention workshops with homeless youth in hostel accommodation (Rotheram-Borus), which demonstrated that the level of change was proportional to the 'dose', with the greatest reductions in unprotected sex amongst those who attended 15 or more sessions during a period of three weeks' residence in a hostel (sessions lasted less than an hour).

Several studies discussed above (see *Social learning* in *Understanding behaviour change* above) also provide evidence of the success and replicability of the skills-based workshop approach (Jemmott). On the other hand, several randomised, controlled studies of group skills interventions show no advantage to participation in such programmes.

A programme for 102 Los Angeles youths with an average age of 12 showed no significant change in 19 of 21 attitudes and opinions about sexual behaviour and condom use. Researchers speculated that the intervention was too short (eight one hour sessions) and that the use of teenage mothers who achieved a good rapport with students may not have discouraged students from early sexual intercourse, but instead glamorised teen pregnancy (Kirby).

Another skills-based intervention which included the use of a comic book, videotape and a group skills curriculum showed no difference in levels of condom use between the intervention group and control group at six months (Gillmore), but researchers suggested that the null result may be attributable to the fact that the people in the sample group were recruited from juvenile detention centres, and may have had no opportunity to practice the skills learnt during the workshops!

The research literature leaves unanswered the question of how many workshops might be adequate in order to sustain behaviour change. Unfortunately, no evaluation exists of the workshop programme developed by Gay Men Fighting AIDS in the UK, which contains many of the elements described above. The Sex Day format has been delivered to several thousand men in the UK since its inception in 1992, but no research evidence has been collected on the behavioural effects of this one-session intervention. It has been argued that a controlled trial of such an intervention would be impossible because it would be difficult to distinguish the effects of the intervention from those of other HIV prevention activities. However, as the studies above show, this problem does not seem to have arisen for researchers looking at other high-risk populations.

References

Gillmore MR, et al. *Effects of a skills-based intervention to encourage condom use among high risk heterosexually active adolescents*, AIDS Education and Prevention 9, Supp A, 1997.

Hobfoll SE, et al. *Reducing inner city women's risk activities: a study of single, pregnant women,* Health Psychology 13(5): 397-403, 1994.

Kelly J, et a. *Behavioural interventions to reduce AIDS risk activities,* Journal of Consulting and Clinical Psychology 57(1): 60-67, 1989.

Kelly J, et al: *HIV/AIDS prevention groups for high risk inner city women: intervention outcomes and effects on risk behaviour,* paper to American Public Health Association, Nov 1992.

Kirby D, et al: *An impact evaluation of Project SNAPP: an AIDS and pregnancy prevention middle school programme,* AIDS Education and Prevention 9, SuppA, 1997.

Individual cognitive interventions

The cognitive interventions discussed above all rely on group formats for their delivery. This makes them labour intensive and unsuitable for large population interventions. However, a number of research teams have reported individual cognitive interventions which have proved effective.

Ron Gold reported a randomised controlled study using individual diaries to encourage men to examine their intentions and self-justifications regarding unprotected anal intercourse. Gay men were randomised to three groups and asked to keep a sexual diary for 16 weeks and send in completed pages each week. After four weeks men were randomised to one of three groups: a control group who received no intervention, a group who received safer sex posters with the request to evaluate

their impact and effectiveness, and a group who were asked to fill in a questionnaire.

The questionnaire group were asked to reflect upon a recent occasion when they had engaged in unprotected anal intercourse, and were given a list of possible self-justifications for having unsafe sex. They were asked to indicate the extent to which each of these self-justifications had been on their mind at the moment they had decided to engage in unprotected anal intercourse. They were then asked to select the self-justifications that had been in their mind most strongly at the time; to indicate how reasonable each of these seemed to them now, looking back on it, an to briefly justify these responses. The men were thus asked to reflect on their thinking in the heat of the moment, and to justify it in the cold light of day.

A significant difference in sexual behaviour emerged by the end of the study period. Whilst there was no significant difference between the three groups in the numbers who had unprotected anal intercourse at least once, there was a significant difference between the self-justifications group and the others in terms of the amount of unprotected anal intercourse that took place during the 16- week study. A total of 42% of the control group and 41% of the poster group had unprotected anal intercourse more than once, whereas only 17% of the self-justifications group had anal intercourse more than once.

Gold argues that the technique may exhibit a greater effect when individuals have unprotected sex after engaging in an examination of why they had unprotected sex. He comments: "Presumably their first post-intervention slip-up provoked and disturbed the men; their perception that they had done it again concentrated their mind on the problem. At that point they really began to absorb the lessons of the intervention."

References

Gold R, et al. *AIDS education: has it gone wrong?* National AIDS Bulletin March, 1995.

Community mobilisation

Community mobilisation is a term akin to community development, but it is used here to distinguish it from community development methods used in other health areas because it has a specific history in the HIV field.

Community mobilisation has been studied in several well-controlled trials in the United States. The most famous example is the Kelly study of opinion leaders, a randomised, controlled trial conducted amongst gay men in paired towns in four US states. The study tested the argument of social diffusion theorists, that if 15-20% of a population adopts an innovation, then it will be conveyed through natural social networking to cause community wide change. Many historians of safer sex have argued that this is how safer sex came to be adopted by gay men during the mid-1980s.

The study utilised `opinion leaders' who were identified as the people most likely to influence their peers. Opinion leaders were identified by asking bartenders to nominate people they considered to be most liked and trusted by patrons. The opinion leaders selected were then invited to attend group sessions at which they were trained in ways of delivering HIV risk reduction messages to their peers. These methods included endorsing the benefits and timeliness of risk behaviour change, recommending strategies for implementing change and correcting risk misperceptions amongst their friends. The men were then invited to initiate twenty conversations amongst their friends over the following weeks.

The study was carried out in four states, with two cities in each state compared, one serving as a control and one as an intervention site. Three months and again six months later, surveys of all men entering bars in the intervention cities and control cities were carried out. The response rate was 85%, and unprotected anal intercourse in the intervention cities declined from 33% at baseline to under 25% at nine months, a reduction of 28%. No change was found in the control group.

The reported incidence of unprotected insertive anal sex fell from 27% to 18% over the same time period in the intervention cities, but the incidence of unprotected receptive anal sex fell more slowly. There was no change in the control cities.

When researchers analysed the results to determine the factors accounting for the changes in behaviour they had observed, they found that men who spent the most time in bars had the highest levels of risk behaviour at baseline. But they also showed the greatest reduction in such behaviour following intervention. Since most peer conversations probably took place in bars, the researchers hypothesised that there was a dose response effect. This was corroborated by men's own reports: those who reported being engaged in the greatest number of risk reduction conversations also reported the greatest reduction in risk behaviour.

Another US project, similar to Gay Men Fighting AIDS and a number of other UK projects in its design, was the Mpowerment project. This was tested by US National Institutes of Mental Health researchers in two West Coast cities, Santa Barbara, California, and Eugene, Oregon, in 1992.

Eugene received the intervention first whilst Santa Barbara served as control, and longitudinal cohorts of gay men aged 18 to 29 were recruited and assessed before and after by mail-back survey.

The project tested the hypothesis that involvement with the process of peer education would have an effect on risk behaviour. By allowing the community to take responsibility for behaviour change efforts, it was hoped to foster a deeper and longer lasting effect than one achieved by professionals.

A core group of 15 self-selected volunteers was recruited and given a brief to design the project, with advice from local academics, public health professionals and AIDS service organisations. The project developed several arms: peer outreach conducted by volunteers in bars, community events and events organised by the group itself. This outreach work also served to recruit other peer educators in a rolling programme of recruitment.

The group also organised a storefront drop-in centre and small group sessions focussing on safer sex information and skill development. The latter were attended by 170 young men in the town (estimated to represent at least 15% of the local gay population).

One year after the intervention a 26% reduction was reported in the number of individuals who reported any instance of unprotected anal intercourse. This included a 45% reduction in respondents reporting any unprotected anal intercourse with non-primary partners and a 24% reduction in those reporting an unprotected anal intercourse with primary partners. In contrast there was no change in these variables in the control city (Kegeles).

A study amongst injecting drugs users provides evidence that such methods need not be confined to gay men. The US National Institutes of Drug Abuse has studied the use of peer educators amongst injecting drug users, and concluded that a project employing volunteer drug users as peer educators and community development facilitators not only reduced the sharing of injecting equipment, but led to fall in HIV incidence in Chicago (Wiebel). However, this is the only controlled study amongst IDUs.

A problem with all of these examples of community mobilisation is the difficulty we have in judging the relationship contexts in which unprotected sex was taking place in these studies. Whilst the Mpowerment study did ask questions about unprotected sex with regular partners, the Kelly studies did not, and critics of the community mobilisation approach have argued that such interventions are only likely to have an effect on those having unprotected sex with casual partners. Those in regular partnerships may see themselves as immune from such messages and may need to be targeted specifically. However, these criticisms ignore the fact that all studies of community mobilisation have been studies of a methodology, not a message.

In order to prove that community mobilisation is an inappropriate way to target men in relationships, it is necessary to design a study which looks at the diffusion of messages about unprotected sex in relationships. This has not yet happened.

Clearly these studies do not answer all the questions which might arise about the distribution of resources in a community mobilisation type project, but they do suggest that the level of contacts achieved need not be analogous to the total population of a district. However, the Kelly studies suggest that dosage and exposure were important elements in the success of the project.

Both studies support the need for knowledge of local sexual and social networks, and sensitivity to the customs and idiom of the local community. The selection of local informants is a crucial first stage in a community mobilisation project: if this goes wrong the project could veer off course.

There is also a danger that culturally-specific problems could arise in replicating community mobilisation-type efforts in other countries. Evidence of this was supplied at a recent meeting of the British Psychological Society by Graham Hart, who reported on a study being conducted by the Medical Research Council's Medical Sociology Unit in Edinburgh and Glasgow, intended to replicate some elements of the Kelly and Kegeles studies (Williamson).

Among men who reported speakingwith peer educators 49% reported thinking about their sexualbehaviour and 26% reported changing their sexual behaviour. Lead researcher Lisa Williamson said that the study "appears to be an effective interventiontool in terms of the uptake of sexual health services, but isless effective in achieving actual sexual behaviour change amonghomosexual men."

Hart reported that local informants were none too keen on the idea of encouraging popular local figures to discuss intimate details of people's sex lives, because their popularity tended to be proportional to their store of local gossip! Many people would be unwilling to discuss intimate sexual matters with such popular but indiscreet figures.

Nevertheless, such evidence does suggest that the general concept of community mobilisation has a valuable contribution to make to HIV prevention activities. However, design and evaluation of future projects should proceed with an awareness of the limitations of current evidence, and should seek to add to the body of research knowledge about community mobilisation strategies. For example, is it adequate to reach 15-20% of the population to diffuse a message, and how would you measure this? What is the best balance of activities within community mobilisation?

References

Kegeles S, et a. *The Mpowerment project: a community level HIV prevention intervention for young gay and bisexual men*, Am J Public Health, in press, 1997.

Kelly JA, et al. *HIV risk behaviour reduction following intervention with key opinion leaders of the population: an experimental analysis*, Am J Public Health 81: 168-171, 1991.

Kelly JA, et al. *Community AIDS/HIV risk reduction: the effects of endorsements by popular people in three cities*, Am J Public Health, 82: 1483-1489, 1992.

Williamson, LM. *The Gay Men's Task Force: the impact of peer education on the sexual health behaviour of homosexual men in Glasgow.*

Social marketing

Social marketing is an approach which seeks to promote an innovation of social utility by using a variety of methods, including free distribution, promotion of the innovation and subsidised sale of the innovation.

Social marketing has had two huge successes in the AIDS epidemic: condom distribution and needle exchange. Needle exchange is discussed in detail above, as is condom distribution.

No research in the UK has yet been designed which is able to evaluate the impact of condom distribution on sexual behaviour, but social marketing theory suggests that well planned free condom distribution will have a number of impacts:

- Maintains the visibility of condoms in settings where people meet sexual partners.

- Models condom use and the acceptability of carrying condoms.

- Allows individuals to initiate conversations about condom use.

- Provides appropriate condoms and lubricants.

- Makes condoms easily available at times of day when people are likely to meet sexual partners.

- Reduces the cost of condom use, and makes them available free.

- Puts condoms into the hands of people who might not otherwise buy them, and who might choose to have sex on the spur of the moment.

Social marketing of condoms should also be backed up by media promotion which highlights each of these characteristics in ways designed to appeal to the target audience. A model example is a feature article published by the gay men's weekly *Boyz*, which interviewed men in the street about carrying condoms, and whether they had ever missed out on sex as a result of failing to carry condoms. The article modelled the acceptability and desirability of carrying condoms, and of ensuring that they were not out of date or damaged. Purchasing of condom distribution should include a plan for media coverage and promotion, and purchasers should ensure that agencies are resourced to deliver such editorial coverage among the target group media as a key part of their role.

Internet interventions

With the success of gay cruising sites like Gaydar and Gay.com, the Internet has become the meeting-place of choice for many gay men, offering as it does, initial anonymity and safety and a chance to get to know prospective partners before meeting them in person.

Researchers in London (Bolding) have found that by 2003 the proportion of gay men in the city who had met partners online had increased to over 50%, and 75% of HIV-positive men had done so. See **D is for disclosure, serosorting and negotiated safety** for more on the internet and its potential role in disclosure and serosorting.

In an article in Positive Nation by this writer in the same year, Sigma Research's Ford Hickson said: "The internet has led to increases in the number of men who have sex with men, and the number of partners they have, and the proportion who have anal sex, protected and unprotected."

The internet therefore offers an ideal place in which both to survey gay men about their sexual habits, and the online survey has become such an important research tool that for 2005's Gay Men's Sex Survey, Sigma Research abandoned their long-established practice of researchers interrogating gay men about their sex lives at gay festivals and for the first time distributed the survey only in two forms, as booklets in gay venues and as an online questionnaire.

The internet also has considerable power, potentially at least, to offer prevention interventions. The question is, what should these look like? The internet is much more than a set of pages on a computer screen. It is a tool for people to conduct their own sexual health research; a 'safe space' for people to explore sexual fantasies and fears; an intimate, dialogue-based meeting place; and the biggest lonely hearts column and porn magazine ever.

In the *Positive Nation* article, Mark Watson, European Director of Gay.com, said that the internet's interactive nature was its greatest strength, but one that HIV prevention organisations had not yet fully exploited.

Gay men's encounters are in real time. The Internet is a 4D area and we have 2D prevention campaigns. Click on the Terrence Higgins Trust's gay men's prevention resources links and you'll get poster pdfs. The internet enables people to meet where they don't feel they will encounter social disapproval if they talk about sex without condoms. That discussion is not about 'deliberate infection.' It's about guys discussing condom use - and being HIV-positive - in a place where it doesn't feel unsexy to do so.

The internet offers various possibilities for prevention interventions:

- Banner ads with click-throughs to sexual health information sites and HIV and STI testing services.

  Example: InSPOT (http://www.inspot.org/), a peer STI partner-notification site whereby people diagnosed with an STI can anonymously notify people they've met online

- Social-marketing sites that aim to give positive messages about HIV prevention

  Examples: HIV Stops With Me (http://www.hivstopswithme.org/), a site, backed by a poster campaign, featuring interviews with HIV-positive people about their life stories, relationships and safer sex strategies. Tagline: "Positive People Preventing HIV"

- Moderated sexual health chatrooms

  Example: the Terrence Higgins Trust now run a 'Health Info' chatroom within the Gaydar chatrooms, only visible to people whose Gaydar profile locates them in England and Wales: HIV Scotland run a 'Scottish Netreach' site for people there.

- HIV and sexual health information sites for people with specific needs such as drug users, ethnic minorities, youth, etc.

  Example: http://www.tweaker.org/, an information and resource site, also offering a discussion board, for gay men who use methamphetamine (crystal meth)

- Moderated or unmoderated internet discussion boards on sexual health and HIV

  Examples: numerous contact sites, such as Gay.com, offer discussion boards on various subjects such as health, relationships, HIV, coming out and lifestyle.

- Contact and cruising sites specifically for people who with to find a partner of the same HIV status or who are specifically seeking protected sex

  Examples: there are a number of contact sites specifically for people with HIV in the USA, but only a few in the UK, such as the Positive Nation personal ads. In the USA http://www.safesexcity.com/ offers a site for gay men who specifically pledge to maintain safer sex.

- Active interventions where sexual health workers engage people seeking unsafe sex or 'PnP' (sex, usually unsafe, with recreational drugs)

  This is a controversial intervention, as this kind of unsolicited contact can annoy internet users and, if the health worker is pretending to be a prospective contact, would be considered unethical by many people. It has been found useful in certain populations such as Spanish-speaking sites for gay men in the USA.

Does all this internet activity help people maintain sexual health? InSPOT is one of a number of sites run by the US consultancy ISIS (Internet Sexuality Information Services - http://www.isis-inc.org/) a not-for-profit organisation that aims to help sexual health providers develop innovative ways of reaching people and offering online help. ISIS developed a syphilis testing campaign (http://www.stdtest.org/) that offered theatre and book coupons in return for getting a test, and banner ads on cruising sites. The banner ads got 32,000 hits in two months on gay.com and 5,000 redeemed their test coupons.

In terms of information provision and discussion, unsolicited messaging via email or chat messages does not usually work. In a 2001 survey of people (of all sexualities) who completed an online survey of sexual risk behaviour (Bull) most indicated they would visit a websitefor STI/HIV prevention information (61%), but fewer would openan E-mail (45%) or chat (30%) about the topic.

One of the most promising ways of using the internet is by using discussion boards to help people provide each other with mutual support and information, thus mobilising a 'virtual community' - something that works for classic car collectors or Star Trek fans, so it should work for people worried about HIV too.

The potential pitfalls of this approach include the internet's well-known tendency to encourage abuse ('flaming') and contributors posting inaccurate or harmful information. For this reason discussion boards need to be tightly moderated - which considerably increases their cost. Marginalised communities like African immigrants with unsettled residency status are also less likely to have the ability to access the internet in privacy which such interventions need.

References

Bolding G. *Sex with casual partners among London MSM: is the Internet more risky?* Fifteenth International AIDS Conference, Bangkok. Abstract WePeC6053. 2004.

Bull SS et al. *Barriers to STD/HIV prevention on the Internet.* Health Education Research 16(6): 661-670, 2001.

Cairns G. *Cybersafersex - Catching HIV in the Net.* Positive Nation 106: 38-39, 2004.

What interventions can be recommended?

A number of conclusions can be drawn from the evidence discussed in this chapter and in other effectiveness reviews.

Community mobilisation methods have been proven to work

Research evidence clearly demonstrates that community-based education efforts which rely on diffusion techniques and the development of skills lead to behaviour change. There are also sound theoretical reasons (see *Social diffusion* above) for assuming that well-planned and carefully managed community mobilisation interventions which are sensitive to the values and the diversity of a community will be successful in reducing the incidence of HIV infection, although no study has yet been designed to test this assumption.

There is a dose-response in HIV prevention activities

A variety of intervention studies provide evidence that greater exposure to HIV prevention messages, skills building and community norms which promote safer behaviour will be more effective than one-off or occasional interventions. This requires the development of a sequence of activities which are co-ordinated to achieve an adequate level of exposure amongst members of the target group, not one-off interventions.

Intervention techniques are adaptable to different communities and risk situations

The medium is not the message. Many of the interventions described in this chapter can be adapted to different communities and to communicate different types of messages. There is no reason why techniques already successfully deployed amongst gay men, African-American youth and injecting drug users should not work with other groups, provided that they are culturally sensitive. Nor is there any reason to abandon tried and tested methods simply because HIV prevention messages are becoming more complex.

Interventions must have a sound basis in research on risk and behavioural change

Much HIV prevention work taking place now is based on a mish-mash of theories about behaviour change and HIV risk factors. All the interventions discussed in this chapter have one thing in common: a clearly thought-out rationale based on a set of research findings about HIV risk and the way that human behaviour can be influenced.

Intervention techniques are adaptable to different communities and risk situations

The medium is not the message. Many of the interventions described in this chapter can be adapted to different communities and to communicate different types of messages. There is no reason why techniques already successfully deployed amongst gay men, African-American youth and injecting drug users should not work with other groups, provided that they are culturally sensitive. Nor is there any reason to abandon tried and tested methods simply because HIV prevention messages are becoming more complex.

Interventions must have a sound basis in research on risk and behavioural change

Much HIV prevention work taking place now is based on a mish-mash of theories about behaviour change and HIV risk factors. All the interventions discussed in this chapter have one thing in common: a clearly thought-out rationale based on a set of research findings about HIV risk and the way that human behaviour can be influenced.

A variety of tools exist for measuring the success of prevention activities: use them

Using a combination of outcome measures may be the best way of evaluating the effectiveness of a programme of interventions. Unless very sound evidence exists of the relationship between one variable and HIV incidence, the value of a project should not be assessed on the basis of changes in one variable alone. HIV prevention needs to develop performance indicators which measure quality hand in hand with quantity of activity.

Interventions should challenge reasoning, not just risk perception

Many of the interventions discussed contained cognitive components designed to make people think about the ways they rationalise risky activities. This is not proof in itself that reasoning needs to be foregrounded in future activities, but it does suggest a potentially useful avenue for research and project development.

How can we get best value for money in HIV prevention now?

It depends which population is being targeted. Amongst gay men, community mobilisation coupled with more interventionist counselling techniques in STI clinics might yield the best returns, together with a continued emphasis on condom distribution. Face-to-face outreach work does not appear cost-effective in comparison with media work and free condom distribution, particularly in large population centres. Research which can identify the reasons for seroconversions, and which can clarify the future role of GUM clinics in HIV prevention is urgently needed, and would be a good investment.

Amongst African communities, diffusion of safer sex messages is likely to be best accomplished by community organisations and community organisers, but the measurement of outcomes is hampered by fact that it will be difficult to judge whether HIV infections have been avoided as a consequence of HIV prevention activities in the UK or in African countries. However, recent evidence gathered by a variety of research projects suggests that there are big variations between African communities in levels of knowledge about HIV, and an investment is needed in action research which can point the way towards more extensive activities.

Amongst injecting drugs users, an investment in treatment and maintenance of injecting drug users together with the continuation of syringe exchange programmes is likely to keep HIV incidence low.

Needs assessment and evaluation: further reading

References

This chapter does not offer detailed guidance on population needs assessment or evaluation methodologies because a wealth of literature now exists on this subject. Amongst the best sources of information are:

Rhodes T. *Risk intervention and change: HIV prevention and drug use*, Health Education Authority, 1994.

Scott P. *Purchasing HIV Prevention: a No-Nonsense Guide for Use with Gay and Bisexual Men*, Health Education Authority, London, 1995.

Scott P, and Warwick I, with Durbin H. *A Pilot Needs Assessment and Evaluation Training Project*, The HIV Project, London, 1996.

Scott P. *Moving Targets: An assessment of the needs of gay man and of bisexual men in relation to HIV prevention in Enfield and Haringey*, a report published by Enfield and Haringey Health Authority, London, 1996.

Warwick I, Orr K and Whitty G. *Local HIV prevention needs assessment for gay and bisexual men: a review and recommendations for action*, Health Education Authority, 1995.

Weatherburn P, et al. *Behaviourally bisexual men in the UK: identifying needs for HIV prevention*, Health Education Authority, 1996.

Woodhead D, Warwick I and Whitty G: *Developing Local HIV Prevention Assessments with Gay and Bisexual Men*, Health Education Authority, London, 1995.

Further sources of information

This review is not an exhaustive discussion of all evaluated interventions in HIV prevention. It raises a number of issues about research into such interventions, and highlights particularly successful interventions. For further information about research in each of these areas, you can go to:

- EppiCentre (Evidence for Policy and Practice Information and Co-ordinating, University of London Institute of Education) (020 7612 6393; health@ioe.ac). Website: http://eppi.ioe.ac.uk/ . In July 2004 the EPPI Centre conducted a systematic review of research relevant to the development and implementation of effective and appropriate interventions among gay men in the UK. This can be downloaded from the website.

Charges apply to individuals outside the North Thames region for EppiCentre services.

- A useful summary of research evidence from the US is available at http:// www.AIDSCAP. Copies of a twenty page review of current data can be downloaded, along with factsheets (somewhat rudimentary and US biased in their data analysis).

- A review article, *Prevention of HIV infection*, by Kyung-Hee Choi and Thomas J. Coates, was published in AIDS, 1994, 8:1371-1389. It includes discussion of interventions in developing countries

- A book, *Preventing AIDS: Theories and methods of behavioural interventions* by Ralph DiClemente and John Peterson (Plenum Press, New York, 1994) provides a useful and detailed overview of interventions reported up to 1994, although its focus is largely confined to US populations

- A supplement to the journal *AIDS Education and Prevention* (volume 9, number 1), on effectiveness of behavioural interventions, was published in 1997

- A review, *AIDS prevention strategies that work: a review of National Institutes of Mental Health-sponsored research*, was published in 1996 by the Office on AIDS and the US National Institutes of Mental Health.

Positive prevention

The idea that HIV-positive people should be the principal target for HIV prevention programmes is not a new one. After all, HIV-positive people form 50% of the people present at any HIV transmission event and yet are a minority of the population. So programmes directed at them will have a disproportionate effect.

Positive Prevention encompasses two ideas: HIV prevention *targeted* at people with HIV, and HIV prevention *led* by people with HIV.

Targeting evidence-based HIV prevention and sexual harm reduction programmes at people with HIV makes sense:

- on an economic level because an HIV-positive person is involved in every HIV transmission event,

- on a legal level because people with HIV are at risk of prosecution for transmission,

- on a human rights level because people with HIV have demonstrably greater sexual and mental health needs.

The idea of positive-*led* prevention comes from the scientific evidence that, once diagnosed, people with HIV do take steps to reduce the risk of infecting others.

Since, as discussed above, it is easier to support and reinforce an existing behaviour than to completely change it, HIV prevention strategies should be advised from the 'bottom up' by what people with HIV and their partners already do. They should be tailored to help people sustain behaviour that supports good sexual health and relationships, and to address barriers to adopting those behaviours (such as fear of disclosure, depression or substance abuse).

One 1999 paper (King-Spooner) comments:

Preventive interventions with positive individuals are likely to have a greater impact on the epidemic, for an equivalent input of cost, time, resources, than preventative interventions focused on negative individuals. A change in the risky behaviour of an HIV-positive person will, on average, and in almost all affected populations, have a much bigger impact on the spread of the virus than an equivalent change in the behaviour of an HIV-negative person.

Yet throughout the history of the epidemic far fewer prevention resources have been directed at people living with HIV than at the uninfected. In a recent paper, the International HIV/AIDS Alliance suggested why:

Most prevention strategies to date have been targeted at uninfected people to prevent them from becoming infected with HIV. Historically, there has been a reluctance to work on HIV/STI prevention with people with HIV because of perceptions that the concept of prevention for people already infected is inherently contradictory.

There have also been justifiable concerns about victimising an already stigmatised group. In addition, there has been a reluctance to acknowledge that people with HIV have sex, and also to get to grips with the complex ethical issues surrounding people with HIV's responsibilities towards others.

'Positive Prevention' is therefore potentially an extremely effective tool against HIV, but not always one that has a positive effect on *people* with HIV.

The paper that contains the quote above was drafted by the International HIV/AIDS Alliance in 2002. It proposes a very wide definition of what 'positive prevention' is, dividing the activity into 17 different strategies as shown in the table below.

What's interesting about this grid of 17 strategies is that it doesn't in any way make any recommendations as to the content or methodology of any of the strategies it recommends. How is voluntary counselling and testing to be promoted, and how voluntary is voluntary? What kind of counselling works best? How does one encourage beneficial disclosure and reduce stigma? What kind of peer support works best and how can it promote safer sex practices? What content should focused communication campaigns have? And, if you involve people with HIV in positive prevention, what will they say they want?

In other words, with positive prevention we are back revisiting the HIV prevention versus sexual health promotion debate. Should positive prevention be a public health endeavour aimed at helping or coercing, by whatever means work best, people with HIV to keep their virus to themselves? Or should it be positive-*led* promotion, a way of helping people with HIV as a shared-interest community develop sexual health strategies and HIV prevention strategies that work best for them?

We have already mentioned above under **Counselling and HIV antibody testing** that one version of 'positive prevention' is the medicalised one currently being spearheaded by the Centres for the Disease Control in the USA which aims to divert funds away from HIV intervention programmes targeting the whole community, or vulnerable communities, and instead use them to get more people tested for HIV and to offer them intensive support - though they are rather vaguer about post-test support.

Responding to political disapproval of community HIV prevention programmes, on 15 April 2003 the US Centers for Disease Control initiated what they called the Serostatus Approach to Fighting the Epidemic (SAFE). This involved a refocusing and reallocation of HIV prevention resources towards people with HIV. Henceforward, the CDC announced, it would focus on a

drive to maximise the number of people tested for HIV - some newspapers, indeed recommended universal testing for all adults. Once people had tested HIV-positive they would be managed by "ongoing case management, medical interventions, and support for other psychosocial stressors."

There is some justification for laying a very strong emphasis on testing as a key element in HIV prevention. According to the CDC's own statistics, there are over 900,000 people with HIV in the USA. About 700,000 know their status. The annual incidence (new infection) rate is about five per cent a year. But if you just count those infected by people who know their status, it is less than two per cent (1.73%). Conversely, HIV incidence in partners of HIV-positive people who do *not* know their status is nearly 11 per cent a year (10.79%) (Holtgrave and Anderson).

The figures above detailing reduction in incidence after testing tell us nothing about whether people with HIV actually modify their behaviour to reduce the chance of infecting others post-testing. And they tell us even less about how to support them in making any behaviour change, if they do.

Testing people with HIV will obviously bring down infection rates in itself because many will be start taking antiretrovirals. A study of gay men in San Francisco (Porco) calculated that the average HIV infectivity of the population declined by 60% after the introduction of HAART.

However other studies have found that this did not result in immediate declines in incidence, but rather increases (Katz); HIV incidence doubled from 2.1% a year to 4.2% a year in San Francisco between 1995 and 1999. Mathematical modelling (Law) has calculated that it would only take a 30% increase in serodiscordant unprotected sex to counterbalance a 50% decline in infectiousness.

This underlines the importance of testing, because it suggests that if incidence in the partners of tested HIV-positive people is indeed less than a sixth of that in the partners of untested people, then a large proportion of HIV must be transmitted by untested people or those infected since their last test.

This has led, in the USA at least, to calls for universal HIV testing - with two surveys (Sanders, Paltiel) showing this would be cost-effective - and more recently with a change of heart in prevention activists leading to the decision to allow the sale of over-the-counter HIV tests. It is more doubtful if universal testing in the UK would be cost-effective, as we still only have a third of the USA's HIV prevalence. And prevention experts and public bodies alike in the UK do not seem to be ready for self-testing.

3.1 Individually focused health promotion	3.2 Sealing up, targeting and improving service and commodity delivery	3.3 Community mobilisation	3.4 Advocacy, policy change and community awareness
Strategy 1: Promoting voluntary councelling and testing	Strategy 5: Ensuring availability of voluntary testing	Strategy 9: Facilitating post-test clubs and other peer support groups	Strategy 14: Involving people with HIV in decision-making for Positive Prevention
Strategy 2: Providing post-test and ongoing councelling for positive people	Strategy 6: Provoding antiretroviral treatment for Positive Prevention	Strategy 10: Implementing focused communication campaigns	Strategy 15: Advocacy for Positive Prevention
Strategy 3: Encouraging beneficial disclosure and ethical partner notification	Strategy 7:Reducing stigma and integrating Positive Prevention into treatment centres	Strategy 11:Training people with HIV as peer outreach workers	Strategy 16: Legal reviews and legislative reform
Strategy 4: Providing councelling for sero-discordant couples	Strategy 8: Providing services for preventing mother-to-child transmission	Strategy 12: Reinforcing Positive Prevention through home-based care	Strategy 17: Advocacy for access to treatment
		Strategy 13: Addressing HIV-related gender-based violence in Positive Prevention	

Source: Adapted from the International HIV/AIDS Alliance, 2002

However the decrease in incidence from tested partners cannot be due entirely to reduced infectiousness as a result of taking HAART. No more than 74% of the tested US HIV-positive population is taking HAART (McNaghten) of which no more than 80% are virally suppressed at any one time. Therefore, at best, one would expect incidence in the partners of tested HIV-positive to be about 40% of those with untested partners. Instead it is about 16% of that figure. In other words the reduction in HIV infectivity accounts for less than half of the reduction in incidence.

So what positive-led prevention should do is to answer the following three questions:

- How did those tested people manage to reduce the number of people they infected post-testing?

- What behaviour changes did they make to achieve this?

- What could be done better to support them in those behaviour changes?

Why positive prevention may look very different

As we said above in the discussion on 'primary and secondary prevention' (under **HIV prevention or sexual health promotion?**), people with HIV have fundamentally the same need for interventions that can help them attain and maintain better sexual health as people without HIV.

However, the motives for maintaining safer sex, and therefore the kind of psychological reinforcement that best supports it, may also be very different.

In November 2000 a CHAPS campaign, "In Two Minds", depicted the rationalisations gay men may make to give themselves 'permission' to have unprotected sex. The head is depicted giving the reason *for* safer sex; the groin giving the rationalisation against it. All but one picture were of models depicting HIV-negative men. The THT wanted to include an HIV-positive man in the campaign, but ran into difficulties deciding what it should depict him thinking.

An extract from a *Positive Nation* article that discussed this campaign is worth featuring because it depicts how different the decision processes are HIV-positive people, and the difficulty of fitting them into a 'One size fits all' campaign. The problem they had was that the HIV-negative men had a clear and identical motive (rationalised away differently) for avoiding HIV, namely fear of infection. But what was the positive man's motive?

Jack Summerside of CHAPS told Positive Nation: "In the first draft of the advert, he was saying '*What if he trusts me to protect him?*' The team did not think this would work because they did not believe that HIV-positive men, realistically, were motivated by pure altruism. So if positive men aren't scared of infection, what are they scared of? Research provides the answer: isolation, ostracism, and being unwanted.

"So in the end we reverted to a line we'd tried out earlier. '*I'll get a hard time if he finds out I've got HIV and didn't use a condom.*'"

The difficulty of finding a wording that fitted with the rest of the campaign typifies the problem of attempting to skirt round the fact that in many ways negative and positive gay men are totally different 'interest communities'. They are united by their gay identity and by personal bonds. But the motives for maintaining sexual safety are utterly different.

If one looks at HIV prevention from the theoretical viewpoint of the Health Beliefs Model, the activity is about reinforcing and reminding people that unpleasant emotions are a consequence of HIV transmission. In this case HIV-negative people are motivated by an emotion - fear - that is caused by contemplating an existential and unvarying *physical* phenomenon - death and disease.

In contrast, HIV-positive people are motivated by an emotion - shame - that is caused by contemplating a contingent and variable *social* phenomenon - stigma and isolation. Campaigns and prevention interventions may run into problems - not least, that of reinforcing stigma - when they try to reinforce this emotion in the same way.

The findings from the Albarracin meta-review that 'threat' messages were not as counterproductive when used to frame prevention messages for people with HIV, as they were for people without, and Jean Richardson's finding that 'loss framed' messages work better for people with HIV, give some credence to this idea.

The other reason positive prevention may look very different is that, historically, the steps people with HIV and especially gay men have taken to contain their infection may look at the time very different from what health-promotion experts are recommending.

The best example of this is the controversy about 'barebacking'.

'Barebacking' originally signified a transgressive, eroticised seeking out and adoption of unprotected sex by gay men as a rebellion against the norms of HIV prevention messages. As well as involving the sexual charge of doing socially proscribed acts, it has also involved an eroticisation of HIV and HIV transmission themselves, with language terms evolving such as 'bugchaser' and 'giftgiver' for men who seek - or who *fantasise* about seeking - to respectively receive and transmit HIV.

These may be seen as attempts to conquer the extreme anxiety of AIDS by controlling it through eroticisation; similarly, sado-masochism may be seen as a way of controlling anxieties about humiliation and inadequacy. Or they can be seen as an extreme version of compensation for the all-pervasive shadow of HIV stigma - defiantly making 'cool' and sexy what is deemed by society to be most sinful and depraved.

Unsurprisingly 'barebacking' created a media furore, with documentary films like *The Gift* (Louise Hogarth, 2002) exploring this apparently self-destructive gay subculture. But what barebacking *was* and what it *did* may have been two different things. Because it involved a way whereby HIV- positive men attempted to make the deeply unsexy (HIV and disease) sexy and thereby conquer their own internalised stigma, it seems to have become in part a *code* for "I'm HIV-positive", if for no other reason that the next question to a barebacker seeking sex in a chatroom is usually "are you poz?"

In other words, it usually involved disclosure: disclosure not as an act of pure altruism or social responsibility, but disclosure in the service of sex, and therefore motivated much more powerfully than pure altruism could be.

In a 2003 paper (Race) entitled "Re-evaluation of Risk among Gay Men", Kane Race of the National Centre in HIV Social Research at the University of New South Wales comments:

It is unknown at this stage whether barebacking has had a positive or negative effect on new HIV infections. While there are sporadic reports that some HIV-negative gay men make sense of some of the unprotected anal intercourse in which they engage in terms of barebacking, the phenomenon tends to be associated with HIV-positive men. Thus, the effect may be to increase, rather than decrease, the degree of seroconcordance in the total number of sexual encounters. Barebacking may have the effect of partner sorting in a manner analogous to negotiated safety. Unlike HIV-negative men, HIV-positive men require only one HIV test to adequately ascertain their HIV status, thus this possible prevention ethic need not occur in the context of a regular relationship.

What this implies is that people with HIV often do seek to reduce the risk of passing on their infection to others, but may do so in ways that are contrary to received public health opinion or run ahead of it and are also extremely difficult to imagine promoting.

An example is serosorting - the restriction of unprotected sex to people with the same HIV status. Although this may be starting to contribute significantly to apparent reductions in HIV incidence in some US cities (Truong), public health workers are not yet ready to promote it as an HIV prevention measure, as it looks uncomfortably like promoting unprotected sex.

In a recent article in the *Bay Area Reporter* (Bajko) Jeff McConnell, an HIV prevention researcher, said: "If you are talking to a guy who uses condoms all the time and has a perfect record, you wouldn't want to counsel him on serosorting.but if you are counselling an individual who cannot use condoms consistently or refuses to use them, you do want to talk to them about serosorting." But co-researcher Dr Robert Grant said: "I think that it may be deemed inappropriate for public health messages to recommend one type of partnership over another."

The way to square this circle, of course, is to provide the kind of HIV prevention that doesn't involve *telling* people to do anything. Positive prevention may have to involve detaching HIV prevention from the idea of 'health promotion' altogether, making it something much more like a combination of community mobilisation and self-efficacy training.

What works in positive prevention?

Two meta-reviews of HIV prevention interventions specifically directed at people with HIV were published in the first few months of 2006, finally amending the dearth of review-level research in the area - although they still concentrate entirely on US studies.

In the first, Nicole Crepaz of the Centers for Disease Control sifted through 310 studies of prevention programmes for people with HIV and filtered out all but the twelve whose standard of evidence stood up to the most rigorous scientific scrutiny. In total 4,052 people with HIV participated in these twelve programmes.

Crepaz concluded that HIV-positive people responded at least as well as HIV-negative people, and possibly better, to prevention interventions. She found a significant reduction of sexual risk incidents in participants in the twelve programmes (Odds Ratio 0.57), and a reduction in the amount of STIs (Odds Ratio 0.21, though only a minority of programmes measured this). Programmes designed to reduce needle-sharing in drug users also produced significant improvements in risk behaviour (OR 0.47).

By comparing one study with another, Crepaz found that the most effective interventions were ones that:

- Specifically taught people how to negotiate condom use and safer sex as their main focus.

- Also included help for other aspects of living with HIV, such as disclosing your status, medication adherence and maintaining self-esteem.

- Were intensive, that is, they involved at least ten sessions delivered over at least three months.

- Were delivered in a clinical setting or at a voluntary organisation that already provided services to people with HIV, rather than in outreach or community settings.

- Were at least partly delivered by professional counsellors.

- And were at least partly delivered on a one-to-one basis.

Crepaz found that the least effective programmes were those which simply delivered information on transmission risk and condom effectiveness.

In the second meta-review, Blair T Johnson of the University of Connecticut analysed 15 studies, some of them ones that Crepaz also analysed. Some of the studies were split into more than one different intervention (including the 'gain frame' and 'loss frame' trial by Jean Richardson cited above) so Johnson was able to study a total of 19 different interventions.

Programmes used varied techniques such as group therapy, support, role-plays, videos, telephone support and one-to-one counselling and lasted from 18 days to 45 weeks.

Johnson found that, on average, they produced an overall increase in condom use of 16% relative to baseline - not as good as Albarracin's 'active' programmes, but as good as or better than her 'passive' ones. Johnson, like Albarracin, used this measure of effectiveness as it was the one used most frequently as the measure of success.

However Johnson found no change whatsoever in the number of partners people had after intervention. Only seven out of the 19 programmes measured whether the number of partners changed, however, and Johnson suggests that this may have been confounded by people doing things not measured by researchers instead of reducing partners, such as serosorting. The most effective, a 2000 programme directed at HIV-positive teenagers in Los Angeles, increased their condom use by 82% compared with a control group. However some were unsuccessful, and the only non-US programme, directed at HIV-positive people in Tanzania, actually reduced condom use by 25%. Johnson found that programmes that worked had three characteristics.

Firstly, they tended to be directed at younger people. Programmes where the average age of participants was 20 worked five times better than ones directed at 40 year-olds. Johnson hypothesised that older people more often tend to be in long-term relationships where sexual habits are harder to shift, and says that better interventions for long-term couples where one partner has HIV need to be devised.

Secondly, the ones that worked were either motivational or taught people behavioural skills, and programmes which did both worked even better. 'Motivational' was the word Johnson used for programmes that provided things that improved participants' overall quality of life such as increased social support or self-confidence.

Programmes that provided information on HIV risk alone had no effect; ones that added in either motivation or behavioural skills increased condom use by 12%; and ones providing all three things increased it by 33%.

Thirdly, and disappointingly, programmes directed at gay men didn't work, by and large and, conversely, ones that excluded gay men were effective, increasing condom use by 42%.

However Johnson doesn't see this as evidence that gay men are uniquely deaf to safer-sex advice and support. He points out that not one single programme directed at gay men provided both ingredients proven to be necessary - they either provided greater social support or taught behavioural skills but not one did both.

Johnson criticises the lack of scientific research into ways of helping HIV-positive people maintain safer sex and reduce HIV transmission. He comments:

Perhaps the most surprising finding of this work is that more than two decades into the epidemic, there have been so few randomly-controlled trials of interventions that focus on people living with HIV, though there have been literally hundreds of studies conducted with uninfected populations. There is an urgent need for research in this area.

References

Bajko Matthew S. *Few health officials ready to promote serosorting.* Bay Area Reporter08 May 2006.

Crepaz N et al. *Do prevention interventions reduce HIV risk behaviours among people living with HIV? A meta-analytic review of controlled trials.* AIDS 20: 143-157, 2006.

Holtgrave DR, Anderson T. *Utilizing HIV transmission rates to assist in prioritizing HIV prevention services.* Int J STD AIDS. 15(12): 789-792, 2004.

International HIV/AIDS Alliance. *Positive Prevention: Draft background paper.* July 2003. May be downloaded from http://www.aidsalliance.org/sw9438.asp

Johnson BT et al. *Sexual risk reduction for persons living with HIV: Research synthesis of randomised controlled trials, 1993 to 2004.* JAIDS 41(5): 642-650, 2006.

Katz MH. *Impact of highly active antiretroviral treatment on HIV seroincidence among men who have sex with men: San Francisco.* American Journal of Public Health 92(3): 388-394, 2002.

King-Spooner S. *HIV prevention and the positive population.* Int J STD AIDS 10(3): 141-150, 1999.

Law MG. *Modelling the effect of combination antiretroviral treatments on HIV incidence.* AIDS 15(10): 1287-1294, 2001.

McNaghten AD. *Gender disparity in HIV treatment and AIDS opportunistic illnesses (OI).* Int Conf AIDS, Bangkok, abstract MoOrC1032, 2004.

Paltiel DA et al. *Expanded screening for HIV in the United States -- An analysis of cost-effectiveness.* N Engl J Med 352: 586-595, 2005.

Porco TC et al. *Decline in HIV infectivity following the introduction of highly active antiretroviral therapy.* AIDS 18(1): 81-88, 2004.

Race KD. *Revaluation of risk among gay men.* Social Research, Issues Paper No. 1. National Centre in HIV Social Research, University of New South Wales, August 2003.

Sanders GD et al. *Cost-effectiveness of screening for HIV in the era of highly active antiretroviral therapy.* N Engl J Med 352: 570-585, 2005.

Truong HM et al. *Increases in "serosorting" may prevent further expansion of the HIV epidemic among MSM in San Francisco.* Eleventh Conference on Retroviruses and Opportunistic Infections, San Francisco, abstract 843, 2004.

Other NAM resources

HIV Treatments Training Manual

It is NAM's unique training resource, this user-friendly, extensive and adaptable training manual is designed to enable you to plan and run your own treatments training sessions. It gives you all the tools you need for training:

- transparencies for use with an overhead projector
- CD-ROM containing power point slides
- speakers' notes
- handouts for course participants
- awareness-raising games and exercises
- flexible learning modules, that can be broken down into short teaching sessions, or delivered as longer courses
- can be used for both one-to-one treatments work and for training sessions with groups
- gives ideas and guidance for managing group work

And it is suitable for a wide range of audiences, including:

- people personally affected by HIV
- health professionals
- other professionals and volunteers working with HIV

HIV & AIDS Treatments Directory

This resource covers all medical aspects of HIV & AIDS, from in-depth background information on HIV, to the latest information on current treatments.

Chapters include:

- The immune system and HIV.
- Options during pregnancy.
- Starting, changing and interrupting treatment.
- Body fat and metabolic changes.

And has A-Z listings of:

- Treatments
- Illnesses
- Symptoms
- Medical tests

It also features a removable full-colour drug chart. This chart helps to make comparisons of:

- Antiretroviral drugs (licensed in the EU)
- Doses
- Pill burden
- Side-effects
- Food restrictions

order form

ORDER FORM (please insert quantity required in box)

NAM Manual - Annual Subscription
☐ £209.00   statutory & commercial organisations
☐ £150.00   voluntary organisations

HIV & AIDS Treatments Directory
☐ £64.95   professionals & organisations
☐ £12.95   individuals affected by HIV

AIDS Treatment Update (annual subscription)
☐ £75   statutory & commercial organisations
☐ £55   voluntary organisations
☐ FREE   individuals affected by HIV

Please circle the format in which you'd like to receive ATU:
paper / email / audio

HIV & AIDS Reference Manual
☐ £54.95   professionals & organisations
☐ £12.95   individuals affected by HIV

HIV & AIDS Services Worldwide
☐ £24.95

UK AIDS Directory
☐ £54.95

Nambase - UK AIDS Services Database
☐ £249 plus VAT (£292.56 inc VAT)

HIV Treatments Training Manual
☐ £249   statutory & commercial organisations
☐ £199   voluntary organisations

Directory of Complementary Therapies in HIV & AIDS
☐ £15
☐ FREE   individuals affected by HIV

Living With HIV
☐ £19.95

Information series - £1 per copy
(minimum order £10/free to individuals affected by HIV)

☐ Adherence
☐ Anti HIV Drugs
☐ Clinical Trials
☐ HIV & Children
☐ HIV & Hepatitis
☐ HIV & Mental Health
☐ HIV & Sex
☐ HIV & TB

☐ HIV & Women
☐ HIV, Stigma & You
☐ HIV Therapy
☐ Lipodystrophy
☐ Nutrition
☐ Resistance
☐ Viral Load & CD4

Please add the following shipping costs onto your order:

	UK	EU	Rest of the world
Orders up to £75	£0	£5	£10
Orders up to £200	£0	£15	£25
Orders over £200	£0	£20	£30

YOUR DETAILS:

Name

Address . . . .

. . . .

. . . .

Telephone . . . .

Email . . . .

TOTAL PAYMENT DUE (including shipping costs):

£ . . . .

Payment can be made by VISA or MASTERCARD, by bank transfer, or by cheque. Cheques payable to NAM.

Credit Card payment details:

Card number . . . .

Card expiry date. . . . .

Cardholder's address. . . . .

. . . .

. . . .

. . . .

Cardholder's name and initials as on card

. . . .

Cardholder's signature:

. . . .

☐ Please do NOT send me the latest information about NAM's full range of publications and services

☐ Please do NOT send me information about NAM's fundraising campaigns